WATCHDOG JOURNALISM IN SOUTH AMERICA

WATCHDOG JOURNALISM IN SOUTH AMERICA

NEWS, ACCOUNTABILITY, AND DEMOCRACY

Silvio Waisbord

COLUMBIA UNIVERSITY PRESS

NEW YORK

Columbia University Press
Publishers Since 1893
New York   Chichester, West Sussex
Copyright © 2000 Columbia University Press
All rights reserved

Library of Congress Cataloging-in-Publication Data
Waisbord, Silvio R. (Silvio Ricardo), 1961–
    Watchdog journalism in South America : news, accountability, and democracy /
Silvio Waisbord.
        p. cm.
    Includes bibliographical references and index.
    ISBN 0–231–11974–7 (alk. paper) — ISBN 0–231–11975–5 (pbk. : alk. paper)
    1. Investigative reporting—South America.   I. Title.
PN4781 .W22 2000
079'.8—dc21   99–058476
∞

Casebound editions of Columbia University Press books are printed on permanent
and durable acid-free paper.
Printed in the United States of America
c 10 9 8 7 6 5 4 3 2 1
p 10 9 8 7 6 5 4 3 2 1

For Sophia

CONTENTS

ACKNOWLEDGMENTS

I began thinking about this book while I was a scholar at the Annenberg School for Communication at the University of Pennsylvania during the 1993–1994 academic year. Under the experienced guidance of Elihu Katz, the scholars' program focused on the public sphere. Although my original project was not primarily about the press, the program offered the chance to discuss questions about journalism and public life that inspired me to write this book. I am grateful to Elihu and the Annenberg School for an intellectually stimulating experience.

Since then, I could not have completed this project without the invaluable help from many people and institutions. To all the journalists who accepted my requests for interviews and let me hang out in newsrooms and archives, I am forever thankful. This book is largely about them, what they do, how they do it, why they do it. Without their participation, this book would have been impossible. I was fortunate to run into some first-rate journalists who kindly opened their phone books and made contacts for me: Carlos Bustamante, Gilberto Dimenstein, Gustavo Gorriti, Gerardo Reyes, Fernando Rodrigues, Blanca Rosales and Alejandro Santos. Special thanks to Alfredo Leuco, my admired cousin-journalist who, as always, was there for whatever I needed. My deepest thanks to friends for the logistical help they provided while I was chasing interviewees and combing libraries: Pablo Gentili, Paula Medeiros and Aline Sordili in Brazil; Helena Uribe in Colombia; Roxana Barrantes, Manuel Glave, and the Chaparro family in Peru. The documentation centers of the FELAFACS in Lima, Peru, and the Universidad Javeriana in Bogotá, Colombia, were real treasures. I benefited enormously from fruitful discussions with colleagues and friends Suzanne Bilello, Cathy Conaghan, Afonso de Albuquerque, Marina Gilbert, Tomas Eloy Martinez, Nancy Morris, Enrique Peruzzotti, Bill Solomon, Linda Steiner, and Barbie Zelizer. John Nerone read the entire manuscript, raised the right questions, and made thoughtful suggestions. My gratitude also goes to scholars who have been sources of intellectual inspiration and helped me shape my understanding of media and politics through the years: John Downing, the late Marjorie Ferguson, Elizabeth Fox, Dan Hallin, Oscar Landi, Heriberto Muraro, Philip Schlesinger, Michael Schudson, and Howard Tumber.

I presented parts of this book at conferences and panels organized by the Freedom Forum Buenos Aires, the International Communication Association, the Latin American Program at Princeton University, the Latin American Studies Association, the Universidad Católica in Asunción, Paraguay, the Centro Latinoamericano de Periodismo in Panama, and the Universidad Di Tella in Buenos Aires. To all these institutions I am grateful for the opportunity to discuss and clarify ideas. Two anonymous reviewers perceptively read the manuscript and gave me useful suggestions to sharpen my arguments. Linda Gregonis did a superb job in copyediting the manuscript. Ann Miller, my editor at Columbia University Press, has provided skillful direction.

I owe a debt of thanks to my colleagues in the Department of Communication at Rutgers University, particularly to my former chair Harty Mokros, who offered support all the way. My gratitude also to institutions that provided financial support for different stages of this project: the Shorenstein Center on the Press, Politics and Public Policy at Harvard University, and the Research Council and the School of Communication, Information, and Library Studies both at Rutgers University. A fellowship at the Media Studies Center in New York in fall 1998 provided essential resources to complete the manuscript. Larry McGill, Bob Snyder and a dedicated staff made sure that everything was perfect and offered the ideal atmosphere to do good scholarship. Deborah Rogers, the librarian at the Media Studies Center, is any scholar's dream librarian: she was always ready with tips and materials. Alex Gross was a diligent research assistant. Fellow fellows, Jamie Campbell, Stephanie Craft, Bob Frye, Todd Gitlin, Anna Husarska, Victor Merina, and Mark Robicheaux offered valuable feedback and camaraderie.

The aforementioned people and organizations challenged me to think rigorously and creatively about journalism and democracy. I am solely responsible for the ideas presented in this book.

My family has been extremely supportive during the long years that it took me to complete this project. I am thankful to Sara, Lázaro, and Fabio for all the love and support. Cindy Baur gave me counsel, love, and a solid emotional safety net. My daughter Sophia was born at the same time that I began conceiving this book. Raising her hasn't been as challenging as doing research in four South American countries simultaneously, and it has certainly been much more enjoyable. She helped me put (academic) life in perspective. Sophia became my own inquisitive watchdog reporter, inquiring about my opinions, questioning my authority, monitoring my acts, and dogging me with real (and imagined) stories that made me laugh and think. To her I dedicate this book.

INVESTIGATIVE REPORTING AND WATCHDOG JOURNALISM

Journalists and political analysts have observed that the vigor of investigative journalism has been one of the most important and novel developments in the South American press in the 1980s and 1990s (Alves 1996; Reyes 1996). Investigative journalism seemingly contradicts the historical record of the region's press, which has systematically shunned critical reporting and opted for complacent relations with state and market interests. Watchdog reporting was relegated to marginal, nonmainstream publications during democratic periods, and to underground, clandestine outlets during dictatorial regimes. Today the situation is markedly different. Investigative journalism has gone mainstream, making strides in media organizations that traditionally sacrificed the denunciation of power abuses for economic benefits and political tranquility. Whether this is a passing fad or will become a regular part of the press in the region remains to be seen. Some journalists see a bright future for investigative reporting; others fear for its failure (Crucianelli 1998; Reyes 1996).

There are unmistakable signs, however, that a journalism who prizes the sniffing out of wrongdoing has become more visible and legitimate in the region. A rare good in the not-so-distant past, there have been swelling numbers of investigative reports. The most influential newspapers in Brazil (*Folha de São Paulo*) and in Argentina (*Clarín*) have produced a number of investigative stories in recent years. Leading newspapers in Colombia (*El Tiempo*) and Peru (*El Comercio* and *La República*) have investigative units especially devoted to uncover wrongdoing. Other dailies (Argentina's *Página/12*, Colombia's *El Espectador*) and newsweeklies (Peru's *Caretas*, *Oiga*, and *Sí*) have not corralled hard-hitting reporting in one cubicle but have at times adopted critical positions in the coverage of specific subjects. Newspapers that historically epitomized conservative interests (Brazil's *Estado do São Paulo* and *Jornal do Brasil*, Argentina's *La Nación*) have lately stepped up investigative reporting. Major newsweeklies (Argentina's *Noticias*, Brazil's *Veja* and *ISTOE*, and Colombia's *Semana* and *Cambio 16*) have produced many high-profile investigative stories. Watchdog journalism is also found in television news, which traditionally has been even more fearful than the print media of frontally criticizing and angering power holders. For example, during 1997 and 1998, Argentina's *Telenoche Investiga* and Peru's *Contrapunto* produced important investigations. In countries where "journalists still get respect," to quote Peruvian editor Gustavo Gorriti's (1998) remark on the differences in public regard for U.S. and Latin American reporters, some of today's most prestigious and well-known journalists have penned explosive exposés and best-selling books based on denunciations originally published in newspapers and newsweeklies. Muckrakers generally receive local, regional, and international press awards. As a result of their work, and in a context of persistent anti-press violence, muckrakers are frequent targets of attacks. If in the past, the most prominent journalists were publishers not characterized precisely for their critical posture, today's journalistic firmament is filled with muckraking stars.

Patterns can be detected across countries. Watchdog journalism is no longer the province of alternative publications but has been incorporated by leading news organizations. In the past, reports frequently targeted government wrongdoing rather than corporate graft or social injustice. The ideals of professional and factual reporting have gained currency and informed journalistic work. Scores of public officials have resigned in the wake of press denunciations. In all cases, news organizations traditionally unwilling to remove the lid of official wrongdoing have become more interested in bringing out cases of corruption and human rights violations.

The contemporary vigor of watchdog journalism is remarkable, considering its rarity in the history of the press in South America. Its emergence and seeming consolidation are particularly puzzling, considering that in the past, political and economics conditions have not contributed to the affirmation of watchdog journalism. Lately, however, even news media that foreswore oversight functions and avoided publishing news that could enrage ruling powers have endorsed a less complacent reporting. The press, in general, seems less afraid of turning some stones. This does not mean that we should sing hosannas and uncritically praise the press, but rather that we should recognize that the new energies of watchdog journalism differ from the media's past trajectory in the region.

These developments stimulate a number of questions. How can we account for changes and similarities among countries? How does investigative journalism in South America differ from its counterparts in developed democracies? What does such journalism reflect about the linkages between media and power in present-day democracies? Considering that a critical press that is critical of political and economic powers is desirable for democracy, how does investigative reporting contribute to improving the quality of democracy in the region? These are the questions that inform the analysis in this book.

This study has three goals: to explain the rise of watchdog journalism in the context of the region's new democracies, to elucidate its characteristics and its differences with past traditions, and to discuss its contributions to contemporary democratic life. In analyzing watchdog journalism outside the better-studied cases in the United States and Western Europe, the study also examines the limitations of exporting models of investigative reporting and journalism in general to contexts that are glaringly different from those in developed democracies. Further, it assesses the strengths and weaknesses of watchdog journalism in developing democracies. The intention is not only to understand the relations between media and democracy in South America, but also to contribute to international comparative studies of media and politics. With that goal in mind, this study is an effort toward building a theoretical framework to analyze the linkages between media and power in contemporary democracies. On the assumption that comparative work allows us to enrich theoretical concepts and reach better grounded conclusions, this study hopes to make a modest contribution toward such a goal by examining how structural factors as well as organizational routines and cultures shape the possibilities for critical journalism in contemporary democracies.

INVESTIGATIVE OR WATCHDOG JOURNALISM?

Writing a study about investigative journalism inevitably requires dealing with matters of definition. Much of the debate surrounding investigative reporting centers on clarifying what sets it apart from other forms of journalism. The bumpy trajectory of investigative journalism in South America, and the fact that journalistic traditions in the region do not easily fit with U.S. and European experiences make it necessary to explain how investigative journalism is understood in this book.

One set of definitions in the U.S. literature emphasizes the methods that reporters use to get information as investigative journalism's distinctive feature (Anderson 1976; Aucoin 1995; Benjaminson 1990; Gaines 1994). Journalist Bob Greene's standard definition states that investigative journalism requires the disclosure of issues of public relevance that results from the effort and initiative of reporters (Ullman and Colbert 1991). Similarly, media scholar Ralph Negrine (1996) considers that investigative journalism requires active reporting, the unearthing and putting together of pieces of information, in contrast to passive reception as in the following of leaks. This interpretation raises a number of questions that deserve attention. Among them, one is particularly important to understanding investigative journalism: If investigative reporting only refers to work that results from reporters' efforts and initiative, how should one consider information leaks, a staple of investigative work? What if information is passed by sources rather than doggedly chased or uncovered by reporters after sifting through documentation? According to the aforementioned definition, this practice would not be considered investigative reporting because the reporter hasn't conducted original work but relied on someone else's information.

South American journalists reject the understanding of investigative reporting in terms of specific methodological requirements that sets it apart from other forms of journalism. They are skeptical about making newsgathering methods one of the salient characteristics of investigative journalism. Investigation is what journalism *is* anyway, they observe, so why make it a unique attribute of some journalists and reports? The statement of a Brazilian journalist represents a widespread sentiment: "I am a journalist and that presupposes some kind of investigation" (Pacheco 1997). Whether journalists actually carry out full-fledged investigations in their daily work is a different matter, but they are reluctant to single out investigation as something inherent to one kind of journalism. Reports typically mix journalists' efforts and information leaks. Sometimes leaks spur investigations, but knowledge that specific reporters are working on particular stories also prods sources to contact newsrooms. Cut-and-dry distinctions miss the fact that both reporters' own work and leaks are essential in newsgathering routines of muckrakers. Moreover, they add, methodology-centered definitions of investigative reporting reflect the working conditions of U.S. journalists that make possible for reporters to rely solely (or mainly) on their initiative and efforts. In South America, the absence of regulations that require filing public documents and authorize public access excludes the possibility of reporters obtaining official information without help from sources. Thus journalists need to combine personal efforts and information supplied by sources.

A different understanding of investigative journalism prioritizes the consequences rather than the methods. A good example of this approach is a study by a Northwestern research team, which defines investigative reporting as "the journalism of outrage" (Protess et al. 1991, 5). This is "a form of storytelling that probes the boundaries of America's civic conscience. Published allegations of wrongdoing — political corruption, government inefficiency, corporate abuses — help define public morality in the United States. Journalistic exposés that trigger outrage from the public or policy makers affirm society's standards of misconduct." Here the emphasis is on the impact of reporting rather than on the procedures. The main strength of this approach is that it opens a new analytical dimension that is more concerned with the linkages among journalism, public opinion, and policymaking than discussions about technique and strategies. It also calls attention to the strong moral component of investigative reporting (also see Ettema and Glasser 1998).

This approach is not without problems. First, even if we could adequately measure outrage (how much, whose, for how long), it is problematic to equate investigative reporting with public indignation. Reporters may expect their reports to shake the public. It is likely that a reporter's work is validated when citizens respond by demanding legitimacy to an investigative story, as Protess and coauthors suggest. Reactions, however, are contingent on a number of factors unrelated to a reporter's work, such as the mood of public opinion, the dynamics of policymaking, and specific ingredients of denunciations. A story can incite controversy or have no repercussions, depending on previous stories or existing beliefs about the subject. In South American societies, where there is widespread skepticism about the honesty of public officials and where denunciations of wrongdoing have become regular in recent years, exposés may have less impact than in situations where government officials are widely expected to obey the law or are seen as decent and trustworthy persons. Some stories have a strong impact, triggering congressional investigations and public mobilization; other exposés barely register on the public radar.

The ingredients of the story also may account for different consequences: A story featuring the testimony of a well-known figure and sensational details is likely to have a wider ripple effect than more technical accounts packed with new data but devoid of tabloid-like elements. Public indifference to denunciations does not suggest moral toleration, as Protess and his colleagues contend, but perhaps saturation, a sentiment of just-another-

news-about-corruption among citizens. The absence of public outcry or active engagement in civic action to combat abuses disclosed by news reports
does not mean that citizens condone corruption. It may actually reflect political disenchantment and apathy. The repercussion of stories, then, cannot
be used as an adequate barometer to determine whether reports are investigative. Even when they fail to mobilize public action, stories may actually
qualify as examples of "investigative journalism" if they disclose corruption
and other forms of power abuses.

The definition advanced by Protess and coauthors presents two other
problematic assumptions. Investigative journalism does not always "probe
the boundaries of . . . civic conscience" and is not the only kind of reporting
that "help[s] define public morality." Investigative reporting, this study hopes
to show, typically *assumes* rather than *tests* moral consensus around certain
issues. When a government official takes bribes, a police chief deals drugs, a
company subjects employees to inhuman working conditions, or a sweatshop
hires underage workers, exposés rarely explore why these actions are morally
objectionable. Instead, such stories invariably take for granted that those behaviors run against "good ethics." If such violations become news, this is because it is assumed that they fall outside common expectations of public
morality, even in societies where unlawful behavior is known to be rampant.
Muckraking commonly accepts a diffusely defined moral order rather than
exploring its boundaries. Nor is definition of the contours of public morality
unique to investigative reporting. Other kinds of stories that do not necessarily "feature investigation" also shape moral boundaries. News about crime,
sexuality, sports, disease, and moral panics in general similarly sketch the limits of acceptable and unacceptable morals (Cohen 1980; Thompson 1998). Investigative work is one form of journalistic discourse that deals with moral
questions, yet it is not the only avenue for journalism to outline, reinforce, or
modify conceptions about public ethics. Investigative reporting addresses
(but not necessarily explores) moral transgressions; but it does not monopolize journalism's treatment of moral issues.

Investigative journalism should not be equated with reporting about information that is relevant to the public, as suggested by Ullman and Colbert
(1991) and others. To incorporate "relevance" into the definition raises a
number of problems that obscure, rather than help, the understanding of
what characterizes investigative reporting. It takes for granted that there is
"important" and "unimportant" information while, actually, this is one of
the least understood and most problematic questions in the literature on
press and democracy. Such a requirement assumes that we unanimously

know what kind of information the news media should provide citizens. But how does the media determine what information is relevant? Who determines what is relevant, reporters or readers? All readers? Aren't issues of public relevance often treated trivially and superficially? Turning the assumption into a question seems more intriguing: What do investigative stories tell us about what press organizations, newsrooms, and readers consider to be relevant news?

And one final point: The idea that investigative journalism is characterized by a "detailed factual exposure" (Miraldi 1990) straitjackets investigative reporting into the tradition of U.S. modern journalism and excludes other possible styles that do not conform to the catechism of objectivity and impartiality. In fact, as the Latin America cases suggest, investigative journalism may adopt different practices according to the traditions and principles that inform news production. The U.S. model of investigative journalism is extremely influential, but it is not the only possible paradigm. It is more fruitful to examine how reporters expose wrongdoing and whether they prioritize or, conversely, eschew journalistic facts.

In summary, the notion of investigative journalism is equivocal. More than particular news-gathering methods or specific public reaction, what characterizes investigative journalism is that reporters dig out information about power abuses. It is the kind of journalism that, as Argentine muckraker Horacio Verbitsky (1997, 16) writes, "disseminates what someone does not want to be known. Its function is to make visible what is hidden, to bother, to throw salt in the wounds." As I hope to show in this study, the meaning of investigative journalism varies according to dissimilar press traditions and conditions for journalistic practice. Because standard definitions of "investigative journalism" reflect experiences and practices in the United States, I have opted to use the broader concept of "watchdog journalism" (and alternately, muckraking) to examine reporting that brings attention to wrongdoing through reporting information that some implicated parties want to keep hidden (see Schultz 1998).

A REGIONAL PHENOMENON

This study originally grew from an interest in press exposés and scandals in Argentina and Brazil in the early 1990s. At that time the Menem administration in Argentina was repeatedly shaken by denunciations of wrongdoing and ensuing scandals, and the Collor administration in Brazil was brought down after disclosures of corruption and congressional investigations and impeachment proceedings. But those developments were not limited to Argentina and Brazil. Press denunciations were surfacing almost everywhere in the region. Dailies such as *Siglo 21* in Guatemala, *La Prensa* in Panama, *ABC Color* in Paraguay, and *Reforma* and *El Norte* and the newsweekly *Proceso* in Mexico, to name a few, also featured "investigative reports." Even in countries such as Mexico and Paraguay where the timidity of the press, its tendency to cozy up to state powers, and its disinterest in monitoring power abuses were legendary, new winds seemed to be blowing (*ABC Color* 1997; Orme 1996). The trends were not limited to watchdog journalism, either. As a result of press denunciations, governments were embattled in political scandals throughout the region. Civilian administrations were forced out of office, including Abdala Bucaram in Ecuador and Carlos Andrés Pérez in Venezuela. Press revelations about the funneling of drug monies into his election campaign weakened Ernesto Samper's presidency in Colombia.

These developments indicated that the analysis, if focused on one case, had to be sensitive to the fact that watchdog journalism was a regional trend. Another possibility was to shift the analytical prism: Instead of taking a case study, the analysis could explore similarities and contrasts in a handful of countries by delving into a handful of cases from each one. This is the perspective that this study takes. The intention is not to offer conclusions that apply to all South American countries, but to consider the experiences in a few countries so as to identify patterns that help us understand watchdog journalism, its causes, its characteristics, and its potential contributions to democracy.

Next, it was necessary to choose which countries should be put at the center of the analysis, considering that press systems in South America, despite sharing many features, are embedded in different traditions and political contexts. The intention was to include cases where similarities and differences could be addressed. The Argentine case was intriguing because the press, after a prolonged slumber during the authoritarian years of the 1970s and lethargy in the first years of democracy in the 1980s, was experiencing important renovations in the early 1990s that were linked to the flurry of press denunciations targeting members of the Menem administration. At the same time, the Brazilian press had also brought to light many cases of wrongdoing, but its reporting presented important differences compared with Argentina. In Argentina, the left-center daily *Página/12*, which practices watchdog journalism and does not disguise its ideological sympathies, was responsible for most denunciations, while in Brazil major news organizations that embraced the ideals and practices of U.S. reporting churned out

investigative reports. Press exposés contributed to the political process that
concluded with the peaceful removal of Fernando Collor de Mello from office in 1992, a novel development in a region accustomed to military coups.

At the same time, watchdog journalism in Peru, which showed signs of life
in the early 1980s soon after the return of liberal democracy, continued un-
abated even after the self-coup by President Alberto Fujimori in April 1992.
The military was unable to squelch investigative energies, and a handful of
news organizations persisted in revealing power abuses. As in Argentina,
watchdog reporting in Peru was close to crusading journalism and press denunciations; although repeatedly aimed at the Fujimori government, did not
trigger major political crises. Both the Menem and Fujimori administrations
not only remained in power but also were reelected in landslides in the mid-
1990s. Watchdog journalism in Colombia also is included in the study. The
Colombian case offers important elements that contrast with Argentina,
Brazil, and Peru. Traditionally, the press in Colombia has been divided along
partisan lines and has not been affected by the chronic rotation of democratic
and military regimes that characterized the political evolution of most countries in the region. In addition, Colombian newspapers pioneered U.S.-in-
spired investigative reporting in South America in the late 1970s.

Because my intention is to address issues comparatively rather than on a
country-by-country basis, this book is organized thematically in three sections. The first deals with the reasons for the current strength of watchdog
journalism. Chapter 1 offers an interpretation of the historical absence of
watchdog journalism in the region. Several conditions have undermined the
possibilities for the consolidation of investigative reporting along the lines of
U.S. journalism. The intertwined political and economic relations between
news companies and the state made impossible the affirmation of the model
of an "independent," "fourth estate" press, a model that views the reporting
of official wrongdoing as one of its priorities and obligations. In countries
where the state remained in control of vital resources for press economies,
rarely were news organizations willing to criticize governments out of fear
that such reporting would have damaging political and economic consequences. Additionally, the persistence of a heavily partisan culture ran
against the consolidation of an "independent" press. News organizations explicitly took sides in the partisan and often violent confrontations that characterized contemporary South American politics. Also, constant political instability and the long absence of extended democratic periods undermined
the prospects for a critical press that would target official malfeasance. Consequently, there were few and isolated examples of watchdog reporting, and
those were relegated to the margins of the press system. The alternative

press, which explicitly defined itself against the orthodoxy of U.S. journalism and instead crusaded in the name of specific ideological causes, almost monopolized the reporting of wrongdoing. Watchdog reporting, then, has historically been attached to a press that eschewed the ideal of independent, objective journalism.

Chapter 2 reconstructs the evolution of major muckraking reports and examines similarities across stories and countries in the last two decades. The analysis suggests that unlike previous experiences, mainstream publications, many of which are part of large media conglomerates, have shown interest in watchdog reporting. This is a significant shift, for it brings in important changes in the thematic agenda and the practices of watchdog journalism. The overwhelming majority of exposés have dealt with official corruption and human rights abuses. Only sporadically did the news media delve into social inequalities or business venality. Reasons for this are examined in subsequent chapters.

Chapter 3 explains the rise of watchdog reporting in the 1980s and 1990s and offers a preliminary explanation for why denunciations commonly single out official wrongdoing. Not all news organizations showed similar interest in denunciations, nor did they expose the same cases. The press is not a single entity but is crossed by economic and political divisions. Watchdog journalism reflects the coexistence of *journalisms*, that is, of different and contradictory understandings and conceptions of reporting. Such differences need to be considered in reaching a nuanced account not only of the conditions that have prompted news organizations to report on abuses or dissuaded them from doing so. Such differences also need to be assessed when examining the repertoire of muckrakers. It would be mistaken, however, to suggest that political and economic factors have been solely responsible for the growing interest of some news organizations in reporting about subjects that were formerly considered taboo (e.g., human rights violations). A fuller explanation also requires the analysis of news-making practices and the emergence of a new journalistic culture.

The second section of the book is concerned with how journalistic principles drive the interest of some news media in publishing exposés and how they shape the thematic agenda of contemporary muckraking. In chapter 4 I argue that although watchdog reporting requires a minimal margin of distance between news organizations and the targets of denunciations, proximity between reporters and sources is also crucial. The analysis looks into the relations between journalists and sources. The existence of obstacles to practicing U.S.-styled investigative journalism (e.g., the lack of legislation to access public records, the half-hearted commitment of news organizations to in-depth investigations) and the prestige that covering official news carries in the culture of South American journalism explain why official abuses are commonly at the center of press denunciations. The fact that watchdog journalism regularly deals with official wrongdoing at the expense of other kind of abuses suggests new ways of practicing politics in South American democracies. Intra-elite conflicts inform press denunciations: They prod reporters and news organizations to bring out wrongdoing and feed leaks that are the basic information in support of denunciations. Such dynamics make it necessary to critically reconsider the idea that a so-called "independent" press is the cornerstone of watchdog journalism. News organizations, regardless of the actual political-economic standing vis-à-vis different actors, maintain tight connections to newsmakers. Information-exchange linkages between journalists and newsmakers are extremely important in the production of denunciations and determine both the subjects and the timing of exposes.

Chapter 5 explores the questions of facticity and objectivity in the context of how journalism manufactures information about wrongdoing. The analysis reveals changes and continuities in the production and treatment of "journalistic facts." Although facticity and objectivity are two pillars of the ideal of professional reporting in the Anglo-American press, the increasing concern with facticity in South American journalism does not imply unanimity about the desirability of objectivity. Here the persistence of *journalisms* becomes evident again. It is expressed in the lack of a consensus about what principles should rule reporting, the different treatment of journalistic facts, and the presence of antagonistic views about the suitability and possibility of objectivity in news production. An examination of these issues offers an entry into the question of the professional identity of contemporary muckrakers. What motivates them to pursue denunciations — personal politics, professional ambitions? As discussed in chapter 6, the interest in facticity suggests the ascendancy of the ideology of professional journalism. Reasons for this process include changes in the educational profile of reporters, the opening of possibilities for careers in journalism, and a growing concern among reporters with professional prestige. As traditional partisan conflicts have cooled off, the model of market-based media became more dominant and the concept of crusading reporting virtually disappeared. Journalism requires a new cultural imaginary to legitimize practices and articulate the identity of journalists. The ideology of professional journalism comes to fill out this void, but competing understandings of journalism have prevented that ideal from being completely embraced.

In the third section of the book, I examine the consequences of muck-raking for the quality of contemporary South American democracies. It is suggested that truth and political accountability are two central ideals that inform the work of watchdog journalists. Denunciations are intended to find the truth about events and are conceived as mechanisms to hold authorities accountable for their acts. Both ideals resonate with classic ideals of the liberal press as well as with political demands in contemporary South American politics. The pursuit of the truth has been a central demand for a myriad of social and political movements; the lack of accountability constitutes a major weakness of today's democracies and one of the most pressing issues to resolve.

In chapter 7 I discuss whether truth actually can be achieved as a result of press denunciations. Journalism's relation with the truth, as understood in realist accounts that articulate the conception of journalistic truth, is problematic. This results from the existence of obstacles inherent to the work of muckrakers and, more generally, the limitations on newsgathering. These difficulties make it necessary to reconsider the potential of journalism to contribute to debates about the truth by taking a perspective that does not jettison the ideal of truth but recognizes its value and desirability in newly democratized countries. Only then it would be possible to value the potential role of the press, not as an institution that monopolizes the truth, but as one that, at best, can stimulate and enrich public debates.

Chapter 8 examines the contributions of watchdog reporting to political accountability in countries where, to many observers, powerful interests continue to be largely unanswerable to citizens. Muckraking is ill-equipped to generate full accountability nor should it be expected to do so. Accountability refers to a system of institutions to check and monitor powers rather than the actions of one institution. Watchdog journalism, however, can add significant efforts to render powerful actors accountable by publicizing information. The availability of information that certain actors want to keep hidden is a crucial requirement for accountability to be possible. Muckraking cannot be examined apart from larger institutional dynamics. Although it has the potential for engaging the public in debates about the functioning of power and inform political and social sanctions, it remains constrained by the political and economic limitations of news organizations, the routines of newsgathering, and the culture of newsrooms.

WATCHDOG JOURNALISM IN SOUTH AMERICA

PART I

THE MAINSTREAMING OF
WATCHDOG JOURNALISM

CHAPTER 1

WATCHDOG JOURNALISM IN A
HISTORICAL PERSPECTIVE

Any discussion about watchdog journalism, or for that matter a democratic press, inevitably entails a debate about press freedom. Timeworn and overused, the idea of press freedom probably deserves to be left alone for a while. In South America, grassroots media activists strive for freedom; reporters and publishers fly the flag of freedom; media moguls praise freedom; and even military juntas justified iron-fisted tactics in the name of press freedom (just as they also defended coups as necessary to achieve true democracy). Press barons accused national-populist generals of violating freedom of the press; the latter retorted by defending their policies as instruments for achieving true press freedom. Press freedom, often used interchangeably with autonomy and independence, is what we defend and what our enemies oppose. We cannot do without press freedom, however. It is hard to analyze the prospects for a democratic press in the contemporary world or to sort out the problems and strengths of the press, without introducing such a big yet seemingly irreplaceable term. Who can be against a value that resonates with one of the most humane promises of modernity?

We all agree that press freedom is better than no press freedom. Answers to the question "who opposes or undermines press freedom," are diverse. These differences correspond to the basic principles that organize competing visions about the relation between press and democracy. Autonomy from the state is the cornerstone idea of the Western liberal tradition of the press, enshrined in the U.S. and South American constitutions and, these days, ceaselessly repeated to justify media privatization and reform. Only at an arm's length from the state can the press monitor government actions. The degrees of separation between press and government best indicate the degree of press freedom. Inspired in the ideals of the modern democratic revolutions, this tradition holds the state under suspicion as being authoritarian and prone to suffocating the press. Consequently, monitoring power means monitoring political autocrats. What better place to watch the state than from a press firmly anchored in the market? Economic independence is the only ticket for arriving at press freedom and making concrete the ideal of a watchdog press.

The necessity of an independent press also rings true for leftist critics. There cannot be a truly democratic press without autonomous news organizations. Embedded in the same cultural *zeitgeist* of modernity, this perspective does not fault liberalism for upholding press freedom as a noble and desirable ideal. Rather, it accuses liberalism of erring in the diagnosis and in the recommendations, of wearing eighteenth-century blinders that ignore the realities of contemporary capitalist societies. The market rather than the state is mainly responsible for keeping the press subordinate. As South American journalists quip about liberal positions defended by press owners, "*Libertad de prensa* (press freedom) means *libertad de empresa* (market freedom)." The ideal of free media is hopelessly utopian or simply false when press organizations regularly succumb to market pressures or wholeheartedly embrace capitalist interests. Monitoring power means monitoring plutocrats and the intertwined relations between capitalist states and business.

In the South American context, these two conceptualizations need to be considered to understand the problems for the existence of a press that can effectively bring the economic and politically powerful to public scrutiny. Although it was coined in the early modern European context of democratic revolutions, liberalism's indictment and fear of the state still seems relevant in fin-de-siècle South America. Even modest bourgeois freedoms (including press liberty) seemed a threat to military despots and civilian authorities, who paid rhetorical tribute to press freedom yet, with a few exceptions, consistently aimed to cultivate a lapdog media. *Contra* liberalism, however, it is necessary to reconceptualize power: It is not a tangible good monopolized by one single institution, but a process in which multiple actors vie for scarce resources. A view that sees power as residing in the towering, all-powerful state is inadequate; it fails to take into account that much of Latin American history is precisely about the unyielding and still unfolding struggles for state-building and domination. And, pace the Frankfurt School and critical political economists, liberalism does not bring to the forefront the power of the market and the interlocked interests between state and market interests in regard to the constraints limiting press autonomy.

Even in South America where, arguably, the state during periods of military rule came closer to the image of an almighty state, the relations between press and power were more complex than what liberalism's theoretical equipment allows for. If press freedom is measured only in terms of the degrees of separation between the Goliath state and the David press, the analysis simplifies an extremely complicated problem. The separation between the state and the press is certainly necessary for watchdog journalism, especially in a historical context of permanent violations of liberal freedoms and news organizations ready to court state powers. There is no question that the affirmation of a liberal press is a seismic shift, but watchdog journalism (and democratic press) cannot be read only in the key of classic liberalism. If autonomy is indispensable for watchdog journalism to evolve, as both liberal and critical positions hold, the rarity of watchdog journalism in the region has been the product of a press historically tied to both economic and political powers and, if willing to take distance, unable to become effectively autonomous.

To make autonomy a requisite for watchdog journalism does not mean to assume a dreamy-eyed vision of independence and press freedom. In its most simple version, this ideal straitjackets the analysis into Manichean oppositions that do not help to capture the complex relations between news and power. The press is assumed to be dependent or independent, free or subjugated, and, conversely, the state is viewed as either interventionist or unintrusive, democratic or tyrannical. As many studies have concluded (and South American journalists overwhelmingly recognize), there is no independent media in the strictest sense; all news organizations are shaped, constrained, informed, subjected to diverse interests, and part of a "network of relationships" (Nerone 1994). To name two extreme examples in terms of business and political muscle, neither the news conglomerate nor the grassroots radio station are truly autonomous. They mediate a complex network of relations among audiences, authorities, advertisers, and other actors, relations that are not immune to politics. For much of its rhetorical force and democratic appeal, the principle of press freedom, so dear to the liberal tradition, often clouds the essentially political nature of the press and the inextricable relation between the press and power. Although it may seem a cliché in times when the ruling dictum is that politics is everywhere, it is still important to bear in mind that all news making is political. The promise and ideal of an independent press uncontaminated by the down-and-dirty world of politics goes against the grain of standard research, which has shown that the press is, above all, a political institution whose functioning cannot be understood separated from larger political dynamics.

To understand what deters and what facilitates watchdog journalism, it is important to bring to the foreground the linkages between the press and economic and political powers. The democratic potential of the news media depends on its capacity as an institution in the public sphere to keep state and market powers at a distance. News organizations that could come closer to the ideal of the public sphere are those that serve as conduits for the expression of alternative public opinions uncontaminated by state and market interests, that is, institutional settings that offer spaces for the critique of official and economic interests. To use media scholar James Curran's (1996) terminology, both "civic" and "professional" media are necessary in this regard.[1] The civic media should sustain adversarial views and publicize the ideas of particular groups; the professional media can be relied upon to maintain a critical surveillance of all power centers in society, and expose them to the play of public opinion (Curran, 1996:110). Problems arise when the civic media are weak and suffer continuous problems to remain alive, and when mainstream journalism has limited degrees of separation from states and markets. Proximity to specific powers makes the press unlikely to be interested in keeping the same interests at bay. It dims the prospects that news organizations can effectively, as Curran (1996:112) hopes, "sustain vigilant scrutiny of government and centers of power." Watchdogs do not bite their owners, as David Protess and colleagues (1991) state nor, we should add, do they chomp neighbors with whom they have amiable relationships. Only when subjects are at a reasonable distance from the targets of investigation, may news organizations be willing to pore over confidential information and implicate political and economic powers in illegal activities. News organizations may be interested in prioritizing relations with one or more different actors for different reasons. They may focus on mass or upscale readers; maintain ties to ruling or marginal political parties; be funded primarily by owner's fortunes, sales, and ads; draw advertising from small or large sponsors; be affiliated with social movements or depend on the largesse of state-owned companies; or opt to privilege relations with prominent politicians or ordinary citizens. All these are political relations that variously shape relations among press, states, and markets and differently affect news making as well as the possibilities and thematic agenda of watchdog journalism.

The different liaisons that news organizations maintain with states and markets make it problematic to discuss the press in singular terms. Moreover, the soundness of approaching the press as a monolithic institution is questionable, given not only unequal articulations between news organizations with political and economic powers, but the fact that they do not pledge allegiance to the same ideological principles, face comparable economic situations, or adopt similar journalistic styles. Broad-brush statements ("the American press has become sensationalized," "Third World newspapers consistently depend on state advertising") are useful for pointing at similarities but at the same time pave over important differences and obscure the complex realities of "the press" in a given country or region. "The press" is an umbrella term that refers to a plurality of organizations that manufacture and distribute news. In turn, news is imbued with different political convictions that are based on different economic situations and that advocate different conceptions of journalism.

Recognition of these distinctions is extremely important to understanding the press in South America where, historically, "the press" has referred to an ensemble of news organizations with dissimilar political sympathies and unequal economic muscle that were influenced by different and superimposed journalistic traditions. Brazilian columnist Alberto Dines (1994, 20) puts it bluntly: "the press, in reality, does not exist. The organizations that pretend to represent it are fictional. The press consists of the sum of the actions of information vehicles." The label "press'" is used to designate newspapers, which are part of a large conglomerate of media and other industrial interests, and the newsmagazine, which survives on sales of a few thousand copies. The bracketing of "the big press" from the "other" press, a distinction commonly found in critical studies about journalism in the region, attests to the differences among news organizations.

The "big press" refers to a handful of politically influential, advertising-rich, and circulation-strong newspapers and newsmagazines, but it can hardly be considered a unified institution. Despite circumstantial agreements and similarities, not necessarily do leading news organizations offer identical coverage or editorial viewpoints. Moreover, the historical coexistence of different understandings about the mission of journalism also makes it problematic to talk about the press as a unified institution. Press scholar Anne-Marie Smith's (1997) observation about the lack of a common identity in the Brazilian press holds true elsewhere in the region. The absence of a consensus about "the role of the press" was not specific or intrinsic to the media but instead reflected wider ideological battles and divisions. Debates about the role and identity of the press were another battleground of the political wars that have characterized South American societies for decades. Informed by and loyal to different press traditions, publishers, editors, and reporters offered diametrically opposed answers to questions such as "what is the function of the press" 'or "what is the role of a journalist?"' No unanimity ever existed about its role, ideals, or norms governing journalistic practices. News organizations might have coincided on some matters and strategic considerations but agreements have not necessarily sealed all cracks.

In this chapter I analyze the traditions and historical conditions that have influenced South American journalism and explain why watchdog journalism has been exceptional in the context of the relations among press, state, and markets. This should help to clarify the family lineage, continuities and breaks with the past, and strengths and weaknesses of present-day watchdog journalism. This chapter can also serve as an introduction for readers who are unfamiliar with the Latin American press by providing a roadmap of countries, newspapers, and historical developments.

PRESS MODELS

Basically, two journalistic heritages have shaped the history of the press in the region: one championed journalism as advocacy and active interpretation of political reality; the other made the principles of dispassion and political independence its cornerstone. The "journalism of opinion" professed allegiance to journalism as political interpretation, and conceived of publications as vehicles for party ideals and journalists as crusaders for party causes. From this perspective, the mission of the press was conceived to be the promotion of party dogmas, the propagation of policies, and the support of candidates rather than turning a profit or delivering "objective" news. This tradition has been represented by newspapers and magazines that expressed the doctrine and platforms of political parties, trade unions, religious, and other civic organizations (Capelato 1989; De Marco 1969; Trindade 1980). These publications were testimonies for the concept of journalism as a political tribune rather than an impartial chronicler of facts, and for the journalist as an activist for specific causes rather than a "neutral witness to history."

This tradition drew inspiration mainly from the European press. English, French, and Italian newspapers in particular have gripped the imagination of South American journalists for decades. Into the 1950s and 1960s, for example, the pervasiveness of belle-lettreism was seen as an offshoot of European journalism. An able prose, a superb command of the language, and storytelling skills were synonymous with journalistic talent. The comments made by José Freitas Nobre, former president of the national union of journalists and congressional representative, accurately describe experiences throughout the region: "Initially, Brazilian journalism had a doctrinal, philosophical, literary tendency, which defined the beginning of the century as a European, especially French, phase" (in Marques de Melo and Lins da Silva 1991, 44). The concept of newspapers as commercial enterprises mainly interested in market success was looked down on, considered unbefitting to the cultural and political missions of journalism. In the mid-1950s, Brazilian journalist Danton Jobim (1954) wrote, "In Latin America nobody is supposed to establish a newspaper as a business, to make money. Money can be welcomed as an unexpected dividend, but a newspaper is founded generally to serve political aims: to defend, for instance, the candidacy of a national leader for the presidency, to fight for political reform, to support a government. Few of those papers become financially strong and stable." The concept of "journalism of opinion or doctrine," particularly of French inspiration (see Chalaby 1997), was another manifestation of the extraordinary influence of European culture among political and literary elites, who have been the social cradle of the most renowned publishers, editors, and columnists.

Inevitably, the fate of the partisan press has run parallel to the up-and-downs of political parties, trade unions, and other organizations. The absence of a well-grounded partisan media in contemporary Latin America is rooted in the ephemeral and intermittent life of political parties, especially in the past few decades. It is no coincidence that partisan publications were more likely to survive in countries where political parties have been able to maintain a longer presence. This explains why news media identified with party interests still exist in Colombia and Uruguay, while elsewhere in the region they had a volatile existence and rarely reached massive circulation. The cleavages that divided societies were articulated in a number of publications whose primary purpose was to serve as intellectual and political forums rather than profitable ventures.

Colombia is as an interesting exception in terms of the resilience of party-identified press in a region where such publications have been relegated mostly to political-cultural pockets in press markets dominated by nonpartisan, business-oriented media conglomerates. The origins of leading newspapers in present-day Colombia hark back to late nineteenth-century and early twenty-century political battles. Confrontations inside and between the Liberal and Conservador parties created today's premier newspapers, including *El Espectador* in 1887, *El Colombiano* in 1912, *El Tiempo* in 1911, and *Vanguardia Liberal* in 1921. In its first edition, for example, the leading paragraph of *El Tiempo* read: "This paper will support the ideas of the Partido Republicano, born in the crisis spawned by the endless and grave confrontations between two political groups." Enrique Santos Calderón (1989, 111), one of the most influential contemporary columnists in Colombia, writes, "All political leaders directed or collaborated in a newspaper, an indispensable tool for political proselytism at the time. . . . Journalism was characterized by its militancy, combativeness, and extreme politicization." Santos Calderón argues that a partisan press that reflected local political wars characterized the first half of the twentieth century. "Politicians and journalists were the same," he points out, "because national journalism is and has been the seeding ground for presidents and party leaders."

In the nineteenth century, twenty presidents had been newspaper owners, publishers, or editors. The tradition of partisan press continues but is more toned down than in the past. Liberal newspapers no longer abstain from mentioning conservative presidents as they did with President Laureano Gómez in the early 1950s. Nor have recent conservative administrations adamantly tried to silence the Liberal press. Nor do conservative militants attack liberal dailies, as they did when they burned the building of *El Espectador* in 1968 (Duzán 1994). Many contemporary leading politicians still exhibit journalistic credentials, such as former president (and later appointed Organization of American States secretary) César Gaviria and President Andrés Pastrana. Although the linkages between party and newspapers have become considerably looser, the partisan sympathies of the press still are unmistakable. The masthead of *El Espectador,* even after the Cano family sold a majority of its stock to the Santo Domingo group, still carries founder Fidel Cano's phrase: "*El Espectador* will work for the goodness of the motherland with Liberal principles and for the goodness of Liberal principles with patriotic principles."

Although the decline of the partisan press is not unique to the region, there are specific factors that have contributed. The recurrent authoritarian regimes decimated political organizations that had developed and sustained partisan publications. For example, Peronist newspapers (many of which received state support) could not have survived after the 1955 coup that ousted General Juan Perón and banned the Peronist party. It is hard to imagine that *La Tribuna,* the long-time newspaper of the Acción Popular Revolucionaria Armada (APRA), could survive after the disastrous electoral performances of the former popular party and the general crisis of traditional political parties in Peru in the 1990s. Rising partisan dealignment in the last decades has made the existence of partisan media difficult if not virtually impossible. This is evident even in countries where there has been a long trajectory of party-affiliated publications. Uruguayan scholar Carlos Filgueira (1994: 90) aptly summarizes this situation: "The rupture of the traditional party press is also rooted in the crisis of the political parties to respond to recent structural and cultural transformations. It is increasingly more difficult for press outlets to compatibilize the partisan-political logic with the [dominant] business logic."

The gradual decline of the partisan model did not mean the complete disappearance of "the journalism of opinion," of a press ostensibly committed to specific political ideas that impregnate the entire coverage and are not relegated simply to editorials and columns. The so-called independent press and the alternative press of the 1960s and 1970s, to be discussed later in this chapter, attest to the continuous attraction of that tradition. Nor has the European press been abandoned as a source of inspiration. It continues to exercise a perceptible influence. In 1987, the founders of *Página/12*, the premier example of watchdog journalism in today's Argentina, found inspiration in the satirical style of France's *Le Canard Enchaine*, in the leftist, non-ideological position of *Liberation*, and in the pluralism and undivided support for democracy in Spain's *El Pais* (Lanata 1987). In Brazil, Mino Carta, founder of the two most influential newsweeklies (*Veja* and *ISTOE*) and former editor of leading newspapers, advocates the European rather than the U.S. model of the press as better suited for his country. "The system of big newspapers, with huge number of copies, many branches, a large workforce, and, consequently, high production costs is good for the United States but it does not correspond to the socio-economic reality of our country. In economic terms, Western European journalism is more appropriate for us and, politically, guarantees the importance of the individual journalist within the machinery of a newspaper." (Carta 1988: 67).

THE MOVEMENT TOWARD A NONPARTISAN PRESS

The slow fading out of the partisan press took place simultaneously with the rise and affirmation of a journalistic tradition that embraced the press model developed in the United States around the early 1900s. This tradition rejected the principles of partisan journalism and declared itself to be independent from party and government influences. It incorporated the principles of objective reporting and other innovations of the modern U.S. press, such as format, design, and newsroom organization. Its intent was to attain commercial success rather than spread partisan gospel and evangelize readers. To this tradition belong the newspapers that gained worldwide recognition as examples of "quality" press, such as Argentina's *La Nación* and *La Prensa*, Brazil's *O Estado de São Paulo*, Chile's *El Mercurio*, and Peru's *El*

Comercio and *La Prensa*. These dailies were owned and controlled by powerful families, the "great names" of Latin American journalism: Edwards of Chile, Miró Quesada and Beltrán of Peru, Mesquita of Brazil, and Gainza Paz and Mitre of Argentina.

Before they turned into flag-bearers of U.S. journalism in the region, these newspapers were essentially partisan, expressing the changing political and economic cleavages during the nineteenth century and early decades of the twentieth century and serving as instruments in intra-elite disputes. In Argentina, *La Nación* and *La Prensa* each were, as the former's masthead announced, "a tribune of doctrine," expressions of intra-elite battles that defined the country's politics in the second half of the nineteenth century. *O Estado de São Paulo* (first called *A Provincia de São Paulo* and later owned by the Mesquita family) defended the Partido Republicano, which represented antimonarchical and antislavery positions in the 1870s (Duarte 1977). Even until the 1940s, the press in the state of São Paulo (as well as in the rest of Brazil) was divided along partisan ideologies and the liberal-antiliberal opposition (Capelato 1989). In Peru, Miró Quesada's *El Comercio* was born as an expression of guano-exporting interests in the 1840s; and Beltrán's *La Prensa* originally was linked to the Partido Demócrata. Whether they were born as ribs to Adam's state or in direct opposition to the government, none of these newspapers were originally tied to the market logic. The business organization was essentially a means to accomplish political goals, as Taschner (1992) observes about the origins of modern Brazilian dailies. With high levels of illiteracy and small markets, these newspapers could not function solely as economic ventures.

The origins of a market-oriented, U.S.-style press occurred in the years when South American economies were incorporated into the international order shaped by the second industrial revolution. Leading newspapers incorporated the latest technological innovations, adopted the services of news agencies, and embraced the values of U.S. journalism. While European dailies were mandatory references before World War I, U.S. press influence became notorious afterwards. The incorporation of U.S.-style news occurred at a different pace in each country, and it coincided with the slow shift from a partisan to a commercial press. This tendency was perceptible as early as the 1920s and 1930s. The result of the merging of two newspapers in the 1920s, Chile's *El Mercurio* explicitly tried to follow the model of *The New York Herald*. Its founders intended to produce a newspaper controlled by entrepreneurs, not by a political group, that would emphasize information and neutrality over doctrine, relegating opinion to the editorial pages (Santa

Cruz 1988). The foundation of *Folha da Manha* and *Folha da Tarde* (that later merged into the *Folha de São Paulo*) in Brazil (Taschner 1992) and the massive success of *Crítica* in Argentina (Saíita 1998), a tabloid that tapped into popular tastes and offered an alternative in a press system dominated by elite newspapers, also hinted at the growing influence of nonpartisan, market-oriented journalism.

Partisan independence was held as the principle that should guide modern newspapers, which expressed the emergence of urban middle classes. In the late 1910s and the 1920s, the opening of international and local advertising companies and market research agencies indicated that news reporting was increasingly being seen as a business. The creation of news agencies and the growing presence of international and domestic wire news services in daily editions suggested the affirmation of a concept of news that privileged fact-gathering and neutral language over opinion. Back from visiting newsrooms in the United States, the top brass of South American newspapers introduced changes to refashion journalistic routines, writing styles, and formats. The coming of mass newspapers had a great impact on the political and cultural life of these countries. With their arrival, the press was no longer restricted to the elite newspapers that had dominated in the "oligarchic period" or the "aristocratic republic." Together with the incorporation of the middle classes into the political system and the beginning of mass political parties, the new press indicated that South American societies were democratizing.

During this time, the United States consolidated its dominant position in the hemisphere while the influence of European powers (politically, economically and culturally) weakened. And the transition toward industrial capitalism, especially in Argentina and Brazil, and the growth of a middle-class readership also stimulated the rise of U.S.-influenced journalism. For press scholar Gisela Taschner (1992), "the transition of Brazil to the U.S. sphere of influence, the [Second World] war, the censorship of the *Novo Estado*, and the presence of a business logic (though subordinated to editorial positions) contributed to the modernization of newspapers, incorporating techniques and products already used by the U.S. cultural industry." For her, this transition could be traced in the overall concept of newspapers. Information, not commentaries or chronicles, became the "main product," hard news was assigned more space, photographs and illustrations became ubiquitous, and dailies featured different sections. Even the Colombian press, which even today remains identified with partisan positions and party leaders, introduced some of these changes. This influence was evident in technical aspects such as "news design, organization of press companies, distribution and marketing strategies, news reporting. U.S. managerial and professional designs began to be a decisive presence in Colombian newspapers. It was an influence in form rather than content, however, for there remained significant differences in terms of the concept of news" (Santos Calderón 1989: 122).

A sure sign of these changes was the growing role of the Inter-American Press Association (IAPA) in the hemisphere. In 1926, the first Panamerican Congress of Journalists held in Washington, D.C., approved a recommendation for the foundation of a regional institution for journalists, thus establishing a basis for the IAPA. Founded in 1943, IAPA adopted professionalism and nonpolitical journalism as its leading principles (Napp 1987). A foremost champion of the U.S. model of journalism, IAPA turned into a leading international forum and chief political and professional referent for premier newspapers. In editorials or at international meetings, editors and publishers of premier dailies have praised the principles of U.S. journalism and condemned government intervention as a violation of press rights. In the name of "freedom of the press," they invoked legislation in the United States and Latin America to rebuke attempts to keep the press on a short leash and opposed policies that promoted state encroachment on the press.

STATE AND PRESS ECONOMICS

The import of U.S. journalism was half-hearted. Its ascendancy was visible in the rhetoric of publishers more than in actual practices and content. Notwithstanding its growing influence, the U.S. model did not become fully incorporated into the South American press. None of the crucial developments that facilitated the rise of a market-based press in the United States existed in South America. Widely different press economies, the absence of political consensus, and the topsy-turvy development of democracy in the region worked against a successful transplant of U.S. journalism to the region.

The modern concept of the U.S. press goes back to the commercial revolution of the early 1800s, when the main interest of newspapers gradually shifted from political ideologies to the mass market. This change reflected a process in which press economies were becoming less dependent on party subsidies and, instead, relied more on advertising and sales. According to several analysts (Schiller 1979; Schudson 1978), the simultaneous growth of

an urban middle class was also essential to the process. Shop clerks and arti-
sans were the target readership of the "penny press." Once press economics
veered toward the nascent mass market, standard positions have argued,
partisan influence receded. Press scholar John Nerone (1987: 391) has questioned this position, arguing that partisanship "was never absent from penny
papers, and it became more pronounced as the penny paper became more
successful." For Nerone, "the penny press did not invent political independence and did not institute neutrality or objectivity." Instead, the growth of
news monopolies was directly responsible for the decline of the partisan
press. It was not until the first decades of the twentieth century that partisanship waned and newspapers began to incorporate the ideals of objectivity (Hallin 1994).

Against arguments that attributed objectivity and partisan detachment to
the coming of the telegraph and other technological innovations, sociological studies have emphasized the importance of changing social and cultural
conditions as responsible for the weakening of the partisan character of U.S.
newspapers (Schudson 1978). The South American cases support this last
position: News wire services and other information technologies that became widely available in the early 1900s were by themselves unable to change
the tenacious grip of partisan sympathies on newspapers. The mass market
of readers and advertisers and the gradual loosening of a partisan political
culture, a process that roughly spanned between the 1820s to the 1920s, became the catalysts for the divorce of news from partisanship, putting in place
the basis of the modern U.S. press.

Similar circumstances are not found anywhere in South America. Mass
market-oriented newspapers have existed since the turn of the century, but
economic and political conditions did not offer a favorable environment to
replicate the U.S. model. Without newspapers that were firmly anchored in
the market or tuned to the needs of advertisers and the demands of readers,
the U.S. model could not succeed. In his insightful analysis on the influence
of "American" journalism in the Brazilian press, Eduardo Lins da Silva (1991)
suggests that "the lack of conditions in the local economy frustrated the will
[to implement an American-inspired press], with only a few exceptions (*Jornal do Brasil, O Estado de São Paulo*)" (see Alves de Abreu and Lattman-
Weltman 1996). A limited number of readers, coupled with small advertising
investments did not facilitate the transition to a market-based press. The
partisan press continued to draw its economic lifeblood mainly from the
coffers of party, union, and religious organizations, and private fortunes.
Only the leading dailies in the capital cities were able to move somewhat into

a market direction. As literacy rates, disposable income, and advertising expenditures were higher in the metropolis than in the interior, newspapers based in resource-rich regions were more likely to throw their economic anchors into the waters of the market. Without exception, however, the state remained crucial for the financial health of the press. Government subsidies and loans have been indispensable for the survival of newspapers and, with a few exceptions, the state has consistently been the main advertiser for print media (Salwen and Garrison 1991; Heuvel and Dennis 1995). This situation meant that the power balance survived almost intact even when the mass market expanded and U.S. journalism became a strong cultural referent for publishers and reporters. State bureaucracies headed by civilian or military officials continued to exercise greater leverage than advertisers or the buying public. Typically, substantial amounts of official advertising have been allocated arbitrarily to favor allies and to penalize opponents. Although it has been a crucial presence in press economics since the second half of the nineteenth century, the state gained more power once it began controlling larger sectors of the economy. The creation of public bureaucracies in the 1930s and the nationalization of huge companies in the 1940s and 1950s reinforced the state's pivotal economic role. Big advertisers such as oil, telephone, water, electricity, airline, iron, coal, steel, and tin companies were in the hands of the state.

The considerable power of the state was not limited to the control of large advertising budgets. Political appointees had monopolized access to other assets that greatly affected the economic situation of newspapers. They controlled the issuing of permits to import machinery and decisions to declare tax exemptions and to forgive debts with state-owned banks and overdue taxes that press firms had to the state (de Lima 1988, Filgueira 1994; Waisbord 1996). The chronic debates and disputes over newsprint best illustrate the entangled relation between news organizations and the state. To cultivate a lapdog media, governments have manipulated the import of newsprint (offering foreign exchange below market value or arbitrarily granting import permits) or formed partnerships with newspaper firms in the domestic production of newsprint. Lins da Silva (1986: 37) writes, "the government determines the quota that each company gets to import [newsprint] in order to put out their newspapers. In this way, it has a permanent control, which does not need to be explicit, over the daily life of the press." Given these conditions, newspaper firms had to court the state rather than the market to achieve commercial success. The small size of both advertising and reading markets in many countries reinforced the dependency upon state favors to survive economically. When newspapers were unable to survive by their own means in the choppy waters of the market, the state was the only lifeguard to save them from bankruptcy.

Consequently the press never attained independence from the state, and for the most part did not try to become separate. The state was too important, politically and economically, to be put at a distance. Cutting ties with the state undermined the interests of newspapers in being close to power. It would have been a suicidal move, pulling the plug that supplied indispensable resources. No wonder, then, that the model of the liberal press, where the white-hatted press needed to be suspicious and distant from the black-hatted state, never became deeply rooted. Instead, a quid pro quo relation between the big press and the state evolved. The power of the press meant proximity to, not distance from, the state. Brazilian observers speak of a press that has been part of the intimate circle of power, historically situated a stone's-throw away from power (Dines 1986; Sodré 1966). Similarly, "the big press [in Colombia] is supported on the power of the state" (Donnegra 1984: 58). To critics, a truly state-independent press never ranked high in the priorities of newspapers' owners. The purpose of launching and maintaining newspapers was not primarily journalistic but to serve other political and economic interests, a stepping-off point to achieve other goals. Newspaper ownership brought the possibility to have a public presence and opportunities to propagate ideas and facilitate the accomplishment of business and political goals. Colombian scholars argue that "in some cases, political and economic interests were more important than support for freedom of expression and the right of citizens to information for publishers" (Arocha et al. 1989:136). Communication scholar Luis Peirano and colleagues rightly indicate that "the majority of the largest [Peruvian] newspapers responded to the interests of the owners to use a daily as complement to political and economic action" (1978: 17).[2]

PARTISAN AND VIOLENT POLITICS

The convulsive politics that have characterized modern Latin America also made it impossible to replicate the U.S. model. Nothing remotely similar to the Progressive movement that contributed to extirpating party politics from journalism ever surfaced. Nor did prescriptions to mold journalism as a "scientific" enterprise, uncontaminated by the world of politics. If hostility to politics is an essential element of the U.S. journalistic culture, as media scholar Dan Hallin (1994) argues, the persistence of a politicized culture in an environment where political negotiations and conflicts between newspaper firms and state officials were constant deterred the affirmation of U.S. ideals as the ruling principles of journalism.

This is immediately obvious in the case of Colombia, where the press has been not just the stage for the chronic confrontations that pitted liberals against conservatives since the late nineteenth century but the victim and, to some critics, the perpetrators of violence. The coming of a conservative administration was a bad omen for liberal newspapers and vice versa. Liberal and conservative publications historically exchanged accusations and insults and, arguably, fanned the flames of La Violencia, one of the most tragic episodes of Latin American history.[3] In the aftermath of the murder of Jorge Eliécer Gaitán, angry liberal mobs destroyed the buildings of conservative dailies *El Siglo, La Defensa, El Figaro,* and *La Prensa* among others. In November 1949, Conservative president Mariano Ospina Pérez "shut down Congress, imposed gag laws, banned long-distance telephone calls, authorized governors to dispose of 'disturbing' media, and even created the office of the censor" (Fonnegra 1984: 45). Conservative militants set fire to the facilities of Liberalism's premier dailies *El Tiempo* and *El Espectador* in September 1952. Partisan allegiances continued to determine press-government relations after General Gustavo Rojas Pinilla took power in 1953. Having supported the coup against conservative Laureano Gómez, the Liberal press was initially exempt of the autocratic tactics of the government. The press did not object to Rojas Pinilla's decision of keeping Ospina's autocratic laws or to the closing of the Gomez-owned dailies *El Siglo* and *Diario Gráfico.* The relation between the press and the dictatorship, which was originally seen as the best guarantee to put an end to popular insurrection that surfaced in the 1940s and 1950s, was not a long-lasting love affair. Many dailies continued to support the government but Rojas Pinilla responded with heavy-handed tactics to Liberal and Catholic newspapers, which, having become estranged from the government, questioned some of its policies and dictatorial methods (Santos 1955).

In Argentina, Brazil, and Peru, party conflicts never bordered on all-out violence, nor were leading newspapers closely identified with political parties like in Colombia. Nonetheless, nonpartisan, politically neutral journalism was inconceivable. The absence of a minimal political consensus, best expressed in highly politicized cultures combined with recurrent cycles of civilian and military governments from the 1930s onward did not provide hospitable conditions for the affirmation of nonpartisan journalism.

Despite their confessed admiration for the canon of the U.S. press, "independent" dailies have practiced a "journalism of opinion," perhaps not as openly as partisan publications but shielded in the mantra of objectivity. To many observers, the passionate defenses of the ideals of impartiality and objectivity made by the publishers of premier newspapers smacked of mere lip service (G. González 1992; Peirano et al. 1978). Robert O'Connor's (1980) observation on the Venezuelan press is applicable to other countries in the region: "newspapers are generally nonpartisan — which is not to say that their reporting is totally objective or fair to all parties at all times . . . they tend to slant toward a major party (rarely toward a party of the left) but without closely following a particular party line."

Although they have not acted as organic mouthpieces for political parties and only circumstantially backed specific political figures and platforms, premier newspapers have not hidden their sympathies, which are often in favor of conservative policies. *La Nación* and *La Prensa* in Argentina have been historically aligned with agrarian interests and flatly opposed the industrial and social policies of Perón's administrations in the mid-1940s. In Brazil, *Folha da Manha* (the early incarnation of today's *Folha de São Paulo*) originally expressed the interests of powerful coffee-growing landowners and combated industrial policies (Taschner 1992). *O Estado de São Paulo,* in the words of former editor-in-chief Claudio Abramo (1989: 35), has been "anti-state, antiworker, anticommunist, and antichurch." In Peru, the Prado family-owned *Crónica* offered unmitigated support for President Manuel Prado in the 1940s and 1950s and defended the family's commercial interests even though it declared partisan neutrality in its founding editorial in 1912 (Pinto Gamboa 1983). *La Prensa* and *Ultima Hora,* owned and directed by legendary publisher Pedro Beltrán, historically have been seen as defenders of free-market ideals and the voice of large landowners and powerful domestic and foreign interests in the sugar, cotton, oil, and mining sectors. As Finance minister, Beltrán headed the Council of Ministers during Prado's presidency.

In situations of heightened conflict, dailies have forsaken any pretense of objectivity and openly defended unmistakable economic and political positions. One of the best-known examples is the frontal war that Chile's *El Mercurio* waged against Salvador Allende's socialist administration in the early 1970s and the paper's active participation in the 1973 coup. Many historical episodes offer evidence that premier newspapers were ready to drop neutrality in the name of national interest such as the confrontations that pitted military-populist regimes against the establishment press in the 1940s and

1950s. In all cases, these clashes resulted in the intervention and expropriation of the newspapers. In Brazil, claiming that the daily kept illegal weapons, the Vargas administration first intervened at *O Estado do São Paulo* and then relaunched it under the direction of the government's Department of Press and Propaganda. In Argentina, the frontal opposition waged by *La Nación* and *La Prensa* against the Perón administration in the early 1950s resulted in the government's decision to close *La Prensa* (Cane 1998).

In the context of the cold war, the rising political temperature in the region during the 1960s and 1970s also drew newspapers to take sides. In Argentina, the main newspapers prioritized "national security" over freedom of expression and strongly supported the military regime that came to power in 1976 (Blaustein and Subieta 1998). A delegation of the Inter American Press Association reported that self-censorship was widespread. It noted that editors were completely risk-averse and that some publishers justified that they didn't print news on kidnappings and violence because they agreed with the "government's campaign against terrorism" and volunteered "to cooperate" (see *Página/12* 1998). *O Estado de São Paulo* and *O Globo*, among other leading Brazilian dailies, vocally supported and applauded the military intervention that dethroned João Goulart in 1964. Members of the top brass of Brazil's premier news organizations (*Diarios Associados, Folha de São Paulo, TV Record, Jornal do Brasil, Tribuna da Imprensa*) participated in the *Instituto de Pesquisas e Estudos Sociais* (IPES), an organization founded in 1961 with "the goal of mobilizing democratic public sentiment against the leftists that surrounded João Goulart" (Vinhas 1994). In contrast, *Ultima Hora*, a nationalist newspaper that had defended moderate reforms under the Goulart administration and had substantially relied on government advertising, was the most visible supporter of the ousted president.

The development of the Peruvian press reached a turning point when the military ousted the Belaúnde Terry administration in 1968. Unlike other authoritarian regimes that took power around that time in the region, which were internationally aligned with the United States and linked to conservative domestic interests, the coup led by General Juan Velasco was influenced by nationalistic ideals and promised to carry out a revolution to transform the structure of Peruvian society. One of its first decisions, the expropriation of the International Petroleum Company, alienated Manuel Ulloa Elias, the owner of the daily *Expreso*. Ulloa and the daily have historically supported conservative causes and were linked to Acción Popular, the party dethroned by the military. As Belaúnde Terry's finance minister, Ulloa had negotiated the oil contract that the military had canceled. *Expreso* responded by accusing communists of having taken over the military and the country. During the first year in power, President Velasco continually criticized the press, portraying the leading newspapers as advocates of oligarchic and foreign interests and manipulators of public opinion to benefit antipopular interests. Velasco's verbal attacks were the preamble to the expropriation of newspapers based on the argument that nationalization was necessary for newspapers to work toward "social interests." The government ordered the intervention of *Expreso* and *Extra* in March 1970 (and a radio station also owned by Ulloa). In an oft-quoted statement, Velasco declared that the expropriated dailies, now in the hands of different organizations, would serve as "hounddogs against the oligarchy."[4] *El Comercio*, guided by the nationalistic sympathies of publisher Luis Miró Quesada, was an early supporter of the coup and of the government's decision to cancel the contract signed by the previous administration with an U.S. oil company. Later, however, it joined the influential *La Prensa* and a host of newspapers (*Crónica, Correo, Ultima Hora*) in their frontal opposition to the Velasco government. All the premier newspapers were expropriated in July 1974. In a letter to the IAPA, Miró Quesada described the situation: The expropriation and arrest of journalists "constitutes an unprecedented decision in the history of Peruvian journalism and probably in America at a time when the independent press was devoted to a decisive campaign to prevent the advance of communism in Peru . . . In this hard moment in which the path of independence, and not subjugation, has been chosen, we reiterate our complaint against totalitarian measures against the press of our country. We thank deeply the valuable help of the free journalism of the world and reiterate our faith in the most precious human freedoms: freedom of expression" (López Martínez 1989: 542).

If the partisan press is defined as publications intended to act as instruments for political parties, then the evolution and consolidation of the big press from the 1950s onward attests to the gradual demise of partisanship. If partisan press means publications that defend political or economic interests (not necessarily represented by party organizations), then partisanship has not disappeared. During the second half of the twentieth century, premier newspapers gradually abandoned their original party roots and metamorphosed into publications primarily concerned with market success. Journalists generally observe that the "independent" press has presented its political sympathies more subtly than the partisan press, but those sympathies are still apparent. The reason for this is that the intensity of South American politics left an indelible imprint on the press. The absence of a political consensus made it impossible to establish a truly independent forum.

Not only were newsrooms heavily impregnated by political sympathies but news organizations also had prominent roles in waging political battles. Publishers often brought their dailies into the political trenches to support or to lash out at different administrations. As discussed in subsequent chapters, the partisan nature of the news media has not disappeared even in times when political parties are in a deep crisis of legitimacy across the region and media companies vigorously try to consolidate and expand market power.

POLITICAL VIOLENCE AND THE ABSENCE OF LIBERAL DEMOCRACY

Finally, political instability and violence were anathema to duplicating the U.S. model of journalism in South America. An independent, politically neutral press was a chimera when civilian and military governments closed down media firms, tightly censored newsrooms and persecuted and killed dissident journalists.[5] The few editors and reporters who took distance from the government and remained committed to watchdog journalism often paid with prison, torture, exile, and death. Most newspapers adopted cautious positions or, in the cases of authoritarian Argentina and Brazil, supported military dictatorships by stifling political dissidence and ignoring human rights violations. More than explicit support for autocratic regimes, failure to report wrongdoing revealed the disinterest of the big press in taking up the role of public watchdog. Justifying the press's position, editorials often stated that when the national interest was threatened it was necessary to close ranks and leave criticisms aside. The much-exalted missions of nonpartisan and watchdog journalism were allegedly put off for the sake of national unity.

When publications did practice critical reporting, the result was the closure of newsrooms, the seizing and burning of editions, and the persecution and murder of dissident reporters. Colombian reporters recall the mid-1950s as particularly terrible for the press. Under the General Rojas Pinilla government, the publication of information that directly or indirectly referred to the armed forces was penalized with heavy fines and prison. Newspapers that did not support official decisions were banned, censored, and their tax returns meticulously examined. Editors were imprisoned and critical reporters were harassed and tortured. Violence against the press in Colombia was not limited to the 1950s, either. Seventy journalists were murdered between 1988 and 1993 in that country.

During the military dictatorships of the 1960s and 1970s in Argentina and

Brazil, publications and reporters that crossed the boundaries outlined by the regime were the targets of state violence. Ninety-three journalists disappeared in Argentina during the 1976–1983 authoritarian regime (Camaño and Bayer 1998). The government expropriated the daily *La Opinión* and its publisher Jacobo Timerman was kidnapped and tortured. Although in Brazil, the military government that ousted President Goulart in 1964 maintained a relatively hands-off position in regard to the media during the first years because the leading newspapers have actively collaborated (or implicitly endorsed) the putsch. The government switched gears after a military faction gained control. Amid growing discontent and civilian opposition, it decided to silence the press (and society at large), shutting down Congress and eliminating democratic rights in December 1968. This decision marked the beginning of the "hard" stage of the authoritarian regime. Fifteen reporters were tortured to death or disappeared between 1970 and 1978. Lins da Silva (1986) observes that the premier newspapers could not report on the immediate effects of the decision, such as the imprisonment of political leaders and repression of union movement, because the police seized the editions. Government censors were assigned to clear stories at *O Estado de São Paulo, Veja, Jornal da Tarde,* and *Tribuna da Imprensa* and self-censorship quickly became dominant in the press at large.[6] Censors were removed after 1975 when the most brutal and repressive phase of the dictatorship ended and the gradual process of political opening began with the coming of General Ernesto Geisel to power. In all cases of press under authoritarian regimes, censorship was virtually unnecessary as the big press engaged in self-censorship and suppressed stories that might enrage the military.

PARTISAN CRUSADING

To recapitulate, none of the factors that originated the modern tradition of U.S. journalism existed in South America. The economic antenna of newspapers was tuned to the state rather than to the market. There has not been a political-cultural movement determined to make journalism less partisan. And military juntas and political violence imposed conditions that negated the fundamental principles of U.S. journalism. The elimination of basic democratic rights, the iron-fist control of newsrooms, the persecution of critical journalists, and the imposition of terror and fear were contrary to the creation and affirmation of a liberal-democratic press that, even within the constrains of a capitalist system, could lay wrongdoing bare.

These conditions also made the presence and affirmation of watchdog journalism extremely difficult. For the most part, the big press has not been interested in scrutinizing political and economic powers, and publications that occasionally dared to lift the rug came under the pressure of market and state interests. The denunciation of business graft was often followed by business punishment. Even rumors that a news organization would break a story investigating prominent companies would be sufficient to trigger a rush of phone calls that ultimately killed in-progress pieces. In solidarity with the company investigated and fearful that investigations could reach them, large sponsors threatened and withdrew advertising. The investigations carried out by Colombia's *El Espectador* on white-collar crime in the early 1980s distinctly illustrate the problems any publication faced if it decided to pursue corruption in business. Investigations on fraud and mismanagement involving Grupo Gran Colombiano, one of the country's major corporations, with holdings in banking, financing, manufacturing, and media industries, resulted in, as María Jimena Duzán (1994: 28) wrote in the mid-1990s, "The loss of advertising revenue and the beginning of an economic struggle for the paper that hasn't ended yet."

The weight of the state in press economies automatically excluded government from being the target of investigations. What could be considered good copy from a professional or commercial standpoint played against a company's financial health. The publication of denunciations could swell readership numbers and potentially draw advertisers but it was likely to anger governments. For much of their apparent editorial or market soundness, such decision was bad politics and, thus, bad economics. An investigation of the illicit activities of a government official, for example, could affect the chances of a newspaper to be rewarded with favors such as official advertising, lower exchange rates for importing newsprint, and broadcasting licenses. As the former editor of an Argentine daily puts it, "To criticize a president, a minister, a mayor or even a low-ranking official is to shoot yourself in the foot. It never fails: you see the consequences when government advertising budgets are allocated." Fears of retaliation from irate government officials often resulted in editors killing stories on sensitive subjects. The journalistic merit of news stories was subject to political calculations.

"News value" did not necessarily mean "commercial value" either. The publication of sensitive news involving government officials could interest readers and increase sales, but a boost in readership numbers, many editors acknowledged, did not become a magnet for large advertisers. Sponsors were concerned that advertising in critical news media might alienate government officials who had power over key decisions that directly affected their own commercial interests such as taxes, large contracts with government-owned companies, and allocation of import permits. These fears explain why sponsors often boycotted news media that investigated public corruption. *Correio da Manha,* the only leading newspaper credited for having opposed the 1964 coup in Brazil, lost a substantial amount of advertising as it resisted the pressures of big sponsors to change its editorial position (Cotta 1997). Also in Brazil, the fate of *Jornal da República* illustrates the economic plights confronted by any publication that throws punches at the ruling order. Founded in 1980 by liberal-minded journalists and investors with the express purpose of offering an opposing view to the authoritarian regime, the paper lasted only five months and it was "systematically boycotted by advertising agencies, sponsors, and the government as advertiser" (Lins da Silva 1986: 41).

Without a press that kept the state minimally at an arm's length, watchdog journalism was virtually impossible. When economic survival or expansion was tied to the state, the press was generally complacent or extremely mindful of pleasing governments in military uniform or civilian clothes. Only on rare occasions did news organizations decide to support the investigation of wrongdoing. Under specific circumstances and for a limited time, some leading newspapers crossed political lines and dared to take a poke at their governments. Brazilian columnist Carlos Brickman (1992) recalls press denunciations of monopolies in cotton markets that involved the state-owned Banco do Brasil in the 1940s, irregularities in the development of Brasilia, the construction of the Rio-Niteroi bridge, and other incidents as evidence of watchdog journalism in the past. In the 1960s and 1970s, *Jornal do Brasil, O Estado de São Paulo,* and *A Tribuna de Imprensa* occasionally criticized the authoritarian regime and even investigated cases that involved government officials, but watchdog journalism remained the exception. Unwilling to ruffle government censors, Brazilian newspapers opted to draw attention to censorship through irony. *O Estado de São Paulo* inserted poems by Luiz de Camões and letters and *Jornal da Tarde* featured cooking recipes at places in their paper that were originally allocated for stories banned by censors. *Tribuna da Imprensa* printed a whole page without any articles.

If practiced, watchdog journalism could not be anything but partisan. When publishers actively took sides in heated political battles and carried their news organizations into their personal crusades, and pressures and persecution were the most likely responses to stories that scrutinized power, the disclosures of abuses were informed by partisan interests. A concept of muckraking couched in liberalism's language of "the guardian of the public interest"' or "the fourth estate" was unimaginable when journalism was traversed by the same political divisions that tore South American societies apart. Muckraking was possible only as crusading journalism when states, commercial interests, and premier news organizations cultivated tight relations; political cultures were fiercely partisan; owners and publishers were at the forefront of national politics; and violence and repression strongly conditioned journalistic work. Watchdog journalism implied a commitment to determined political causes rather than to the democratic ideal of checks and balances. It responded to the political orientations of owners and reporters and functioned as a strategy to advance specific agendas. It did not intend to wrap itself around the flag of balanced reporting and the defense of public good.

REBELS WITH A CAUSE

The "alternative press" best illustrates the partisan character of watchdog journalism. "Alternative press" refers to publications that bloomed under authoritarian regimes in the 1960s and 1970s that were conceived to exist outside the boundaries of the big press and to escape the trappings of mainstream journalism (Reyes Matta 1983). In his detailed study of the alternative press in Brazil, Bernardo Kucinski (1991: xiii) suggests that "alternative" alludes to "something not linked to dominant politics, a choice between two mutually exclusive options, the only exit in a difficult situation, and the desire of the generations of the 1960s and 1970s to protagonize social transformations." When spaces for public expression were closed and tightly controlled in Argentina, Brazil, and Peru, alternative publications were spaces of resistance to military rule and communication instruments for political parties, social movements, and other organizations. In Colombia, they were envisioned similarly, as alternatives to a two-party system controlled by liberals and conservatives who defended establishment interests and exclude forces of change. These weeklies and monthlies expressed the ideals of social change in the 1960s and 1970s incarnated in leftist and popular organizations and counter-cultural movements. They responded to the efforts of journalists, political activists, and intellectuals to gain political presence and resist the dominant political regime (Mello Mourao 1987). With a few exceptions, most were poorly funded and had limited circulation, with rarely more than a few thousand copies.

What made the alternative press alternative? In a broad sense, it was a journalism at the margins of the dominant order that opposed ruling political, economic, and social structures. Alternative only makes sense in terms of what set those publications apart from the dominant press: It was the *imprensa nanica* (midget press), as it was called in Brazil, in opposition to the big press. One of the key differences between them was their different positions vis-à-vis the state. While premier newspapers historically sought to maintain close relations with the state, the alternative press opposed the state. In fact, numerous alternative publications could only exist clandestinely. They were neither conceived as an offshoot of the state nor did they depend on official funds for survival. Having no economic aspirations, they were not interested in propagandizing official messages or courting prominent officials. Nor did they eagerly wait to be rewarded with official advertising or broadcasting licenses for good behavior. The economics of alternative publications resembled the situation of the partisan press in previous decades: Neither aimed to become commercially successful but, instead, to champion specific political causes. Party coffers and personal monies, barely sufficient to keeping them alive, provided economic resources. Under adverse economic and political conditions, the alternative press was closer than the big press to achieving autonomy from the government.

The approach to politics and journalism also made these publications "alternative" to the big press. They espoused what in Brazil is called *jornalismo de causa,* a journalism primarily concerned about propagating political views rather than achieving market success. In contrast, as many critics have observed, the big press consistently prioritized business interests over political agendas, ideologies, and personalities. The difference was not that alternative publications were "political" while the big press was not. As mentioned earlier, the political sympathies of premier newspapers have been unmistakable, although they declared to be committed to political neutrality. The differences lay elsewhere: Alternative publications were in the business of politics while the big press historically played politics to do business. Kucinski (1991: xix) writes, "they were moved by an anticapitalist spirit. They did not have market goals. They repudiated profit-making. When *Pasquim* [a leading alternative publication] began to sell more than 100,000 weekly copies, it generated profit and had the opportunity to buy printing facilities at sale prices . . . Jaguar [*Pasquim*'s editor-in-chief] refused, fearing the prospects of becoming owner." In his study of the alternative weekly *Opinião,* Pinheiro Machado (1978: 121) writes, it "had from the beginning the intention to devise a commercial strategy that did not depend on advertising. It would not reject ads, which were thought to strengthen [the publication], but, it aimed to serve readers and that readers would support it. It wanted to establish a policy similar to *Le Monde*: the advertising budget from big sponsors and agencies would not surpass twenty percent of billings to avoid dependency."

For alternative publications, journalism and politics were indivisible. Journalism was not a disinterested activity, separated from partisan and commercial interests, but it was politics by other means. Colombian Nobel-laureate Gabriel García Márquez's thoughts on why he participated in *Alternativa* represent the spirit that animated many journalists who worked in alternative publications: "In *Alternativa*, I think, I have found a form of political participation [*militancia*] that I sought for years. Serious journalistic work, deeply and clearly committed to reality'" (1978: 31). Not surprisingly, alternative publications followed the tradition of partisan or interpretive journalism that premier newspapers had abandoned decades earlier. Nothing was more foreign to a press ostensibly committed to political ideologies than the ideal of journalism as a discourse guided by the principles of objectivity and partisan detachment. In terms of cultural referents, the alternative press was closer to Albert Camus's *Le Soir Républicaine* or *Combat* during the French Resistance, revolutionary Cuba's *Granma*, or to new journalism in the United States rather than to the liberal gospel of U.S. journalism admired and glorified by the big press. It defined its mission in terms of defending and championing specific causes such as democracy, human rights, social justice, national interests, and socialism. Some of the best-known publications explicitly stated in their titles this concept of journalism such as Brazil's *Pasquim* (Pasquinade), *Opinião* (opinion), *Movimento* (movement), *Politika* (politics), *Resistencia* (resistence) and *Critica* (criticism), and Colombia's *Alternativa* (alternative) and *La Nueva Prensa* (the new press).

More than employment opportunities, extremely limited and poorly (if rarely) remunerated, alternative publications functioned, above all, as channels for political participation. For reporters (and intellectuals)-cum-political activists, these publications were one of the few opportunities for participating in politics at a time of political proscription. Those who held jobs in leading newspapers could publish ideas that were vetoed in mainstream publications. Those who could not get reporting jobs due to political reasons and were forced into a professional exile found in alternative publications the only available outlets for writing. These publications were the only possibility for journalists and writers who had been fired from newspapers and academic jobs, blacklisted, or considered to be "risky" for any mainstream newspaper. Hamilton Almeida (in Medina 1987), who worked for several alternative periodicals, recalls, "I spent a year without work because when I showed up at newsrooms people said 'Don't come here. It doesn't look good.'"

The birth, expansion, and gradual demise of the alternative press followed similar paths and timing in the region. The different characteristics of the ruling political order coupled with the specific makeup of political organizations shaped the distinctive characteristics the alternative press had in each country. Brazil, for example, had more alternative publications than anywhere else in the region, the publications stimulated by the long tenure of the authoritarian regime in power (1964–1985) and the vitality of social movements in the gradual process of *abertura* (political opening) (Kucinski 1991). In Peru, the weekly *Marka* was one of the best examples of the alternative press. Its foundation in 1975 responded to the intention of a group of journalists to create a journalistic alternative to the state-owned press and to champion socialist ideas. *Marka* steadily grew and became a best-selling political magazine. Its success stimulated the creation of *El Diario de Marka,* a newspaper that, as Juan Gargurevich (1991) indicates, explicitly defined itself as a leftist newspaper in contrast to the tradition of "independent" journalism advocated by establishment newspapers.[7]

Aside from specific characteristics in different countries, the alternative press functioned as a political and literary public sphere, a space for critical reflection and dissident voices, wedged between the state and the market, free from the political and business calculations of the big press. Readers were conceived not as consumers but as citizens, as members of a political community. Its intellectual muse were Antonio Gramsci's thoughts on the role of organic intellectuals and Lenin's writings on political organization, readings avidly discussed within the Latin American left at that time. Despite different ideological affiliations, alternative publications were conceived to function in ways somewhat analogous to the salons, clubs, and coffeehouses in eighteenth-century Europe. They were public spaces for democratic debate outside the limitations imposed by the state. They expressed the efforts of political and cultural organizations to carve out a buffer zone equidistant from authoritarian regimes and media business and to assist in the formation of a critical public opinion. Certainly the alternative press did not match Habermasian standards of bracketing political interests or advancing the force of the best argument. Quite the contrary: It was unabashedly partisan as it pushed to express the voices excluded from a public sphere that, under authoritarian regimes, could only live in alternative and underground spaces.

The democraticness of the alternative press lay not on measuring up to a yardstick of democratic discursive conditions but in its efforts to stimulate public life and oppose the attempts of the state to suffocate civil society.

With no state and business strings attached, alternative publications effectively functioned as spaces for monitoring wrongdoing and taking stabs at ruling powers. The alternative press set out to challenge power (Almeida 1980). Rodolfo Walsh, one of Argentina's preeminent investigative reporters, best expressed a concept that equated journalism with watchdog journalism. On Walsh, Uruguayan writer Angel Rama has said, "the denouncer-journalist [is] only committed to the truth and discovers secret dealings. He is the guardian of honesty, the incorruptible server of justice" (quoted in Pacheco 1985:4). In 1956, Walsh penned a series of articles for two small partisan publications *Revolución Nacional* and *Mayoría*. The articles were expanded and published the following year in *Operación Masacre*, a book that, to many analysts, pioneered new journalism before Truman Capote's 1964 *On Cold Blood*. Two features are particularly striking in Walsh's work: nonfiction writing that wove real events (journalism) into a fictional narrative (literature) and the concept that journalism necessarily was committed to specific political causes. Walsh investigated and denounced the kidnapping and shooting of Peronist militants in the aftermath of the 1955 military coup in *Operación Masacre* and the murder of a union leader in *Quién Mató a Rosendo?* in 1968 (these reports were originally published in the publication of a dissident union organization). His work clearly distilled his political inclinations, "the identification with the weak and the persecuted," as journalist Horacio Verbitsky (in Villalba 1991) puts it. Unlike the traditional "journalism of opinion" that was driven by journalists' beliefs rather than "journalistic facts," Walsh's accusations drew from extensive collection of information.[8]

In the 1960s and 1970s, alternative publications and journalists pushed watchdog journalism amid difficult economic and political circumstances. Sustained by meager means, publications lacked economic resources that could allow reporters to spend unlimited time marshaling information. In authoritarian contexts, public records were neither available nor accessible to reporters, and potential leakers were fearful of passing information. Against these conditions, alternative publications persisted in denouncing human rights abuses, government repression, and the mismanagement of public funds at a time when the more resourceful and powerful big press shrugged off critical reporting. In turn, denunciations triggered persecution and, ultimately, contributed further to undermine the continuity of the alternative press. As the cold-blood murder of Walsh at the hands of a death squad in broad daylight in Buenos Aires in 1977 and the 1976 bombing of the offices of Colombia's *Alternativa* painfully illustrated, alternative journalism was a prime target of state-sponsored violence.

Political persecution and economic difficulties, the same conditions that insulated the alternative press from the pressures and interests of the big press, plagued its evolution and contributed to its demise. Under government pressure, most alternative publications had a short life span and an on-and-off existence (Nassif 1997a). Although they could keep their heads above choppy political waters, persistent economic difficulties ended up drowning them. On the fate of the alternative press in Colombia, Santos Calderón (1989) writes, "The chronic scarcity of economic resources revealed a lack of advertising, that vital support for the news media in capitalist countries." Those able to survive the most brutal years of violence and repression lost their original missions after civilian administrations replaced authoritarian regimes in the 1980s. A press purposely created as an alternative to a big press (that refrained from oversight functions) and that prospered under dictatorial conditions necessarily had to shift purposes once the political context changed. The virtual disappearance of the alternative press in present-day South America indicates the difficulties most surviving publications confronted after liberal democracy settled in. Most importantly, the political impetus and cause celébres of the 1960s and 1970s that originally motivated their creation declined in post-authoritarian and post-cold war times. The resistance against military dictatorships in Argentina, Brazil, and Peru has given way to new political agenda after civilian administrations were elected. The vast array of leftist, nationalist, insurrectionist, and counterculture movements that gained momentum in past decades have dwindled due to devastating repression, internal differences, political apathy, and other processes that have profoundly reshaped the political and cultural environment that engendered and sustained them.

CONCLUSION

Historically, the deck has been stacked against watchdog journalism. When the press tried to stay close to the state and was prone to give a kid-gloves' treatment to officials, blowing government secrets open was inconceivable. It would alienate officials eager to punish those who stepped out of line as well as large advertisers who were not interested in angering governments, the source of much-needed resources and substantial contracts. In fairness to publishers and journalists who were interested in critical journalism at a time when colleagues chose other priorities or acquiesced to state and market requirements, political violence, stimulated by domestic confrontations and cold-war ideologies, did not offer suitable conditions. In this context, watchdog journalism could only have a chance when newspapers decided to battle governments and were ready to deal with consequences such as the lack of access to state advertising, official contracts, undervalued exchange rates, cheap newsprint, broadcasting licenses, and official information. This chapter has shown that, in the interests of keeping the presses rolling, newspapers rarely opted to take a more dangerous and uncertain road. And when they did, state repression inevitably quashed the chances that official dealings could be steadily monitored.

The intensity of political confrontations made the occasional bursts of watchdog reporting deliberately partisan. The lack of a hegemonic model of journalism meant that not all suspected or known acts of wrongdoing would be equally considered subject to press denunciations. While some publications investigated and publicized illegal dealings, others downplayed, ignored, or even implicitly justified them. The absence of a common understanding about the mission of the press and the existence of diametrically different positions about what acts needed to be monitored and denounced expressed the absence of political consensus. Partisan politics could not be stripped away from reporting when the same fault lines that divided the political landscape also separated news organizations.

The upsurge of press denunciations in the 1980s and 1990s insinuate the possibility that at least some obstacles to undressing emperors have been removed. If so, what conditions have encouraged the press to disclose wrongdoing in recent years? Is this seemingly invigorated watchdog journalism still partisan? These questions are tackled in the chapters that follow.

CHAPTER 2

DENOUNCING WRONGDOING

In this chapter I offer brief sketches of the main stories and a summary of the recent trajectory of watchdog journalism in Argentina, Brazil, Colombia, and Peru. The goal is not to provide an exhaustive account of all cases, which would be impossible within the limits of this book. Rather, my intent is to show examples that attest to the vitality of watchdog journalism and to offer a preliminary description to ground the analysis. I hope that a bird's-eye view will serve as both a first approach to the historical context and an introduction to the subjects and contents of stories. The overview shows that two subjects have dominated the thematic agenda of watchdog journalism: official corruption and human rights violations. After a country-by-country summary of the main denunciations, this chapter concludes by suggesting reasons why muckrakers regularly focus on government misdeeds and only sporadically delve into corporate venality and social problems. A consideration of the issues that the press has paid attention is important to frame the analysis in subsequent chapters regarding the rise and the characteristics of watchdog reporting in contemporary South America.

ARGENTINA

The Argentine news media have unearthed dozens of cases of wrongdoing since the return of democracy in 1983. Reporters have investigated the actions of the military juntas during the 1982 Malvinas/Falklands war soon after the battles ended and the responsibility of military and police officers in the persecution and disappearance of citizens during the "dirty war" in the 1970s. In the 1990s, *Clarín* published several reports documenting the making of the 1976 coup and the design and instrumentation of the persecution of political dissidents. Based on the testimony of a Navy captain,

Página/12 columnist Horacio Verbitsky (1996) authored an investigation into the "death flights" in which death squads regularly dumped people live from planes in the 1970s.

Exposés have also targeted government corruption. Although some denunciations had targeted members of the Alfonsín administration in the 1980s, the Menem administration has been beset by a string of exposés and scandals. In January 1991, the daily *Página/12* featured a story that included a letter signed by then-U.S. ambassador Terence Todman that was sent to then-Finance Minister Erman Gonzalez and then-Foreign Affairs Minister Domingo Cavallo a few months earlier (see Verbitsky 1991). The U.S. State Department backed the document. The letter responded to a concern among U.S. companies that "subject[ed] to strict reporting requirements regarding 'commissions,' gifts, and other enticements used to secure business, [they] are at a distinct disadvantage vis-à-vis competitors from elsewhere who have less compunction about paying up" (*Latin American Weekly Report* 1991). Todman's letter suggested that an anonymous government representative asked a U.S.-based company (later identified as Swift-Armour) for a bribe in exchange for activating a file involving tax reductions and speeding up the importation of machinery. The reports pointed at Emir Yoma, president Menem's brother-in-law and close political ally, as a key actor in the operations. The letter also mentioned difficulties that other U.S. companies had encountered in doing business in Argentina.

A few months later, *Página/12* hit again with an exposé about the participation of government officials in drug-money laundering operations. The accusations pointed at Amira Yoma (Menem's appointment secretary and former sister-in-law), Ibrahim al Ibrahim (Yoma's former husband), and Mario Caserta. The story and the subsequent investigations and political scandal were dubbed "Narcogate" and "Yomagate" (Lejtman 1993). Initially, two reporters for the Spanish newsweekly *Cambio 16* informed *Página/12* about an in-progress story that featured the testimony of a convicted drug-dealer who implicated relatives of President Menem in the dealings of a drug-trafficking organization. Madrid judge Baltasar Garzón was investigating this drug ring. On March 6, 1991, the Argentine daily reproduced the *Cambio 16* story. The revelations jolted the government. Attributing the charges to "an international conspiracy," the Menem government worried that denunciations could damage relations with the United States at a time that it was trying to cultivate close relations with the Bush administration that had prioritized the "war against drugs" in its Latin America policy.

The judiciary process started a few days later. According to *Página/12*, the government encouraged the accused officials to testify in a federal court, fearing that the Spanish judge might ask for their extradition if there were no judicial process open in Argentina. Judge María Servini de Cubría was put in charge of the legal process, even though her nomination didn't go through the customary lottery system used to assign judges to causes. Throughout the process, *Página/12* uncovered several transgressions committed by Servini de Cubría and reported that she had close relations with the government, including President Menem. When the judge flew to Spain in March 1991 to meet judge Garzón and dealer-turned-informant Andrés de la Cruz, *Página/12* suggested that Servini de Cubría's trip had two purposes: to find out what the turncoat knew about Menem's role and whether the latter was included in the legal process. It was reported that Menem had attended a birthday party where Ramón Puentes, the presumed boss of the drug organization, also was present.

Página/12 kept churning out stories with information from its own reporters and investigations by *Cambio 16* and Judge Garzón. It revealed a document where Puentes wrote down the names of Amira Yoma and Ibrahim al Ibrahim and the amounts of money they had carried from New York to Buenos Aires. Caserta, who resigned his government post soon after the story broke, was called to testify and was put in jail. Yoma and Ibrahim testified a few days later. Ibrahim's testimony was stunning. He defined himself as a government envoy and mentioned names of several top officials who had asked him for favors. Although he could barely speak Spanish and could not read or write it, Ibrahim had been appointed advisor to the chief of customs at Buenos Aires international airport. Reportedly, his position was crucial to facilitate the smuggling of suitcases loaded with money. *Página/12* revealed that president Menem issued the decree that created Ibrahim's job and that Vice President Eduardo Duhalde had signed the appointment papers. Duhalde's signature violated a series of rules: no selection process was ever conducted and the Syrian-born Ibrahim had not been an Argentine citizen for more than two years (as the law mandates for naturalized citizens to be able to hold any official post). Ibrahim had received his Argentine citizenship in the record time of two weeks in March 1989.

New revelations kept cracking the stonewalling attempts of government officials. *Página/12* reported that Servini de Cubría had a copy of Judge Garzon's request to Interpol to capture Yoma, Ibrahim, and Caserta but had not reported it to the prosecutors. Weeks later, the daily published a leaked conversation between Khalil Hussein Dib and a judge. Admitting his friendship with Ibrahim, Dib offered details on the activities of Yoma, Ibrahim, and

Caserta in the drug-money laundering ring, justifying his decision not to testify before Judge Servini de Cubría because "he heard that Yoma and Ibrahim said that [she] has been bought off," and declared that Menem's personal aides had tried to bribe him.

Before the dust of Narcogate had settled, and while the judicial process was occurring, *Página/12* continued scrutinizing the antics of the Menem administration. Its next subjects were Miguel Angel Vico, then one of Menem's personal aides, and Carlos Spadone, a known entrepreneur and presidential advisor. According to investigations published on October 1991, Vico and Spadone owned two companies that had provided rotten milk to a social program run by the Ministry of Health and Social Action. The reports suggested that the bidding process for providing foodstuff to the program favored Menem's close aides and that Vico's dealings were incompatible with his government position. The contract also violated a decision of the Central Bank to ban Vico from owning any business after he had declared bankruptcy a few years earlier. It also was revealed that Spadone's company Summum won the bidding to provide 2,000 tons of milk even though Sastre, the factory that produced the milk, could not produce more than 20 tons per day. Also, the company sold milk to the state program at a cost twice than the regular price. Even though he initially rejected any involvement in these transactions, Vico later admitted that his family had previously owned Sastre. He also was found to be part owner of ERA, the factory that supplied the technology to Sastre to meet the quantity that Summum had committed to the Ministry of Health and Social Action.

Beginning in 1994, the newsweekly *Noticias* started publishing a number of denunciations. In November, it published an exposé about Armando Cavalieri, the head of the business workers' union that has the largest membership in the country (*Noticias* 1994). More than the revelations about his suspected wealth, the disclosure that Cavalieri tried to bribe the journalists in exchange for killing the story caused a major commotion. With the help of a team of lawyers, reporters audiotaped and videotaped the meetings with Cavalieri's representative who offered the money. They also recorded telephone conversations with Cavalieri in which he volunteered to lobby companies to advertise in the magazine and offered advertising monies from the union's health services department.

Noticias published several exposes on Alfredo Yabrán during 1995 and 1996. The disclosures were published simultaneously with the frontal attack that then-Finance Minister Domingo Cavallo launched against Yabrán, a businessman reportedly involved in shady dealings that implicated government officials. In his high-tone tirades against government corruption, Cavallo, who was considered the architect of the plan responsible for Argentina's "economic miracle," accused Yabrán of linkages to Mafia-like organizations that involved politicians and judges (Gonzalez and Michi 1996). *Noticias* also denounced former navy personnel who had participated in the *Escuela de Mecánica de la Armada,* one of the most infamous torture centers during the military dictatorship, owned and staffed by security agencies linked to Yabrán (Zunino and Goldman 1996). The denunciations reached a dramatic point in January 1997 when *Noticias* newsphotographer José Luis Cabezas was found dead in a burned car in Pinamar, a fashionable sea resort where political and economic elites congregate. At the time, Cabezas was on assignment working on a Yabrán story. A year earlier, he had taken the picture that was featured in the cover of one of *Noticias*'s issues that had exposed the reclusive businessman.[1] As the investigation on the ghastly murder of Cabezas began to circle among police officers linked to Yabrán, *Noticias* disclosed the latter's relations with police departments and the Executive. A March 1997 story dubbed him "a man without limits [who] protected by political power builds a parallel state and even his own army" (Zunino 1997: 26). It stated that Yabrán's business interests included the printing of national identification cards, passports, and voting rolls, in duty free shops, the manufacture of license plates, one of the country's largest transportation companies, private security, private mail companies, an airline, and a hotel chain. Simultaneously, the newsweekly also published other high-profile denunciations such as the involvement of police chiefs and police departments in corruption and drug dealing, and an exposé revealing that then-minister of Justice Rodolfo Barra had been a member of a Nazi organization in the 1960s. The last denunciation was particularly relevant in the context of the problems surrounding the judicial investigations of the bombings of the Israeli Embassy in May 1992 and the Jewish cultural center in July 1994, which, at the time of this writing, have not yet concluded.

Another important journalistic investigation dealt with the murder of army private Omar Carrasco and the cover-up of the assassination by military hierarchies. The relevance of the story was twofold. It pored over the brutal treatment of privates in army barracks, a topic that the press never investigated in a country where the armed forces had a dominant presence throughout history. The denunciation also was important for it initiated the process that concluded with the elimination of the 1901 law that established the mandatory one-year military service for 18-year-old males. The story became national news on April 1994 when several news media, but especially

La Nación, revealed that Private Carrasco had disappeared on March 6, only three days after he joined the army in the southern province of Neuquén (see Urien Berri and Marín 1995). When Carrasco's parents inquired about their son, they were told that he had deserted. Soon thereafter, they contacted a local newspaper and reported the events. A month after Carrasco was reported missing, army authorities announced the discovery of his mutilated body. Changing the original statement that Carrasco deserted, the army issued a communiqué suggesting that the private had died of natural causes but it left unclear where the corpse was found. This version was replaced by another explanation according to which Carrasco escaped, was killed by a gang outside the barracks, and then his body was thrown inside army property. All versions were later dismissed when it was proven that Carrasco was beaten to death inside the garrison where he served. Investigations revealed that Carrasco's nervous smile infuriated an officer who, with two privates, punched and kicked Carrasco to death. Judge Rubén Caro later was charged with having ignored evidence that compromised members of the army brass.

A year later, the armed forces were at the center of another journalistic investigation. On March 1995, the daily *Clarín* broke the story that Argentina had sold seventy-five tons of weapons to Ecuador during the Ecuador-Peru war in February. The sale violated the arms embargo issued by the United States and the guarantors (Argentina, Brazil, and Chile) of the 1942 peace treaty. Obviously, the fact the Argentina had exported weapons to one of the warring parties was incompatible with its diplomatic status. The exposé stated that airplanes of the Miami-based Fine Air had transported the shipment to Guayaquil, Ecuador, in the midst of the war. In a later story, *Clarín* revealed that a decree signed by President Menem, Defense Minister Oscar Camilión, Foreign Affairs Minister Guido di Tella, and Finance Minister Domingo Cavallo had authorized the company Hayton Trade to act as the intermediary in the sale of weapons to Venezuela, not to Ecuador. According to the initial reports, Maxino Pirela Avila, who was initially presented as the owner of Hayton Trade, was being investigated by the Venezuelan government for illegal dealings. Pirela Avila's legal situation, however, did not prevent him from been appointed as a representative of Fabricaciones Militares, the state-owned company that manufactured the weapons and was under the authority of the Ministry of Defense. When the news story surfaced, officials of the Ministry of Defense insisted that the weapons were sold to Venezuela, and they accused Hayton Trade of having lied about the destination of the shipment. Top Venezuelan military officers and diplomats quickly denied any involvement in the transaction. They argued that the shipment included arms that Venezuela already had produced, that the caliber of Argentine cannons was different from the ones used by the Venezuelan forces, and that if they were interested in purchasing Argentine weapons it would have been cheaper to do the transactions without an intermediary. In April 1996, a document released by Prodefensa, the Ecuadorian company that purchased four shipments of Argentine weapons, undermined the argument of Argentine officials who insisted that they had ignored the fact that the weapons were bound for Ecuador. Prodefensa asserted that the shipments were incomplete and that the weapons were old and lacked parts. One of the most damaging revelations was that Fabricaciones Militares had offered weapons from several countries (including Iran and Russia) to compensate for not having delivered the fourth shipment, which was canceled after the story broke. The statement revealed contacts between Argentina and Iran at a time when the Menem administration was seeking for a close alignment with the United States. The story has not concluded and judicial investigations continue at the time of this writing (see Santoro 1998).

BRAZIL

Brazilian reporters often mention *Folha de São Paulo* columnist Janio Freitas's exposé about kickbacks in the building of a major railroad system in Rio de Janeiro as the first major journalistic investigation in the post-authoritarian era. The project was one of the main public works planned by the Jose Sarney administration (1985–90), the first democratic government after more than twenty years of military regime. Freitas was informed that the public bidding for the selection of the companies would be manipulated. Instead of denouncing it before the decision was made, Freitas decided to publish a classified ad with the coded information. When the names of the companies were later announced, *Folha* proved that the results were already known. As a consequence of the outcry that followed the revelations, President Sarney decided to cancel the bidding. Since then, the press has disclosed a number of cases of wrongdoing, among them favoritism in the allocation of advertising contracts for government-owned companies, corruption in the creation of the Plan Cruzado (which benefited banks that declared bankruptcy), kickbacks in the building of Rio de Janeiro's metro system, monopolistic practices in public transportation, irregularities in the banking system, child prostitution, manipulation in the bidding for public works contracts, trafficking of children and body organs, shady dealings with treasury bonds, and corruption in the implementation of agrarian reforms and in the process of privatization during the Collor de Mello and Franco administrations.

No doubt the most celebrated investigations were the disclosures about the illegal deeds of former President Fernando Collor de Mello. According to *Folha de São Paulo* (1997), the gradual evolution towards a more critical journalism during the 1980s culminated with the impeachment of president Collor in 1992. Many journalists suspected that his 1989 election campaign was riddled with corruption, and they suspected that the candidate was directly involved. *Folha de São Paulo* and the newsweekly *ISTOE* initially published a series of exposés about shady deals that involved people close to him. They focused on the activities of Collor's alleged point man, Paulo Cesar (PC) Farias, his influence-peddling network of bank accounts and companies to funnel extorted monies, and Farias' sudden enrichment after Collor came to power (Krieger, Lobato, and Cipola 1992). According to an editor, representatives of Farias pressured *ISTOE* to kill the story, in exchange for bribes (Fernandes in Jose 1996). The denunciations did not get much public notice. *ISTOE*'s reputation and considerable circulation were not sufficient to provoke a strong reaction. Its previous support for former governor of São Paulo (and Collor's electoral opponent) Orestes Quercia in the presidential election, arguably undermined the potential repercussion of the exposés. Furthermore, the reports hovered around Collor but did not implicate him directly.

This drastically changed after *Veja*, Brazil's leading newsweekly, published an interview with Pedro Collor, the late brother of the former president, on May 10th, 1992. Pedro Collor's declarations did not add substantially new information to what *ISTOE* and *Folha* already had published, but sales of nearly one million copies indicated that the new focus brought unique ingredients that were responsible for the greater impact. An on-the-record testimony by the president's brother was surely decisive. Also, the interview offered a peek into the tawdry side of politics. Titillating details about Fernando's supposed cocaine and womanizing habits that peppered the accusations of influence-peddling offered celebrity voyeurism and gossip about the Collors that gripped public attention. Furthermore, *Veja*'s reputation as the leading newsweekly granted legitimacy to the accusations. Its status as indispensable reading among political elites and its larger readership guaranteed both an inevitable impact among decision-makers and a wide reach. Pedro Collor chose to go public through a highly visible and credible medium.[2]

In the following weeks, *Veja* featured testimonies by the former president of Brazil's national oil company, the leader of Collor's congressional bloc, the president of the Bank of Brazil, and Collor's former secretary. The fact that prominent sources representing political and economic interests went on the record to add information about a corruption scheme that involved the president, coupled with the beginning of congressional investigations, suggested a political shift. In a country where media coverage is commonly interpreted as a sign of larger political interests, *Veja*'s gung-ho attitude to unearth hard-hitting evidence, and its condemnation of Collor before any judicial decision was reached, insinuated a gradual repositioning of forces in Brazilian politics (Neto 1994a). The political floor of Fernando Collor, who until a few weeks earlier remained the darling of establishment forces, suddenly was cracking open. The fact that accusations were regular front-page news in newspapers and newsweeklies between June and September 1992 signaled rough times ahead for him. In an interview with newsweekly *ISTOE*, driver Eriberto França provided the "smoking gun." França declared that he had regularly deposited monies from Farias' companies in bank accounts that belonged to Collor's secretary. The story was a major coup for *ISTOE*: It was seen as a demonstration of journalistic patience and perseverance that affirmed the newsweekly in its head-to-head competition with *Veja* in the coverage of the scandal.

A year after Collor's resignation, the press uncovered an extensive kickback network involving members of the Budget Committee in Congress. *Veja* published an extensive interview with the former director of the committee, who accused several representatives of having mounted an influence-peddling network fueled by federal funds. The publication of denunciations prodded Congress to investigate the charges.

Another important investigation was journalist Caco Barcellos's exposé about human rights violations by São Paulo military police. It revealed that the cold-blooded murder of suspects was a practice intrinsic to the police rather than isolated cases or the "excesses" of individual officers. It also documented that whites and middle- and upper-class neighborhoods rarely were the targets of police brutality; the majority of the victims were blacks and mestizos. Other journalists conducted investigations into police brutality in other cities. *Jornal do Brasil*'s reporters Renato Fagundes and Wilson Aquino, for example, disclosed a rise in the number of deaths at the hands of members of the military police in the state of Rio de Janeiro. Their investigations revealed that the police had a system of rewards intended to work as an incentive for officers to commit murders. If the number of victims of police violence was falling in São Paulo after a series of reforms, the reports argued, the situation in Rio had worsened in recent years.

In April 1997, *Folha de São Paulo* published a series of investigations disclosing a vote-for-money scheme to support an amendment that paved the way for the reelection of president Fernando Henrique Cardoso. Entitled "Mercado do Voto"' [Market of Votes], the series was based on taped conversations in which representatives discussed the terms of the agreement and mentioned the names of members of Congress and two state governors involved in the operations. According to the conversations, the late Minister of Communications Sergio Motta was involved in diverting funds for the bribes. *Folha* reporter Fernando Rodrigues investigated the story and collaborated with an individual (initially known as "Senhor X") in recording the conversations.

COLOMBIA

In a region ruled by military governments between the 1960s and early 1980s, Colombia (together with Venezuela) was the exception. Except for a brief military period in the late 1950s, the Liberal and Conservative parties have alternated in government and have dominated the country's politics. As a result of the country's liberal democracy, contemporary watchdog journalism developed earlier in Colombia that in other South American countries. In August 1978, *El Tiempo,* the country's most influential newspaper and historically identified with the Liberal party, decided to create an investigative unit. Between the late 1970s and early 1980s, the period some journalists call the "golden years of Colombian investigative journalism," *El Tiempo* exposed several cases of wrongdoing. The denunciations included a number of subjects, among others, illegal trade of wild animals; corruption in local government, the country's leading airline company, and land appropriations; fraud in state lotteries; illegal contracts for public works; the antics of a top public prosecutor; bribes in the bidding for the provision of telephone services; and the importation of clothing made out of carcinogenic fabrics. Between 1978 and 1989, the daily produced over 130 investigative reports (Santos Calderón 1989). The investigations of the workings of Congress resulted in two best-selling books that tracked and analyzed the records of representatives and political candidates (Samper et al. 1982, 1986). Alberto Donadío (1983, 1984), one of the founders of *El Tiempo*'s investigative team, penned several books based on his investigations about corruption in the banking system and embezzlement of contributions to workers' funds. The success of *El Tiempo*'s investigations stimulated a boom in investigative journalism throughout Colombia. *El Espectador* in Bogotá, *Vanguardia Liberal* in Bucamaranga, and *El Colombiano* in Medellín and other newspapers decided to create investigative units, while other papers, without setting up sections specifically devoted to investigations, also began publishing stories about graft. Many of these investigations had important political consequences. For example, the investigations spearheaded by *El Espectador* about illegal operations in the largest banks (the Banco de Colombia, Banco del Estado, and Banco Gran Colombiano) together with the findings of the overseeing agency precipitated the crisis of the banking system and the decision of the Belisario Betancur administration to intervene with the banks and to nationalize the Banco de Colombia.

This budding tradition of investigative reporting suffered a severe blow in the mid-1980s, as Colombia's endemic violence reached new heights. State terrorism linked to the repression of left-wing guerrilla movements, when added to the wave of violence launched by the Medellín cartel, exponentially raised the risks for practicing investigative work. The cartel's fury targeted particularly *El Espectador,* the liberal daily that had revealed that Medellín boss Pablo Escobar, who was a Liberal representative in Congress at that time, had a criminal record for drug-trafficking. Guillermo Cano, the publisher of *El Espectador,* launched a crusade against the cartel and regularly lashed out at drug barons in his weekly columns. The paper assigned top reporters to uncover the complex architecture of drug trafficking and its connections with political and economic interests. The cartel initially responded by intimidating journalists and waging an all-out war against *El Espectador.* It was responsible for the murder of publisher Cano in December 1986 and the bombing of the newspaper's building in September 1989. The cartel took responsibility for the assassination of the circulation and distribution managers of *El Espectador* in Medellín and the kidnapping and execution of prominent journalists such as Sylvia Duzán, who had done extensive reporting on teen-age assassins hired by drug lords and paramilitary bosses.[3] Maria Jimena Duzán, Sylvia's sister, who had investigated the links among landowners, the military and drug barons for *El Espectador,* also was the target of attacks. The paper did not seem to flinch. The day after its building was bombed, it answered by keeping the presses rolling and by running the defiant headline, "We will carry on."

As violence and threats became common, investigative journalists suffered threats and went into exile, such as *El Tiempo*'s investigative unit founder Daniel Samper, *El Tiempo* columnist Enrique Santos Calderón, and journalists Alberto Donadío and Fabio Castillo (1987, 1991), who reported for *El Espectador* and authored two best-selling exposés on drug trafficking. Located in the crossfire between paramilitary and police groups, drug barons, and leftist guerrilla organizations, reporters either turned away from denouncing wrongdoing altogether or shifted attention to less risky subjects. Forty-seven reporters were killed in the late 1980s. Top editors were chauffeured to work in armored cars and wore bulletproof vests (Eisner 1990). The investigation of drug-trafficking or human rights violations by security forces automatically increased the probabilities of getting killed. By contrast, the denunciation of white-collar crime was less likely to meet violent responses. One journalist notes, "the only journalists who survived didn't report just drug trafficking" (M. Rodriguez 1996).

In recent years, Colombian reporters have disclosed a number of abuses such as public officials involved in racketeering, favoritism in the auction of fishing ships, irregularities in a public hospital and in the national office of customs, linkages between the former top public prosecutor and the Cali cartel, and waste in the state-run television network. To many observers, this tradition of active journalism reached an important point during the investigations about the contributions made by the Cali Cartel to the 1994 Liberal election campaign. On June 21, 1994, two days after Liberal Ernesto Samper was elected president, the newscast *24 Horas* led with a story about taped conversations between the Rodriguez Orejuela brothers, the bosses of the Cali cartel, and one of their closest aides. The conversations dealt with monetary contributions to the Liberal campaign. The following day, Andrés Pastrana, the frustrated candidate of the Conservative party in 1994 (who was elected president in 1998), called a press conference to announce that he had a tape revealing that drug money has been funneled into the Liberal campaign. He urged the newly elected president to resign if charges were proven to be true. Although they were interpreted and somewhat discounted as "wounds of electoral loss," the denunciations carried enough legitimacy to be taken seriously and confirmed early rumors about the presence of drug monies in election campaigns (Santos Calderón 1994). A few weeks later, several media made public the existence of other tapes in which one of the Rodriguez Orejuela brothers and their security chief Alberto Giraldo talked about meetings with Liberal campaign treasurer Santiago Medina and commented on Samper's "gestures of friendship."

On July 18, the newsweekly *Cambio 16* (Caballero 1994) featured a story that the Comando Especial Conjunto de Cali (CEC) raided an office linked to the Cali Cartel and found documents with instructions to deliver payments to a list of names of former representatives and government officials with a copy to the Rodriguez Orejuela. The report refrained from publishing the names. The CEC, also known as "Bloque de Búsqueda," was an organization to fight the Cali Cartel that had been created by the Gaviria administration with the participation of intelligence, military, and police forces. In a second report three weeks later, after President Samper had been sworn in, *Cambio 16* did include the names of the politicians plus statements made by off-the-record sources about military officers who also were on the cartel's payroll. An unidentified member of the Drug Enforcement Agency was quoted as affirming that the politicians included on the list were just a small number of "the 50 or 75 percent of the Colombian congress influenced by the Cali Cartel" (*Cambio 16* 1994: 22). The second report immediately generated strong reactions. It confirmed what many already suspected about the complex and long relations between prominent politicians and drug barons. Former Liberal senator Eduardo Mestre Sarmiento and former government counselor Rodolfo Gonzalez García, who were mentioned in the lists reproduced in the stories, sued the newsweekly and labeled the journalists "irresponsible."

The investigations hit a lull after outgoing top prosecutor Gustavo de Greiff decided to shelve the narcotapes case. De Greiff stated, "fortunately for Colombian democracy, it was decided that the presidential campaigns did not receive monies from drug cartels." His departure in August 1994 generated much speculation. In a much-debated decision, the Supreme Court lowered the retirement age for prosecutors to sixty-five. To many observers, this move expressed the political discontent both in Colombia and in the United States with De Greiff's decision to grant safe conducts to drug barons and about his advocacy for the legalization of drugs (Donadío 1995).

The nomination of Alfonso Valdivieso as top public prosecutor was a turning point in the evolution of journalistic investigations; it drastically changed the course of events. Valdivieso proved to be extremely active in investigating the linkages between the Cali cartel and politicians. The change in prosecutors was relevant for two reasons. First, Valdivieso decidedly investigated the charges and crusaded against the Cali cartel. In December 1994, he announced that the investigation would be reopened and the modest sentences that drug traffickers received would be reviewed. Convinced that the office of the prosecutor in Cali was hiding documentation crucial to his investigation, he petitioned to move the case from Cali to Bogota, the capital city. It was then that the case became known as "*Proceso 8,000*" (the

original number of the file). Second, the change also had important implications for the work of investigative reporters, as Valdivieso's office provided
the press with a steady stream of leaks that informed many denunciations.

In January 1995, *Cambio 16* (1995) published a key document with a list of
names of politicians and two columns of numbers. Two names were immediately recognizable: Santiago Medina, the former treasurer of the Liberal
campaign, and representative Rodrigo Garavito. When asked about the list,
Medina replied: "It could have been money that somehow entered the different campaigns. But it didn't directly. Those numbers must be codes. They
could be t-shirts! Yes sir, because they gave me about 20,000 t-shirts in my
house." Medina contended that the Cali cartel may have decided to donate
other goods after he rejected monetary contributions and suggested that the
t-shirts were taken to his house, not to campaign headquarters, because his
house is spacious. The article also included excerpts from an interview with
Garavito: "The office of the public prosecutor was in charge of that five
months ago. Then I was the president of the judicial commission in Congress. Prosecutor de Greiff told me that the list was dated in June and made
references to some t-shirts. He said it was in a file and gave me a copy but I
didn't keep it. During the time of the 'narcotapes,' they told me it supposedly
was a list of t-shirts they would give. But I never received t-shirts, especially
in the month of June after the congressional elections. Do you think I would
sell myself for 3,000 t-shirts?"

According to de Greiff, who after stepping down from the prosecutor's office became ambassador to Mexico, he did not give a copy of the list to Garavito and suggested that the CEC had it. He stated: "I asked [Garavito] why
he was included and he said it was advertising." These testimonies jolted
Colombian politics. Members of the Samper administration reacted angrily
and accused the newsweekly of hurting the country's image. Others recognized that many officials already had or knew about the documents.

This story stirred up debates and prodded further investigations, but
press revelations basically dovetailed with the actions of prosecutor Valdivieso. With a few exceptions, most revelations essentially sponged off leaks
from judicial investigations. Beginning in mid-April 1995, Valdivieso filed a
lawsuit against Medina and the representatives who appeared in the lists
found by the CEC. Medina testified at the end of July and directly implicated
President Samper and Minister of Defense (and former campaign manager)
Fernando Botero. His full testimony was published in *El Tiempo*. Samper rejected the charges and declared that if drug monies had entered the campaign, it happened "behind his back." A few days later, new events added fur-

ther tension. On the one hand, the capture of drug boss Miguel Rodriguez Orejuela sent a signal that the government was making efforts to go after the Cali cartel. While some high members of the cartel were captured, others surrendered. On the other hand, the newsweekly *Semana* published a transcript of a conversation between President Samper and Elizabeth Sarria, wife of a former police officer with links to drug traffickers. This story added further evidence that the government had close relations with drug rings. The friendly tone of the conversation between Samper and Sarria was striking and, to some observers, it confirmed suspicions about the president's knowledge of the funneling of drug monies into his campaign.[4] Medina's initial testimony and press revelations accelerated the decision of Minister Botero to present his testimony to the public prosecutor. After his deposition, Botero was put under arrest on August 15. In January 1996, in a televised interview, Botero affirmed that Samper knew about the participation of drug monies in the campaign and denied any involvement in the operations. *El Tiempo* and *Semana* unearthed more details on the drug connection of the Sarrias. *El Tiempo* (1996a) investigated air flights that transported monies donated by front companies owned by the Cali cartel to regional offices of the Samper campaign (similar information already had been published in a regional newspaper). Another story revealed how the boxes with the funds were distributed among local politicos. The news media continued investigations on possible donations made by the Sarrias to the Liberal campaign.[5] After more than a year of investigations, prosecutor Valdivieso prepared an official denunciation against President Samper in February 1996.

PERU

In the 1980s and 1990s, a number of human rights violations implicating military and intelligence forces and illegal dealings involving government officials occupied the attention of Peruvian muckrakers. The investigations conducted by the newsweekly *Caretas* about Vladimiro Montesinos in the 1980s sparked and set the tone for subsequent exposes. According to *Caretas*, Montesinos, an army captain, had been an aide to General Edgardo Mercado Jarrín, prime minister and armed forces commander during the Velasco Alvarado government in 1974 and 1975 (Gorriti 1994). Montesinos was suspected of having leaked information to U.S. intelligence services about Velasco's activities and about government's dealings in the purchase of military equipment from the Soviet Union. After army higher-ups who supported him were ousted, Montesinos was assigned to a remote military outpost. He returned to Lima and falsified a travel permit that allowed him to fly to the United States. Upon his return to Peru, he was arrested on charges of falsification of documents and abandoning his duty. He was dismissed from the army and sentenced to a year in prison. While in jail, he studied law, and he graduated soon after being released. One of the most sensitive revelations was that, taking advantage of his contacts with judges, army intelligence and police departments, Montesinos was a legal advisor to drug traffickers and racketeers. After the exposé, Montesinos fled the country when an army counsel resuscitated the 1976 criminal case. He returned a year later but was banned from entering military property. *Caretas* put the spotlight on Montesinos again in a 1986 series of investigations about a drug trafficking organization that included prominent police and army officers as well as politicians. It disclosed that Montesinos coordinated the legal defense of the organization. In 1990, a few months after President Alberto Fujimori was sworn into office, *Caretas* published a report warning about Montesinos in his new job as presidential advisor, and indicated that he was responsible for purges in the police.[6]

The newsweeklies *Caretas* and *Si* played a central role in an investigation of killings in the poor neighborhood of Barrios Altos in Lima in November 1991. Military forces assaulted a house where a *pollada* (a chicken barbecue) was taking place and killed fifteen people (including one child) who were later identified as street vendors and relatives. Apparently, the attack originally targeted a nearby address where, according to the confession of a Shining Path member, the guerrilla organization held regular meetings (Valenzuela 1995). Press investigations hinted that the party responsible was the "Grupo Colina," a death squad comprised of military officers with a record of brutality and illegal activities. In subsequent years, the newsweeklies unearthed further details suggesting that military personnel were involved in the murders. The attackers used an army truck and two pickup trucks stolen from government offices; the bullets corresponded to rifles used by several military units; and the descriptions provided by unidentified witnesses interviewed by *Caretas* matched the features of the suspected military officers. Montesinos reportedly had authorized the operation.

In July 1992, the disappearance of nine students and a professor at the University of La Cantuta shook public opinion. The event was widely interpreted as an indication that, in the aftermath of President Alberto Fujimori's self-coup in April, security forces had launched a frontal attack and repression of citizens suspected of links to the Shining Path. The Cantuta case returned to the front pages a year later when a team of *Si* reporters conducted a search for human remains in the outskirts of Lima. Although the remains initially were unidentified, it was later confirmed that the bodies of the students and the professor were buried there. In a telling example that some South American journalists do more than simply report the news, then editor-in-chief Ricardo Uceda and two reporters conducted the search for the bodies. Following a tip and a map provided by military sources, they looked for the area where the corpses were presumably buried and, later informed local and international authorities and human rights organizations about the findings.

The ghastly discoveries confirmed leaks from military sources and gave credibility to stories published months earlier by *Caretas* and *Si* about the participation of the Grupo Colina in the massacre of La Cantuta (Lauer 1993). The major newsweeklies (*Caretas, Oiga,* and *Si*) extensively pursued different aspects of the story that contradicted the arguments presented by military and government officials. They disclosed details about past activities of Major Santiago Martín Rivas (the head of the Grupo Colina), the connections between members of the squad and the offices of army and national intelligence, other murders attributed to Colina members, the reluctance of military forces to collaborate in the investigations, the governmental delay in submitting the remains for forensic examination, the attempts to cover up the murders and to blame them on the Shining Path, and the fact that military personnel harassed students who had witnessed the murders at La Cantuta campus (Marticorena 1996).

In the early 1990s, the news media also reported on fraudulent dealings committed during the Alan García administration in the 1980s. As a spillover of the "tangentopolis," the name for the investigations of illegal activities and finances that implicated prominent politicians in Italy, the Peruvian press disclosed shady deals between former president García and powerful Italian politicians, including former Prime Minister Bettino Craxi. According to the investigation, Craxi struck a deal by which the García administration granted a multimillion dollar contract to Italian companies to build an electric train in Lima. The project was overvalued and, reportedly, members of the Peruvian government (including the former president) had accepted bribes. After he went into exile in Colombia after his presidential term concluded in 1990, García continued to be the target of investigations in a number of cases: the Bank of Credit and Commerce International (BCCI) scandal, contacts with an arms dealer in the purchase of Mirage warplanes from France, and the sale of passports to Chinese immigrants.

García was also implicated in another major journalistic investigation that delved into the illegal operations of Alfredo Zanatti. An entrepreneur with good contacts with the García administration, Zanatti obtained a foreign exchange rate at a third of the real cost (the so-called "dólar MUC" [Mercado Unico de Cambio]) to purchase engines and parts for Faucett and Aeronaves del Peru, two airline companies he partially owned. At the end of its term in office, the García government had authorized several companies to receive subsidized dollars to compensate for state-imposed price controls. In the case of the airline companies, the rationale was that they were to be compensated because fares were being maintained at artificially low levels. At the beginning of 1991, investigations revealed that Zanatti had committed fraud against the Peruvian government. It was reported that Zanatti did not use the subsidized dollars for the ends specified by the government but, instead, had transferred a substantial portion of the twenty-five million dollars assigned to his companies to bank accounts in "fiscal paradises." Zanatti admitted to having paid a $200,000 bribe to García. In addition to disclosing this circuitous corruption scheme, the newsweeklies *Oiga* and *Caretas* as well as the dailies *El Comercio* and *La República* called attention to the Fujimori administration's ambiguous stance on the investigations. They documented that top government officials, who showed a penchant to investigate graft during the previous government, had regularly maintained personal contacts as well as business and political connections with members of the García administration who had been accused of corruption. There were speculations that members of the government had spoon-fed information to news organizations with the hope of keeping attention away from the Fujimori administration's own antics.

The administration was at the center of several press denunciations in 1996 and 1997 (Conaghan 1998). TV Global's newscast *La Clave,* with host César Hildebrandt, disclosed that a well-known drug trafficker had funneled monies to high-ranking government officials, included shadowy advisor Vladimiro Montesinos. News programs such as Channel 2's *Contrapunto* and Channel 4's *La Revista Dominical* also brought out connections between druglords and military officers. *Contrapunto* broke a story that military officers had taken apartments that had been confiscated from druglords. The reports angered official and military hierarchies (Arrieta 1998). The bombing of an affiliate of TV Global, which broadcast Hildebrandt's show, in the southern city of Puno in October 1996 was interpreted as a sign that the revelations were not quietly accepted by military and intelligence services. *Contrapunto*'s revelations were striking, considering that Channel 2 had hitherto been a staunch supporter of the Fujimori administration. This was the beginning of a fierce battle between the station and the government: The former aired several denunciations and increasingly stepped up the tone of accusations; the latter reacted by dismissing the charges and intensifying pressure on journalists.

La República's investigative unit exposed intelligence plans to muffle and intimidate the critical press (the so-called "Bermuda plan," a word play meaning "to see the press mute"). The developments took a macabre twist when the body of Army intelligence officer Mariela Barreto was discovered. In a dramatic interview with *Contrapunto* at the hospital where she was recovering from torture, intelligence agent Leonor La Rosa stated that Barreto was killed by fellow agents for leaking information to the press about the Bermuda plan. La Rosa also said that agents had tortured her. *Contrapunto* did not stop firing heavy accusations on the government. It disclosed that Montesinos's tax return showed astronomical earnings even though as a government official he was not allowed to continue his law practice. The government answered by bringing legal demands against journalists and threatening to take away the Peruvian citizenship of Channel 2's majority owner Israel-born Baruch Ivcher. Before Ivcher was stripped of his citizenship, *Contrapunto* reported that the government had tapped the telephones of 167 individuals, including members of the opposition, scores of journalists, and former presidential candidate and former U.N. secretary general Javier Perez de Cuellar. Shortly thereafter, progovernment minority shareholders took over control of Channel 2, the combative journalists that worked in *Contrapunto* resigned, and Ivcher left the country.

WHAT IS NEW?

The reconstruction of the main stories of watchdog journalism in recent years shows two important characteristics. First, watchdog journalism is no longer restricted to the alternative press but has attained mainstream status. In Argentina, *Página/12* has carved out a niche as a hard-hitting daily, a remarkable development given not only the paper's persistent economic difficulties but also the historical absence of a market-oriented, center-left newspaper widely read among political elites. *Página/12* no longer monopolizes critical journalism. Its incisive style has spread to other traditional newspapers such as *Clarín* and *La Nación*, which, historically have stayed away from investigative journalism, but recently have published investigations. *Noti-*

cias, the flagship of one of the largest publishing houses, also has featured exposés. In Brazil, *Folha de São Paulo,* the country's largest and most influential newspaper, has practiced investigative journalism, especially since the transition from authoritarian to democratic government in the mid-1980s. *Folha's* investigations have influenced other newspapers that traditionally have avoided aggressive journalism. A number of dailies in the interior have taken risks in disclosing wrongdoing. *Veja* and *ISTOE,* the leading newsweeklies, also regularly run exposés. Colombia's *El Tiempo* has maintained an active investigative unit since the late 1970s, whereas *El Espectador* consistently pounded on drug lords in the 1980s. Political and financial newsweeklies such as *Semana, Cambio 16,* and *Dinero* also have published reports on various abuses. In Peru, the newsweeklies *Caretas, Si* (in the early 1990s), and *Oiga* (until it folded in 1995) housed the most important journalistic investigations conducted in the 1990s. *El Comercio* and *La República* created investigative units, and the daily *Expreso* has featured denunciations of corruption.

In summary, while practiced almost exclusively by the alternative press in the 1970s, watchdog journalism is now found in the mainstream of the South American press. News organizations that supported military juntas in the past and avoided hard-hitting reporting have lately reported on wrongdoing. Of course, this does not signify the existence of an entire press that unflinchingly and continuously reports on wrongdoing or that all kinds of wrongdoing have been investigated and reported. Only a few news organizations have intermittently and selectively revealed illegal practices. This raises two questions: What explains the mainstreaming of watchdog journalism? And what has changed in the treatment of the information, once watchdog journalism has been adopted by mainstream news organizations? Subsequent chapters will tackle these questions.

The majority of stories have dealt with public officials embroiled in corruption and human rights abuses. Despite dissimilar editorial positions and journalistic styles, news organizations typically put the spotlight on government malfeasance. The portfolio of Argentine muckrakers is packed with stories about the violation of human rights, drug-money laundering, and government officials involved in influence-peddling and kickbacks. The Brazilian press has exposed fraudulent dealings in the bidding for public works, military and police violence, money-for-votes schemes, and the influence-peddling scheme that finally drove Fernando Collor de Mello out of the president's office in 1992. In Colombia, the mainstay of journalistic investigations has been official corruption, the operations of drug lords, and the linkages between high-powered politicians and the Medellin and Cali cartels in the last decade. The Peruvian news media have generally reported on corruption during the 1985–1990 administration of Alan García and human rights abuses committed by military and police forces during the Fujimori government. In summary, watchdog journalism often tells two kinds of stories: government officials abuse power and public resources for private benefit, and military and police officers are responsible for human rights violations.

Rarely have investigations pried open social inequities, zeroed in on wrongdoing committed by economic powers, or disclosed legal transgressions that do not directly involve the circles of high politics. As Peruvian muckraker and managing editor of Panama's *La Prensa* Gustavo Gorriti (1995) points out, "investigative journalism has been opposed to government and the state." Similarly, a Colombian reporter notes, "journalism has been critical of the political class, not of the economic structure of the country" (M. Rodriguez 1996). It could be argued that the trail of business corruption inevitably ends in government, yet these connections are rarely explored. Instead, the focus has been on graft, influence-peddling and human rights abuses that implicate government officials. Only occasionally do the news media make forays into corporate delinquency, like Colombia's *El Espectador* revelations about illegal dealings in financial institutions in the early 1980s. Also, rarely do exposés focus on social plights as journalist Germán Castro Caycedo (1976) did in his admirable reporting on poverty and exploitation in the Colombian countryside for *El Tiempo,* Gilberto Dimenstein (1990, 1991, 1992) did in his work on child prostitution in northern Brazil, *Folha de São Paulo* (1995) did in its investigation about racism in Brazil, or Argentina's *Telenoche Investiga* did in its denunciation of the illegal use and manipulation of chemicals that caused several diseases among mostly illiterate tobacco farmers.

TOWARD A WORKING EXPLANATION

Why do investigative reporters typically pay less attention to social and economic issues and, instead, tend to direct their energies toward government wrongdoing, namely corruption and human rights abuses? To suggest that this preference is directly proportional to the existence or systemic character of official wrongdoing (and the scarcity of economic and social wrongdoing) does not take us far. But how does one pin down, measure, compare the magnitude of wrongdoing? Few could question that official wrongdoing has been pervasive in South America but, although crucial, it is not a sufficient reason to account for its magnetic pull on investigative reporters. The latter do not, in a Willie Suttonesque mode, uncover official wrongdoing just because "it's where wrongdoing is." Official wrongdoing has been endemic; investigative reports about it are only spasmodic. If the magnitude of a state-controlled economy were allegedly responsible for wrongdoing, how does one explain the flurry of investigative reports in times when many administrations have decided to privatize vast sectors of the economy? If corruption has been rampant in the process of privatization, as some analysts have concluded, why has the press barely reported on it? If violations of human rights were not inaugurated by the dictatorships of the 1960s and 1970s, but have been a painful historical legacy, why did they become an important subject of journalistic investigations only in the past decade? Wrongdoing and the denunciation of wrongdoing do not travel the same road. They may run in adjacent lanes, occasionally merging, but they can exist separately. They are related but not identical. Not all forms of wrongdoing are reported and, sometimes, not all reports of wrongdoing are necessarily grounded in actual illegalities. The issue is, then, why have specific forms of wrongdoing become regular news in recent times?

Anyone minimally familiar with Latin American history knows that neither corruption nor human rights violations are news in the strictest sense. Corruption harks back to colonial times. In contemporary times, military and civilian governments have reeked of corruption. The invocation of "widespread corruption" has been a staple of post-coup speeches to justify the ousting of civilian leaders and, in turn, corruption was found to be rampant in the same military governments that allegedly intended to clean up the house. The motto "steals but gets things done" is part of the political folklore of electoral campaigning. Popular culture is full of jokes about corrupt officials. The lives of Latin Americans are packed with anecdotes of petty corruption in daily situations such as bribing police officers to avoid speeding tickets and city officials "to speed the process."

Corruption is a contested term (De Leon 1993; Klitgaard 1988; Walter 1992). It can take multiple forms including officials who buy political support, accept kickbacks to favor private parties, ignore existent stipulations in the granting of public contracts, engage in or protect illicit activities, manipulate regulations, mount influence-peddling organizations, evade taxes, misappropriate public funds, commit electoral fraud, use unlawful mechanisms to raise campaign funds, or act as middlemen for private companies. In all cases individuals committed unlawful actions, induced by bribery or other incentives that work to their own personal benefit.

The shift from authoritarianism to liberal democracy has not eliminated corruption. Quite the contrary, according to some observers (Burgos 1995; Cepeda Ulloa 1994; Fleischer 1996/1997; Geddes and Ribeiro Neto 1992; Saba and Manzetti 1996/1997; Sives 1993). New sources of graft have developed in the 1980s and 1990s, stimulated by the privatization of state-owned companies, politicians' need to raise funds for campaign financing, and the magnitude of the drug economies throughout the region. Concurrently, government corruption has become an important concern. The Colombian Congress passed an anti-corruption law in 1995, which applies mainly to cases of drug trafficking (Cepeda Ulloa 1996). There have been regional initiatives, such as the Inter-American convention to examine possible ways to fight government corruption. Business organizations have called attention to this issue at several fora. At the World Economic Forum in 1996, government representatives and corporate executives supported the formation of an anticorruption group in the Mercosur, the trade agreement among Argentina, Brazil, Paraguay, and Uruguay, to identify cases of graft and to find solutions at the domestic and regional levels. The annual rankings of corruption produced by *Transparency International*, which are based on perceptions among business leaders, receive great attention in the press.

Nor is the violation of human rights a new development in the region. Such abuses also go back to the foundation of modern societies and branded much of the political evolution of the region. There is wide consensus, however, that the coming of military governments in the 1960s and 1970s was responsible for the escalation of human rights violations to unprecedented levels. The harassment, kidnapping, torture, and disappearance of citizens were not isolated cases, "excesses" committed by individual police and military officers, but part of plans systematically organized by military rulers to persecute and intimidate anyone suspected of links to leftist parties and/or insurrectionary organizations. Not exclusive to military-ruled societies, such abuses also were prevalent in Colombia, where the last military president stepped down in the late 1950s. In the historical context of unending violence, Colombian intelligence and military forces have quashed insurrectionary movements and peasant uprisings and have violated the human rights of scores of citizens in the past decades. There is no need for reporters to step outside newsrooms to come across such abuses. For them, the violation of human rights has often hit home, as antipress violence continues throughout the region, particularly in the interior of Colombia, Peru, and Brazil.

Although the situation of human rights has improved in some regards after liberal democracies replaced authoritarian regimes, the political transition has not spelled an end to abuses (Panizza 1995). Reports of regional and international organizations have documented extensively that the state no longer coordinates and methodically executes the persecution, disappearance, and murder of citizens but different forms of abuses persist. The harassment and assassination of citizens suspected to have links to guerrilla organizations continues. Police brutality has grown in some countries and frequently targets poor citizens.[7] The number of prisoners of conscience has grown exponentially. The torture of prisoners is an extensive practice. Death squads and vigilante groups staffed by military, paramilitary, and intelligence and police officers routinely murder street kids and adolescents, slum dwellers, and peasant activists. These practices have been grouped under the label of paralegal violence: The state does not engineer the systematic repression of citizens, but it is unable to control the violent activities of Mafia-like organizations staffed by security officials and often connected to politicians, private individuals, landowners, and drug barons.

Considering the history and recent record of corruption and human rights abuses, journalists turn the magnifying lens to official wrongdoing for a fairly obvious reason: Historically, Latin American governments have been rife with wrongdoing. The petty corruption of low-ranking public officials is a tangible reality. To the victims of violence by military and security forces, human rights abuses are not merely news but personal tragedies. Journalistic investigations of corruption and of linkages between drug cartels and prominent politicians are grounded in the exponential growth of the drug economies in Latin America (Sage 1989). Only in the mind of an absolute relativist would such forms of wrongdoing be considered simply social constructions, devoid of any objective referent in the world "out there." No need to embrace philosophical relativism, however, to shed doubt on the possibility of a somewhat perfect correspondence between the reality of the press and the reality of official wrongdoing. Falling trees do not make any noise if ignored by the press. With a few exceptions, mainstream news organizations have published revelations about human rights violations during authoritarian periods only after the military went back to the barracks. The spiral of corruption fostered by the behemoth size of the drug economies has been investigated only minimally. Although some observers concluded that corruption was widespread during the process of privatization in the 1990s, the press focused largely on other cases of wrongdoing. Revelations about the brutality of paramilitary and police squads are generally considered to be just the tip of the iceberg. The harassment and murder of colleagues is more likely to prod reporters to write about it than, let's say, violence against poor and marginal citizens: The latter often happens worlds apart from newsrooms, while the former occur within earshot of journalists' desks and directly affect their own lives.

The question becomes why the investigative scanners of newsrooms typically register very specific acts of wrongdoing out of a virtually unlimited spectrum of cases. The next chapter analyzes what conditions have made watchdog journalism possible, and what factors shape its agenda.

CHAPTER 3

Why Watchdogs Bark

What conditions have made watchdog journalism possible in contemporary South America? This question warrants an examination of two factors: the interest (or disinterest) of the press with regard to putting the spotlight on wrongdoing, and the availability (or absence) of information about wrongdoing. As previously discussed, the press typically avoided watchdog reporting because it was unwilling to endanger political and economic relations with power holders. The seesaw evolution of democracy also accounts for why watchdog journalism never took hold and press denunciations came out only sporadically. Intolerant of any form of critical reporting, military dictatorships either suppressed or simply liquidated publications and journalists who, uninterested in courting official powers, disclosed corruption. Against this background, the recent proliferation of exposés hints at changes that may have prodded some news media to become more disposed to lift government rugs and to turn watchdog reporting into a regular presence in the news. Why is the press seemingly more willing to put its government relations at risk?

DEMOCRACY AND WATCHDOG JOURNALISM

Although watchdog journalism became in vogue in many countries after the publication of the Pentagon Papers and Watergate (Schultz 1998, Sparks and Splichal 1994), it could not make significant strides in South America as military dictatorships came to power in the 1970s. The fever of investigative journalism that caught news organizations in many Western democracies in the 1970s only belatedly arrived to most countries in the region governed by military rule.

In the 1980s and 1990s, the shift from authoritarian to democratic regimes has been unquestionably the major political transformation in the region. Civilian administrations have replaced authoritarian regimes that ruled in the 1960s and 1970s. The democratic domino of the 1980s tumbled down military governments and resulted in seemingly stable liberal democracies. In countries historically subjected to cycles of civilian and military governments, this is a remarkable development considering that the only exception has been President Alberto Fujimori's auto-coup in Peru in 1992.

It would seem obvious to argue that watchdog journalism is linked to the stability of liberal democracies. In theory, democracies offer better conditions than military rule. To put it simply, the suspension of constitutional rights and widespread censorship during authoritarian regimes chilled critical reporting. Whether they ardently defended government policies or offered complacent coverage, large news organizations typically have eschewed controversial reporting that might have alienated the military in power and its political supporters. The consequences of disclosing official misdeeds ranged from withdrawal of vital state economic support to physical attacks against publishers, editors, and reporters. As discussed in chapter 1, the alternative press, instead, carried the banner of watchdog journalism, acting as a bastion of dissent and the parapet for opposition voices during authoritarian rule. The precarious, underground existence of those publications, however, meant that watchdog reporting was intermittent and ignored or gingerly kept at a distance by the big press. The stuttering life span of critical reporting under military dictatorships was the consequence of the chronic economic difficulties of alternative publications and the state repression that, not coincidentally, targeted muckrakers.

The institutional design of democracies introduces more hospitable conditions for critical reporting. In principle, there is a natural fit between democracy and watchdog journalism. Democracies are better equipped to protect and facilitate watchdog reporting (and journalism in general). Authoritarian regimes, by contrast, discard constitutions, treat critical journalism as a nagging problem, and doggedly crush any signs of media dissent. The existence of constitutional freedoms, however, does not automatically unleash investigative journalism. Can we suggest a direct and immediate relation between liberal democracy and investigative reporting considering that Watergate, the preeminent case of contemporary watchdog journalism, was an anomaly in a country where democracy has endured for more than two centuries and the press consistently has celebrates itself as the alert monitor of government actions?

The correlation between constitutional rule and investigative journalism is not self-evident or immediate. Contemporary South America demonstrates that there is a gap between the promise and the reality of political democracy. Democracy does not inevitably bring optimal conditions for journalism. It is estimated that 116 journalists have been murdered in the region between 1985 and 1995. Consider the case of Colombia, where liberal democracy has managed to exist for much of the twentieth century, despite the country's chronic and spiraling levels of violence. Together with Venezuela, Colombia was immune to the outbreak of military coups that spread throughout the region in the 1960s and 1970s. Democracy, however, has not offered the most supportive conditions for investigative journalism. Beginning in the late 1950s, censorship lasted almost for forty years and was formally ended in July 1982. But then the violence that has characterized Colombia's tragic history intensified. Confrontations among political parties, drug cartels, guerrilla movements, and military and police forces made investigative reporting virtually impossible. A death toll of 133 journalists murdered between 1978 and 1997 has made Colombia one of the most dangerous countries for journalists in the world. Eighteen journalists were killed in 1986 at the peak of drug trafficking-related violence.

History shows that South American democracies do not have a spotless record in terms of respect for constitutional rights and tolerance for hard-hitting reporting. The spasmodic periods of civilian rule before the last wave of military governments in the 1960s and 1970s did not offer suitable environments for reporters. Many democratic administrations showed contempt for basic press liberties and, in a less systematic and violent manner than military juntas, also persecuted dissident reporters and publishers. Nor do contemporary democracies offer nirvana-like conditions for journalism. Existing legislation, reporters complain, makes it easy for officials implicated in press denunciations to counteract by bringing lawsuits against reporters and news organizations.[1] Lawsuits apply economic burdens that ultimately asphyxiate newspapers and reporters. Moreover, facing mounting denunciations and aiming to tighten relations, governments tended to pass gag laws to stifle watchdog journalism.

Aside from legal obstacles, the recurrent episodes of violence against reporters challenge any rosy portrayal of the contemporary conditions for journalism in the region. Violence has ebbed since the military went back to the barracks, but it has not stopped (Waisbord 1998b). Death threats, physical attacks, and the kidnapping and murder of journalists have continued in the 1990s. In Argentina, 884 cases of intimidation against journalists were recorded between 1989 and 1997. There have been bomb attacks on radio stations and an opposition newsweekly, and police raids of newspapers. In 1993, a reporter who worked for the press workers union was initially reported missing and his body was later found floating in a river. The murder of news photographer José Luis Cabezas in January 1997 sent chills throughout the country. His torture and assassination, and then the burning of his body resembled the practices used by paramilitary organizations during the last dictatorship. After receiving Argentina's most prestigious media award, journalist Santo Biasatti (1997) diagnosed the condition of the freedom of the press as being in "intensive care."

Brazil's regional press has been particularly vulnerable to attacks, notably small-town newspapers and editors who uncovered corruption in local governments. Reporters investigating military abuses and environmental issues have been roughed up and shot to death. The situation has been somewhat better in big cities, where journalists only occasionally have been the victims of antipress violence. In some cases, however, journalists who dared to criticize powers accustomed to complete impunity have suffered the consequences of engaging in critical reporting. Caco Barcellos, author of a bestselling expose about killings by members of the São Paulo military police, was harassed soon after his book was released.

Antipress violence has not been uncommon in Peru either. Scores of journalists have been harassed and many went into exile during the 1990s. Antipress violence intensified after the April 1992 coup when the Fujimori government ordered the intervention and closure of the newsweeklies *Caretas, Oiga,* and *Si,* the dailies *La República, El Comercio,* and *El Nacional,* and television stations (Instituto Prensa y Sociedad 1994). Detained soon after the coup, investigative journalist Gustavo Gorriti left the country after being released. Eighteen journalists, mostly reporters for provincial newspapers, were assassinated between 1990 and 1996. In 1997, there were eighty-nine cases of violence against journalists, including two murders and twenty-three physical attacks (*La República* 1998). Some journalists investigating the Fujimori administration and the armed forces have been threatened and beaten; others abducted and murdered. The newsweekly *Caretas* (1993), which published several exposés on the government, assessed the situation in grim terms: "[Press freedom in Peru] is a sick freedom. Sick of lawsuits, of persecution, of threats, of police harassment, of arrest warrants, of Habeas Data."

Official impatience with watchdog journalism was best expressed in the existence of plans to intimidate and silence critical news organizations, plans that were reported by *La República* in December 1996. Members of the *La*

República investigative unit, for example, have been primary targets of threats and harassment. AP reporter David Koop (1997) describes the life of one of its investigative reporters: "Each morning Angel Paez changes paths to go to work, always watching that there are no strange cars following him or new street vendors in his neighborhood. He doesn't have a regular schedule and sleeps in different apartments each night, often on friends' couches. He knows his telephone has been tapped, as he heard his own taped conversations, and unknown intruders have raided his apartment without stealing anything. Paez is no spy or a leftist rebel; he is a reporter, the head of the investigative unit of the daily *La República,* the main opposition newspaper." Peruvian and international organizations that monitor press rights accused intelligence services of masterminding antipress attacks in 1998 and 1999. Reportedly, intelligence agents fed information to a number of tabloid newspapers (the so-called *prensa chicha*) and maintained an Internet Web site of the Association for the Defense of the Truth (APRODEV) that published inflammatory (and libelous) articles about *La República*'s publisher Gustavo Mohme Llona, members of the daily's investigative team, and other print and broadcast journalists who had reported illegalities committed by the Fujimori government, particularly military and intelligence agents. Against the backdrop of a long list of previous attacks, these episodes patently attest to the difficulties of practicing critical reporting and the continuous failure of Peruvian democracy to guarantee even minimal rights for press freedom.

Throughout South America, muckrakers have been more likely to be targets of violence than other journalists. Most attacks have been perpetrated against reporters who worked on or published exposés of high powers. Watchdog reporting is, in the mind of journalists, like "being a war correspondent" (Duzán 1996); a Brazilian reporter called it "kamikaze reporting." Reporters share a sense that conditions remain dangerous, regardless of the ebb and flow in the number of attacks, because violence against journalists is rarely, if ever, punished. Most attacks have not been solved, and only in a few instances have suspects been tried and convicted. It is striking that while reporters and editors associated with metropolitan media have been frequent targets of attacks, the majority of murdered journalists reported for small-town and provincial newspapers. Without the visibility and prominence given by metropolitan news media and without effective checks on local powers, regional reporters are more exposed to deadly attacks (Waisbord 1998b). There are slimmer chances that the murder of little-known reporters working for a small-time publication in the impoverished Brazilian interior or in the Peruvian highlands would trigger tremendous repercus-

sion (Franciscato and Campos 1995). But investigative journalists with national and international reputations and contacts are not free from attacks
or harassment. Critical reporting turns well-known journalists into common targets of intimidation and harassment; their prominence inside political and journalistic circles somewhat shields them from lethal attacks.

If the historical record is less than promising and democracy has not
spelled an end to violence against journalists, how does democracy contribute to watchdog journalism? Even considering the fact that existing
democracies do not bring in perfect conditions for journalism, the return of
the military to the barracks brings about important, substantial changes.
Liberal democracy puts an end to the systematic persecution of reporters by
the state, to military censors who patrolled newsrooms and cleared stories,
and to the suffocating atmosphere that prevailed under military rule. These
differences are not inconsequential. Conditions under military rule are
markedly worse than even when democratic administrations fail to guarantee constitutional rights and wage verbal attacks against journalists.

The consolidation of investigative reporting in Colombia in the 1970s,
earlier than elsewhere in the region, suggests that the most violent democracy in the region offers better conditions than authoritarian regimes, even
when the latter reach their gentler, kinder, and final days. Colombian convulsive politics has not made investigative journalism easy, especially after
the Medellin cartel declared an all-out war against the press in the 1980s. Yet
the absence of "the culture of fear" (Corradi, Fagen, and Garretón 1992) that
dominated Southern Cone countries under military dictatorships seems to
have made a big difference in prodding journalists to investigate. In past
decades, the culture of fear was particularly prevalent in newsrooms, which
for the most part were not subjected to direct official censorship yet opted to
suppress information considered too sensitive to be published (Smith 1997).
Democracy is fundamental for investigative journalism to prosper, even
when contemporary South American democracies are distant from being
political regimes where constitutional rights are fully and consistently observed. It is no coincidence that an investigative tradition grew in Colombia
in the late 1970s while elsewhere in the region such journalism was virtually
absent.

The newly arrived stability of liberal democracy throughout South America has contributed directly to the renewed energies of investigative reporting, principally by ushering in a better environment for journalistic work.
Without that environment, investigative work would be simply unimaginable. Democracy per se does not guarantee complete "freedom of the press,"

but it brings an end to state-sanctioned and perpetrated violence against reporters and puts an end to military monitoring of newsrooms. Government censorship was virtually eliminated once the military relinquished power. The overall situation has improved considerably amid the relaxation of the suffocating atmosphere that dominated when the juntas ruled. This shift does not necessarily guarantee a more critical, hard-hitting reporting. Changes are incremental rather than immediate, and watchdog journalism requires other conditions too. News organizations have cautiously tested the new political waters, and journalists only gradually shed fears. Self-censorship, mandatory for survival in times of indiscriminate repression, does not fade quickly. Notwithstanding changes in political conditions and a situation generally more conducive to journalistic investigations, as one Argentine journalist observes, reporters only cautiously and belatedly explore the new boundaries (Ciancaglini 1996).

In other words, the relationship of democracy to watchdog reporting is far from simple. Watchdog journalism neither completely disappears during military rule, nor does it automatically flourish after the first elections are held. Still, political democracy offers better conditions for journalism, opens room to tackle controversial issues red-lined by military censors or vetoed by editors, and makes it possible for reporters to take jabs at state officials without necessarily fearing for their physical integrity. Against the historical background of systematic violation of human rights, political democracy provides minimal conditions that leaven hard-hitting reports. Democracy is a necessary but not a sufficient condition to stimulate investigative reporting. Once democracy arrives, news organizations do not rush en masse to investigate issues and not all subjects suddenly become the target of investigations. So what does drive news organizations to adopt watchdog journalism?

MARKET SHIFT?

Considering that South American muckrakers typically zero in on government wrongdoing, it is worth exploring whether the historical relations between news organizations and the state have experienced any modifications. It is hard to imagine that news organizations would be interested in monitoring official secrecy when economic and political strings keep them attached to the state.

Classic liberalism asserts that the press can effectively check government only when it gains independence from the state. Market control of the press is the best alternative to counter state interventionism and its shortcomings. Profits make possible a financially independent press. From this perspective, there seems to be an obvious affinity between the market and watchdog journalism: Only an economically solvent press can rail against government. Read along the lines of free-market liberalism, the growing ascendancy of the market in press economies in the region may potentially disentangle the tight connections between press and governments and, consequently, open the possibility for press scrutiny of government actions. Let us consider the merits of this argument.

From Mexico to Montevideo, governments have implemented economic reforms following neoliberal policies that aim to reduce state participation in the economy. Although their purpose is the transformation of the postwar economic order following plans for economic stabilization and state reform, these policies may have unintended consequences, namely, they may contribute to changes in state-media relations. The privatization of state-owned companies shrinks the pool of advertising resources that government officials hitherto controlled. Smaller government advertising budgets, arguably, take chips away from officials who sit at the bargaining table with media owners. Control or influence over leaner budgets translate into fewer resources to reward or punish news organizations. If true, rolling-back-of-the state policies favorably impact press-government relations and potentially open up new possibilities for reporting that scrutinizes official illegalities. Historically, state-owned companies consistently have been the largest advertisers in the region, in economies where states controlled vital industries and depressed advertising markets. State officials decided the allocation of substantial resources that were crucial for media economies, considering that advertising expenditures in the region have been substantially lower than in industrialized democracies. Control over advertising allocations has traditionally put officials in a very favorable position vis-à-vis media organizations, allowing them to manipulate resources according to whether news organizations went along or opted to criticize them. This ingrained philosophy was best expressed in former Mexican president José López Portillo's memorable phrase "*no pago para que me peguen*" ("I don't pay to be hit"). It reflects a concept that regards public resources as private funds and a belief that the allocation of official advertising essentially functions as a way to advance political interests by punishing enemies and rewarding allies. There do not seem to be strong indications that such a concept has suffered substantial changes. For example, consider the repeated threats of the Menem administration to cut off advertising to *Página/12* and the heated disputes between the Fujimori government and opposition media over advertising monies.

Despite privatization, governments still control sizable advertising budgets. Consider the case of Brazil, the largest advertising market in South America, where expenditures totaled U.S.$6.6 billion in 1994 and $8.5 billion in 1995. Media allocations are distributed roughly as follows: television 50 percent, the press 34 percent, radio 5 percent, outdoor 1 percent, and 10 percent to other outlets (Bastos de Quadros 1998). In 1994, government advertising totaled U.S.$210 million. Among the largest official advertisers are telecommunication giant Telebras with U.S.$49 million, the Health Ministry with $20.6 million, and the federal government with $26 million. State and local governments also are important advertisers. The São Paulo governorship spent U.S.$90 million and the municipality of the city of São Paulo allocated $11.6 million, while the state of Rio de Janeiro assigned $22.1 million (Instituto Gutenberg 1995). In 1997, official advertising expenditures added up to $475 million. The largest sponsors were state-owned Petrobrás with $91 million, Telebrás with $88 million, and Banco do Brasil with $82 million (*Veja* 1997). These numbers reflect the fact that even in a large advertising market, the government taken as a whole continues to be the largest single advertiser. Governments also are able to manipulate the allocation of legal official ads and the advertising budgets of remaining state companies which, especially outside metropolitan and advertising-rich areas, provide much-needed resources for news organizations (*Meio & Mensagem* 1994).

The advertising prowess of governments at different levels requires some moderating of the claim that officials have lost an invaluable means of pressuring news organizations to acquiesce to their demands. Instead, the analysis needs to be sensitive to the fact that various government offices have different economic capacities to relate to news organizations, which, in turn, do not rely on official advertising in the same ways. As the Brazilian case shows, total advertising budgets have increased, and may create conditions that, interpreted from a market perspective, contribute positively to press independence and to investigations of state secrecy. Yet states are still important advertisers, and officials are not empty-handed if willing to deter news organizations from scrutinizing their antics. In Peru, for example, an official in charge of assigning government advertising publicly admitted that budgets were used as instruments of pressure on the news media. He revealed that he received orders about where to allocate monies and that in meetings with opposition media he stated "if anyone hits me, I don't give money. You should hit me less and I will advertise more" (in Burgos 1997). Also, privatization of large sectors of the economy does not guarantee better conditions for critical reporting or the separation between news organizations and the state, as a number of critics have observed. This is particularly true in South America, where business opportunities for local and foreign companies are often contingent on cultivating good relations with governments. Companies expecting to benefit from government decisions on privatization and liberalization in diverse industries are not likely to support with advertising those news organizations that denounce officials who wield influence over those decisions.

In addition to advertising, government officials also can pull other levers that affect press finances, such as tax breaks and import duties, which are of considerable importance to news companies in countries where news organizations generally depend on imported resources (printing equipment, computer technology, newsprint, ink). These issues have become even more central, given the economic difficulties caused by stagnant or dropping sales. In Peru, the García and Fujimori administrations threw economic lifesavers to the press, such as subsidized exchange rates to import newsprint and loans from state-owned banks to dailies in financial dire straits. The so-called *dólar MUC* (*Mercado Unico de Cambio*) made newsprint substantially cheaper and facilitated the multiplication of print outlets during the García administration in the late 1980s. In Brazil, loans with federal banks have been the life support for the *Jornal do Brasil,* once the country's most influential national daily, but which has been in tatters in the last decade.[2]

Government officials also control the granting of licenses for telecommunication and broadcasting services. The privatization of formerly state-owned media and the extraordinary growth of cellular telephony and cable and satellite television have opened new areas for media businesses. Administrations dangle the carrots of future biddings for cellular telephony and broadcasting licenses to dissuade media organizations from adversarial reporting. Uninterested in causing ripples with powerful officials, news companies may ignore or downplay sensitive information or, as reporters observe, sometimes opt to send the watchdogs to bring out the antics of rival bidders.

The rarity of watchdog journalism in television indicates that government control of broadcasting licenses discourages media owners from endorsing critical reporting. Only a few broadcast news organizations have investigated corruption and human rights abuses. The caution of television stations in the uncovering of government wrongdoing is even more pronounced around the time when licenses are up for renewal or when new ones are to be granted. Many Colombian journalists observe that television license auctioning was still pending during the *Proceso 8,000,* dissuading the news media from probing government wrongdoing (Rodriguez 1996). The Samper administration ably wielded licenses as a Damocles' sword that would fall if news organizations were to investigate linkages between the political class and drug traffickers (Restrepo 1996).

In Peru, the weight of state advertising on television is a powerful deterrent to hard-hitting reporting. The newsweekly *Caretas* (Vivas 1999) reported that the state is the largest advertiser, doubling the investments of the leading beer company and the leading telecommunications corporation. Practicing watchdog journalism in television has been extremely dangerous. Journalist César Hildebrandt, host of the influential political talk-show *En Persona* and producer of numerous no-holds-barred reports on government corruption and human rights abuses, has received intimidations and threats. The events surrounding Channel 2's *Contrapunto* reporting on government wrongdoing in 1997 also patently reflect the risks of broadcast watchdog journalism. *Contrapunto* angered prominent powers with several stories, including the broadcast testimony of intelligence agent Leonor La Rosa in which she accused intelligence members of torturing her for allegedly leaking information to media organizations; a report stating that presidential advisor Vladimiro Montesinos was paid U.S.$700,000 in 1995; and a denunciation implicating the government in massive telephone tapping. With the argument that the station's accounting presented tax irregularities, the Fujimori administration decided to revoke the citizenship of Israeli-born Baruch Ivcher, Channel 2's main stockholder. This automatically meant that Ivcher could no longer remain at the helm of the station, for only Peruvian citizens can own broadcasting licenses. In addition to broadcasting licenses, governments still decide other issues that directly affect media business. It is unconceivable that a newspaper would investigate the same administrations that grant loans for upgrading printing facilities or approve bidding for telephony services. This does not mean that official control of media legislation and tax policies spawns a completely tame press, afraid of causing any ripples that may compromise the present and future of their economic situation. Not all news media have similar business and political interests, and consequently, expectations about government policies are not identical either. Dissimilar interest in government media policies reflects preexisting divisions within the press and set different limits and possibilities on watchdog reporting. Moreover, discretion or unwillingness to spotlight corruption in government offices that decide over media matters does not exclude the possibility that the news media may spotlight corruption in other units.

Interlocked political and economic interests make questionable the argument that the surge in watchdog reporting is a business strategy of news organizations to capture readers and advertisers in a more competitive media environment. Journalist Gino Lofredo (1993) suggests that investigative journalism "attracts readers . . . and sells advertising." Brazilian journalist Gilberto Dimenstein (1993) contends that "investigative journalism became a matter of survival due to competitions among [news] companies. Nobody wants to lose readers to the competition." A former editor of *Folha de São Paulo* observes that the expectation of higher sales prompted the media to investigate (Lins da Silva 1996). For a *Folha* columnist, "Newspapers started to stimulate [investigative journalism] to grab readers during the battle for the impeachment" of President Collor de Mello (Nassif 1997b). Truly, even one exposé can single-handedly increase sales, especially if packed with salacious information about prominent officials, titillating details about politicians who straddle the worlds of politics and entertainment, or extremely sensitive information. *ISTOE* interview with Eriberto França, the driver who gave decisive details on the shady dealings of former president Fernando Collor, brought a huge jump in sales for the Brazilian newsweekly (Alzugaray 1993).

The argument that watchdog journalism responds to business goals presents some problems, however. It is no coincidence that Brazilian journalists, more often than reporters from other countries, trace the rise of watchdog reporting to the consolidation of a competitive media environment. Watchdog reporting can drive up sales in Brazil, where the size of the advertising market offers sufficient incentives and economic safeguards for news organizations and, as the editor-in-chief of *Folha de São Paulo* states, leading newspapers are intensely competing for readers and advertisers (Frias Filho 1993). In advertising-rich Brazil, government advertising ranges between 5 to 10 percent of the total (Alzugaray 1993). After dropping in the early 1990s, media advertising investments have increased. Since 1993, anti-inflationary plans directly contributed to the growth of advertising expenditures. Simultaneously, newspapers have increased their share of total advertising investments from 24 to 34 percent in that period.

Elsewhere in the region, the situation is markedly different. There is no

MEDIA ADVERTISING INVESTMENTS, BRAZIL,
IN MILLIONS OF DOLLARS.

MEDIUM	YEAR				
	1990	1991	1992	1993	1994
TV	1,314	1,069	1,137	1,350	1,983
Dailies	588	525	467	604	904
Magazines	220	176	161	183	294
Radio	109	98	93	93	149
Other	61	45	60	70	155
Total	2,292	1,913	1,918	2,300	3,485

SOURCE: *Meio & Mensagem* (1994).

question that competition exists among news organizations in metropolitan areas in Argentina, Colombia, and Peru. Flat or dwindling sales prompted print media to launch efforts to capture readers and advertisers such as marketing wars among newspapers. With the intention of stopping the loss of readers, newspapers have introduced color ink and have offered compact disks, books, encyclopedia, lotteries, games, and other goodies. A substantial jump in sales proved those marketing decisions to be wise business decisions. The soundness of watchdog journalism qua marketing strategy, however, is less evident. It may increase readership but the political and business costs outweigh potential market revenues. The managing editor of Peru's *La República* observes, "There are safer ways to increase circulation numbers than revealing the peccadilloes of a cabinet member" (Rosales 1995). Large advertisers do not exactly rush to advertise in watchdog media. They are rather cautious or simply refuse to sponsor publications that feature exposés on government wrongdoing, even if denunciations might attract readers or audiences with a desirable socioeconomic and demographic profile. Sponsoring publications that dig up government secrets might alienate key contacts in high official places. Even when articles touch on government (not corporate) wrongdoing, sponsoring muckraking would send the wrong signals to officials who can be extremely helpful in expediting tax breaks or influencing the allocation of substantial government contracts. A seasoned Argentine muckraker notes that sponsors often punish watchdog reporting by not assigning or by withdrawing advertising from investigative media (García Lupo 1996).

Furthermore, living off the latest scandalous story is an extremely complicated and dangerous method to sustain sales. At best, attention-grabbing exposés give temporary boosts to sales, but they do not contribute to consolidating a larger base of readers. There are plenty of examples showing that sales return to past levels after exposés fizzle out. *ISTOE* sales returned to usual numbers after the França story (Alzugaray 1993). Denunciations do not always generate a substantial increase in sales. *Folha* journalist Fernando Rodrigues (1997) says that sales increased only marginally when daily editions featured investigations. Also, quality suffers when a publication becomes dependent on regularly dishing out shocking stories. It is impossible to produce daily or weekly exposés featuring carefully checked and new information. This is especially difficult when resources for investigative work are limited and when much of investigative reporting sponges off information leaks from high circles of power, as discussed in chapter 4. Stories based on thinly documented information and not carefully checked with different sources are Biblical apples: tempting, but with damaging consequences. Sales might temporarily increase and news media can boast scooping competitors. Lawsuits and loss of prestige, however, might follow when information does not sufficiently support claims made. Aside from concerns about quality and potential legal headaches, publishers cannot bet on reporters regularly stumbling onto different yet equally gripping exposés. When exposés become routine and stale news, reporters have a hard time topping them or shocking readers who have become used to revelations.

MARKET-POWERFUL MEDIA

From a free-market perspective, the commercial consolidation of a handful of media companies also tilts the balance against states. Doubtlessly, the media business in the region is a far cry from past times. A handful of media conglomerates with diversified industrial interests has become consolidated in each country. The situation of the media industry hardly fits standard conclusions about the "lost decade" of the 1980s, when large foreign debts and a combination of stagnation and hyperinflation characterized South American economies. Fueled by technological innovations and laissez-faire legislation, major media companies sought horizontal and vertical expansion. There has been a decline in the numbers of newspapers and readers. Yet the expansion of the television audience, the privatization of broadcasting stations, and the explosion of cable and satellite television have made the media industry highly dynamic and extremely profitable for powerful conglomerates. The politics of economic stabilization also benefited large media companies as advertising revenues have increased while inflation is under control and there is economic growth. Market-powerful media companies have consolidated as a result of these processes coupled with deregulation and privatization.

Take the case of *Folha de São Paulo,* Brazil's largest newspaper. Between 1984 and 1995, its daily sales have grown from 220,000 to 620,000 copies. In 1986, *Folha* surpassed *O Globo* as the newspaper with the largest circulation. Simultaneously, the number of advertising pages jumped from 3,000 to 23,000 between 1980 and 1995 (Leite 1996). With annual billings of U.S.$500 million, *Folha* ranked 150th among the 500 largest Brazilian businesses in 1995. The building of a U.S.$120 million printing center, touted as the most technologically sophisticated in Latin America, attests to its good economic health. Official advertising comprises only 3 percent of *Folha*'s annual revenues (Costa 1997).

Argentina's *Clarín* also has experienced a steady climb in sales and advertising revenues since the mid-1970s, which, coupled with the falling fortunes of other newspapers, turned it into the largest and most influential daily in the country. At the same time, it has steadily expanded into other media sectors, becoming Argentina's dominant media firm. The lifting of media cross-ownership regulations in the late 1980s, together with the introduction of new technologies, spawned *Clarín*'s unmatched horizontal expansion. *Grupo Clarín* controls interests in radio, publishing, cellular telephony, cable and broadcast television, a news agency and newsprint production. Its annual revenues were U.S.$1.14 billion in 1995 (Waisbord 1998a). Brazil's newsweekly *Veja* is the flagship of the *Abril* group, a U.S.$1.2 billion annual revenue company that publishes around 200 titles, has interests in cable and satellite television, and prints telephone directories, among other interests (Katz 1996). With 1.2 million copies, *Veja* is the world's fourth largest weekly newsmagazine, with U.S.$250 million in advertising and sales (Querido 1995). *El Tiempo* is not only Colombia's premier newspaper, but has been the launching pad for expansion into different media industries. With a daily circulation of 230,000 copies, the paper is the flagship of a media conglomerate that controls interests in publishing and cable television. A recent ranking places *El Tiempo* eighty-fifth among the one hundred largest Colombian businesses (see Herrán 1991; Restrepo 1996; Ruiz 1996).

What all these news organizations have in common is that they are part of economic powerhouses. Yet this does not mean that there has been a complete shift from the state to the market. Only a few news media, not the press as a whole, have consolidated a market position that may allow them, partially and circumstantially, to take distance from government units. In the interior of South American countries, where political bigwigs generally control or exercise influence in local media, and private advertising is mostly low in poor areas, the traditional pattern has changed very little. In addition to formidable economic power, massive reach and political clout make the largest news outlets extremely important for any political career, in times when the mass media increasingly have become central to South American politics. The rising centrality of mediated politics in the region reinforces the power of the dominant news media. In an age when media visibility is indispensable for any upcoming or established politician, officials face an uphill battle in confronting media giants that scrutinize their shady dealings. Being shut off from news space or airtime or receiving negative coverage can be extremely harmful for their political aspirations.

Equipped with economic power and political influence, premier news media can take a jab at governments without fearing potential financial damages. They can emerge relatively unscathed after exposing a minister entangled in influence peddling or a police chief involved in drug trafficking. When government advertising is not vital for the financial health of newspapers or when state-owned banks do not wave unpaid loan debts at publishers, reporters can produce reports that are unthinkable in other circumstances (such as when the grapevine informs that a presidential decision to cut newsprint taxes or the "goodwill gesture" of a cabinet member to flush the paper with advertising introduces tangible limits). News organizations can investigate a cabinet member or military officer without fearing government retaliation in the form of cuts in state advertising or rejection of requests for tax exemptions.

The active role of the aforementioned news organizations in the disclosure of government wrongdoing apparently confirms the precept that market strength provides an indispensable economic cushion to support watchdog journalism. Brazil's *Folha de São Paulo* best illustrates this case. In the early 1980s, growing economic might allowed the daily to switch political gears: from passive supporter of the regime to ardent advocate of direct elections. As Gisela Taschner (1992: 199) writes, "the adoption of a business logic and lack of a firm editorial line [allowed *Folha*] to implement that logic to an extreme and explore all opportunities that the process started in the 1960s opened for its consolidation." At a time when the news media still maintained close ties to the authoritarian regime, *Folha* embraced the prodemocracy movement. Taschner states, *Folha* "began to defend, initially timidly and later more defiantly, modern capitalism and the democratization of the political system. It became the vanguard of the mass media in the defense of the prodemocracy movement that had sprung up in the country, which reached its zenith during the 1984 *Diretas-ja* campaign (1992: 186).[3] Yellow banners across its front-pages urged readers to wear yellow, the prodemocracy movement color, in support of direct elections. The daily became known as "the paper of the *diretas*," given its strong identification with the movement for direct elections. *Folha* pioneered exposés in the post-authoritarian years and continued churning out denunciations in the 1990s. Columnist Janio Freitas exposed illegal dealings in the construction of a railroad system that involved the Sarney administration in 1985. In February 1992, months before the Collor scandal broke out, *Folha* reporters disclosed that the wealth of Collor's right-hand man has ballooned simultaneous to Collor's political rise (Krieger, Lobato, and Cipola 1992). Soon after Collor took power, *Folha* revealed that the government had assigned with previous bidding the advertising accounts of oil-giant Petrobrás, the Caixa Economica Federal, and other state-owned and advertising-rich companies. The investigations angered the Collor administration, which reacted by bringing two lawsuits against the newspaper and sending the federal police to raid the newspaper's building in March 1990. The police imprisoned two executives and the secretary of the editorial board. The government justified the decision on the basis of financial irregularities (Rossi 1990). After Collor's fall, *Folha*'s reports contributed to two major scandals that focused on Congress: corruption in the budget commission in 1994, and money-for-votes dealings to pass an amendment to allow presidential reelection in 1997.

Other market-strong news organizations have also put the spotlight on government wrongdoing. *Clarín* churned out reports involving President Menem's aides in corruption, disclosed the sale of weapons during the Ecuador-Peru war that violated diplomatic agreements, and published documents proving that the military juntas systematically organized the repression and persecution of political dissidents in the 1970s. *El Tiempo* has not only been credited for pioneering investigative reporting in Colombia in the late 1970s but also for disclosing more than a hundred cases about wrongdoing in different local, state, and national offices. Advertising-rich newsweeklies have also exposed corruption. *Noticias* has excavated many antics of the Menem administration and even frontally denounced the president himself. *Veja* and *ISTOE* produced decisive exposés during the Collor and Budgetgate scandals among other cases. *Semana* and *Cambio 16* are also credited with publishing important revelations during the *Proceso 8,000* in Colombia.

THE POLITICS OF EXPOSÉS

The foregoing examples seem to provide evidence for the argument that the market builds the strongest defenses against government interference and bolsters critical reporting. Profits have apparently laid the groundwork for watchdog journalism, spawning a politically confident press uncompromised with government interests. Where historically it had been unlikely that premier news organizations would bite the same hand that fed them, it is now possible for them to profile wrongdoing. To turn these cases into conclusive evidence that watchdog journalism thrives when press economies shift to the market is problematic, however. Market-solid news media have not adopted an all-out defiant position: Some have prudently targeted investigations at specific institutions and individuals, while others still favor conciliatory relations with governments and downplay press denunciations. If the market allegedly strengthens press independence and puts news organizations on equal footing with the state, why does the behavior of advertising-rich media fall short of such expectations? Opting for a head-in-the-sand approach when other media published denunciations, or putting the spotlight on carefully chosen targets hardly makes the case that watchdog journalism prospers when the market gives economic reassurance to the news media.

The role of the media in the rise and fall of Fernando Collor de Mello in Brazil, for example, suggests that market power neither warrants hard-hitting reporting nor is sufficient for prodding watchdog journalism. During the 1989 presidential campaign, Collor counted on the undivided support of the major media. Many analysts have argued that the one-sided coverage and explicit backing from media organizations practically hatched Collor's candidacy politics and shepherded him into the presidency. News organizations launched Collor, a little-known governor from the state of Alagoas, far removed from the São Paulo — Rio de Janeiro media axis, into national prominence. For the media (as well as for dominant economic interests), Collor appeared, not as the ideal candidate, but rather as the best hope to prevent the leftist Partido dos Trabalhadores from winning the presidency. Media powerhouse *Globo* visibly threw its support behind him. Globo's *Jornal Nacional,* the most-watched newscast in the country, described him as "a young governor battling the oligarchy in Alagoas." *Jornal do Brasil* nicknamed him "Indiana Collor." alluding to the bravery of the movie character Indiana Jones in confronting evil. *Veja,* Brazil's top newsweekly, called him "the maharaja-hunter" in reference to his fight against parasitic bureaucracies that lived off state contracts and corruption. Only *Folha de São Paulo* kept a distance from the ballyhooed candidate and early on perused his resume.[4]

After backing him during the campaign, *Veja* gradually moved away from its original position. The publication of the tell-all interview with Pedro Collor, piggybacking on previous revelations about the shady activities of Fernando Collor's front-man, was interpreted as a sure sign that not only *Veja* was shifting positions but that the political-economic coalition that carried Collor into office was showing cracks. Globo's *Jornal Nacional* continued looking the other way and allocated minimum time to the coverage of the denunciations and the congressional investigations. On July 11, 1992, it devoted more than twenty-five minutes to Brazil's foreign debt agreement and only a minute and a half to the congressional debates on PC Farias. Its decision to cover the scandal more extensively in late July, two months after it hit the newsstands, was a sign that there were more fissures in Collor's pillars and that the political tables were turning. Tardiness didn't seem surprising considering that *Globo* also, as owner Roberto Marinho declared, belatedly covered growing dissatisfaction with the military government and the surging impulses for democracy in the 1980s.

Media coverage of Collor's wrongdoing does not confirm the argument that market muscle breaks the bonds between government and media organization and unleashes watchdog journalism. The rise and/or absence of this complex phenomenon do not boil down to economics. True, economics does shape linkages between news organizations and the state (or any other potential subject of monitoring) and expands or limits the space for watchdog journalism. It does not provide, however, a comprehensive answer to why news organizations patrol or praise governments.

News organizations in economic difficulties that keep pounding on powerful interests contradict the thesis that market solidity kindles watchdog reporting. Colombia's *El Espectador* persisted in investigating white-collar crime in the early 1980s, even though such reporting damaged advertising revenues. The Grupo Gran Colombiano, then one of the most powerful Colombian companies controlling large advertising resources, boycotted *El Espectador* after it produced a series of reports about financial irregularities in the company (Santos Calderón 1989). Reeling from economic difficulties, the daily adopted an intractable position against drug trafficking later in the decade, notwithstanding obvious problems and threats. It is hard to suggest that economics propped intransigent reporting or that *El Espectador* slammed the Medellin cartel in order to attract advertisers. Followed by like-minded reporters, publisher Guillermo Cano was personally committed to rail against Pablo Escobar and fight the transformation of drug-traffickers into a dominant power in Colombia, even though his daily was in economic dire straits and the disclosure of drug-trafficking activities was potentially deadly. The murder of Cano in 1986 and the bombing of *El Espectador*'s building in 1989 patently proved the political risks of waging a print war against the Medellín cartel.[5]

Argentina's *Página/12* suggests that market muscle is not mandatory for watchdog journalism to flourish. Founded in 1987 as a spin-off of *El Porteño*, an alternative monthly founded during the authoritarian regime, the daily has become synonymous with watchdog journalism in contemporary Argentina. Since President Carlos Menem took power in July 1989, the daily continually has published exposés and broken major stories about official wrongdoing. Its 1991 report that high-powered officials had asked U.S. companies for bribes kicked off a string of exposés. *Página/12* reporters authored the investigations about the Yomagate, which involved Menem's former sister-in-law and secretary, her husband, and associates in drug-money laundering. And they dug up information about the cover-up and the ties between Menem and the judge appointed to the case.

Página/12's investigations and style have had a remarkable influence on the media at large. Signs of its mordant, explosive, informal, and critical reporting as well as its creative, fun-poking, satirical headlines can be found even in button-down newspapers (Leuco 1997). Aside from stylistic matters, one of its main contributions has been to put watchdog journalism at the center of the Argentine media and to push other dailies to produce investigations. Having adopted an all-out opposition role, the paper has been a thorn in Menem's side. In turn, the government has launched a counteroffensive to press charges. It has threatened repeatedly to cease placing legal advertising in the paper. President Menem and members of his administration brought lawsuits against editor-in-chief Ernesto Tiffenberg and columnist Horacio Verbitsky. Government officials have also waged a verbal war against the daily. In his frequent attacks on the press, President Menem has singled out *Página/12*. He accused it journalistic delinquency (when the paper broke the story about a government official who had solicited bribes from Swift-Armour), yellow journalism (when it uncovered the Yomagate scandal), terrorism, being paid by drug-traffickers, and printing lies. Few could doubt that when Menem declared he had "defeated the opposition and the press" after winning reelection in May 1995, *Página/12* was one of the targets of the president's remarks.[6]

Página/12 hardly fits the mold of a market-solvent newspaper. Its roller coaster economic situation has spawned persistent rumors of folding or buyout. Had the government threats of halting advertising been implemented, the paper certainly would have suffered. Official advertising ranges between 20 to 25 percent of advertising revenues (*Somos* 1991). In the context of media concentration, the newspaper stands out for not being a division of a media behemoth or an industrial group with media interests. *Página/12*'s thumping at the Menem administration cannot be attributed only to the fact that its owners do not expect government officials to reward complacent coverage with business opportunities. Politics also shape the watchdog agenda of *Página/12*. Although guest contributors bring different political perspectives and partisan affiliations, the political sympathies of *Página/12*'s columnists and reporters fall in what broadly can be identified as center-left causes. Its tenth anniversary marked a unique development in the history of the Argentine press: the consolidation of a center-left daily with mass appeal and with a great deal of influence among decision-makers. In its first issue, publisher Fernando Sokolowicz defined the paper's goal "to express pluralism and debates in a democratic society in transition. always within the defense of human rights." The defense of human rights and the critique of the policies of state reform and privatization implemented by the Menem administration are commonly found in its columns and impregnate its overall reporting. In fact, *Página/12* rejects U.S.-styled objective journalism and endorses specific political causes. The political orientation of the paper is inseparable from the subjects of denunciations.

The experiences of *El Espectador* and *Página/12* are particularly illuminating, for several reasons. Watchdog reporting does not require the whole press or even a majority of news organizations to be committed to disclosing wrongdoing. It is sufficient that one newspaper stakes out territory and hammers on drug trafficking or government corruption. Other news media may or may not follow suit, but even one politically influential newspaper may blaze the path. As discussed in chapter 2, only a few newspapers and newsweeklies had an active role in breaking sensitive information and carrying denunciations forward. *El Espectador* and *Página/12* indicate that watchdog journalism is not necessarily associated with economically strong news media. The loudest salvos against white-collar crime and drug trafficking in Colombia and human rights abuses and government graft in Argentina have come from newspapers with wobbly economic legs. Not only have news media with lesser economic muscle sniffed out wrongdoing, but in regard to specific subjects they have done so more strenuously than large media companies.

The market does not seem imperative as the springboard from which exposés vault into the headlines. Press independence is not based on rock-solid economics. The complex logic of watchdog journalism and the heterogeneity of news organizations that have disclosed wrongdoing make such an argument questionable and require us to cast a wider analytical net. Free-market arguments overestimate economics, oversimplify media-state relationships, and disregard other factors that may inform watchdog journalism. Even if we assume that market prowess provides enough confidence to dig up information, in no case does watchdog journalism proceed solely from the possibility that media owners believe that they do not need to be closely associated with entire administrations.

Political commitments and economic interests as well as personal disputes between publishers and officials drive a wedge between news organizations and potential targets of denunciations. Partisan politics, confrontations over economic resources, and individual animosities shape relations and may animate denunciations. For many powerful conglomerates, as Colombian columnist Javier Darío Restrepo (1996: 237, 238) writes, "The media are important not a source of income but to put pressure and hold power. The media as business are not an important business." The causes for why press organizations would disrupt relations with powerful institutions and individuals are rooted in the reality of divided political interests and idiosyncratic personal hostilities, rather than in the romantic ideals of press freedom spawned by market muscle. The model of a press comfortably perched in the security of the market and the impartial fourth estate elevated over ordinary political quarrels is in contrast with the pragmatic interests of political and economic groups and even petty personal rivalries that result in journalistic exposés. The press cannot rise above the same politics that articulate its mission and practices. It is not detached but is deeply enmeshed in political conflict. Watchdog reporting, then, reflects the multifaceted relations that different news media maintain with different government units and officials as well as heterogeneous interests that divide the press.

THE AGENDA OF WATCHDOG REPORTING

Different political and economic positions influence the attitude of news organizations vis-à-vis wrongdoing and denunciations of wrongdoing. Consider the dissimilar positions of the liberal and conservative press during the *Proceso 8,000* in Colombia. In a country where historically the press maintained close linkages to party leaders, it would be expected that conservative

news media would eagerly have covered the denunciations that the Cali cartel donated funds to the presidential campaign of Liberal Ernesto Samper.
After Conservative Andrés Pastrana announced that he had a tape with a
conversation that put in evidence the connections between Liberal politicians and drug lords, the Conservative press kept the story alive and urged
President Samper to step down while the investigations were under way.
Television newscast *TV Hoy,* owned by the Pastrana Arango family, allegedly
had access to the tapes that revealed conversations between Liberal politicians and drug barons, but decided not to make the tapes public. The rationale was that it was unnecessary to throw a "news grenade." Although
polls showed that Pastrana, the family scion and presidential hopeful, was
not a shoo-in for the presidency, Conservatives were confident in an electoral victory. Also, the possible reverberations of such explosive information
were impossible to predict and could potentially backfire. The now-defunct
La Prensa, whose publisher was the candidate's brother, as well as the Conservative *El Siglo* flogged the story and did not hide their position. *La
Prensa's* headlines included "Ernesto Rodriguez Orejuela" (mixing Samper's
first name and the last name of the Cali cartel barons) and *"El fin esta Serpa"*
("Serpa" plays with *"cerca"* [near] and it reads "the end is near." Serpa was
Samper's loyal minister of interior and repeatedly declared the president's
innocence).

On the Liberal side, the positions that the news media adopted also
showed partisan colors, but in more complex ways than in the Conservative
camp. There were no consensus or straightforward condemnations of the
Samper campaign, but different attitudes. The newsweekly *Semana* had an
important role in bringing out many denunciations. To many observers, *Semana's* position expressed the political sympathies of its owner and main
editors enrolled in a Liberal faction opposite to Samper. The position of *El
Tiempo,* a firm supporter of Samper during the campaign, varied. Initially, it
warned about rushing to conclusions after the first tapes with conversations
mentioning links between Liberal politicians and drug barons were publicized. A few days after the scandal erupted, one of its main columnists categorically stated "the tapes don't prove anything" (Santos Calderón 1994). A
rift opened between the investigative unit and the editorial board of *El
Tiempo.* The former began playing a more important role in investigating
"hot monies" in the Liberal campaign. The editorial page maintained a cautious position and gradually shifted positions. The late publisher Hernando
Santos Castillo was reported to have discouraged editors from aggressively
covering the subject.[7] Only as new revelations were made public and it

seemed undeniable that Samper knew and participated in the operations with the Cali cartel did *El Tiempo* urge the president to resign.

As a reflection of dissimilar political allegiances, press organizations reached different verdicts after prosecutor Alfonso Valdivieso concluded the investigations in December 1995. *La Prensa* snapped with the headline "OJ Samper" in reference to the presumed culpability of both celebrity O.J. Simpson and the Colombian president. In contrast, the headline of the newsmagazine *Cromos* read, "The End of a Big Calumny," and it declared the case closed, as President Samper could not be linked to the Cali Cartel's alleged funding of the Liberal election campaign (*Cambio 16* 1995). *New York Times* correspondent Diane Jean Schemo (1996b) observed that the unflagging support *Cromos* gave to Samper responded to the corporate interests of the Santo Domingo group, which, in addition to owning the weekly, has interests in several industries (food, aviation, banking, and television). The group is the largest business in Colombia and Julio Santo Domingo personally donated funds to the Samper campaign.

The watchdog agenda of the Peruvian media in the 1990s is also evidence that a combination of politics and economics determines what stones are turned and which ones are left still. The daily *Expreso* has defended President Fujimori's economic policies and praised the government for its actions against guerrilla insurrection. Although editorials and main columnists asserted that democracy should have been preserved, the daily, in general, justified Fujimori's decision to lead a self-coup in April 1992. The justification was based on the argument that the government had no alternative but to bypass the opposition in Congress that stonewalled any attempt to pass market reforms, one of *Expreso*'s pet projects. *Expreso* insisted that former president Alan García was responsible for having cemented a congressional majority that tied Fujimori's hands and made impossible the modernization of the Peruvian economy. *Expreso*'s staunch support for Fujimori contrasted with its piercing criticisms and investigations of skeletons in García's administration. For Fujimori's opposition, *Expreso* has been the government's mastiff, particularly during the first years of his administration, exposing corruption during the APRA government as a smoke screen at a time when the administration has been embroiled in many scandals. Pounding on García was, to many reporters, beating a dead horse. Newsweeklies have already blown open many scandals directly involving García and some of his close associates.[8]

Expreso's exposés didn't bring any startling revelations nor did they add anything new to what was already known about graft during the García administration. They point to *Expreso*'s resuscitation of the Vittor story as an example of how investigative stories about corruption in previous administrations can serve the political goals of the current government. To Francisco Igartua (1995), owner and publisher of *Oiga* (a newsweekly that cracked many stories about García's illegalities before folding in 1995), the government has been extremely interested in bringing out information about shady dealings during the APRA government. To many reporters, many of *Expreso*'s exposés are based on information spoon-fed by the government and intelligence agencies. In a 1995 interview with the author, *Expreso* editor Jaime de Althaus acknowledged that readers were less interested in García's peccadilloes but the story continued as plenty of information was made available. Representative Henry Pease García (1994), former presidential candidate for the opposition party *Izquierda Unida* (United Left), states that *Expreso* has virtually ignored cases of corruption or human rights violations by the present government.

In contrast, the newsweeklies *Caretas, Oiga, Sí,* and the daily *La República,* have churned out investigations critical of the Fujimori administration. *Caretas* and *Oiga* belong to what is known as the tradition of personal journalism, as their identity and positions are inseparable from their publishers and owners (Gargurevich 1991).[9] Although the relation of these two newsmagazines with past governments has not always coincided, they have similarly opposed the Fujimori government in the 1990s. These publications have shed light on taboo topics. Among other stories, they have investigated the activities of death squads, the linkages between drug lords and the political establishment, and military officers involved in corruption. Not that they ignored corruption during the García administration; in fact, some of the cases later extensively uncovered by *Expreso* originally were brought to the surface by the newsweeklies. What sets apart these publications from other news organizations is that they are basically journalistic enterprises without diversified interests in other media industries.

The daily *La República* also has been sharply critical of the Fujimori administration. Its editorial positions as well as electoral support have changed according to struggles among the main stockholders. Gustavo Mohme Llona, leader of the Popular Socialist Action party and the daily's publisher, currently holds the majority of stock. As a reflection of his politics, *La República* has markedly opposed Fujimori on different fronts. Its denunciations unmistakably express its political sympathies. These revelations have put the daily at the center of Fujimori's criticisms. After *La República* revealed the existence of an official plan to stifle the press, Fujimori fired back by accusing the paper of lacking credibility and participating in a campaign against the government. The daily responded: "There have already been past attempts of blaming journalists for official corruption or for the mistakes of the government. Finally, the truth came out. The murders of the students at La Cantuta and of Barrios Altos are just a proof" (*La República* 1996b).

One of the best examples that the Peruvian press strongly differs on what stones should be unturned was the antithetical reactions to the revelation that President Fujimori was not born in Peru. In August 1997, *Caretas* produced a stunning report stating that Fujimori was born in Japan and that his birth certificate had been forged. These findings not only directly challenged his right to the presidency (naturalized Peruvians are not eligible for high office) but hinted at maneuvers to install and maintain Fujimori in power. As expected, such earth-shaking revelations brought a torrent of reactions that split the news media along the Fujimori divide. Consistent with the antigovernment tone of previous reports, journalist Hildebrandt's television show *En Persona* devoted extensive attention to the exposé and, conversely, *Expreso* and the newsweekly *Si* vigorously challenged the reports on the basis of the political motivations behind them. Neither publication minced words in condemning the exposé and the journalists involved. One of *Expreso*'s main columnists accused the denunciation of frivolous aspects and of rushing to conclusions (Ricketts 1997); *Si* called the episode "a dark page for our journalism" and a "pathetic 'investigation'" and scorned Hildebrandt and *Caretas* journalist Cecilia Valenzuela.

This episode is evidence that the press is not a seamless institution, especially in cases when press denunciations spawn heated political conflicts. It does not unanimously advocate or underplay the disclosure of wrongdoing. Political and economic divides across the press make it impossible to pin watchdog journalism on one cause. A sense of unity or commonality can hardly be adjudicated to the press when it is composed of news organizations with different interests. Not all news media are equally interested in pursuing leads or investigating the same stories. Editorial concerns and interests limit reporters' interests in disclosing different cases of wrongdoing. A survey of journalism in five countries conducted by researchers at Florida International University found that reporters categorically deny that they have complete freedom to investigate corruption. The "lack of independence" from editorial interests was indicated as the main problem that journalists confront in most countries (Virtue 1995).

The existing fissures in the South American press are the backdrop to understanding why two kinds of watchdog journalism emerged in the 1980s and 1990s: one practiced by well-established and traditional news companies that are part of multimedia conglomerates, and another illustrated by newly established publications that are not divisions of large conglomerates. In the context of liberal democracy, the economic consolidation of media corporations made possible a kind of journalism that, circumstantially and with limitations, investigates official wrongdoing. In the past decades, the most influential dailies became horizontally integrated media conglomerates. A wide advertising basis coupled with unmatched political influence provides them with a solid economic platform that can absorb the potential shocks that may result from economic retaliations ordered by exposed officials. Unlike underfunded and smaller newspapers that either chronically depend on official advertising or are under direct influence of political bosses, large news organizations have less to fear from revengeful officials. The fact that they are divisions of companies that control interests across media industries (and in other economic sectors), however, raises questions about how far they are willing to go in uncovering corruption. Here the paradox of watchdog journalism (Boyce 1978; Schultz 1998) becomes apparent: news organizations that fundamentally aim to achieve commercial success and depend on market profits for survival are assigned the task of serving the public interest by bringing out wrongdoing. With a few exceptions, large dailies have not pursued all kinds of transgressions but generally have focused on government corruption. The exceptions were reports that resulted from the efforts by editors and reporters to get the green light from the upper brass (like many stories produced by the investigative unit of Colombia's *El Tiempo* in the late 1970s and early 1980s) and from the commitment of publishers and entire newsrooms (like the denunciations of financial graft and drug trafficking done by Colombia's *El Espectador* in the 1980s). Still, it is unlikely that big news organizations would investigate government wrongdoing in toto considering that official policies are decisive for their business projects. Also, commercial pressures and a complex network of interests that weave news organizations with other industries dissuade aggressive reporting on corporate crime.

Reasons for why leading dailies decided to break stories of corruption are not always self-evident, and newsroom grapevine is full of speculations. It is widely believed that, as Brazilian columnist Luis Nassif (1997) puts it, "newspapers aligned with the government use denunciations to hit adversaries; and that those that are critical of the government use denunciations to hit the government." For news organizations that reject the tradition of partisan journalism and closely identify themselves with the nonpartisan tradition of

U.S. investigative journalism, as expressed in public statements by the Inter-American Press Association, the ideology of the fourth estate is often mentioned to justify the need and merit of watchdog reporting. The exposure of corruption finds legitimacy in the catechism of Western journalism that states that the press should monitor government. In practice, such rationale actually hides a sort of "non-partisan partisanism," that is, news organizations couch political interests in a language of political neutrality.[10] Non-partisan partisanism determines not only what issues get exposed but which ones go unexamined. Disclosures typically focus on subjects that either directly affect news organizations or have little political or economic relevance. Not surprisingly, exposés that delve into wrongdoing that compromises the interests of parent companies are unimaginable when profits are prioritized over public interest.

Newly established left-center newspapers have offered an alternative to the model of watchdog journalism represented by "the big press." Political and economic reasons set apart dailies such as Argentina's *Página/12* and Peru's *La República* from older news organizations, and mold a different kind of watchdog journalism. Because they are not part of media conglomerates with wide-ranging business holdings, they are subject to fewer pressures and interests. This does not mean that they are autonomous and embody the noble ideal of the free press. As Jorge Lanata, *Página/12*'s former editor-in-chief, acknowledged "there is no such a thing as truly independent journalism." Still, the fact that owners have more modest business ambitions than press barons means that newsrooms are less burdened by multiple interests vying to influence reporting. They have exposed not only official corruption but also human rights abuses and, occasionally, corporate wrongdoing. For leading newspapers, these issues are too touchy; any reporter willing to uncovering them would likely step into many political and editorial toes.

The watchdog agenda of left-center newspapers reflects not only different economics but also different politics and journalism. Unlike the "independent" press, they do not disguise political sympathies in the ideology of the fourth estate, but openly let readers know where they stand on a variety of issues. Although their editorial politics can hardly be pegged to ideological causes, they clearly represented anti-government positions particularly in regard to human rights violations and neoliberal economic plans during the 1990s. Neither *Página/12* nor *La República* has minced words in confronting the Menem and Fujimori administrations respectively. Their thematic agenda and journalistic style make them heirs to the tradition of al-

ternative journalism, a tradition that reached a crisis (and apparently an ir-
reversible decline) simultaneous to the crisis of social and political movements in the post-authoritarian period and in the post-cold war order. Journalists who, in past decades, used to report for mainstream publications to
make ends meet and moonlighted for alternative publications to have an
outlet for their political views, no longer have that option. Consequently, a
large number of journalists who originally honed reporting skills in a variety of alternative publications in the 1970s and early 1980s currently staff
newsrooms of mainstream news organizations. Some founded and originally staffed publications such as *Página/12* and *La República,* while others
found employment in the big press as leading newspapers became more interested in journalists with hard-hitting reputations as they opened room to
report on subjects that until recently were unthinkable. The migration of
journalists from the alternative press to established news organizations fostered the mainstreaming of watchdog journalism.

CONCLUSION

A convergence of several factors has fueled the recent crop of exposés. The
fact that watchdog journalism has crested in the past few decades simultaneously with the return of democracy in the 1980s and the rolling-back-
the-state policies in the 1990s, appears to be a union made in free-market
heaven. It would appear that the wedding of democratic freedom and market-strong news organizations has provided suitable conditions for watchdog journalism.

It certainly is no pure coincide that exposés have proliferated after the political pendulum swung back to democracy in the region. Democracy offers
more benign conditions, but its connection with watchdog journalism is
more intricate than what it may seem. First, basic constitutional rights are
not fully observed in South American democracies. The persistence of violence and human rights abuses, which repeatedly target investigative journalists, casts doubts on the idea that democracy ushers in a truly paradisia-
cal order for watchdog reporting. Nor is democracy per se sufficient for news
organizations to spotlight power abuses. The affirmation of constitutional
rule breaks down the dominant atmosphere of terror and censorship during
authoritarian rule, but it doesn't encourage all or some news media to disclose government wrongdoing. Other conditions are required too.

The reduction of state participation in the economy, and the growing economic might of a handful of media companies seem to confirm the argument that only a press grounded in the market can maintain some distance from the state and, consequently, act effectively as government watchdog. The press finds political breathing space and is able to bring government secrecy to public view only when it secures economic independence from the state. This explanation rightly directs our attention to the consequences for watchdog journalism of changes in press economies. In a region where leading news organizations and the state generally have maintained close-knit relations, market power may provide at least some news media with enough confidence to take a jab at government offices without fear of cabinet members axing advertising allocations or risk-averse advertisers massively migrating to other news outlets. This argument applies to specific cases, but it fails in other regards. It does not account for why economically feeble news media have insisted on colliding head-on with governments and powerful individuals, even when such attitudes further damaged their economic solvency. Nor does it explain why market power has not emboldened news organizations to dig up official dirt. Nor does it recognize that not all forms of wrongdoing become tender pastures where reporters may graze freely. The growing control of market economics in media industries is not problem-free and has, at best, ambiguous consequences. The fact that official decisions might have a lesser impact on some economically solid news organizations is an unprecedented departure in the history of the South American press. Newer limitations on watchdog agendas are introduced and intensified. These constraints, familiar to press critics in developed democracies, reflect the weight of market interests. The ascendancy of the market may dim the formerly potent light of the state, but it also makes the shadow of market forces loom larger. Trading the state for the market as the mechanism that controls press economies, arguably, potentially allows the press to scrutinize government misdeed. But it does not shake off all constraints, and it brings new ones. It is hard to imagine that a truly democratic press interested in "afflicting the comfortable" would find optimal conditions amid the growing conglomerization of media resources and media ownership in a handful of families and businesses. Within these limitations, it is important to note that, considering the historical context of tight relations between the state and the big press in South America, the market strength of a few news organizations has important consequences for journalism and, particularly, for the agenda of watchdog reporting. When the market becomes the main economic bloodline for a few newspapers and newsmagazines, the old circle is not broken but perhaps shows some fissures.

Without addressing the politics of news organizations, the picture of watchdog journalism is incomplete. Neither politics nor economics alone fuel press denunciations. In the 1970s the lack of economic connections to the state and allegiance to opposition politics was fundamental for the alternative press to lift the rug under authoritarian governments. Conversely, political sympathies and economic relations with dictators made the big press overlook human rights violations and official corruption. In the 1980s and 1990s, both politics and economics also need to be addressed to grasp the situation of watchdog journalism. Dissimilar positions of news organizations vis-à-vis journalistic revelations of wrongdoing reflect a diversity of political and economic relations that they maintain with the targets of investigations. Hence no single answer can be offered to the question whether changing press-state relations have contributed to press denunciations. Relations between media organizations and government present variations and hardly can be summarized in terms of press freedom or subjugation. A newspaper can delve into the drug-trafficking activities of a police chief, the influence-peddling network of a cabinet member, the abuses of a drill sergeant, or the venality of a judge, but it may have little interest in scrutinizing other offices or the whole police, the executive, the army, or the judiciary.

Regardless of specific motivations, the existence of political, economic, and personal differences offer breeding grounds for watchdog journalism. In this chapter I have argued that political and economic conditions facilitate or impede watchdog journalism. A structural interpretation alone, however, fails to address the complexity of news production by which news organizations manufacture news about wrongdoing. Publishers may be interested in excoriating political rivals and newsrooms may have a receptive ear to certain leaks, but denunciations would not necessarily come out. Although differences and separation from subjects of disclosures make it possible for news organizations to catch government officials red-handed, exposés also require factual information that documents that wrongdoing has been committed. In a journalistic culture that gradually is moving away from the tradition of journalism of opinion to fact-based reporting, exposés require not just political will and economic strength but also what newsrooms determine to be factual information to flesh out denunciations. If the news media produce pictures of wrongdoing that repeatedly show official malfeasance, that is not only the result of splits along the government/media fault lines. It is also the result of reporters typically shooting with a narrow-angle lens, of a journalistic culture obsessed about the dealings of government and that consistently applies identical patterns to unveil wrongdoing. The regularity of official wrongdoing as the dominant theme of exposés requires not only the recognition that some news organizations are particularly interested in pulling the rug out from under government officials, but also an examination of newsgathering processes, particularly the relation between newsrooms and sources in the production of disclosures. This is the subject of the next chapter.

PART II

THE SOCIAL ORGANIZATION AND CULTURE OF NEWSMAKING

CHAPTER 4

THE POLITICS OF SOURCES

In the previous chapter I argued that distance between news organizations and government officials is fundamental in feeding or chilling watchdog reporting. Watchdog journalism is unlikely to prosper when news organizations and states form an indivisible alliance. It has no breathing room when publishers opt to wholeheartedly support officials for political or economic reasons and military governments quash even news organizations' attempts to maintain a critical distance. To understand the rise of watchdog journalism and explain why it focuses on government wrongdoing, this chapter examines the flip side of that situation: closeness between journalists and official sources is also indispensable for the media to delve into official wrongdoing. Reporters lack access to evidence to support denunciations if they are far from power centers. Proximity to subjects reduces the chances that news organizations can reveal secrets but close contacts inside the same institutions that are exposed are also necessary. Without distance, news media are prone to offer complacent coverage; too much distance deprives reporters to have access to inside sources. Proximity, I argue, results from the organization of news-making and a journalistic culture that highly prizes official news. While adversarial reporting requires the willingness of news organizations to be at arm's length from the state, newsgathering routines tie them at the waist. Watchdog journalism, then, has an ambivalent relation vis-à-vis its targets. The rise of watchdog journalism as well as the content of exposés are the consequence of this seemingly contradictory situation: Economics and politics may open a breach between some media and some officials, but the dynamics of news-making and the cultural templates of reporting still keep news organizations and the state together. To explain watchdog journalism, it is fundamental to pay attention not only to the political economy of news organizations but also to the social organization and the culture of news production.

Official wrongdoing is another form of official news and, as such, is more likely than other forms of wrongdoing to become the subject of journalistic investigations. Journalistic routines and values are more attuned to the circulation of information coming from official corridors rather than corporate boardrooms or poor neighborhoods. Watchdog reporting expresses the same professional culture that impregnates other forms of reporting. Even media organizations with weak economic and political ties to governments function similarly. Their newsgathering routines are also linked with the interests of elite sources and also focus on official news. Although watchdog journalism reflects the decision of some news organizations to break away from a pack-journalism mentality, covering subjects that others are not interested in and carefully avoid, such mentality persists. Those organizations embrace a professional culture that elevates official news to the highest pedestal of the journalistic world and that basks on closeness to officials at the same time it claims to pull the rug out from under them. Adversarial reporting does not challenge what Stuart Hall and co-authors (1978) have called the bias of journalists toward elite groups and the dependence and deference to recognized authority. Moreover, it feeds off the unequal access that powerful sources have to newsrooms and their strategies for getting media coverage.

At a theoretical level, the dynamics of watchdog journalism attests to the complexity of press/state relations that are not circumscribed to economics and politics but are also linked through news-making routines. The many layers of such relations cannot be fully grasped if we simply take a perspective that sees them along a continuum of independence and subjugation, freedom and domination, adversarialism and acquiescence. Separation rooted in economic and political reasons, indispensable for antagonistic reporting, coexists with close-knit relations, give-and-take information exchanges between reporters and government sources.

In the context of the importance of official news and official sources in the daily practices of South American journalism, the decisions of political elites to wage battles in the media ring are also crucial in driving news organizations, like moths to light, to swarm around official wrongdoing. Unlike ordinary citizens who lack "definitional power" (Schlesinger 1989), official sources have recognition and fluid contacts with newsrooms to pass information that compromises enemies and to shape the repertoire of watchdog journalism. In this regard, the motives and the strategies of official sources in leaking information bears consideration, for their cooperation or negligence in giving information is crucial to trigger press denunciations, especially in countries where newsrooms confront important legal and political barriers in having access to information.

THE SOURCES ABOUT WRONGDOING

To paraphrase sociologist Joe Gusfield's (1981) observation about social problems, not all forms of wrongdoing become public ones. It is necessary to examine who has access, power, and ability to shape the definition of wrongdoing as a public problem. The fact that corruption and human rights violations have been rampant is not sufficient to explain why official wrongdoing has become the bread-and-butter of press exposés. How are they transformed into news? As many studies insist, reporters do not simply write about news out there but instead, manufacture news through standard and routine practices (Fishman 1980; Tuchman 1978). There is no wrongdoing in a raw state just waiting to be discovered, but rather journalistic mechanisms that process corruption, favoring some events and underplaying other kinds of wrongdoing. Media scholars David Paletz and Robert Entman (1981: 24) argue that "much of the news is determined less by external 'reality' than by the internal logic of media organizations and personnel." This logic, I argue, is responsible for why government wrongdoing, rather than other forms of wrongdoing, absorbs the attention of watchdog journalists. Reporters rarely stumble into it but, more typically, receive information about it, thanks to being plugged into an information-gathering system. And even when they do observe it first-hand, they are more likely to resort to testimonies of other witnesses.

The reporting of official news enjoys high prestige among South American journalists (Noblet 1995). The reliance on official sources is an extended practice. A Brazilian editor notes, "Easy access to a source is key because we run against the clock. We call who we know, with who we are in constant contact. . . . The press is tuned to a very restricted part of the population, the players. Only those who have a certain position are of interest. Taxpayers or consumers do not enter the news." (*Radar* 1995). *Folha de São Paulo* editor-in-chief Otavio Frias Filho (1993: 39) observes: "All of us have been educated professionally according to the idea that the government is the main source of information, that everything that happens with it is important. . . . That's the journalistic law of the least effort. It's faster and easier to practice journalism based in the world of government than putting emphasis on what's happening in society."

The same newsgathering system that privileges information emanating from public offices also prioritizes the reporting of wrongdoing involving government officials. News routines that regularly put the spotlight on officials develop echo chamber-like conditions that emphasize the peccadilloes of politicians, judges, and military and police officers as news events. News about wrongdoing, like news in general, are "organized and produced substantially around the views of the dominant political group in . . . society" (Glasgow University Media Group 1982: 111). If regular assignments equally prized other news, we can hypothesize, it would be less likely that much of watchdog reporting would single out government misdeeds out of a wide spectrum of possible acts of corruption.

The prestige of government news carries over to the reporting of government corruption. A telltale sign that unearthing government corruption carries more prestige than shedding light on illegal operations of corporations or abuses on the ordinary citizens is the extended perception among reporters that "investigative journalism is worthless if it doesn't sack a minister," as Argentina's *Clarín* managing editor puts it (Kirschbaum 1996). A Brazilian reporter observes that exposés about congressional corruption bring more prestige to a reporter than a denunciation of social injustices (Lobato 1997). The exposure of social problems is more likely to bring recognition in specific circles (universities, nongovernment organizations), but shouting "gotcha" to a prominent public official catapults a reporter to higher levels among audiences, peers, and, most notably, among official sources. Among these publics, news about racism or poverty, instead, ranks lower than news of government wrongdoing in the hierarchy of newsworthiness. Journalists observe that middle-class readers and audiences, the main consumers of newspapers and newscasts that produce investigative reports, rarely respond with a great deal of interest to reports on issues that affect poor and marginal citizens. For example, according to one of its producers, *Channel 13*'s exposé about diseases among impoverished tobacco workers caused by the unlawful use of chemicals in Argentina's northeastern province of Misiones did not trigger any public response, unlike the much-discussed denunciations of corrupt mayors and police chiefs, observes the story's producer (Elguezabal 1999). In Brazil, a country where the majority of citizens are blacks and mulattos but newspaper readers are overwhelmingly white, *Folha de São Paulo*'s extensive investigation about racism had little repercussion among readers, says an editor (Rodrigues 1997). Also, the culture of newsrooms is decisive in shaping attention to some and not other forms of wrongdoing. It is not just a matter of the prestige and visibility of official stories somehow rubbing off on journalists' work and providing professional recognition by contagion. It is also linked to the perceived difficulty of investigating different subjects. Journalists observe that some social exposés are often dismissed by colleagues as easy stories for anyone comes in daily contact with, let's say, poverty or street children, while not too many citizens or journalists have access to information about wrongdoing inside the folds of power. The prominence of the actors involved also determines what stories command more prestige among elites. The professional status of a reporter rises proportionally to the political and economic status of the individuals implicated in the exposés and the visibility of the known or suspected informers.

The interest of officials in divulging information is also important in determining the subjects of denunciations. The anatomy of exposés shows that the cooperation (or reluctance) of highly placed sources has enormously facilitated (or conversely stalled) the work of muckrakers. Watchdog reporting, like journalism in general, is not self-sufficient: it requires the active collaboration of sources. They are indispensable to find out incriminating evidence and get the go-ahead from editors. High-powered officials have been key in sharpening the interest of the press in government wrongdoing, tipping and prodding reporters to investigate. If "investigative journalists place a great deal of faith in information, especially documents, from official sources," as David Protess and co-authors (1992: 207) suggest, it is because investigative stories essentially deal with transgressions committed by official sources. In all the major stories chronicled in chapter 2, nonofficial sources rarely had a pivotal role in journalistic investigations such as in *ISTOE*'s exposé, based on the testimony of driver Eriberto França, who admitted to have transported funds linked to the illegal operations of Collor de Mello. Generally, however, watchdog journalism depends on inside jobs to open the safe of official information. Without it, most exposés would not have surfaced, as high-placed sources monopolize information that implicates other officials. And, conversely, if they are silent about specific issues and obstruct access, there are few chances that even widely suspected cases of corruption would rise above rumors in newsrooms and political circles.

Reporters talk of being inundated with not-so-mythical anonymous phone calls with hot tips, especially once stories gain wide visibility and affect prominent figures. Some journalists call it "the snowballing method" (Donadío 1998): initial investigations and disclosures prompt other sources to volunteer information. In this way, reporters quickly gain expertise in a given subject and become magnets for tips and outlets for behind-the-scene sources. This situation forces them to be extremely discriminating among sources. The interests are many, the stakes are high. The chief concern is to preserve their own credibility, which strongly depends on the credibility of the sources consulted, as a Brazilian reporter notes (de Carvalho 1997).

Wide acceptance of off-the-record information heightens the role of official sources in fueling stories about wrongdoing. Although it is practically impossible to measure their use and influence, reporters confess that "offs," as they call them, are central to watchdog journalism. When relying on testimonies from anonymous sources, reporters often stress their trustworthiness to bolster their own credibility and ask readers to believe them even though no specific names are mentioned. Peruvian muckraker Angel Páez, for example, describes an informant in the denunciations about the plans of intelligence agencies to harass journalists as "a safe and known military source" (*La República* 1996b).

The wide acceptance of anonymous sources encourages a perverse relation of mutual advantages and benefits. Reporters do not have to reveal their sources and the latter are able to steer coverage. Rarely, if ever, do newspapers and reporters inform readers about the origins of the information or rectify previous mistakes when off-the-record sources were found to be wrong (Buarque de Gusmao 1993). This practice contributes neither to making the workings of journalism more transparent nor to raising awareness among readers about the origins of information. Instead, it legitimizes the interests of powerful sources in spilling information without revealing their identity, and it allows journalism to disclose wrongdoing without disclosing its own practices. The public, then, is left without knowing who passes information and why. Only insiders, deeply immersed in and cognizant of inter-elite disputes, are able to decipher the interests behind the denunciations and the motivations of sources to blow the whistle. Not surprisingly, then, military officers are the primary readers of military exposés, politicians are the primary readers of political denunciations, and so on. The newsmaking process remains largely obscure at the same time that the news media pursue to shed light into the secret affairs of the state.

Facing a large number of sources eager to provide details and versions of the same story, reporters choose different strategies. Some prefer to keep the number of informants to a minimum to avoid being drowned in a sea of accusations; others lend ears to anyone willing to talk in order to maximize information. During Colombia's *Proceso 8,000*, for example, the editors of the newsweekly *Semana* admit to have regularly consulted a handful of sources (Lesmes 1996; Vargas 1996). The main investigative reporter for *Cambio 16*, however, recalls having received and checked information from around fifty informants (Caballero 1996). Regardless of the specific issue under investigation, reporters often check a handful of sources that are considered mandatory according to editorial politics. In different newsrooms, specific names of political, business, military, and ecclesiastical figures are implicitly required to be consulted, whether or not they or their institutions are implicated in the stories.

Some reporters avoid relying on a single source even when she or he seems credible and familiar with the story. A symbiotic relationship can turn journalists into mouthpieces for specific interests. Buying tips from out-of-the-blue informants or sources without any credibility is also problematic. Reporters prefer to massage information out of familiar sources to lower risks. Working with a handful of credible sources is often the safest way to avoid costly mistakes that can deeply damage professional credibility. Sources considered authoritative and known to editors enjoy a natural advantage. Consulting long-time, trustworthy sources who may be out of the loop on the specifics of the story under investigation but are able to report on rumors circulating in influential circles is also considered mandatory to sounding tips and hearsay.

Official sources often dictate the tempo of investigations by being reluctant or eager to feed information and go on the record. In Brazil, widespread suspicions about corruption in Collor's election campaign were insufficient to publish accusations that would directly implicate the then-president. Editors feared the impact and legal consequences of the stories. The investigations could not go further without the cooperation of sources with first-hand knowledge. In the early investigations carried by the newsweekly *ISTOE,* the information mainly came from entrepreneurs who paid the bribes that fueled what became known as the "PC scheme." Angered about demands to pay bribes of 33 percent compared to the historic rate of 10 percent, entrepreneurs became whistle-blowers (Fleischer 1996/1997). Former *ISTOE* reporter Bob Fernandes (in Jose 1996: 159) observes, "the scheme was too expensive for those who paid." For journalist Augusto Fonseca (in Jose 1996: 159), "the Collor-PC scheme abused the patience of the traditional elites, charging astronomical bribes for the 'ethical' standards of our entrepreneurs." But without key sources close to Collor's operations, *ISTOE*'s investigations could not progress. "Politicians from inside Collor's kitchen, implicated up to their necks, kept their beaks shut," Fernandes recalls. The story was stalled as high-powered sources and hard facts explicitly involving Collor were unavailable. Sources wielding "smoking guns" had not appeared, nor had documents revealing Collor's approval of corruption. Editors were reluctant to give the green light without inside sources and/or documents backing accusations.

This situation changed once Pedro Collor granted an interview to the newsweekly *Veja*. Even though he had previously contacted several newsrooms and promised journalists to pass hot information, off-the-record information was not sufficient. Before he went on the record, Collor had sent a dossier that included the number of foreign bank accounts with the signature of PC Farias a month before. The dossier did not include any proof of his brother's wrongdoing but it promised to give them if necessary. According to a *Veja* reporter, the information, mailed from the Collors' home state of Alagoas, was "thrown in the garbage" as the documents had no signature and reporters suspected that only a few sources could have access to such important information (Alcantara 1996). Even though making denunciations without solid proof is not unusual in Brazilian journalism, news organizations were unwilling to implicate then-president Collor de Mello.[1] His political status and the possible ramifications of the story required more than grapevine rumors or thin facts to corroborate suspicions. *Veja*'s interview with Pedro Collor moved the investigations into a new phase, almost erasing the fact that other media had previously exposed the illegal dealings the president's brother narrated.

TYPE OF SOURCES

Which official sources are more likely to be consulted by reporters? Different sources exhibit different credentials to become informants. There are those with sufficient political prestige to gain wide attention (regardless of how much information they have or are believed to have), those close to individuals suspected of wrongdoing, those assumed to have direct knowledge of corruption, and those with first-hand information about congressional and judicial investigations.

Sources with recognized political status carry enough credibility to kick off a story and confirm the suspicions of reporters and editors. In Colombia, there were plenty of rumors in newsrooms about the links between the 1994 Liberal campaign and the Cali Cartel yet the story did not break. Without "journalistic facts," a point to be further explored in chapter 6, editors were reluctant to go forward. The editors of newsweekly *Semana* remember that they "often regretted the amount of loose information they gathered but could not disclose as they lack confirmation or because the story will be denied and the magazine didn't have facts to demonstrate that the story was true" (Vargas, Lesmes, and Tellez 1996: 138). Reporters faced the dilemma of finding solid evidence to tell the complete or partial story without risking credibility if implicated officials declined any responsibility and sued them for libel. This impasse quickly changed once Andrés Pastrana, the defeated conservative presidential candidate, called a press conference to confirm a newscast story about taped conversations hinting at the funneling of drug monies into the Liberal campaign. Pastrana's political visibility and status as member of a political and press dynasty not only made his declarations newsworthy but, most importantly, jump-started denunciations.

The towering presence of the United States in domestic affairs in South American countries makes U.S. officials much-sought sources. In Argentina, the U.S. embassy almost single-handedly triggered the "Swiftgate" investigation. Even though the collaboration of government sources was important in leaking the ambassador's letter originally sent to President Menem, the political weight of the U.S. embassy made additional testimonies confirming or disproving the document almost unnecessary. In Colombia, a handful of U.S. government organizations and individuals were extremely influential in the unfolding of the *Proceso 8,000*. Even though no organization ever publicly claimed responsibility for producing the tapes that detonated the process, journalists generally subscribe to the version that Colombian and U.S. intelligence services worked together in wiretapping people close to the Cali drug barons and that U.S. officers passed the first recording to a U.S. journalist who, in turn, handed it to Andrés Pastrana.[2] Reportedly, CIA and DEA officials were key informants throughout the journalistic and judicial investigations (Lesmes 1996; Vargas, Lesmes, and Tellez 1996).

Sources close to individuals suspected of corruption are also obviously attractive to reporters. Reporters intensely contacted Fernando Collor's brother even before he finally decided to go on the record. The legitimacy of Pedro Collor did not stem from holding any political office (which he did not); his credibility derived from the assumption that family ties and past business partnership gave him first-hand knowledge of the president's antics. Moreover, unlike other potential sources, his testimony could not be suspected of having political interests, of being, in the words of *Folha de São Paulo* columnist Clovis Rossi (in José 1996), "*petista*, revengeful, or the devil."[3] It is certainly impossible to guess what could have happened without Pedro's testimony. Although reporters remained firmly convinced that Fernando Collor was deeply involved in the PC scheme and even had several not-for-attribution declarations, the exposé had reached a dead end. But

Veja's interview confirmed suspicions, unleashed further investigations, and set in motion the scandal that culminated in the impeachment of the president four months later. Only after the interview did other high-placed sources also went on the record confirming that Fernando Collor fully knew about Farias's activities.

Reporters also pursue sources that directly participated in wrongdoing. Some are widely believed to have been involved given their role in the organizations and activities under investigation. In Colombia, campaign treasurer Santiago Medina was allegedly a key source before and after his deposition to chief prosecutor Alfonso Valdivieso. Once Medina publicly admitted that the suspected linkages between the Liberal party and the Cali cartel were not limited to minor and regional party leaders, the investigations closely circled around the party's upper brass. His declarations confirmed what journalists had suspected and known for months — that the Cali cartel donated a substantial amount of money — yet could not publish because there were no top sources inside the Liberal campaign willing to go on the record.

Less familiar sources, whose responsibility in wrongdoing is not immediately obvious to reporters, can also be important informants. As their credentials and information are unknown, reporters cautiously cross-examine them. They are initially used as sounding boards to check information (as well as credibility) and eventually can move to the status of primary informants. The testimony given by former captain Adolfo Scilingo to Argentine columnist Horacio Verbitsky was the basis for the latter's best-selling exposé detailing the regular flights in which corpses and semiconscious people were thrown into the ocean. Many of *El Espectador's* chronicles about drug trafficking in Colombia were reportedly based on information handed out by informants inside drug organizations.

Reporters also consider it indispensable to maintain regular contacts with sources in the offices of public prosecutors and congressional committees investigating charges. In Colombia, the office of chief prosecutor Valdivieso was a constant source of information (Ronderos and Cortés Fierro 1996). "Much of investigative journalism was based on judicial information, without naming the source," remarks a reporter (Gómez 1996). Then-minister of Interior Horacio Serpa (and later Liberal presidential candidate in the 1998 elections), who ardently defended President Samper, openly criticized deputy prosecutor Adolfo Salamanca for leaking classified information. In the cases of scandals in Brazil and the *Proceso 8,000* in Colombia, some observers conclude that once public prosecutors and congressional committees started poring over accusations and gathering testimonies, investigative reporting took the backseat. Reporters carried out little, if any, original investigations and, instead, followed the actions and fed off on information from members and aides of the prosecution and congressional committees (Nassif 1997b). Many justify this decision as the only way to jump over the problems of having limited access to official sources of information. Not infrequently, then, journalists team up with prosecutors or with sources who are considered to be "the healthy part" of the institution under scrutiny and collaborate in extracting and exchanging information.

DENUNCISMO: QUICK AND EASY REPORTING

The dependence of investigative reporters on tips and documents passed by officials engenders *denuncismo*. This refers to facile denunciations that lack sufficient evidence and are the product of information passed by one or two sources. *Denuncismo* is a debased form of investigative journalism that features little independent investigations and depend on the cultivation of informers. Other monikers commonly used, "dynamite journalism" (reports published chiefly to make a big noise) and "desk-journalism" (reports based on just a few phone conversations or information handed down by influential sources), similarly dismiss *denuncismo* as a quick and easy form of investigative reporting (Reyes 1996; Vivas 1995). According to reporter Fernando Rodrigues (1997), author of many important investigations for *Folha de São Paulo:* "Many times, the journalist is sitting in the newsroom and receives a telephone call from someone telling a story and offering proofs. Most times, those crazy callers do not have evidence to prove what they are saying. But, in some cases they do and the story is good. And presto! There you have investigative journalism. Also, there is 'sourcism,' good sources, faithful to specific journalists [who pass information]." Peruvian muckraker Angel Páez (in López Chang 1995: 57) observes, "with a few exceptions, most investigative stories aren't the result of investigations."

An expression of the leading role that sources hold in source-reporter relationships (Bennett 1996; Gans 1980; Sigal 1973), this form of reporting puts in evidence the proximity of the press to government sources. The political clout of a few sources, rarely quoted or only cryptically mentioned, is often sufficient to print stories, making it unnecessary to comb other potentially knowledgeable parties or to search for alternative sources of information. It is clear that here the limits between standard understandings of investigative journalism and information leaks become blurred. For media scholar Ralph

Negrine (1996), the former requires active reporters while the latter means that journalists are mere recipients of information. In the South American context, however, such clear-cut differentiation hardly applies. The boundaries between enterprising reporting and sourcism, investigations and leaks, are blurred.

There have been many criticisms of *denuncismo*. Columnist Rafael Santos (1996) has observed that the inability of Colombian journalism to keep its distance from official sources during the *Proceso 8,000* made reporters prone to manipulation. Reporters have been scoffed at as *sicarios sociales* [social assassins-for-hire]. Many Brazilian journalists have raised questions about *denuncismo,* alluding to news organizations that claim to practice investigative journalism based on groundless accusations. The lack of solid evidence undermines the credibility of denunciations and, eventually, of the press (Nogueira de Sa 1993). Columnist Luis Nassif (1997a) has charged the Brazilian press with "not developing parallel investigations, elaborate explanations, analyze alternative hypothesis of investigation [during the impeachment of former President Collor]. Simply hitting the information bag of a legislator was considered sufficient." Alberto Dines (1994), former *Jornal do Brasil* managing editor, concluded that the impeachment of President Collor was "the victory of *denuncismo* . . . shoot first and then ask. The press prejudged in the Collor case. It made him guilty before judgment. The press created Collorgate before the CPI [Congressional Investigative Committee] was appointed. It does not mean that I am in favor of Collor or consider that he had any dignity. . . . The press did not investigate. It emotionalized. . . . It did not use resources of investigative reporting but of crusading journalism, of *opinionismo* [opinionism]."

Folha columnist Gilberto Dimenstein (1993) warned, "The exchange of investigation for facile denunciation is one of the greatest dangers to be avoided in the post-Collor era." *Folha* managing editor Josias de Souza (1997) notes, "[Brazilian journalism] makes bad investigations. It is highly influenced by 'cabinet information' and simply relies on quick telephone calls. It's easier to do. After Collorgate, anything was a denunciation and was published in the papers." Government officials have also criticized *denuncismo*. A Minister of Culture charged *Folha* of printing accusations without evidence after the daily fingered members of President Cardoso's entourage for wasting time and public resources during the 1996 official trip to France (Moisés 1996).

Underlying these criticisms is the idea that *denuncismo* is solely driven by the intention to inflict political damage on specific individuals rather than to produce quality, critical reporting. Press critic Sérgio Buarque de Gusmão

(1993) has argued that "instigative journalism" is a travesty of "investigative journalism" that responds to the political and business interests of news companies. Evidence of wrongdoing is secondary to waging campaigns against individuals. Superficial denunciations are not the responsibility of reporters, he argues, but the result of "business dynamics and press competition" (1993: 29) that are mainly concerned with the political consequences of the exposés rather than their journalistic merits. With a few exceptions, news companies are not interested in devoting resources to gather rock-solid facts to support charges. Good investigative reporting is expensive. The gathering of proof requires money and time. Insinuations, instead, are deemed to be sufficient to go ahead with a story. But even when denunciations are found faulty or thinly supported on shreds of evidence, the damage has been already done. News organizations may retract and acknowledge mistakes, which they rarely do, and accused individuals may get a chance to offer their viewpoints but it's hard to repair the damage. "A kilo of accusation weighs more than a kilo of defense," Buarque de Gusmão (1993: 12) observes. Many Brazilian journalists mention the cases of public officials and institutions that became publicly identified with corruption and crimes even though neither the press nor courts presented solid evidence of wrongdoing (Ribeiro 1995). *Folha de São Paulo* columnist Luis Nassif (1997d) writes, "There is a widely practiced style of journalism, one that shows that there are no differences between the professional defects of journalism and of the military police. Some kill people, others kill reputations. Both ordinarily used their weapons to shoot people or reputations."

Several factors feed *denuncismo.* First, the tradition of investigative journalism is lacking in the region. The former editor of Colombia's *El Tiempo* investigative unit comments, "investigative journalism is a little understood ghetto" (Santos 1996). Recent successes and awards have, at best, spawned the belief that investigative journalism is necessary but did not stimulate a culture that wholeheartedly embraces it. Assigning journalists to follow a story for an extended period of time is an idea that still escapes the imagination of most publishers and managing editors, reporters comment. Nor are most journalists sufficiently trained in the arts of investigative reporting. The habit of "reading documents" is missing, an Argentine reporter points out (Santoro 1996).

Second, South American societies lack a tradition that holds government information to be a common good, available to any member of the public, rather than a private booty for officials to appropriate and wage political wars with. This tradition is expressed in the absence of legislation that conceives official information as a matter of public interest and also in a history of judicial decisions that favored government officials rather than investigative reporting. Even if documents exist, there are no legal resources to demand access. Laws for public access are non-existent, weak, or ridden with loopholes. In the U.S. context, press scholar Timothy Gleason (1990) has argued that it is impossible to understand the watchdog concept of journalism without addressing the significance of press laws and the interpretation of such legislation by the courts. Not only legislation but also court decisions that gave special protections to the press have made watchdog journalism possible. This requires conceiving the press as *primus inter pares:* An institution that, although privately owned and driven by profit-making, needs special legal treatment to serve effectively the collective good. Without legal defenses or without courts willing to back the right to access and publish information without government intervention, watchdog journalism would have had wobbly legs, Gleason argues.

In South America, the lack of similar legal protections and the ambiguous standing (and at times outright opposition) of courts to the liberal concept of the press continue to be major obstacles for investigative reporting. It would be wrong to assume that the existence of First Amendment legislation, the bedrock of the liberal model of watchdog journalism, is the panacea that would solve all problems and inevitably guarantee ceaseless investigation on abuses of power in different realms. It is important to recognize, however, that its absence constrains the possibilities for investigative journalism and shapes certain reporting practices that are not problem-free. The managing editor of Argentina's *Clarín* observes, "there are serious difficulties for having access to information. There is no legislation like in the United States. The diffusion [of official documents] is punished. Confidentiality is not protected." (Kirschbaum 1996, 1998). Even in countries where constitutions explicitly define official documents as public and grant the right of access, such stipulations are systematically ignored and are largely ineffective in assisting journalists in investigations. A recent survey among reporters in the region has found that 30 percent of the respondents believe that the refusal of public offices to accept request for access to information is the main obstacle for investigative journalism (Virtue et al. 1995).

The situation in Colombia is somewhat different from other countries. Alberto Donadío (1995: 21), cofounder of the *El Tiempo* investigative unit, writes, "A 1913 law was still in the books. That law gave access to the investigations of the Chief Prosecutor about public officials, airplane crashes, expenditures and appointments in the Senate. . . . In 1984, the minister of government submitted a proposal to Congress that set the basis for the 1985 law that enforces the publication of official acts and documents, the equivalent of the Freedom of Information Act in the United States." The efforts of *El Tiempo* muckrakers were key in this regard. Donadío (1998) observes: "If access to official archives is legally recognized today and there exists a constitutional article that protects requests [for access], it is because of the demands that I, sometimes with other people and with other members of the unit, presented to the courts and the favorable decisions that followed. In many cases, we invested as much time in litigation as in the investigations."

Still, problems persist for Colombian journalists to have access to official information. In describing the numerous obstacles in reporting drug-trafficking, journalist Maria Jimena Duzán (1994: 51) writes, "we were having difficulties in obtaining access to official documents. Although Colombia has a law that is the rough equivalent of the US Freedom of Information Act, it was not effective in getting us the material we needed. The bureaucracy involved was daunting and obstacles were always thrown in our way." Even when documents are available, reporters often find out that they suddenly disappear, states *El Tiempo* judicial editor (Torres 1996). Facing these difficulties, journalists say they have no other way to produce denunciations but by scrapping together leads and secret documents collected from anonymous sources.

Third, the scarcity of resources also fuels *denuncismo*. Notwithstanding the ongoing vigor and prestige of watchdog reporting, journalists are rarely assigned to follow a story for an extended period of time, but instead are expected to churn out articles regularly. Without sufficient human and monetary resources, well-researched and exhaustive stories are extremely difficult to produce (Donadío quoted in Padilla 1995). For a Peruvian editor, "reporting is done without resources, using low-cost methods" (Barraza 1995). Brazilian journalist Jose Hamilton Ribeiro observes: "Investigative journalism is expensive. If, for example, a newspaper would do a life story of a candidate, it would need at least fifteen to twenty days. It's not something you get in twenty-four hours, go in the morning and bring it at night. It requires patience and money. You would have to search for information in registry offices, real estate agencies, public offices, and listen to many people. The companies don't want to pay this price" (in Marques de Melo and Lins da Silva 1988:49). Although having an investigative unit and producing critical reports may bring prestige to a newspaper, many reporters observe that management often prioritizes, for example, technological investments over the allocation of monetary and human resources to investigative reporting. A Brazilian columnist quips, "newspapers offer support, moral support" (de Freitas 1997). Given these circumstances, most in-depth denunciations are inspired by reporters' interests and are a personal gamble. They express the convictions of journalists (more than of news organizations) and are the product of after-hours work. There is no solid editorial commitment but cyclical support in specific moments, often stimulated by the firecrackers and sporadic booms generated by explosive reports.

Lastly, the wide acceptance of not-for-attribution quotes in South American journalism also tills the ground for *denuncismo*. Sources can remain behind the scenes while throwing daggers at their political rivals. Journalists can produce explosive stories without having to pressure sources to go public. Such dynamics work for the benefit of sources and reporters, editors, and publishers and consolidates you-scratch-my-back-I-scratch-yours practices that facilitate the trading of information. Granted, in cases such as the reporting of drug trafficking and human rights violations, the pervasive use of off-the-records results from the inevitable dangers that sources and reporters face. "On-the-records are paid with your job or life," notes Colombian journalist Maria Cristina Caballero (1996) who investigated the linkages between politicians and drug cartels and the activities of death squads.

Certainly it would be foolhardy to expect full disclosure and complete rejection of anonymity in the reporting of topics where the difference between quoting or not quoting sources is a matter of personal survival. This also goes to the nuts-and-bolts of the culture of journalism: the identity of sources is one of journalists' best-kept secrets, an essential trick of the trade to scoop colleagues and to negotiate with sources. The problem arises when the use of anonymous quotes becomes common rather than a sparsely used recourse considered valid only in specific circumstances. As María Teresa Ronderos and Ernesto Cortés (1996) observe, "violence and fear have led many [reporters] to practice clandestine, faceless journalism. But what was a necessity in life-or-death situations became a general norm."

The danger of *denuncismo* is ventriloquism: Press exposés often speak for concealed sources. No question, they typically express the convergence of the interests of sources, news organizations, and journalists. But while news organizations and journalists (except when they don't include their bylines because of security reasons) assume public responsibility for denunciations, sources are able to pursue political goals without being publicly identified. The paradox is that while aiming to shed light onto political and economic practices, watchdog journalism facilitates the perpetuation of the politics of secrecy by which political wars are waged underhandedly. Public officials throw stones and hide their hands without ever publicly committing to words and deeds. Who passes information? Why are sources interesting in disclosing secrets? How was the information obtained? *Cui bono* from revelations? Journalists constantly ponder these and similar questions but rarely invite a public conversation about such matters. They invoke professional secrecy and shield laws when confronted with judicial demands to identify sources. They justify such legal protection to answer demands from accused individuals and judges to reveal sources, demands that, no doubt, are often inspired by the intention to muffle investigations more than to make journalism accountable. Some reporters find refuge in the fact that such practices ultimately lead to a greater good and, consequently, are ethically justified from an instrumental perspective that considers that the morality of means depends on the pursuit of desirable ends.

Aside from whether such arguments are justifiable, a point to which I shall return in subsequent chapters, what is troublesome is that journalism rarely questions the consequences of *denuncismo,* namely, what kind of political practices are legitimized as a result of frequently relying on information from anonymous sources. Certainly, journalists are not blind to the political intentions of sources but their main concerns are strictly journalistic: to verify that sources are knowledgeable and have corroborating evidence of wrongdoing. The dominant attitude is "to check and publish," as an Argentine muckraker puts it (Lejtman 1996), rather than considering whether a story merits publication on the basis of the reasons that prompt informers to pass information. If the information is solid and does not hit editorial and legal snags, it is secondary whether individuals leak information for personal or political motives or who actually benefits from those revelations. Journalists are inclined to think that making information public, regardless of its origins, is better than no information. As a rule of thumb, they admit, all sources should be distrusted, all information leaks are always motivated by self-interest, and manipulation is assumed to be intrinsic to source-reporter relations. What is important, grizzled journalists warn, is to scrutinize the credibility of sources, the soundness of the information, and the evidence to back up accusations. The paramount concern is to take precautions to avoid being manipulated with "rotten information." The solidity of the evidence is the yardstick for separating the wheat from the chaff of sources, particularly in situations where muckrakers become the dumping ground for all kinds of informers to unload information after they become experts in certain subjects and gain visibility after disclosing several cases of wrongdoing.

These concerns are primarily relevant to the needs and practices of journalism but not necessarily to the process of democratic communication. What mainly matters is whether the information fits newsroom expectations and standard practices. Reporters and editors care about checking the credentials of unknown sources, in contrasting information, in sounding out other sources, and so on. Whether that information actually helps citizens to understand politics better or whether newsgathering routines reinforce the power of recognized (yet invisible) sources are questions subordinated to journalistic criteria. Journalism rarely sets out to maximize public knowledge about the context and conditions that breed and facilitate denunciations but, instead, operates on the assumption that revelations contribute to the public's right to know.

The challenge for watchdog journalism is, what are the implication of publicizing illegal affairs without making newsgathering procedures public? Isn't the press a central institution of the same public life that it allegedly seeks to make more public? If these questions have barely received attention, it is because the newsgathering process is hard-wired to deal with questions about reporting, not to probe the merits and the impact of journalistic routines on democratic life. Bringing out information about power abuses is, few could doubt, desirable and admirable, particularly in countries where journalists face plenty of obstacles. "Bringing the news at any cost" and regardless of the intention and identity of sources, however, is hardly satisfying when such practices raise a host of complex issues that are at the core of public life. It is necessary to explore the apparent contradiction of a journalism that sets out to make things public but reveals little about its own workings and is often subservient to the politics of sources that pour gas into the engine of watchdog reporting. The problem is not just about journalistic transparency but also about newsgathering routines that legitimize and perpetuate insidious practices that reinforce inequalities in media access.

POLITICS BY OTHER MEANS

The rise of muckraking reflects new political dynamics by which official sources choose to battle enemies through media denunciations. Conflict among high-powered sources is central to explain why watchdog journalism

has recently gained momentum as well as its tendency to focus on government wrongdoing. Several authors have already called attention to the need
to understand changes in news coverage in relation to elite confrontations.
Philip Elliott (1978) concluded that press disclosures are the result of "disaf-
fection and disagreement between different centers of power." Paletz and
Entman (1981) observed, "when elite sources conflict, the press will contain
a diversity of views about issues, problems, events. . . . Elite conflict is a
prime cause of the nature of the news reports of any event or problem: the
more conflict, the more coverage, the more varied the views stories contain."
Similarly, Dan Hallin has suggested that changes in media coverage of the
Vietnam War expressed shifts in the opinions and positions among policymakers: "The behavior of the media . . . is intimately related to the unity
and clarity of the government itself (1986: 213). Along the lines of these arguments, watchdog journalism in South America also needs to be analyzed
in connection to the lack of unity in government. Conflicts are key to make
information about wrongdoing available and feed adversarial news. Given
that media coverage is tightly dependent on authoritative sources, agreements and disagreements among power-holders can open or close opportunities for watchdog reporting.

To paraphrase political scientists Benjamin Ginsberg and Martin Shefter
(1990), the ascendancy of watchdog journalism suggests the rise of "politics
by other means" in contemporary South American democracies. They argue
that the politics of RIP (revelations, investigation, and prosecution) in the
contemporary United States has resulted from the inefficacy of traditional
political mechanisms (specifically, elections) to resolve conflicts and constitute governments. The political stalemate resulting from party decline and
electoral deadlock introduce other forms for carrying out political confrontations. Institutions such as the courts and the media gain a more central role as arenas for doing politics by other means. Taking Ginsberg and
Shefter's insight, I argue that the elimination of military coups as a recurrent
formula to gain access to power has changed the mechanisms by which powerful actors have historically tried to influence decision-making processes
and shape the public agenda in South America. Once military interventions
are no longer a viable option, other institutions become potentially more
important.

Democratic institutions such as political parties and Congress, however,
have been inefficient in becoming solid channels for mediating conflict and
spaces for political communication. They have been unable to incorporate

and adequately express public opinion and interests. In turn, the shortcomings of traditional institutions have catapulted the media to an increasingly central position in the political process. More and more political confrontations are played in the fishbowl of front pages and television newscasts. As Peruvian columnist Mirko Lauer (in Burgos 1997) observes in regard to investigations that implicated the Fujimori administration, "This is the conclusion of system in which there are no political parties and different camps inside the government borrow a stage [from the media] to fight over internal affairs." Such practices are facilitated by the inclination of the media to shield charges in the anonymous rubric of highly placed sources and the possibility for interested sources to get quick and wide attention by circumventing party structures and other institutions. The prominent status of powerful sources as newsmakers makes possible to draw attention to government wrongdoing and to play mediated politics.

The crisis of political representation and the centrality of the mass media in Latin American societies usher in new forms of political communication and political practices. Unequal power positions determine that such practices are different for political elites and citizens. Without media contacts, ordinary citizens have to resort to other mechanisms to get airtime and print space. Citizens demanding land rights, protesting police abuses, or asking authorities for investigation and justice commonly resort to rallies and demonstrations, for example, to receive media attention. Getting media access through other forms is difficult if not impossible for those who lack "definitional power." For political elites, the path to newsrooms is smoother than for the majority of citizens. The need of reporters to cultivate sources in key official places reinforces the privileged position of the powerful as newsmakers. The fact that official information is a news staple, the nearness of government sources to behind-the-scenes events and classified information, and the authoritative status of officials, enormously facilitate the access of political elites to newsrooms. Consequently, information about corruption involving government officials is more accessible than, for example, about companies that do not pay taxes or about working conditions in sweatshops. Certainly, news organizations may frown upon disclosures on such crimes for they may contradict business and political interests. The problem is also that at the level of daily newsgathering practices, reporters usually maintain steady contacts with government sources rather than with business executives, sweatshop workers or families of abducted children.

The interests of sources in passing information are also decisive in shaping the repertoire of watchdog journalism. Studies have indicated that different motivations prompt sources to leak information: to promote or harm a certain person, organization, or idea; to satisfy their ego; to try possible reactions to possible actions (the so-called trial balloons); or to blow the whistle. They also have specific goals vis-à-vis journalists: to cement relations, to return favors, to hush, saturate, or bribe reporters with information (Hess 1984, 1996; Limor and Caspi 1997; Schlesinger and Tumber 1994). Argentine reporters talk about "the politics of the dossier" (Lejtman 1996; Majul 1996); that is, powerful sources systematically keep files documenting the antics of allies and rivals and are ready to leak them in specific circumstances. The not-so-invisible hand of official sources was perceptible in the major stories that revealed corruption inside the Menem administration. Deep-seated rivalries among opposite factions and figures of the government reportedly stimulated journalistic denunciations of wrongdoing. According to several testimonies (*Noticias* 1992) that were confirmed in my interviews with journalists, leaks to the press in the most prominent exposés came from cabinet officials and high members of the opposition. Susana Viau (1996), who penned many investigative stories for *Página/12,* comments that "[government officials] generate personal hatred" that seeds the ground for political vendettas that are acted out through information leaks.

In Colombia, journalistic investigations about drug-trafficking relied upon, "members of Congress disgusted with the corruption around them . . . guerrilla informants . . . mysterious police agents and investigators, some motivated by moral outrage and some by vendettas against drug bosses who had crossed them" (Duzán 1994: 51). Press coverage during the *Proceso 8,000* heavily depended on information passed from a variety of official sources: conservative and liberal politicians, drug-trafficker turncoats, and the upper brass of intelligence services and military forces. *El Tiempo* reporters María Teresa Ronderos and Ernesto Cortés (1996), co-authors of an award-winning series about media coverage of the *Proceso,* observe, "The same way drug-trafficking infiltrated politics, sources infiltrated the media. Friends interested in President Samper remaining in power and enemies who wanted him out, all used the media to give orders." The Peruvian daily *La República* (Páez 1996) acknowledged that military intelligence sources passed confidential documents that were the basis of its denunciations of corruption in the purchase of aircraft equipment.

In Brazil, information and documents passed by a member of Collor's personal security were crucial in the first investigations done by the *Folha de São Paulo* on the then-president in March 1991. Newsweekly *Veja* received documents that raised doubts about the finances of PC Farias from members of the opposition party *Partido dos Trabalhadores* (PT) and bank employees union (Giannotti 1992). Rivalry between the military police and the civil police in Rio de Janeiro allowed reporters of the *Jornal do Brasil* to have access to archives where they found evidence of the sudden growth in the numbers of deaths committed by trigger-happy members of the civil police (Aquino 1997). Although there were endless speculations about why Pedro Collor decided to go on the record, several observers concluded that his decision was motivated by fears that business dealings between his brother Fernando and PC Farias would endanger his family's media interests in the state of Alagoas.

Tipping newsrooms as way to fight rivals is not a practice limited to domestic officials. U.S. military intelligence officers fed information about illegal operations in Peru's purchase of military equipment from Eastern European countries. U.S. government officials publicly expressed concern about Colombia as a *narcodemocracia* and attentively watched the unfolding of the investigations. In times when both the Bush and Clinton administrations have given priority to the "drug-problem" in hemispheric relations with South America, U.S. officials had vested interests in revelations about issues connected to drug-trafficking. In January 1995, U.S. Ambassador Myles Frechette deemed it unlikely that his government would grant certification to Colombia in the fight against drugs. A few weeks later, then-U.S. Secretary of State Warren Christopher characterized as "not completely satisfactory" the attitude of the Colombian government against drug trafficking. In an article that had wide repercussions in Colombia, the *Dallas Morning News* published an interview with "Maria," a woman who had presumably witnessed conversations between the Cali cartel and Ernesto Samper in the 1994 presidential campaign. Many reporters point out that the growing attention of press exposés about government-drug-trafficking connections in South America is inseparable from the priority that the U.S. government has given to drug issues in hemispheric relations.

No doubt, the practice of leaking information was not absent during authoritarian governments, but such practice finds more conducive conditions in a democratic context basically because the plumbing system is different. When administrations aggregate dissimilar interests and civilian leakers are less likely than military leakers to face harsh punishment, government becomes, as journalist James Reston once put it, "the only known vessel that leaks from the top" (in Hess 1996: 69). In authoritarian regimes, the organization of government along the lines of military structures places built-in conditions that discourage such practices. Under military rules, any act of whistle blowing becomes an act of insubordination and treason that could result in punishment, demotion, or ejection. Civilian informers, instead, are not tied to such institutional codes and, arguably, power is less hierarchically organized. There are no institutional sanctions against leaking. The relaxation of the culture of fear is also important: Potential leakers are less intimidated by fears of retaliation (the case of Peruvian intelligence agents and Colombian drug-traffickers tortured and murdered for passing information to journalists seems exceptional). But leaks could not go far without a press more interested in sensitive information. Despite anti-press violence, the overall improvement in the conditions for journalistic work makes newsrooms more interested in lending an ear to leaks and in publishing them. No longer do military censors check daily editions. Fears about personal safety and self-censorship don't completely disappear but gradually wane.

In summary, watchdog journalism provides stages for inter-elite battles in which information is leaked by powerful sources with the intention to harm rivals (Dimenstein 1993). Such conflicts have been crucial in the proliferation of press denunciations. To argue that journalistic denunciations mostly reflect confrontations among powerful actors should not lead to the conclusion that the news media simply function as transmission belts for the interests of sources. News organizations also have their own interests in bringing out specific acts of wrongdoing. The range of elite confrontations constrains the repertoire of watchdog journalism. The fact that watchdog journalism rarely touches on business malfeasance or social inequalities is not only the result of editorial disinterest in those subjects, but also of newsgathering conventions. It is not just that denunciations may affect political and economic interests that news organizations are uninterested in enraging. Exposés also reflect the boundaries of the disputes among powerful actors over turf and interests. Such disputes do not question social inequalities and are focused on individuals rather than on structures or institutions.

Despite these limitations, it is necessary to recognize that conflicts among "primary definers" (Hall et al. 1978) open important possibilities for watchdog reporting by ushering in dynamics typical of liberal democracies, which in the region that has historically experienced spasmodic periods of democracy, are certainly novel. Those possibilities are not unlimited precisely because of journalism's acute dependence and reverence to recognized sources. Given that journalism overwhelmingly pays attention to wrongdoing involving high-powered officials and that newsgathering routines are intertwined with government actions, official sources wield tremendous power in delineating the limits of news disclosures. The parameters of elite confrontations set the boundaries for watchdog reporting. In this sense, watchdog journalism does not challenge the "primary definers" but, more frequently, offers conduits for "primary definers" to wash dirty linen in public. The subjects of investigative reporting as well the dynamics in the origins and evolution of the stories are another manifestation of the dominant power that authoritative sources have in news-making.

NOT THE LONE RANGERS

Muckraking stories are, no doubt, grounded in a long past and present of official abuses, some taking place a stone's throw away from reporters, others in corners where only few individuals have access. Although it is the raw material of watchdog reports, government wrongdoing per se is not enough to spark a welter of journalistic disclosures. The codes of newsgathering dictate that influential, credible, and well-connected sources combined with political interests are indispensable for a given case of wrongdoing to turn into the subject of press denunciation.

The dependence of watchdog journalism on authoritative sources offers grounds to challenge the myth of muckrakers as lone rangers determined to uproot corruption from public life. The notion of a neutral, impartial press underscores the image of reporters who stubbornly ferret out corruption against all odds. The most serious problem with such a romantic portrayal, enshrined in the popular imagination and repeatedly cultivated by reporters and news organizations, is that it depoliticizes what is essentially a political institution and overlooks the multiple ways in which news organizations relate to power holders. Media scholar Robert Entman's observation applies to watchdog journalism: "Restricted by the limited tastes of the audience and reliant upon political elites for most information, journalists participate in an interdependent news system, not a free market of ideas" (1989: 3). There is no absolute independence or dependence between media and powerful interests, but rather multilayered and contradictory relations that produce openings and closures for adversarial reporting.

Newsgathering dynamics are chiefly linked to the affairs of the state and only partially to the rumbles of civil society. Surely, the misappropriation of public funds, the violent treatment of army privates, or police brutality directly affects the lives of millions of citizens. Most denunciations originate somewhere else, not where most citizens' lives daily evolve, but in the offices of politically influential figures. Revelations typically reflect high-powered rivalries rather than the woes and concerns of average citizens whose lives are situated far from official quarters and newsrooms and orbit too low to be sensed by journalistic radars pointing at the high spheres of power. It is also a matter that when publicized, abuses that affect ordinary citizens rarely command much attention from the public or have a large impact among policymakers. The majority of watchdog reports reveal intrigues and infighting inside government, often in a subtle tone and only evident to political cognoscenti. For a journalism mesmerized by official news, official sources bear an irresistible attraction. As insiders (especially if located in the heart of the executive), they have relatively easy access to newsrooms to unload information; as witnesses, they function as authority proxy for reporters who rarely, if ever, have the chance to observe wrongdoing first-hand.

In conclusion, watchdog journalism has complex relations vis-à-vis its targets of investigations: Proximity reduces the chances that news organizations can pry secrets open, but close contacts inside the institution under investigation are indispensable for information that is not otherwise available. Without distance, news media and journalists are prone to offer complacent coverage or ignore wrongdoing. Far from the reported subjects, however, they have difficulties in getting information. Distance allows but also prevents disclosures; proximity facilitates but also constrains the repertoire of muckrakers. Not to be underplayed, the lack of legislation permitting access to public documents and the absence of a tradition of public record-keeping makes investigative work not only difficult but also highly subservient to the decision of powerful sources to spill information. The half-hearted commitment of most news organizations to in-depth investigations contributes neither to enlarging the reporting menu of muckrakers nor to producing well-grounded and extensive reports. The negligence to allocate more resources to investigative reporting, the lack of legislation that protects reporters and promotes the compilation of public records, and a newsroom culture that cherishes official news explain why government wrongdoing is the typical subject of exposés. The same factors account for why information leaked by high-powered officials frequently constitutes the facts of watchdog reports. When the deeds and misdeeds of official sources are news, the typical facts are off- and on-the-record testimonies as well as documents slipped by high-powered and authoritative informers. When reporters cannot devote extended periods of time to follow a single story, when there is neither legislation allowing access nor records available for public inspection, when telephone calls are quicker than shoe-leather reporting, information dished out by official sources becomes the bread-and-butter of exposés. The thematic agenda of muckraking largely reflects the social organization of journalism, and, as argued in the previous chapter, political and commercial interests. A journalism more attuned to corruption and turf battles among the politically powerful than to other forms of wrongdoing is also the product of news organizations that equivocally support investigative reporting and often, based on political and economic calculations, cautiously turn some stones and leave others unturned. The professional rules of journalism, as I analyze in the next chapter, also put limitations and shape the workings of contemporary muckrakers in South America.

CHAPTER 5

PARALLEL IDEALS:
FACTICITY AND OBJECTIVITY IN EXPOSÉS

South American journalists recognize a growing sensibility to the idea that exposés should foreground facts over opinion in newsrooms. In contrast to past times, they observe, suspicions gathered through the rumor mill and even confirmed by colleagues are deemed insufficient to publish denunciations. Consensus among journalists that wrongdoing has been committed is considered to be insufficient to proceed with a story if authoritative sources do not come forward with information. Without the nod of credible sources, editors are unwilling to give the green light to a story. More and more, to paraphrase the defense attorney in Hollywood's *A Few Good Men* who had been challenged with finding the facts of crime, what reporters believe is not important. What matters, instead, is what they can prove. And what they can prove is not what they agree in informal discussions but what "legitimate" sources are interested in backing up with personal assertions and documents.

The growing importance given to fact-based muckraking raises questions about the definition of journalistic work. How do reporters construct the facts that ground press denunciations? What information qualifies as facts? What is the extent of the preoccupation with facticity? Are facts consistently at the center of watchdog reports? These questions are particularly relevant considering that antagonistic traditions have informed journalistic practices in South America. As analyzed in chapter 1, the models of journalism of opinion and objective reporting have been historically present. An analysis of the conventions in contemporary muckraking allows us to reflect upon how these traditions shape the practices of watchdog reporting. This chapter examines this question by analyzing the issues of facticity and objectivity in watchdog stories.

THE IDEAL OF OBJECTIVITY

The concept that news reporting essentially involves the reporting of facts is identified with the tradition of objective reporting, "the fetish of American journalism" to use James Carey's (1969) expression. In his study of this historical development of the U.S. press, sociologist Michael Schudson (1978: 6) defines objectivity as "a faith in 'facts,' a distrust of 'values,' and a commitment to their segregation." The ideal of objectivity conceives the gathering and reporting facts as the central tasks of journalism. Only when factuality becomes a ruling principle is balanced and detached reporting possible. Facts are the antidote for opinion. In the tradition of modern U.S. journalism, facticity and objectivity are the twin sides of the same ideal, one that negates subjectivity and political bias and emphasizes the impartial recording of facts as the raison d'être of reporting.

Objectivity, however, is not identical to other forms of factual reporting such as "naïve empiricism" that simply assumes that facts speak for themselves without any subjective intervention. Objective reporting, instead, presupposes that subjectivity is inevitable and, consequently, journalists actively construct news rather than merely presenting facts that exist independently from any human action. For Schudson (1978), journalists' belief in objectivity is grounded not on naïve realism but, rather, in the recognition that subjectivity prevails and cannot be overcome. Objectivity in journalism is not associated with the adoption of philosophical realism, the idea that a reality exists out there and can be represented as it is. Instead, it corresponds to the use of determined procedures and conventions to apprehend reality.

This idea reflected journalism's ambitions to gain respectability as a valuable form of knowledge at a time where the model of the natural sciences was dominant in the early decades of the twentieth century. The adoption of objectivity in U.S. journalism happened simultaneously with "the rise of science as a cultural paradigm against which all forms of discourse came to be measured" (Hallin 1994: 25). At a time when the press was becoming more distant from partisanship, and the scientific paradigm gained legitimacy as synonymous with "true knowledge," journalism adopted scientific techniques to render objective accounts of the world. To use Allan Megill's taxonomy, journalistic objectivity meant "procedural objectivity" instead of "an absolute sense of objectivity," that is, a set of specific rules to minimize the influence of subjectivity. "Rules provide an alternative to personal judgment. They substitute for personal judgment. In a situation where values are in conflict and consensus elusive, such rules may well be the only thing that permits agreed-upon public action" (Megill 1994: 11). Objective reporting hinges on the use of scientific methods such as observation and fact-gathering techniques that, if they do not exclude subjective impulses completely, certainly temper them. In emulating the scientific paradigm, journalism displaces values and beliefs and turns rigorous observation and narration of facts into the primary task of reporters.

Despite the long-standing influence of the U.S. press, neither objectivity nor "journalism as science" acquired the status of *über*principles in South American journalism. The view that news reporting implies a double process of assembling facts and separating facts from opinions never attained a dominant position. Consequently, the distinction between facts and opinion has been murkier than in U.S. journalism. Conventions of news reporting remained ambiguously defined. Freewheeling writing, *ensayismo* (essayism), factual reporting, storytelling, and fact-grounded stories have been considered different and equally acceptable forms of practicing journalism. Not even after press barons imported and vigorously championed the model of U.S. journalism, notably in the post-World War II years, did South American journalism reach a consensus around the principles of objectivity and fact-gathering. The tradition of journalism of opinion maintained its influence. At any given time, news organizations that viewed journalism as impartial gathering of facts and as political advocacy shared newsstand space. Consequently, journalism in South America has been crossed by antithetical expectations and demands and, to quote media scholar Paolo Mancini's (1992: 47) observation on Italian journalism, "incapable of defining an organic, consolidated, and consensually acceptable body of ethical and professional principles."

If U.S. journalism has been torn between the science and the literary model, as Phyllis Frus (1994) has argued, South American journalism has unequivocally kept its roots in both the literary and the political worlds. Memoirs as well as personal interviews attest to the belief among journalists that reporting has long been attached to literary ambitions and political endeavors. In the eyes of journalists, the view than reporting is modeled after the scientific paradigm seemed impossible, absurd, and even undesirable. No wonder, then, that objectivity was a foreign concept, whether defined as a realist conviction of a world existing independent from human consciousness or as a set of procedures to observe reality. And, conversely, relativism, the antithesis to journalism's positivism, has been accepted rather than condemned in the name of objective reporting. The idea that human bias could be excluded from reporting in order to provide impartial accounts of reality was considered nonsensical when journalism was chiefly viewed as "doing politics by written means" and as "literature with deadline," as a Brazilian columnist quipped (Dines 1986).

The presence of different and even contradictory concepts of reporting expressed the lack of a consensus about the practices and principles that should define journalism. There has not been a single and culturally unified journalism but *journalisms,* that is, the coexistence of a myriad of understandings about what principles should guide reporting. Instead of common answers, journalists have given diverse responses to issues such as defining the function of the press or the role of journalists. No unanimity ever existed about journalism's role, ideals, or practices. To define a number of enduring core values in South American journalism, as sociologist Herbert Gans (1979) has done for U.S. journalism, would be impossible.

Such issues are concerned with the rules and practices that define journalism as a "knowledge community." This concept draws from press scholar Barbie Zelizer's (1992, 1993) notion of "journalism as interpretive community." Journalists define their identity through discursive work. "Journalism as interpretive community," Zelizer writes, refers to "a group that authenticates itself through its narratives and collective memories" (1992: 9). In her study of the coverage and journalists' stories about the coverage of the Kennedy assassination, Zelizer has persuasively demonstrated that journalists are involved in a permanent process of affirming and reaffirming authority and community building through narratives that speak about their role in specific news events. The notion of journalists as knowledge community directs our attention to the presence and change in the conventions that journalists accept and reject as valid to produce information. This includes the "whos, whats, whens, wheres, whys, and hows" of news routines, newsgathering techniques, and ethical behavior.

In this sense, journalism can be considered a "knowledge community" held together by a common paradigm when reporters, to paraphrase Thomas Kuhn's (1970: 11) well-known formulation about scientific communities, "are committed to the same rules and standards for [journalistic] practice." For Kuhn, paradigm refers to an epistemological discourse that rules and regulates practices in a scientific field. It could be argued that journalism is not a scientific community, for its purpose as well as overall approach to knowledge is entirely different from that of scientists. No doubt, journalism is not concerned with asking research questions or testing theoretical formulations. Yet the point here is not to identify journalism with the model of the natural sciences as comparable forms of knowledge but as a specific *form of knowledge* that may (or not) be governed by certain unified assumptions guiding reporting practices. The ideals of journalism imply an epistemology, a theory of knowledge as press scholars Robert Hackett and Yuezhi Zhao (1998) argue. The question is, then, whether journalism as a knowledge community subscribes to the same paradigm.

In taking this approach, we could think of the possibility that journalism, following Kuhn, could experience "revolutions" when a new paradigm replaces a previous one. Hypothetically, this paradigm shift may happen when members of a journalistic community agree on the merits of an emergent model as more suitable to define the identity and mission of reporting. Consensus over a shared paradigm exists when practitioners intersubjectively agree on a set of practices and values that distinguish good from bad reporting, acceptable from unacceptable techniques, or admissible from illegitimate ethics. Only when a model is widely considered to be better than any alternative, journalists coalesce around certain principles.

Historically, the difficulty of journalism in South America to reach an epistemological consensus about what paradigm it should embrace meant that different and contradictory paradigms continued to exercise powerful influence in defining reporting practices. As a knowledge community, journalism has been torn between competing definitions about what methodologies and principles should be upheld as the right ones, valid to all news organizations and reporters regardless of political orientations and editorial positions. Neither "news as social construction" nor positivist approaches, to mention two influential and contradictory paradigms of newsgathering, have dominated the canon of reporting. Neither the gate-keeping model nor the advocacy paradigm (Janowitz 1975) was able to displace each other and gain dominant status.

What accounts for the lack of consensus about journalistic paradigms? The fact that South American journalists did not undergo a common training can, arguably, be seen as responsible for such absence. In effect, as discussed in more detail in chapter 6, individuals with disparate backgrounds have typically staffed newsrooms. Most working reporters lacked formal education in journalism. Only recently, simultaneous to the consolidation of journalism schools and the passing of accreditation requirements in some countries, a growing number of reporters show similar backgrounds and diplomas in journalism. But reasons for why journalism never converged around a single paradigm cannot be reduced to training. In fact, a majority of journalists may have similar background and have experienced a common education process but would not necessarily agree on conventions and procedures about news reporting. Training programs may declare allegiance to different values and lessons, but such values may clash with the realities of newsrooms (as critics of journalism schools often argue). More importantly, again following Kuhn, is the existence (or absence) of informal communication channels through which journalists define a "discipline matrix." The force of a paradigm is contingent less on what journalists have been told in schools or newsrooms and more on the exchanges and conversations with peers in which they define and redefine identities and commit themselves to certain requirements, habits and practices. Not to be neglected, educational canons and daily practices can be enormously influential in circulating ideas and setting limits. Curricula, style manuals, or codes of ethics or editorial directives certainly do sway journalism in one direction. But the capacity of powerful organizations to institutionalize a given paradigm is not sufficient without members of a journalistic community actually agreeing on certain principles and the force of news organizations in institutionalizing certain practices. Such agreement results from discursive processes and the capacity of newsroom to impose those practices.

A particular journalistic ethos in South America is the result of political and cultural processes rather than technological factors or commercial development. Skepticism about objectivity as *the* towering principle of journalism has persisted even though news organizations have regularly incorporated technological innovations that allowed for the adoption of objective reporting. Histories of U.S. newspapers have suggested that the introduction of the telegraph in the 1830s and photography in the 1890s facilitated and supported claims to objectivity. Telegraph transmission standardized news language and conveyed the same wire information to newspapers. Photography was later incorporated in reporting and strengthened claims to objectivity on the basis that it was a technology that provided an undistorted view free of human bias. In this way, news photography further cemented journalism's intention to wrap itself in the flag of scientific realism.

In South America, however, even after newspapers incorporated wire services and photography in newsgathering, journalism still remained crossed by contradictory ideals. Nor was objectivity adopted as the ruling ideal even after news organizations gradually shifted economic gears in the first decades of the twentieth century as their finances increasingly became more dependent on the market. The model of commercial journalism gained presence in South America around the 1920s and 1930s simultaneously with the development of a consumer market and the rise of a middle class with growing economic and political influence. The emergence of non-elite readers and consumers fueled the emergence of newspapers oriented to the market (rather than to elite politics) and prompted changes in established dailies willing to capture this emergent public. Neither objectivity nor any other ideal, however, achieved dominant status.

Answers to why there has not been a single knowledge paradigm that dominated South American journalism can be found in the larger absence of a political consensus in the region. The absence of agreement on a paradigm was not specific to journalism. Ongoing political controversies made it impossible for any paradigm to become hegemonic. Journalism's inability to agree on a given model reflected a much larger history of bitterly and violently divided interests. It could not escape the turbulent politics that shaped larger conflicts between populist and conservative, leftist and reactionary, democratic and authoritarian projects. News organizations have been at the forefront of the very same confrontations that crisscrossed the political evolution of contemporary South America and, arguably, contributed in delineating and maintaining political rifts. In times when publishers openly brought newsrooms into the political trenches and the fate of news organizations was subjected to changes in the political winds, it was inconceivable that journalism would become unified around any grounding principle.

The fact that South American politics have never undergone a process of departisanism explains the inability of the paradigm of objectivity to define the identity of journalism. For Schudson, a move away from partisanship contributed to the rise of the ideal of objectivity in the 1920s. Journalists began clinging to the paradigm of objectivity after newspapers abandoned partisan sympathies and thus left them culturally loose and in need of professional orientation. In an era when the press was moving away from the partisan model, journalists required a new cultural framework to orient and legitimize their work. The absence of a similar process and even the intensification of partisan confrontations throughout the twentieth century meant that South American journalism could not be organized around the principle of objectivity. The idea of journalists as "observers stationed on an Archimedean point above the fray of political life," as Carey (1969: 335) puts it, has been antithetical to the reality of politically committed news organizations and the prevalent notion that journalism should champion political causes.

JOURNALISTIC FACTS

Against this background, the present interest of journalists in grounding watchdog stories in facts raises the question whether the model of journalism associated with the U.S. press has lately found better conditions to develop and thus influence reporting. My interviews with journalists and my reading of exposés show a concern about facts that is unusual in the history of South American journalism. Contemporary reporting seems far closer than in previous periods to following the claim of Claudio Abramo (1989), the late and influential Brazilian editor, that "the role of journalists is to narrate facts."

Under the model of objectivity, watchdog reporters are expected to offer facts as evidence that something has happened. What counts as a journalistic fact? Facts are "assertions about the world open to independent validation. They stand beyond the distorting influences of any individual's personal preferences" (Schudson 1978: 5). If we take a "news as social construction" position, facts are contingent on what journalists consensually agree to define as such. But precisely because news can be constructed differently according to subjective preferences, journalists are urged to provide facts that are above any doubts, facts that can be presented as irrefutable evidence of wrongdoing. From a positivist perspective, journalistic facts confer immediate access to reality. The muckraker establishes her professional authority by removing herself and letting the facts speak as indisputable evidence of wrongdoing. Reporters are cast as neutral conveyors of evidence, recorders of facts who stand above suspicions. The underlying assumption is that there is no difference between reality and accounts of reality. There is no mediation but transparent representation. Accounts are assumed to be unbiased and suspended on a web of facticity. In taking this empirical outlook, reporters submit facts for public consideration, facts that cannot be suspected of being tainted by personal preferences or fabricated. The facts of wrongdoing are assumed to exist independent from human subjectivity or intentionality. Like any "scientific demonstration," the attribution of causality hinges on facts impervious to human subjectivity. In doing so, muckrakers are expected to "make a convincing argument by communicating the 'illusion of reality,'" to use cultural historian Carlo Ginzburg's (1994) observation about the tasks of both historians and lawyers. Facts are thought to be plain evidence upon which reporters construct arguments about events and responsibilities.

In constructing news stories, journalism operates according to the familiar distinction between "facts" and "evidence." Historian of science Lorraine Daston (1994: 243) writes, "Facts are evidence in potentia; mustered in an argument, deduced from a theory, or simply arranged in a pattern, they shed their proverbial obstinacy and help with the work of proof and disproof." Facts become evidence only when organized according to a certain claim.

But under objectivity qua naïve empiricism, facts stand for themselves rather than constitute links in a chain of argument. If suspected of being in the service of anything other than "reality," they automatically lose legitimacy as neutral evidence.

Evidence is understood as facts that journalists present to determine actions and responsibilities in a given case of wrongdoing. Taking into consideration that what constitutes evidence varies across different disciplines and professions, it is important to consider the paradigms that frame the definition of facts in watchdog reporting. As Peter Phelan and Peter Reynolds (1996: 110) put it, "The requirements of evidence and consequently the specification of what counts as evidence may differ according to the context in which the evidence is being used."

As mentioned earlier, the scientific paradigm has been extremely influential in shaping the definition of facts in contemporary journalism. In watchdog journalism, however, legal definitions of facts and evidence are particularly important. What can be admitted in court as evidence is what often defines journalistic facts. An Argentine muckraker states, "I want proofs, legal proofs" (Zunino 1999). The concerns of news organizations and reporters about potential lawsuits that may result from exposés and the possibility that public prosecutors can request information from journalists to be used in their investigations, make newsrooms particularly sensitive to legal definitions of facts. The threat of multimillion dollar libel lawsuits coupled with the potential loss of credibility are important concerns for news organizations. This is why they hire lawyers to comb denunciations for statements that may bring legal troubles in the future, especially when, as it has happened in recent years in all countries here studied, individuals implicated in denunciations typically resort to libel laws and other legal actions to squelch investigative energies.

The framing of "journalistic evidence" as "legal evidence" also results from the fact that reporters' investigations often evolve simultaneously, and are in constant dialogue with prosecutors' actions. During Colombia's *Proceso 8,000*, for example, journalists were interested in finding facts that could be used in a court of law to prove that President Ernesto Samper had participated in the funneling of drug monies into his 1994 election campaign. They were after journalistic evidence that could double as legal proof. Journalists observe that information that is typically considered "factual" in newsrooms would not necessarily be used in exposés if, for example, lawyers decide that it does not fit legal definitions or presents too many ambiguities that could cause legal headaches. This does not mean that news organizations are consistently careful and take all precautions by making sure that facts always match legal requirements. In many cases, they went ahead with hell-of-a-story denunciations driven by the possibility of pulling a journalistic coup and not intimidated by potential legal repercussions.

Still, the legal paradigm of evidence has markedly become more important as the context of justification that determines the nature of journalistic facts. Media scholar Richard Campbell (1991) has rightly noted that the metaphors of science (fact gathering, objectivity, information) impregnate journalism. Although such language certainly permeates reporting, the concerns and the mind-frame of South American muckrakers seem to be primarily legal rather than scientific. They are ultimately concerned with whether findings could pass legal, rather than scientific, tests. Rarely do other reporters verify a colleague's evidence or question whether someone has used the right methods to secure proofs. The facts of reports, however, could be eventually judged on legal merits. This does not imply that legal and scientific paradigms are incompatible in regard to understanding what constitutes evidence. This is not the place for delving into this complex matter. Suffice to mention that, as a body of legal studies has examined, central tenets of the scientific model have articulated modern concepts of legal evidence (see Jackson 1996; Shapiro 1991). What is important to note is that legal definitions of terms that are found in other varieties of discourse (proof, evidence, witness) have made significant inroads in the vocabulary of South American investigative reporters. This has been the result not only of news organizations' preoccupation about legal outcomes of denunciations, but also of reporters' proximity to legal professionals, comparing notes and relying on leaks from prosecutors and judges. Journalism's realism, which resonates with principles of the scientific model, informs its approach to facticity; muckraking's concept of "facts as evidence," however, is increasingly embedded in legal discourse.

THE FACTS OF WATCHDOG JOURNALISM

Legal concerns coupled with a journalistic culture heavily oriented toward official news explain why official testimonies are one of the main facts of watchdog reporting. Official declarations are considered facts because official sources are viewed as, to use legal parlance, expert and eyewitness evidence. Expert evidence is often presented in so-called "background," "deep background," and "off-the-record" statements. Identifying the experts by name is not deemed necessary, as analyzed in the previous chapter. The acceptance of quoting unnamed sources further promotes *denuncismo*. Such practice puts in place conditions that favor powerful informers who are able to leak information and set news frames without having to be publicly identified. Reporters also benefit because they can break and follow a story relying on a few informers who passed newsrooms' credibility checks. The name of a prominent official as a source of information is often enough to get the go-ahead from editors. When information comes from second-level officials, two or three checks are considered sufficient for publication. Journalists and news organizations are sometimes reluctant to build stories on feeble (legal) evidence, especially when dealing with "hell-of-a-story" exposés. The likelihood of political and legal repercussions deters them from going ahead simply equipped with not-for-attribution information. Under these circumstances, "hard" or "on-the-record" facts become indispensable and are submitted as conclusive evidence that sustains claims.

Eyewitness evidence is offered by featuring identifiable official sources in stories. Only on exception are the testimonies of non-official eyewitnesses considered evidence. *ISTOE*'s interview with driver Eriberto França stood out not only because it provided crucial facts in the judicial process against former president Collor de Mello but also because França was not a prominent source. For journalists, the credibility of witnesses lies in the assumption that they have first-hand experience in wrongdoing. Pedro Collor de Mello in Collorgate and Santiago Medina in the *Proceso 8,000* fit this requirement. Although journalists harbored doubts about why they were willing to come forward and blow the whistle, Collor's and Medina's testimonies were great journalistic coups for newsweeklies *Veja* and *Semana*.

Although statements by public officials are widely considered journalistic facts, they are different from "fixed information," that is, testimonies that are constant, uniform, and tangible. Words are fickle and can be easily forgotten or denied, but they become "fixed" when recorded in paper or caught in audio or videotape. Reports assume fixed information will resist the passing of time. Whether the information was produced five years ago or last week, it stays unadulterated. In this way, sources are anchored to statements and reporters can avoid potential problems of backtracking and denials. Fixed information conveys the sense that regardless of the subjectivity of reporters and the public, the information remains unchanged. It is concrete and visible to anyone, not just to the reporter or to eyewitnesses. Thus, journalists are interested in presenting "fixed symbolic materials" as credible information that is beyond any doubts. To sociologist John B. Thompson

(1997: 52), "by using certain technical media of communication — paper, photographic film, electromagnetic tape, digital storage systems, etc. — the context of symbolic exchange can be fixed or preserved in a relatively durable fashion." This makes possible to untangle facts from personal biases, peg them to objective reality, and remove completely human agency. Notwithstanding examples that show that fixed information can be altered, such as the erasure of segments of audio tapes, the incomplete publication of taped conversations, or the manipulation of photographs, journalists remain convinced about the solidity of such techniques for preserving content. Watchdog reporters rely on three kinds of fixed information: paper trails, visual facts, and sound proofs.

Paper Trails

Manuals of investigative reporting emphasize the combing of a variety of public and private records. Audit reports, bank records, birth and death certificates, legal notices, credit card information, income tax forms, business directories, and telephone records are some forms of documentation that provide key information and greatly assist investigative reporters (Anderson 1976; Benjamison 1990; Gaines 1994). Peru's *La República*, for example, featured transcripts from classified intelligence and military reports in exposing corruption in the purchase of military equipment. Investigations about Argentina's illegal sale of weapons to Ecuador drew extensively from reports elaborated by Peruvian and Ecuadorian intelligence services (*Clarín* 1995). In unraveling the web of corruption linking then-president Collor de Mello and businessman PC Farias, the Brazilian media made public several written records that stood as evidence of linkages between Farias' business and Collor. Unlike U.S. reporters, who either have immediate access to such records or can legally petition access to documents, their South American colleagues face a different situation. Some of those records do not exist in most countries (e.g. individual tax forms), or if existent, they are outdated and incomplete (e.g. business directories). Public offices and private companies are reluctant to provide access. Neither there is an established tradition of record keeping in public and private worlds nor, with exception of a few countries, legal recourses to request access to available information (Donadío 1995; Reyes 1996). For any public official, giving out public information carries severe penalties. Without legislation similar to the First Amendment and with courts that generally side with officials that are at the center of press denunciations, reporters face difficult battles if they decide to use leaked public records. Certainly some of those records do exist and access, though difficult, is not impossible. Getting that information requires adequate training, perseverance, and resources. But, journalists observe, reporters are not adequately trained in the arts of investigative journalism, lack much-needed patience and interest in sifting through files, or face daily deadline pressures from news organizations unwilling to assign time and money to follow potential bombshells. Given these obstacles, exposés typically feature written materials (official announcements, phone logs, letters, faxes, and memos) leaked by inside sources.

Visual Facts

Watchdog journalists also use audiovisual facts as real evidence of wrongdoing that allows readers or audiences to judge for themselves. In this case, no source is needed to tell what happened; the public is offered seemingly unmediated access to wrongdoing. Despite the possibility of altering and staging images, journalism still subscribes to a visual empiricism that sees photographic objectivity as able to bring out reality without intermediaries. Technological innovations make possible to record facts and submit them as unambiguous evidence of wrongdoing. The underlying assumption is that technology is neutral and reliable, unaffected by personal biases. The principle "the camera does not lie" is one of the cornerstones of watchdog journalism. Visual clues are displayed to demonstrate wrongdoing or authenticate claims.

If we are living in a post-photographic, postmodern era, as W. J. Mitchell (1992) argues, watchdog journalism stands as one of last bastions of modernism. According to postmodernist arguments, images kill reality. For modernist muckrakers, however, images bring out reality and make it transparent. Muckraking's solid conviction in the capacity of images to present reality "as is" goes against the grain of much scholarship that interprets contemporary media images as the postmodern subversion of the positivist belief in photography. The belief in facts and in a single, objective reality that can be recorded represents the perpetuation of a modernist approach to reporting. Recent studies have detected in different forms of contemporary reporting the signs of postmodernism, the blurring of the border between fiction and fantasy, and the displacement of real by media images. Watchdog journalism, however, incarnates the tradition of naïve realism that assumes that the real exists and can be apprehended. If the real is not visible, this results from lying and hiding. Journalism's task, then, is to extricate and render reality visible. Watchdog journalism has no room for blurring images and reality but retains an undivided loyalty to the idea that photography can record and render reality visible. The modernist principle of "knowledge through seeing" continues to guide its mission. Watchdog journalism assumes that reality can be presented as if there were no human intervention, as if humans could be disengaged from the very act of knowledge. It celebrates the power of images to make the real visible. It embraces the idea that we are able to grasp reality through vision. It remains stubbornly modern, unshaken by the postmodern argument that we have entered a time of "the death of photography" (Robins 1996). Digital technologies, as postmodern positions suggest, make images suspect and throw into question the merit of vision to apprehend a reality superseded by a plethora of images. Clinging to positivism, nevertheless, watchdog journalism incorporates visual technologies to demonstrate that reality does not disappear under the reign of the image but is actually rendered visible thanks to technology.

John Hartley (1992) has defined journalism as "the art of televisualization" for it offers a vision of reality through visual images. Metaphors of sight such as eyewitness news, watchdogs, spotlight, insight, discovery, and revelation' are central to journalism, Hartley observes. Although most studies have underscored the importance of images in yellow journalism (see Dahlgren and Sparks 1992), muckraking as a form of serious news also relies on visual cues as testimonies of reality. But, unlike yellow journalism, muckrakers use images not to throw reality into question but to make it visible to the public eye. Watchdog reporters assemble texts from written and visual elements to bring out reality. Optical visibility affirms the ideal of facticity. The underlying assumption is that there can be no doubts that events have happened or that certain individuals are responsible, if they are visually documented. Images are offered not merely as clear evidence supporting a reporter's story but also as anchors of professional credentials. They prove that reporters are faithful to reality.

The underlying principle is that seeing-is-believing. To journalism's naturalistic position, images are "direct, unmediated transcriptions of the real world" (Schwartz 1992: 95). Visual cues are incontestable evidence of reality. Visuals are not a representation *of* but actually *are* reality. Photography allows to present evidence as objective evidence, untouched by personal influence. It conveys the sense that reporting transparently and objectively reveals that wrongdoing has been committed. It strengthens the claim that the reporting of the facts is an impersonal process, free of human bias and opin-

ions. Pictures are assumed to eliminate subjectivity and render an uncontaminated portrayal of reality, to be solid proof that something has happened
beyond any doubt.

The assumption that images are "toll of documentation" free from
human intervention (Zelizer 1995: 149) informs the use of hidden cameras in
television watchdog journalism. *Telenoche Investiga,* a segment of Channel
13's evening newscast in Buenos Aires, Argentina, *Contrapunto* in Peru, and
Rede Globo in Brazil have resorted to undercover cameras to denounce police brutality, corrupt mayors and judges, police chiefs involved in drug trafficking, abuse of minors, graft in social programs for senior citizens, and
other forms of wrongdoing. The underlying assumption is that visual
footage allows capturing reality without any distortions.

Newspapers and magazines typically assemble words and images in
watchdog reports as irrefutable evidence of wrongdoing. For example, pho-
tocopies of checks, bank statements, and receipts may be used as evidence of
shady money transactions. In Collorgate, Brazilian journalists needed to
show a web of personal-business connections that funneled money from
campaign donors to private pockets. This was not an easy task: it required
access to records kept by banking institutions reluctant to volunteer information. When the information was finally obtained, the documents were
published as evidence of the elaborate influence-peddling network controlled by PC Farias, Fernando Collor's campaign fund-raiser. *Folha de São
Paulo's* (1995) investigations included copies of financial documents tracing
the flow of funds from companies to banks to ghost firms headed by Farias.
A few weeks later, *Veja* (1992) featured copies of PC Farias' tax returns in the
story "X Ray on [Farias']Wealth," a title marking the appeal of visual
metaphors in journalism. During Collorgate, journalists faced the problem
of showing the connections between Farias and Collor de Mello. In early July
1992, the newsweekly *ISTOE* published a story featuring a copy of a check
signed by an unknown Maria Gomes that had been deposited in the account
of Collor's wife. The reporters found that Gomes's identity number was the
same as Ana Maria Acioli's, the former president's personal secretary. Later,
Eriberto França affirmed in an *ISTOE* interview that Farias' secretary regularly deposited monies in Acioli's account and admitted that he had driven a
car rented to one of Farias' companies to transport the monies to the bank.
The same week, *Veja* also published stories entitled "The Proofs" and "Banking Proofs" that displayed photographic reproductions of bank statements
of accounts in the name of Gomes and Acioli.

Argentine journalists faced a similar problem in investigating the illegal sale of weapons to Ecuador in 1995. One of the main challenges of the investigation was finding out who knew and how much they knew about the operations. *Clarín* found a "smoking gun" in a presidential decree authorizing the export of weapons to Venezuela. At a time when it was speculated whether President Carlos Menem knew about and directly approved the arms deals, a photographic reproduction of the decree seemed to offered unambiguous evidence that the executive was aware of and endorsed the negotiations. What was still missing was documentation that the government also knew that the final destination of the weapons was Ecuador. It was a three-point operation: Venezuela was only an intermediate point to bypass the ban on selling weapons to countries involved in military conflicts. Likewise, the publication of a photocopy of the permit issued by *Fabricaciones Militares,* the state-owned weapon-producing company, to the company Hayton Trade to serve as mediators in the arms deal (*Clarín* 1995).

Press denunciations offer a wide range of visuals. *Veja* published photos of Fernando Collor's sumptuous residence that worked as, what semioticians may consider, an "indexical sign" of the former president's suspected illegal wealth.[1] Reports on the *Proceso 8,000* in Colombia frequently featured images of checks, bank statements, personal memos, and typewritten lists with names and numbers. The intention was to support claims about linkages between drug traffickers and Liberal politicians. *Clarín*'s (1996) report about *Operación Claridad,* a plan designed to persecute intellectuals and artists during the last military government, included reproductions of alleged blacklists. Images of the documents were presented as confirmation of what critics of the regime had long claimed and high-ranking military officers denied. Persecution and blacklisting existed. Moreover, such persecution followed a systematic plan masterminded and instrumented by the military juntas. This assumption is also found in exposé books, which typically include appendices featuring reproductions of documents that buttress the arguments presented.

Photographic reproductions of scribbled notes and official decrees acquire meaning within a larger Barthesian "structure of meaning." They can be used for many purposes but they only acquire status of evidence, as W. J. Mitchell (1992: 193) puts it, "when somebody finds a way to put it to work." Visual facts turn into evidence of wrongdoing after being incorporated in an argument. By themselves, they can be interpreted in multiple ways and do not necessarily stand as evidence. Reporters anchor and narrow down the meaning of visual facts in a larger narrative that strings together images and texts are put together in a string of meaning. In isolation, they are facts but become evidence in a structure of meaning.

Sound Proofs

Audio materials, such as taped conversations and transcripts of recorded words, are also used as facts and evidence. The release of taped conversations, for example, launched the *Proceso 8,000* in Colombia after the 1994 election campaign. Copies of the tape were given to then-president Cesar Gaviria and attorney general Gustavo de Greiff a few days before election day. Reportedly, the dailies *El Tiempo* and *El Espectador,* the television newscast QAP, and the *Dallas Morning News* correspondent in Bogotá had also received copies. No one, however, released the information. On July 21, two days after Liberal Ernesto Samper defeated Conservative Andrés Pastrana, *24 Horas,* a newscast linked to Conservative politician Alvaro Gómez, decided to make public segments of the tape. The tape contained conversations between journalist Alberto Giraldo, known to be close to the Cali cartel, and one of the Rodriguez Orejuela brothers, the cartel's bosses. They discussed money dealings and commitments, and mentioned names that were presumed to be of prominent politicians and influential businessmen. The following day, the newspapers carried the story and Pastrana gave a press conference in which he urged Samper to resign if suspicions that his campaign received funds from drug-traffickers were proven.

Three more *narcocassettes,* as they were dubbed, were released in subsequent weeks. One tape included a passage many regarded as evidence of connections between President-elect Samper and the Cali cartel:

> Giraldo: That Samper is showing to be a good friend
> Rodriguez Orejuela: Hope that the heart of this son of a bitch doesn't get
>   hurt.

Regardless of how much or little the tapes confirmed speculations, the press approached them as conclusive evidence that well-known politicians were named in conversations between highest-ranking individuals in the hierarchy of the Cali cartel. The same position was adopted when newsweekly *Semana* (1995a), after many months of internal debates, published transcripts of taped conversations between Samper and Elizabeth de Sarria, who was married to a retired police officer suspected to be a drug trafficker. A columnist called the surfacing of narcotapes "the James Bond trend" (Pombo 1995), a sign that different organizations — drug agencies, intelligence services, the military — had regularly recorded a large number of phone conversations in Colombia.

In May 13, 1997, *Folha de São Paulo* published a series entitled "The Market of Votes," a denunciation of a money-for-votes scheme in Congress to pass a constitutional amendment to allow presidential reelection. The articles were based on five taped conversations made over five months that featured congressional representatives talking about sums of money, checks, payments, and names of politicians (including members of Congress and the late Sergio Motta, then-minister of communications). While in the Colombian case the tapes were allegedly produced by domestic and U.S. intelligence agents, the recordings that fed *Folha*'s revelations were made by an unidentified individual called Senhor X (Mister X) who had participated in the conversations. What was also different in the Brazilian case was that *Folha* actively pursued and participated in the recording of the conversations. According to journalists, the Brasilia press corps widely believed that a number of representatives were involved in money-for-votes dealings. Even some members of Congress admitted in off-the-record conversations the existence of such negotiations. There were no "facts" such as written documents or on-the-record statements to go ahead with the story, however, so the newspaper decided to find someone willing to tape conversations. Fernando Rodrigues (1997), *Folha*'s Brasilia editor and author of the series, states that the individual not only agreed to participate but also accepted other conditions, to wit, that the tape recorder and the tapes belonged to *Folha* and the recordings would be turned to Rodrigues soon after they were completed (Instituto Gutenberg 1997). *Folha* and Senhor X were in constant contact during the time the conversations were taped. The material was published only after several recordings with different representatives. According to Rodrigues, any ambiguous information was not included. The tapes were presented as facts of wrongdoing. On whether the newspaper "denounced" wrongdoing, Rodrigues said: "*Folha* does not make a denunciation. *Folha* publishes facts. *Folha* published a fact: the content of tapes that demonstrate, according to representatives, that votes favoring [constitutional] amendment have been bought and sold."

These cases show that journalists (reporters, news photographers, camera staff) and sources (e.g. official and foreign intelligence services) are able to produce audiovisual facts. The availability of an arsenal of surveillance technologies such as lipstick-size lenses and tie-mikes has certainly made it easier to create (and sometimes recreate) the facts of wrongdoing. Sometimes, reporters intervene to capture facts as in the Senhor X story or when they use undercover video and photo cameras; other times, they rely on videotaped footage and sound materials such as Colombia's *narcotapes* leaked by official sources. The existence of a vast intelligence apparatus tracking down the activities of public figures and private citizens makes it possible to manufacture "fixed information" that fits the requirements of factual news coverage. As Thompson (1997: 53) states, "fixed symbolic materials provide forms of evidence which may not be entirely conclusive, but which are much more difficult to deny or explain away than unwitnessed and unrecorded conversations."

The widespread use of audiovisual facts raise a number of ethical and legal issues, which are discussed in chapter 7. For the purposes of this chapter, it is important to note that technological innovations restructure the understanding of facts and potentially can make written facts less important to watchdog reporting. Journalists can manufacture facts, and violate laws, if they doctor writing. If they invent quotes, named sources would likely deny assertions and bring legal actions. The availability of pint-size audiovisual technologies and the persistence of a legal limbo about the uses of those technologies in South America offer the opportunity to make facts. Certainly, journalists have always manufactured facts (and still do) by picking and choosing sources, testimonies, and events that warrant becoming news. Today, cameras and tape recorders allow them to produce facts that otherwise would not exist. These practices deserve attention particularly in countries where there is neither legislation facilitating access to public information nor electronic databases containing official records that journalists could use. Given these conditions, computer-assisted reporting, the latest call of investigative journalism in the United States, seems difficult. But the availability of miniature recording technologies offers the temptation to bypass old reporting techniques such as chasing a reluctant source to go public or combing documents, and turning to the construction of the journalistic facts of wrongdoing. In these cases, reporters do not just report, but can also produce the news.

Although verbal testimonies scribbled in reporters' notebooks and paper trails of wrongdoing continue to be used, reporters seem inclined to prefer audiovisual facts. This can be interpreted as a corollary of the trend toward visualization in the mass media. For television reporters, visual footage of wrongdoing is a rule of thumb. In print journalism, images have became central, too; they are no longer circumscribed to newsweeklies that are typically more visually oriented than newspapers. This preference is also linked to the specific working conditions faced by South American journalists. Without legal mechanisms to gain access to written records, and when written records are privately and tightly controlled or are nonexistent, catching crooks in film or on tape offers a way to secure facts. When reporters cannot extricate hard evidence from informers or when a story is stalled because no sources are willing to give information, filming and recording wrongdoing helps to bypass such obstacles. The inclination to get images and sounds is particularly strong when reporters lack sufficient resources and time to follow stories. The fact that surreptitious wiretapping, filming, and picture taking remain legally undefined and, if sanctioned, are rarely punished, encourages such practices as well.

Also, the credibility attributed to the sights and sounds of audiovisual facts makes them extremely appealing. The camera and the tape recorder are deemed to be mightier than the pen of written facts and off-the-record statements. They offer the possibility to peek and listen to perpetrators of wrongdoing caught in the act. A Peruvian journalist, who produced many broadcast exposés, asserts, "The people want to see, to watch, the [illegal] act. There have been many reports that were impossible to put them on the air. I would say that 60 percent had to be shelved because of the lack of visuals" (Arrieta 1998). Even when there may be lingering suspicions about doctored images and tapes, snippets of visual footage and recorded conversations seem more believable than written reproductions of official statements and writings. The issue of credibility of audiovisual facts is decidedly important in democracies where distrust of public officials runs high and verbal and written leaks can be equally suspected of serving interested parties. Audiovisual facts, instead, offer the sense of unmediated information that gives audiences direct access to wrongdoing. Despite persisting doubts about their authenticity, such facts convey the impression that audiences can see (and hear) with their own eyes (and ears). This transforms any reader or viewer into an eyewitness to wrongdoing and avoids potential credibility problems that emerge when it is merely expert witnesses or official eyewitnesses of dubious credentials who provide the information. The authority of audiovisual facts lies precisely in appearing to remove both sources and journalists from reporting and turning audiences into vicarious witnesses of wrongdoing.

This mechanism for legitimization seems particularly convincing because, as discussed in chapter 4, journalists rarely explore or acknowledge the reasons that motivate certain sources to produce video and audiotapes documenting wrongdoing and leak them to newsrooms. By not presenting the motivations of leakers and the process of selection and interpretation in newsgathering, journalism eliminates traces of human interest and intervention in the presentation of audiovisual facts. Subjectivity, which shapes the choices that journalists make in covering stories, is effaced. In regard to news photos, Stuart Hall writes, "They seek a warrant in that ever pre-given, neutral structure, which is beyond question, beyond interpretation: the 'real world.' At this level, news photos not only support the credibility [of the news media]. They also guarantee and underwrite its *objectivity* [emphasis in the original] (that is, they neutralize its ideological function" (1978: 188). Although one could argue that such an assumption underlies the presentation of all journalistic facts, Hall's observation is particularly relevant to analyze how audio and visual facts are used to bolster claims to "objectivity as facticity" in South American countries where news organizations are generally believed to be aligned with specific political interests.

This is also important considering that journalism rarely informs readers about how reporters select and manufacture news. Readers rarely get a peek into "the conditions of production of knowledge" (de Certeau 1983) in journalism. In his observations about historiography, de Certeau describes media representations as products "of certain milieu, of a power structure, of contracts between a corporation and its clients, and of the logic of a certain technicality." Yet, he adds, "the clarity and simplicity of the information conceal the complex laws of production that govern its fabrication" (1983: 132). By presenting the real in the form of facts the media closes the possibility of questioning the information offered as if it had real existence. A number of questions are not asked, much less answered: How were facts obtained? Which ones were available but rejected? What interests lie behind information leaks? What facts are missing? Informing readers about the process of getting the facts and the politics behind the facts is less important to journalists than submitting those facts as unequivocal proof of wrongdoing. In South American journalism, this practice coupled with the wide acceptance of information leaks further promotes *denuncismo*. When facts cannot be secured, even when considerable time and monetary resources have been invested, journalists find it hard to resist to the multiple allure of audiovisual facts as evidence of wrongdoing.

FACTICITY WITHOUT OBJECTIVITY

The preceding analysis confirms the change that reporters recognize in South American journalism: Facts are increasingly considered indispensable for exposés, and fact-finding increasingly defines contemporary reporting. This cannot be interpreted as a radical departure from previous journalistic practices, however. The concern about facticity does not imply that facts are consistently the backbone of press denunciations. A Colombian journalist, member of *El Tiempo*'s original investigative team, observes: "Latin American journalism accepts literary license and sacrifices facticity. It paraphrases rather than cites sources. It doesn't believe in quotes. It interprets without facts. Journalists do not resist the temptation of resolving the country" (Reyes 1995). If we consider the frequency of *denuncismo,* Reyes's observations are warranted. Watchdog stories that are thinly supported on facts or that draw on equivocal and incomplete evidence suggest that the idea that reporting should be fact-grounded is not shared by all reporters. On the other hand, one could interpret the criticisms of these practices precisely as a sign of an emerging recognition that watchdog journalism *should* be grounded in facts. The criticisms leveled against *denuncismo* hint at that sensitivity especially, as journalists observe, in contrast to past times when exposés were not often judged strictly upon factual merits.

What is important to note is that, in the mind of South American journalists, facticity and objectivity are not identical. Facticity may have recently made inroads. But adhering to the paradigm of objectivity as a whole is quite different. In the tradition of U.S. journalism, factual reporting and objective reporting are the flip sides of the same coin. They are part of the same tradition. But in South America, both principles do not travel the same road. Although journalists may agree that muckraking should foreground facts, this does not bring consensus about how facts should be reported. Fact-grounded reporting may be considered the defining element of journalism but this does not necessarily lead to the belief that objectivity is desirable or possible. Instead of rejecting or adopting it, South American journalists are still ambivalent about the possibilities and merits of objectivity.

Can watchdog journalism be objective? To some analysts, objectivity only belongs to straight reporting not muckraking journalism (Gauthier 1993); for others, investigative journalists maintain allegiance to objectivity but inevitably rely on narrative strategies because "facts do not speak for themselves" (Glasser and Ettema 1993). Answers to this question vary according to how objectivity is understood. The remainder of this chapter analyzes how reporters deal with facticity and objectivity by examining the language used in bringing out wrongdoing. I argue that there is no single approach to news reporting. News organizations offer different and incompatible approaches in reporting wrongdoing and journalists remain skeptical about objectivity.

These differences reflect the persistent lack of consensus about one ideal that could unify reporting.

JUST THE FACTS

Some reports follow the orthodoxy of journalistic objectivity understood as naïve empiricism by presenting facts in an adjective-free, unadorned language. This assumes that journalists are able to show wrongdoing by being faithful to facticity without any stylistic additives, by showing a deep commitment to straight facts. According to this view, facts are sufficient evidence that illegal behavior has been committed, obviating the need to pass judgment or to add adjectives. "Facts speak for themselves. . . . Adjectives are not necessary," says a *Clarín* journalist who investigated Argentina's unlawful sale of weapons during the 1995 Ecuador-Peru war (Santoro 1996). A former editor of Colombia's *El Tiempo* investigative unit states, "Denunciations should be more concise, direct, obsessed about details." (Santos 1996). Here is a concept of journalism that illustrates the belief that objectivity requires the elimination of authorship, a so-called clinical detachment characterized by "flat tone, avoidance of drawing the moral, excessive detachment, impersonal narration, monotonous recording of details" (Frus 1994).

This approach is found, for example, in Colombia's *El Espectador*'s exposés on drug trafficking. Although the daily was publicly known for its vocal opposition to the drug barons, its reports distilled facts without adjectives. Facts condemned drug lords as criminals. Reports about Pablo Escobar Gaviria, the late boss of the Medellin cartel, were packed with information about his activities and associates, amounts involved in different transactions, registration numbers of airplanes and ships, the location of airports used to transport shipments, and plenty of numbers about Escobar's extraordinary wealth. They meticulously described Escobar's attempts to bribe security agents, the assassination of detectives investigating his activities, and intimidations and executions of judges involved in the investigations. Reports about other cartels were full of information about the activities and possessions of drug barons, criminal records, and connections with political bigwigs. Stories also teased out the complex structure of drug money-laundering organizations and identified owners as well as names and addresses of companies. None of the stories expressly call Escobar or other drug barons criminals or delinquents. The underlying assumption was that the information plainly showed that, indeed, they were involved in illegal activities.

The same assumption is found in a report published by a team of *Clarín* journalists that featured documents proving that the *Operación Claridad*, the plan of the last military government to persecute political and cultural dissidents. The report was published on the twentieth anniversary of the March 1976 military coup. Until then no documents had been published showing that the dictatorship had systematically organized the persecution and blacklisting of artists and intellectuals. The report detailed a number of government memoranda that suggested the need to infiltrate schools and universities. It also named officials involved in the preparation and distribution of the lists and execution of the plan.

Journalist Gilberto Dimenstein (1992) also used a fact-centered approach in his investigation of child prostitution in ten Brazilian cities and towns. His series was based on descriptions of the conditions in the brothels, life histories, and interviews with girls, pimps, and social workers. Dimenstein expresses no opinion on who was responsible or why child prostitution is morally repulsive. There was no need to embellish his account with adjectives. The testimonies, vignettes, and photographs portraying lives full of atrocities, violence, disease, abuse, drugs, corruption, and death spoke for themselves.

THE PROOF LIES IN COMPARING THE FACTS

Journalists take a different approach when they set facts against the testimonies of individuals under investigation or suspected of wrongdoing. Wrongdoing is exposed not through simply offering the facts, as in the earlier cases, but rather as a result of the difference between what was said and what the reporter reveals. Journalists seem to be saying, "This is what so-and-so say but if we look at this information then we can deduce that it's not true." During Collorgate in Brazil, for example, bank account statement linking PC Farias' business with the President's secretary were submitted as evidence that Collor de Mello had lied when denying any involvement in the kickback scheme. Brazilian journalist Caco Barcellos opted for a similar strategy in investigating the murders of poor youths at the hands of the trigger-happy military police in São Paulo. His denunciations emphasized the obvious contradictions between the facts he presented and the testimonies of police officers. When asked about the deaths of individuals in unclear circumstances, the police typically said that the suspects were armed, had initiated gunfire, and had been taken to the hospital. Against this explanation,

Barcellos built a case based on testimonies of parents of the victims, the police pages of the tabloid *Noticias Populares,* and records at the *Instituto
Medico Legal.* His investigation showed that rarely, if ever, there were suspects who survived fire exchanges. Civilians were captured only in 28 out
more than 3,200 cases in a twenty-year period. The contrast between the official version and the journalistic facts is often shown through irony. With a
rate of one wounded person for every 265 deaths, the police "deserve an
award for efficiency against the enemy" (Barcellos 1992: 117). Barcellos went
on to observe that, "If the military police tells the truth when they say they
help wounded individuals, it means that hundreds of doctors in São Paulo,
even first aid stations in the outskirts [of the city], were unable to save even
1 of the 3,546 people wounded in gunfire who were taken to the hospitals"
(Barcellos 1992: 132). Internal police documents revealed that the killings
were actually encouraged and rewarded by police hierarchies.

STRETCHING THE FACTS

A third narrative strategy is to present facts and to use them as the basis for
speculations. Reporters do not just convey facts but also offer an explicit analytical framework to interpret them. Nor do they make a subtle invitation
to read between the lines of events or camouflage their political biases behind an adjective-free language. Rather, they overtly suggest possible connections, ramifications, and interpretations that are otherwise not explicit in
the facts that are known. The reporter does not take a position above political interpretation and interests at stake but explicitly takes sides, pushing the
facts and indicating inconsistencies in official testimonies.

Press scholars Theodore Glasser and James Ettema describe how U.S.
journalists use irony with a similar intention, to cue readers about the meaning of news stories. Irony offers a way to be loyal to "the norms of neutrality
and steer readers away from what the facts 'obviously' mean" (1993: 323).
Without violating the codes of objective journalism, reporters reach out to
irony to make evaluative judgments. Winking an eye at the informed reader,
the one who knows how things really are, they tell what facts mean beyond
what they say. This is done obliquely, so as not to violate the commitment to
objectivity. But South American muckrakers are less constricted than U.S.
reporters by journalistic norms and can twist the orthodoxy of journalistic
objectivity by peppering stories with analysis and speculations without having to adopt an impartial pose.

Argentine journalist Jorge Urien Berri's reporting of the murder and cover-up of an army private offers a good example of this strategy. The reporter does not merely offer the facts, instead he makes connections and guides the reader through the analysis. In one of his many articles in *La Nación*, Urien Berri (1995) writes,

> While waiting for conclusive evidence against the three main suspects of having murdered Omar [Carrasco], the Carrascos' lawyers petitioned to process former soldier Jorge Anzorena as coperpetrator and sergeant Mario Guardia for cover-up. . . . The lawyers believe that Anzorena . . . was one of the three soldiers who hit Omar. They are based on secret declaration by former soldier Miguel Angel Villanueva, to whom someone told that in the night of March 6, [lieutenant Ignacio] Canevaro tied Omar to a water tank and three soldiers hit him. The problem with the secrets of Villanueva is double and very serious: the murder would have happened at least six hours after the disappearance and near Omar's barrack. Also, it partially contradicts the sudden testimony of sergeant Carlos Sánchez, which was as sudden as lieutenant González's. Last year Sánchez changed his declarations after changing lawyers. Then he affirmed that [soldier Victor] Salazar confessed to him to have hit Carrasco together with [soldier Cristian] Suárez following orders from Canevaro. But Sánchez suggested that the beating took place in a bathroom, twenty meters from the barracks, not at the water tank. . . . The interest of [the Carrascos'] lawyers to process Guardia for cover-up is striking. If Guardia were the only assassin, the Army would have given him up without question. It's easier to surrender a sergeant with a spotted record rather than a lieutenant [Canevaro], the brother of a mayor and a captain and the son of a colonel who commanded the same garrison.

The decision of two officers to declare on the case and change previous depositions was presented as a "sudden testimony." In writing, "the interest of [the Carrascos'] lawyers to process Guardia for cover-up is striking," the reporter hints at the possibility that unidentified interests were responsible for those decisions or that there was foul play in the trial of the case.

Peruvian journalist Cecilia Valenzuela adopted a similar approach in her investigation of the killings at La Cantuta University. Her report contains facts, which are mostly based on testimonies from military and intelligence sources, but also offers guidelines to understand developments. Valenzuela (1993: 14) writes,

There are different versions and many obscure points about the events at La Cantuta. But there are many facts that now seem to beyond any doubt. The nine students and the professor were kidnapped and murdered. Versions about self-kidnapping and escape are rejected. The perpetrators were active military officers. They were not only in a site surrounded by the army but the denunciations of General Robles and the denunciations by congressional members also suggest so. Alberto Fujimori's confirmation that four officers are being held also confirms it. If this is true, then there are few doubts that aside from the authors Santiago Martin Rivas and the Colina group [the death squad's name], higher-ranking officers are also implicated. Even if the murder was Martin's "crazy act," it is hard to believe that he and his people were able could access La Cantuta and take ten people away without the authorization of higher-ranking officers. The army clearly devised a cover-up strategy. Even if the hypothesis that Martin acted alone, the commanders of DIFE [Division of Special Forces], SIE [Service of Army Intelligence], DINTE [Office of Intelligence of the Armed Forces], SIN [Service of National Intelligence] and the army commander-in-chief had to know about the situation. No one collaborated in the investigation.

Here Valenzuela not only offers the facts but also invites readers to think through the events, weigh possible developments, and note inconsistencies in official testimonies. The weaving of facts with opinion and analysis is common in *Caretas*'s exposés. The newsweekly commonly interprets facts without hiding its editorial positions.

This is perceptible not only in the reporting of official narratives and written facts but also in the treatment of visual facts. Rather than relying on straight photography to render an objective account of reality, *Caretas* often uses photomontage to provide ironic comments that denote editorial judgment vis-à-vis certain events. For example, the decision of the Fujimori administration to exonerate Alfredo Zanatti, a member of the Alan García administration who was involved in influence-peddling in the purchase of military equipment, was received by the newsweekly with a cover showing a halo over Zanatti's face and the headline "What a joke! Former fugitive on his way to beatification without even opening his secret [bank] accounts" (*Caretas* 1995b). *Oiga* (1991), another Peruvian newsweekly, also used photomontage to construct facts. When it denounced the connections between former president Alan García and a Middle Eastern arms dealer and fraud in the purchase of Mirage warplanes during the Garcia administration, its front cover featured an image of García dressed in a dark tunic and his head covered in a *kefiah* with the headline "The one and a thousand of Alan and El Assir."

The Brazilian newsweekly *Veja* (1993) also superimposed images when it "dressed" PC Farias in a black-and-white stripped uniform on its cover. After a judge ordered the capture of fugitive Farias, *Veja* featured a photo of the face of Collor de Mello's "partner in crime" attached to a hand-drawn black-and-white striped outfit. The cover story concluded, "Prison is the right place for Paulo Cesar Farias" (1993: 23). Similar to the Peruvian newsweeklies, *Veja* did not intend to present the image as a truthful representation of reality. Farias was not in prison nor has he been photographed wearing prisoner's clothing. Such stretching of the boundaries of facticity is noteworthy considering that, unlike the Peruvian newsweeklies, *Veja* generally stays away from satire or openly disclosing its editorial sympathies. The photographic jailing of Farias could be interpreted as a falsification of reality: It created a fact that did not occur. What the newsweekly did, instead, was to present the reality of believed facts. After a barrage of media disclosures on his illegal activities during Collorgate, the recognizable face of Farias became the public symbol of corruption in contemporary Brazil. *Veja* was not risking its claims to facticity by portraying Farias as a prisoner but, rather, it aimed to echo widespread sentiment that Farias was guilty and deserved prison.

These examples reveal how some news organizations resort to photomontage, a narrative strategies typical of tabloid news, artistic vanguards, and advertising (Ades 1986), to disclose wrongdoing and report "serious news." In featuring images with additions and rearrangements, they dismiss the constraints of objectivity and blur the distinctions between reality and fiction, fact and opinion, neutral reporting and other journalistic and aesthetic styles. The information is explicitly colored by editorial sympathies. The combination of images is intended not to falsify reality but to interpret reality in a certain way, taking "real" facts' and slanting the analysis through the use of visual collages.

AN UNFINISHED DEBATE

The preceding examples show the impossibility of concluding that South American watchdog journalism either *follows* or *does not follow* the ideals of professional journalism as defined in the canon of the Anglo-American press. This ambiguity partially results from the multiple meanings of some of professionalism's central ideals. If understood as involving a series of procedures to report facts, watchdog journalism seems to be converging around objective reporting identified with "empirical, 'U.S.-style" reporting. To Eduardo Lins da Silva (1996), former managing editor of *Folha do São Paulo,* "investigative journalism [follows] the U.S. tradition of no opinion but facts and documents." According to *El Tiempo* editors, U.S. journalism is associated with "scientific rigor and verification" (Santos 1996) and "an effort to be rigorous" (Torres 1996). But if it is defined in terms of philosophical realism or related to the possibility of disinterested reporting, objectivity is rejected.

Although the idea that journalism should foreground facts has made visible strides, journalists remain skeptical, if not opposed, to the possibility of impartial reporting. Brazilian journalist Jose Hamilton Ribeiro (in Marques de Melo and Lins da Silva 1986) observes: "That business of objectivity is a disgraceful stupidity. What is important is an honest report of reality." Likewise, Argentine journalist Luis Bruschtein (1997) writes: "The idea of objectivity is anachronistic and has been replaced by that one of veracity: not lying or hiding information. A news medium is not objective from the moment it confers different relevance to different information according to its criteria and the same thing goes for writing and editing. Those criteria are ideological, personal political and economic." Mino Carta (1996a), former editor-in-chief of two leading Brazilian newsweeklies, observes: "Before invoking press objectivity is necessary to claim honesty. We narrate facts as observers from our modest and not very important viewpoint." "We believe very little in objectivity," notes a Colombian editor (Vargas 1996).

Journalists argue that political reasons make it impossible to embrace the ideal of disinterested reporting. Maria Jimena Duzán (1996), one of Colombia's best-known investigative reporters, states: "'I do not believe the *gringo* theory of neutrality. Distortion is inevitable. Our journalism is subjected to the reality of the country." Likewise, Cesar Hildebrandt, a Peruvian television talk-show host who disclosed numerous cases of wrongdoing involving the Fujimori administration, declares: "I am against objectivity. Without constitutional tribunal and with disappearances, torturers and uncertainty about the country, there is no alternative but journalism in the trenches. Neutrality is not possible" (*Caretas* 1997). Argentine editor Hector Timerman (quoted in *La Nación* 1998) says, "I'm neither neutral nor impartial. I do not agree with the theory of giving two or three versions. I'm in favor of one [version] that I want to push forward."

Objectivity as philosophical realism is also deemed impossible insofar as editorial interests limit journalistic autonomy. What stories reporters may be able to disclose are inseparable from their employer politics and editorial positions vis-à-vis specific institutions and individuals. Journalistic autonomy refers to "freedom from external social control of clients and employing organizations" (Sparks and Splichal 1996). As long as reporting is tightly constrained by editorial interests, professional autonomy is elusive. Journalists unanimously believe that editorial lines cannot be trespassed; there is little, if any, room to push boundaries (Virtue et al. 1995). They do not hold a dreamy-eyed belief in journalistic independence but, instead, show a pragmatic attitude that assumes that constrains are inevitable and vary across media. Not all media offer the same degrees of autonomy, observes the former managing editor of *Folha de São Paulo* (Lins da Silva 1996). Paraphrasing a popular adage, a Colombian journalist asserts, "Tell me for who you work and I will tell what you can write about" (Rodriguez 1996).

Top decisions do not trickle down in memos explicitly stating what can or cannot be the subject of critical examination. Instead, reporters themselves come to recognize editorial limitations. They speak of having radar to sense what subjects and treatments of stories would hit editorial snags or be frowned upon by the upper brass. The repertoire of possible and impossible, touchable and untouchable topics is not stapled to employment contracts but it is learned through breathing the cultural air within a given news organization. Nor are limits set in stone, determined once and forever. They may shift according to different circumstances. Therefore, reporters need to poke at boundaries to see how flexible they are. Sometimes they are even encouraged by editors to write about topics that were previously redlined. If it becomes known in coffee rounds that a member of the editorial board dines with a local police chief, the reporting of abuses in the nearby precinct may have a long shot in getting the green light. If confrontations between the publisher and the city mayor are in the open, an in-progress story about favoritism in bids for trash collection has better chances of getting published, especially after the local police is sent to comb accounting files in search of proof of tax evasion. It would be inconceivable that reporters can dig up wrongdoing that contradicts the interests of owners, publishers, and their political allies.

The point here is not that personal commitments run against objectivity, but that the political and cultural milieu that may breed a consensus about journalistic principles is absent. As historians of U.S. journalism have observed, the ideal of objectivity is based on the recognition that human beings cannot be objective and that subjectivity needs to be subjected to standard practices (Streckfuss 1990). Schudson writes, "[Objectivity] became an ideal

in journalism, after all, precisely when the impossibility of overcoming subjectivity in representing the news was widely accepted *because* [in the origi-
nal] subjectivity had come to be regarded as inevitable" (1978: 157). "Journalists came to believe in objectivity, to the extent that they did," he adds,
"because they wanted to, needed to, were forced by ordinary human aspiration to seek escape from their own deep convictions of doubt and drift"
(Schudson 1978: 159).

If understood as the balancing of sources, objectivity seems possible in
the mind of South American journalists. If objectivity means impartiality,
instead, they are highly skeptical. The former is considered feasible (though
not necessarily observed); the latter is impossible. Objectivity is possible in
the reporting rather than in the newsgathering process. Subjectivity is inseparable from the selection of subjects to be exposed but reporters can "let
the facts speak for themselves" and give voice to different positions in the reporting. This perception of objectivity is illustrated in the views of a *Folha de
São Paulo* editor, "Objectivity and neutrality do not exist. What is possible is
to aim for objectivity and neutrality. That is what I do. I never publish a criticism without listening first to the individual who is the target of the attacks"
(Rodrigues 1997).

Objectivity as neutrality is considered antithetical to the dominant conviction among reporters and news organizations that journalism, and politics at large, implies taking sides as a member of a community of interests.
Philosopher Richard Rorty argues that objectivity requires that a person sees
herself as distant from a community, not as a member of a group but removed from it. Detachment from group membership makes possible universal, scientific viewpoints defended by the "partisans of objectivity" (Rorty
1991: 34). But as long as journalism is conceived as a participant in battles and
aligned with partisan politics, objectivity remains elusive. Objectivity *as* impartiality sounds hollow when news organizations are not interested in carving out a space away from "communities of interests." Consequently, there
are no conditions that may prompt journalists to reach a consensus around
objectivity.

Reasons indicated in the literature for why objectivity was originally attractive to U.S. journalism as a way to circumvent the inevitability of subjectivity are still missing in South America (Allan 1997; Hackett 1984; Soloski
1989). The scientific method does not seem to have become more appealing
as the paradigm that rules journalism qua knowledge community. Fears of
government manipulation are accepted as part of the game rather than
mechanisms that make necessary to find shelter in neutral reporting. Jour-

nalists do not view objectivity as a way to downplay emotional and sensational coverage. Nor there has been a commercial process in the press that
could have forced news organizations to throw out partisan reporting and
embrace objectivity as a reporting strategy to achieve industrial discipline in
the newsroom.

Journalists widely accept that institutional and personal values, explicitly
or implicitly but always necessarily, intervene in news selection. News judgment trumps objectivity. Objective facts are selected on the basis of different
considerations. Partisan distortions are inevitable: Journalism is shaped and
conditioned by larger political calculations even in times when news organizations are not primarily conceived as political mouthpieces. Facts are
judged not just as a representation of things the way they are, but are molded
and chosen according to diverse interests. Journalist Luis Majul (1996), author of two best-selling books exposing the business practices of wealthy Argentines, states: "I take positions with facts." Majul's statement encapsulates
the ambivalent position vis-à-vis objectivity in South American journalism.
If understood as accuracy, factuality, and balanced reporting, it is considered
desirable and possible. Defined as reporting that stands above the fray of political confrontations, it is deemed to be impossible, since personal and editorial preferences inevitably slant news. Rather than a complete shift in
knowledge paradigms, this ambiguity reflects both changes and continuities
in contemporary journalism. Fact-grounded reporting is becoming increasingly accepted but the persistent lack of consensus about a single journalistic model makes it necessary to analyze South American muckraking as re-
flecting competing ideas of journalism. These ambiguities are further
explored in the next chapter.

CHAPTER 6

PROFESSIONAL CRUSADERS: THE POLITICS OF PROFESSIONAL JOURNALISM

The preceding chapters point out the complexity and contradictions of the professional status of watchdog journalism in South America. Consider the issues of autonomy, facticity, and objectivity, all ideological pillars to the Anglo-American press (Golding and Elliott 1979; Elliott 1978). Chapter 3 shows that the politics and economics of South American news organizations have a decisive influence in deciding which skeletons to rattle. In so doing, editorial concerns exert powerful and tangible limitations on journalistic autonomy. Journalist Mario Diament (1994: 32) writes, "The perception among Latin American news business is that their interests are better served by a controlled rather than an autonomous newsroom." Chapter 5 addressed two aspects of professionalism: the growing importance of facticity as a measure of technical competence and the persistent doubts about objectivity as a possible or desirable principle of reporting. The coexistence of opposite judgments about facticity and objectivity attest to the fact that the meaning of professional journalism remains contested. No single journalistic canon is embraced by all journalists and news organizations.

From the previous chapters, then, the emergent picture is one of South American journalism being pulled in different directions. The increasing acceptance of facts as central to watchdog reporting suggests the adoption of U.S.-style professional journalism, but facts are treated in multiple ways, objectivity is suspected and questioned, and the idea of professional autonomy rings hollow when editorial positions tacitly or openly intervene in determining the repertoire of watchdog reporting. If professionalism requires shared norms that ground the behavior of journalists, as press scholar John Soloski (1989) argues, then is professionalism possible in South America, a region where journalists hold different opinions about what defines journalism?

This chapter explores this question by interrogating the professional status of watchdog journalism. Is it a form of political crusading antithetical to a notion of professional reporting? Or is it professional muckraking concerned with disclosing facts to prove wrongdoing? Is it straight politics played through journalistic means or a profession guided by the ideals of impartial reporting? Can it be both? Is it half-hearted professional journalism? Is it journalistic crusading with a professional face?

In this chapter I analyze changes that are manifest in the increasing adoption of the standards of "professional journalism" in watchdog reporting. The entrance of college-trained reporters, the opening of better remunerated positions, the growing significance of market dynamics for media careers, and journalists' search for legitimization and recognition suggest the increasing professionalization of the field. But these transformations cannot be considered synonymous with the affirmation of professional journalism, because there is ambiguity surrounding the idea of professional reporting, and limitations on U.S.-styled professional journalism persist in the region. Notwithstanding a recent movement toward "professionalization," the professional identity of journalists continues to have multiple meanings, journalism is pulled in different directions, and muckraking straddles different press traditions.

AMBIGUITIES OF PROFESSIONAL JOURNALISM

Traditionally, South American journalists have held ambivalent views about whether journalism is a profession. While some have defended the professional claims and status of journalism, others frown at the idea that journalism is (or can aspire to be) a profession. Many journalists have long believed that journalism is, to use Jeremy Tunstall's (1971) expression, an "indeterminate" occupation, for it includes a wide "range of expected tasks." Not all reporters are expected to have the same skills and training in the process of news production. The observation made by Luis Miró Quesada, the late publisher of Perú's *El Comercio,* reflects doubts among South American journalists about the status of journalism: "Depending on how it is practiced, journalism can be the most noble profession or the most despicable craft" (in Martínez 1989: 544). It is not unusual to find journalists who still assert that journalism, above all, is not a profession but "an art, a vocation" (Pedreira 1992). "Journalism, the Best Craft in the World," is the title of a widely cited article by Gabriel García Márquez (1996), a towering figure in Latin American literature and journalism. In it he hints at a concept that places journalism closer to other crafts, rather than to law and medicine, the archetypal modern professions.

Asked whether journalism has become more "professional" than in the past, journalists I interviewed consistently give affirmative answers. Argentine reporters are seen as embracing a professional culture separated from ideologies, less driven by political passion, and more interested in information and in writing without adjectives (Pasquini Durán 1996; Rodriguez 1995; Santoro 1996; Tenembaum 1995). New generations of Brazilian journalists are judged as less ideological and more influenced by U.S. journalism (Dimenstein 1996; Kucinski 1997; also see *Imprensa* 1993). Colombian journalists are described as more driven by empirical not ideological journalism, more committed to facts, and less involved in partisan battles than in the past (Lesmes 1996; Santos 1996; Torres 1996). Peruvian journalists speak of their colleagues as being more independent and less politically committed, more professional and less interested in intellectual debates (Adrianzen 1995; Barraza 1995; Paredes 1995). A veteran editor says: "while journalism used to be conceived as an art and a craft, reporters now do their job like any other job" (Igartua 1995). An Argentine journalist, who authored several award-winning exposés, says "Journalists used to be divided between establishment and critical journalists. Now I define myself professionally" (Ciancaglini 1996). Put together, these self-descriptions coincide in portraying today's reporters as better prepared, more pragmatic, more interested in fact-grounded reporting, and more driven by career values. These characteristics are associated with professional journalism, which to *Folha de São Paulo* managing editor, "is what the market demands, 'complete' journalists who are well-trained, know Internet, speak two or three languages, and are non-partisan, capable of separating politics from passion" (de Souza 1997).

In marking off these features, however, these observations make disparate assumptions about the defining elements of professional journalism. They reflect the multiple meanings associated with the concept of professional journalism. Is formal training necessary? Should accreditation, the mandatory bar of quintessential liberal professions, be required? Does remuneration set apart amateur from professional journalism? Can professional autonomy be possible when most reporters are salaried employees in large bureaucratic organizations? Is careerism a decisive ingredient? Should the espousing of the ethics of public service be a requisite? Can professionalism journalism, no matter how it is defined, be similarly understood in the context of South American and Anglo-American journalisms?

The haziness surrounding the idea of professional journalism derives, in part, from the ambiguity of professionalism as an analytical category (Abbott 1988; Freidson 1986; Johnson 1972). Sociologist Sheldon Rothblatt (1995: 194) observes, "The subject of professions is exceedingly complicated. There are far too many vocations by that designation, many national variations on common themes, and plentiful examples of professions that share only a few common traits." Conditions specific to journalism are also responsible for the difficulty, if not impossibility, of reaching a conclusive definition (Broddason 1994). Answers to the aforementioned questions vary according to how professionalism is defined and what requirement(s) are weighed more heavily in defining the professional claims of any occupation. The literature on professionalism provides a number of defining elements that put together would form an ideal-typical model of professions: autonomous and remunerated work based on the monopoly of a certain knowledge provided by systems of higher education and that observes certain ethical principles. The next sections examine these requirements to analyze what professionalism means in the context of South American journalism.

PROFESSIONS AS MONOPOLIES OF KNOWLEDGE

Some studies identify the monopoly of knowledge received through exposure to higher education as a distinctive feature of professionalism (Freidson 1986). Training in formal knowledge certifies individuals as capable of performing certain tasks. Educational institutions function as filters and legitimizers for they hold powers over accreditation, and credentials are understood as incontrovertible proof of professionalism. Diploma-granting institutions testify that, having mastered certain knowledge, individuals are professionals.

Applied to journalism, then, this would require not only that reporters should be certified by journalism schools, the institutions that monopolize the capacity to grant degrees, but also that news organizations require such credentials. When the boundaries between journalism and other activities are too fluid, the bases for professionalism are weak. When journalists not only have diverse backgrounds but also arrive in newsrooms via multiple tracks, journalism can hardly make claims to professionalism. Professionalism requires establishing boundaries separating who is and who isn't a journalist. Press scholars Colin Sparks and Slavko Splichal understand this approach to professional journalism as one that "conceives of professions as self-conscious groups acting to impose or monopolize a certain niche in the labor market and seeking to maximize social and economic benefits by restricting access and opportunities to a limited circle" (1994: 43).

If we follow this understanding, the entrance of new generations of graduates from journalism schools into the newsrooms suggests a gradual professionalization of South American journalism. Beginning in the late 1960s, the foundation of schools of journalism coupled with the push for licensing has arguably contributed to turning college diplomas into the dividing line between nonprofessional from professional reporting. From a viewpoint that sees professionalism in terms of academic credentials, a reporter fresh out of journalism school is a professional while a twenty-year newsroom veteran without a college diploma is not. Such conclusion, expectedly, does not sit well with a good number of journalists who continue to prize newsroom experiences rather than college education as decisive in conferring journalistic credentials, especially as journalism education in the region has been long criticized for prioritizing theoretical rather than empirical knowledge.

The question of credentialism has been a topic of constant controversy in South American journalism (Knudson 1996). Even in countries such as Brazil and Colombia where journalistic diplomas are required, there is still no consensus on whether college education and licensing are the defining elements of professionalism. Unions have vigorously defended *colegiación*. For them, licensing limits the entrance of reporters into the labor market and thus benefits journalists in two ways. It protects job security and prevents the fall of wages that otherwise result from the existence of a large pool of reporters (Valverde 1990). Critics of pro-licensing positions include the Inter-American press association, owners' organizations, as well as prominent journalists who attack *colegiación* for imposing inadequate standards to decide what qualifies a reporter and for setting up a situation that favors autocratic governments' ability to manipulate the press and muffle freedom of expression (Seaton 1990).

A recent exchange between the head of the journalist's union and a prominent columnist in Colombia fairly represent the main points of the debate. For the unions, credentials means professionalism, a system for recognizing that an individual has received journalistic training, an instrument with which to defend social rights and income levels, and a mechanism to exclude those "who parachute in [journalistic jobs]" (Tamayo de Echeverry 1998). Other observers believe that credentialism gags independent journalism, is used by different powers to control the press, and is abused by those who are accredited (Caballero 1998). Three decades after the system of *colegiación* was implemented, similar positions and controversies can be found in other countries such as Brazil and Venezuela.

Journalists agree that the changing profile of reporters attests to growing professionalism. Gone are the days when newsrooms were staffed by a menagerie of individuals with disparate backgrounds but no formal training in journalism. In the past, reporters were not expected to bring, and indeed rarely had, journalistic skills and training into the newsroom. Writing talent, creativity, or contacts with the editorial upper brass, rather than degrees in journalism, were the typical credentials. García Márquez (1996: 14, 15) remembers the old days when "the craft was learnt in the newsrooms, in the workshop, in the coffeehouses, in the parties. The motto was 'Journalism is learned by doing it.' Students who failed in disparate classes or were searching for a job to crown their academic careers, or professionals graduated in anything who discovered their real vocation, were in the newsroom." The testimony of a Peruvian journalist and poet describes the archetypal reporter of the past: "Like everyone else, I started in journalism while developing my writing skills for other (literary?) pursuits. But I stayed and still continue" (Orrillo 1986: 5). Newsrooms of the past are remembered as staffed by bohemian reporters, struggling novelists, and poets who could make a steady income writing for a publication, and graduates from a wide range of professions who found in journalism an outlet for literary inclinations. The former editor-in-chief of Peru's *La República* recalls, "There were no schools of journalism back then. An M.D. closed the first page, another directed the political section, there was an engineer here, a lawyer there" (Thorndike 1995). Journalists did not have professional ambitions and did not exhibit credentials certifying them as bona fide professionals. Remembering his father's journalism, a noted Brazilian columnist observes, "Journalism used to be an odd job . . . a good excuse to arrive home late" (Cony 1993).

The recollections of one Brazilian journalist are worth quoting in length:

> The journalistic family was a highly varied fauna. There were the poor and the rich, the badly dressed and the dandies, the illiterates and the educated, the veterans and the rookies, the corrupt and the dishonest and the blackmailers. To be a professional journalist was an oddity full of dramatic deprivations. [News] companies could not pay even the low salaries, therefore those who did not have another job, and most didn't, were in big trouble. I, for example, lunched for free in one restaurant and had dinner

in another thanks to advertising deals. At the company level, there was a lack, even in the upper echelons, of a solid professional ethic (with a few exceptions). Turn-of the-century habits persisted: writers and intellectuals lived off monies selling their mediocre literary production to caudillos and political bosses. Those were dismal times; journalists were connivers in search of small advantages. Only later, after the imposition of professional wages and the regulation of work laws, journalism became decent and respected. The commercial expansion of [news] companies inevitably produced a new professional model. The classic press bohemian, an irresponsible individual, often drunk without the bosses caring about it, was condemned to disappear. Now, the professional journalist is gaining strength. In the past, the journalist had parallel professions to survive: lawyer, doctor, judge, teacher, public official, bank clerk, salesman, advertising man or employee. (Motta 1975)

This professional ambiguity belonged to a time when literature and politics shaped the identity of journalism. Literary liberties were more accepted and factual rigor was less important. Poetic enhancements and embellished writing were not simply accepted but actually valued as superior attributes of a gifted journalist. The accomplished wordsmith with encyclopedic knowledge, rather than the fact-minded reporter, better describes the typical journalist of the past. In bookish and iconoclast newsrooms, familiarity and mastery of literary trends, philosophical treatises and political discussion were prized over methodological rigor. This was possible in the context of a press more interested in serving as a political tribune than as a business operation. Not without a tinge of nostalgia, veteran journalists recall those as the good old days, when profit making was secondary to other pursuits at both the editorial and reporting level. A Peruvian publisher describes it as a time when journalism was more of a romantic enterprise devoid of the commercial drive prevalent in the contemporary press (Igartua 1995).

Recent crops of reporters are markedly different. Although, as journalists admit, it is difficult to generalize especially given the lack of census information at the regional level, the general impression is that today's young reporters are greatly different from journalists in the past. For once, they are more likely to be graduates of college-level journalism schools. A 1993 study showed that 76 percent of reporters at the *Folha de São Paulo* held degrees in journalism and communication while the rest had graduated in different social sciences and humanities (Cunha Pinto 1993). Compared to previous generations, young reporters are more influenced by the U.S. tradition of facticity and careerism, more skeptical of partisan politics, less likely to accept old-time corrupt practices (e.g., receiving bonus wages from government offices or selling advertising), less interested in following old practices that minimized individual work (such as writing articles by simply transcribing official communiqués), and more concerned and eager to receive and update professional skills. If the idea of professional journalism means reporters with such attributes, then, there are unequivocal signs of growing professionalization. A Brazilian journalist recalls the time when his newspaper "inaugurated the first newsroom destined to follow the school of Rio de Janeiro's *Jornal do Brasil*: journalism as profession. Journalists with professional concerns. No sideline jobs. No corruption. Just high sense of professionalism" (Chagas, Mayrink, and Pinheiro 1992).

PROFESSIONALISM AS REMUNERATED WORK

Studies have also indicated that monetary compensation defines any profession. Elliot Freidson (1986: 24) notes, "Profession refers to all kinds of occupations that one engages in for a living." In her path-breaking study, sociologist Magali Sarfatti Larson (1977: 209) writes, "Modern professions organize to exchange their services for a price." Applied to journalism, the reporter who receives a paycheck for her work is a professional while someone who contributes to a magazine or a newspaper without remuneration is an amateur. If we take this approach, then, neither education nor expertise but remuneration defines professional reporting. From this perspective, South American muckrakers are, indeed, professionals: they are salaried journalists toiling for profit-making news organizations rather than amateurs reporting about wrongdoing in their spare time.

The opening of opportunities for muckraking to be better remunerated is partially the result that better-paid jobs in journalism are more available than in the past. Journalists agree that there are more chances for journalists to be better paid. Brazilian journalist Mino Carta (1996b) states, "until the 1970s, journalists knew they couldn't make much money." This has made possible the consolidation of careerism in journalism. Bledstein (1976) has indicated that careerism and mobility are central to professionalism. Journalists observe that it is not unusual to find, in contrast to previous times, colleagues interested in working for news organizations on the basis of strictly professional rewards and are ready to change jobs if other publications pay better salaries or offer positions with higher responsibilities or more prestigious than their current positions. They see their colleagues as willing to work for news organizations regardless of editorial sympathies. The availability of well-paid positions has stimulated a careerist mentality markedly different from the previous journalistic worldview.

The possibility of earning higher salaries does not mean that journalists are better compensated overall. The Latin American Association of Journalists portrays the situation in grim terms. 20 percent of journalists are unemployed, 40 percent hold informal jobs, and their monthly average salaries that range between $200 and $800 hardly suggest affluent economic times (Tijman 1995). Journalists confirm this gloomy portrayal. They say that although there are more opportunities for earning decent incomes, salaries widely vary across news companies and broadcast and print media, as well as between metropolitan and rural areas (Virtue 1995; Vomero 1999). With a few exceptions, the majority of reporters are still badly paid. The former managing editor of an Argentine daily observes that to keep employment costs low, news organizations prefer to hire young and inexperienced staffers, especially female reporters who overall earn less than male reporters (Diament 1996). The feminization of the newsrooms, he observes, responds to wage considerations rather than to the intention of redressing the balance of gender representation.

Although most reporters continue to face difficult economic conditions, muckrakers can potentially make additional income by netting royalties for best-selling exposés. In recent years, many exposés originally published as individual pieces in newspapers and magazines have appeared as books. This situation is different from past decades when it was more difficult for exposé books to generate money for journalists. An Argentine editor observes that Gregorio Selser, a journalist-essayist who extensively investigated the activities of the CIA and transnational companies in Latin America in the 1950s and 1960s, "published forty books but never made any money" (Pasquini Durán 1996).

It would be hard to offer a comprehensive list of the industry of the "books about crooks" that have been published in the last two decades but several noteworthy examples can be mentioned. In Argentina, Horacio Verbitsky's *Robo para la corona,* a denunciation of corruption inside the Menem administration, single-handedly started the boom of investigative books and sold close to a quarter million copies. Gabriela Cerrutti's *El jefe* revealed details of President Menem's life and political trajectory. Luis Majul's best-selling two-part *Los dueños de la Argentina* lifted the rug under the wealthiest individuals in that country. Jorge Urien Berri's *El ultimo colimba* exposed the murder and cover-up of an army private. In Brazil, Gilberto Dimenstein authored a number of exposés including *As meninas da noite* (about child prostitution) and *Conexão Cabo Frio* (about corruption in the ministry of foreign affairs), Caco Barcellos denounced police violence in *Rota 66*, and three *Folha de São Paulo* reporters penned *Os donos do Congresso* about illegalities in Congress. In Colombia, a list of best-selling exposés includes *Por quien votar 1982?* and *Por quien votar 1986?*, two critical studies of the profiles of candidates and congressional members written by members of *El Tiempo*'s Unidad Investigativa; Alberto Donadío's *Banqueros al banquillo* and *Por que cayó Jaime Michelsen?*, investigations of fraud in the banking industry, and *El espejismo del subsidio familiar*, a denunciation of the misuse of workers' funds; Germán Castro Caycedo's *Colombia amarga*, a grim look at the lives and working conditions of ordinary citizens; several books about drug-trafficking such as Fabio Castillo's *Los jinetes de la cocaína* and *La coca nostra*, Luis Cañón's *El patrón*, and Edgar Torres's *Mercaderes de la muerte*; and *El Presidente que se iba a caer*, a chronicle of the *Proceso 8,000* written by three editors of the newsweekly *Semana*.

What motivates the publication of these books? For major publishing groups and smaller editorial houses, the attractiveness of such books is obviously commercial. Piggybacking on the success and the commotion caused by stories written by the same authors, many books topped best-selling lists. Perhaps the exception is Peru, where fewer "exposé books" have appeared despite the existence of a brawny watchdog journalism. A smaller market than in Argentina, Brazil, and Colombia and persistent threats on critical reporters have, arguably, deterred the publication of such books in Peru. For journalists, books are appealing for various reasons. They reach a massive readership, can potentially reap significant earnings, and offer an outlet for writing full-length exposés that include information left out from the original versions. An Argentine journalist who penned several best-selling exposés states, "It is possible to present the most pure information in books. Publishing houses are not subjected to conflicting interests [as news organizations are]" (Majul 1996). In cases of stories butchered due to time and space constraints, toned down or only partially approved due to editorial concerns, books give the opportunity to present information that was not originally included. Journalist Gerardo Reyes (1996) observes that reporters think of books as opportunities for writing "what news organizations don't let me publish." This does not mean that publishing houses, especially major groups, are not concerned about the potential political and legal troubles that may result from no-holds-barred exposés. Although they take precautions by having legal advisors carefully combing the content of the books, journalists observe, there are fewer constraints than in newspapers and newsweeklies.

PROFESSIONAL PRESTIGE AND POLITICS

What motivates a reporter to pry open wrongdoing — professional calling, personal politics, awards, salary increases? It is impossible to reach a single answer valid for all cases: not only do different reporters practice watchdog reporting for different reasons, but sorting out professional from political motivations is also complicated. The issue is worth exploring, to show the complexity of the concept of professional reporting in South American journalism. It is not a matter of concluding that investigative reporters are apolitical professionals or lyrical crusaders uninterested in professional satisfactions, but to examine how professionalism and personal convictions are intertwined in watchdog journalism.

Professionalism assumes, we are told, that reporters suppress subjectivity and follow the rules of objectivity, omit personal convictions and put professional standards first. The question "How is professional journalism possible?" has received a great deal of attention and discussion in Anglo-American journalism. The canon of modern reporting states that opinions have no room in the newsroom or, if admitted to, need to be strictly separated from factual reporting. Personal politics have little, if any, influence in news-gathering precisely because of the weight of the culture of professionalism. Adherence to professional norms explains why the argument that the personal convictions of reporters are responsible for news bias is incorrect. Such a position ignores that professional rules and ambitions coupled with organizational routines, rather than personal politics, shape news content and reporting practices (Gans 1979; Schudson 1995).

What happens in journalistic cultures where the meaning of professionalism is deeply contested and, as the previous chapter argues, the rules of objectivity are not consistently followed? When journalists remain skeptical about the feasibility and desirability of "professional journalism," how are tensions between personal politics and professional expectations resolved? This question is particularly relevant in watchdog journalism, more perhaps than in any other journalistic genre, because it foregrounds the ethical dimension of reporting. Watchdog journalism does not deal with straight news but with acts believed to violate certain legal and/or ethical principles.

This opens the possibility that personal politics, rather than just professional standards, determine what acts of wrongdoing need to be denounced. My interest here is examining whether professional and personal concerns drive journalists to report wrongdoing.

The prospect of professional distinction associated with breaking hell-of-a-story exposés is, no doubt, a big incentive. Muckraking journalism heightens professional reputations and gives credibility to fourth estate claims. Both reporters and news organizations can boast that they knocked down cabinet members and show a record of practicing hard-hitting, "independent" journalism. As *Folha de São Paulo*'s managing editor says, "from a marketing perspective, independence is the best place for journalism to be. It gives prestige to the newspaper. . . . It's a managerial more than a journalistic rationale." (de Souza 1997). Ideological motivations are important too. It would be hard to argue that primarily professional ambitions drove Peruvian journalists to investigate the workings of the Shining Path, the activities of death squads, and illegalities inside the Fujimori administration; motivated Argentina's *Página/12* journalists to expose a myriad of cases of corruption involving members of the Menem government; or inspired Colombia's *El Espectador* to go after the Medellin cartel. Any of these topics is too sensitive and hotly political to be investigated just because of professional interest, especially in countries where there are lingering suspicions that politics, rather than just a pledge to professional values and ideals, are always behind the production of exposés.

Asked about why they practice watchdog reporting, journalists say that journalism has a "social commitment." One Colombian journalist asserts: "To be a journalist is not like being a plumber. It works towards the social good. The main goal shouldn't be profit but the general good" (Gómez 1996). "Journalism has to provoke society and create consciousness; otherwise it is just supermarket ads," says another (Torres 1996). "Journalism is a profession of adventurers who have a mission of goodness and justice" says a Brazilian columnist (Hamilton Ribeiro 1991). A Peruvian muckraker contends, "We, journalists, have the moral obligation to denounce, to criticize certain behaviors. The impunity of certain people makes me sick, [to see] what they have done to our country" (Arrieta 1998). It is not traditional political rallying cries that inspire contemporary muckrakers.

Amid general disenchantment with partisan politics, journalists are not the exception. A Colombian journalist who authored several exposés during the *Proceso 8,000* affirms: "All political parties are the same *sancocho* [stew]. Dirty, garbage politics'" (Caballero 1996). Instead, larger moral or philosophical convictions seemingly drive the work of muckrakers, a kind of liberal humanism that finds repulsive the abuse of human rights, the activities of drug traffickers, and widespread corruption in societies plagued with poverty and hunger. In my interviews, muckrakers consistently talk about disclosing political wrongdoing at a time when politics has become publicly delegitimized and more citizens are indifferent to partisan conflicts. They express similar personal feelings about organized politics: most reject any identification with political parties or other political organizations and many even refuse to vote for any party out of the impossibility of taking partisan sides. What endures, they recognize, are certain ethical principles among both the public and muckrakers. Those principles determine that certain behaviors are wrong. Graft, murder, and other forms of power abuse clash with moral, rather than partisan, convictions. What prompts a reporter to disclose corruption is not partisan calls, especially the ideologies that informed the muckraking work of alternative publications in the 1960s and 1970s, but the desire to reinforce certain moral values, to moralize politics while jettisoning partisan attachments.

To some journalists, personal convictions are fundamental to understanding why some reporters disclose wrongdoing despite several obstacles. Harassment and threats from military and police officers, government officials and drug-traffickers makes muckraking extremely dangerous. Personal and family safety is at risk. Peruvian journalist José Arrieta (1998), who went into exile after intelligence sources warned him that his life was in danger, remembers: "I have three children. I used to be armed. I never had lunch or dinner in the same place. It was not a life, but I did it because of principles." Some journalists even joke that more than some degree of insanity, rather than personal convictions, is necessary to cover touchy subjects such as intelligence activities and drug trafficking.

Personal convictions also make reporters willing to push a story when human and monetary resources assigned to investigations are scarce, particularly in cases when executives and editors fear that certain stories may enrage powerful interests. In resource-poor newspapers such as Argentina's *Página/12*, reporters observe that the lack of generous budgets for investigations and exposés (ironically these were staples of the daily) was overcome by an esprit-de-corps mentality, a collective perception that some stories were worthwhile and politically important. Nor is watchdog journalism always personally rewarding. Many journalists say that expressions of support from the public are invigorating: Peruvian journalist Cecilia Valenzuela (1997) says, "there is satisfaction when people who don't have means to say what I say ask you not to give up." Pessimistic feelings, however, are wide-spread among journalists when exposés do not meet a great deal of public interest or encourage other institutions to conduct further investigations. There is little satisfaction when denunciations are ignored by judicial and congressional powers or get lost in the limbo of Byzantine legal systems. Moreover, intense legal persecution and burdensome lawsuits brought up by individuals accused of wrongdoing, fuel further pessimism and cynicism.

Convictions also motivate journalists to propose specific topics of inves-tigation to higher-ups who are not always particularly interested and are fearful of watchdog reporting. Here the question of personal interests in spe-cific investigations is linked to the problem of journalistic autonomy. All journalists do not have similar cachet to propose topics and carry investiga-tions forward nor do news organizations offer identical degrees of auton-omy to reporters (Cardoso 1995). A Colombian journalist says, "There is al-ways a battle you have to wage against the source, the lawyers, the editor. You are willing or not to fight. It's your own commitment more than the editor telling you 'we have to do this and that.'" (Rodriguez 1996). For a Peruvian editor, "Autonomy is the space that you achieve for yourself and depends on the chemistry between publisher and journalist" (Barraza 1995). Journalist Gerardo Reyes (1996, 57), an original member of *El Tiempo*'s investigative unit recalls, "We had to fight with diverse obstacles. We took advantage of the facts that the managing editor was absent, the solidarity of sons and nephews [of the publisher] with our work, and the neutrality of some board members vis-à-vis some subjects. [Team member Alberto] Donadío wrote, 'inventing resources and strategies to guarantee that [our articles] would be published became part of the routine.' The obstacles got us tired and eventually were responsible for our resignation."

If a journalist reports for a news organization whose editorial politics are somewhat similar to hers, she would likely run up against fewer limitations. For example, *Página/12* reporters speak of the freedom to report about dif-ferent topics in a newspaper where "we all thought alike" (Rodriguez 1996), especially in comparison to colleagues in other news organizations. But, in most cases, the situation is quite different from *Página/12*'s, as the personal beliefs of reporters do not always coincide with editorial positions, and news organizations are typically not interested in waging moral or political cru-sades against specific subjects. A Colombian reporter recalls that when she insisted on disclosing different cases of corruption, an editor warned her that the mission of the newspaper was "to inform not to stage campaigns" (Caballero 1996). In similar situations, then, reporters make different decisions about how much and often they are willing to confront editors. Tired of stories being consistently axed or topics redlined, journalists tell personal stories of changing jobs.

Not surprisingly, all news organizations do not share the same interest in one single exposé. A story about corruption in municipal government is likely to be frowned upon if the newspaper is politically aligned with the local mayor, but it may be better received if the paper supports one of the mayor's electoral rivals. The sensitivity and potential explosiveness of a subject matter also affects acceptance or rejection in pursuing a story. A newscast or newsweekly may be interested supporting the investigation of environmental disasters or police corruption but may find revelations about drug trafficking that may implicate prominent officials too risky. The timing of an exposé also matters. Editors may be reluctant to keep pounding on a cabinet member if they have recently published a series of revelations on him and/or his party. An Argentine editor observes, "You have to remain equidistant. If I talk about someone all the time, it becomes a persecution" (Zunino 1999). Interested in wrapping themselves in the flag of independent journalism, they fear that their news organization may be seen as too biased against a specific individual, and criticized for ignoring the rules of neutral reporting and warn about the dangers of converting journalism into an ideology. Such a position patently reflects the intention to abandon muckraking as crusading journalism and, instead, to embrace nonpartisan, "nonideological" reporting, one of the central tenets of U.S.-style professional journalism.

Ideological convictions also help to explain the decision of news organizations to denounce crimes. Consider the decision of *El Espectador* to disclose corruption involving Colombia's biggest banks and to wage a prolonged and persistent war against the Medellin cartel in the 1980s. The Cano family, then owners of the newspaper, as well as journalists knew perfectly well that exposing financial fraud would have lethal economic consequences. They also were aware that aiming the investigative arsenal at the powerful cartel would put them in the bull's-eye of boss Pablo Escobar, who was known for his inclination to retaliate violently against anyone who criticized him. *El Espectador* continued, however, even after advertising decreased, threats became regular, the paper's building was bombed, and publisher Guillermo Cano was assassinated. It was clearly a case of a publisher and journalists openly committed to a specific cause who decided to go after major political and economic power holders.

In contrast to positions that foreground the relevance of personal beliefs, other reporters stress the appeal of professional carrots dangling in front of investigative journalists. "Circumstances make you get involved. There is no altruism. [Journalism] is a vice, pure adrenaline," observes the former managing editor of Colombia's most influential newsweekly (Vargas 1996). "It makes you happy. There is adrenaline, a feeling of combat," observes an editor for the Argentine newsweekly *Noticias* (Zunino 1999). Writing a shocking exposé brings the satisfaction of scooping colleagues, earns respect, heightens the professional stature among sources, and may potentially bring the prospects of better jobs. "Awards and prestige, not money, prod a reporter," says an Argentine journalist who disclosed the illegal sale of weapons to Ecuador (Santoro 1996). Watchdog journalism may catapult reporters to journalistic stardom. In cases of high-profile stories involving prominent officials that receive a great deal of media attention, muckrakers can even become celebrities or, at least, achieve fifteen minutes of fame. Radio and television talk shows invite them, politicians comment on their reporting, and colleagues reward them with prizes and accolades.

The significance of professional rewards cannot be understood apart from the rise of the culture of journalistic celebrity. First, the growing importance of individual bylines has boosted the visibility of watchdog journalists. In past decades, reporters did not always sign stories. An Argentine journalist recalls, "Newsrooms in the 1940s and 1950s were staffed by reporters who didn't believe what they wrote thus preferred not to sign. Peronist newspapers had nonperonist journalists. Only columnists, who were often identified with the editorial line, signed" (Garcia Lupo 1996). State censorship and persecution also deterred the signing of stories. Aware that critical reporting would meet negative reactions from government officials, reporters opted to play it safe and leave out sensitive information. Also, when stories were butchered by censors or considerably toned down by editors, reporters were reluctant to include their signatures. They were not interested in signing stories that didn't fully satisfy them.

Violence also deterred journalists from signing. Individuals implicated by exposés can certainly find out the identity of the author when they want to let the author know that revelations did not sit well with them. Nonetheless, reporters frequently decided not to sign exposés on touchy subjects out of personal interest or when advised not to do so by publishers and editors. Anonymity increases security. In the late 1980s, the decision of Colombian drug bosses to retaliate against individuals and organizations that publicly criticized them made the situation considerably difficult for journalists, especially for those who reported on drug trafficking. Convinced that drug barons would not hesitate to attack, many journalists opted to submit reports unsigned. Under the leadership of *El Espectador* publisher Guillermo Cano, major news organizations teamed up to produce and publish collaborative exposés that were likely to enrage drug lords. This was done, for example, with the publication of the criminal record of Medellin cartel boss Pablo Escobar. The rationale was that if all published the same information, drug traffickers would not retaliate against one news organization (Duzán 1994). Even during the *Proceso 8,000*, some reports in the newsweeklies *Semana* and *Cambio 16* were not signed for fear of retaliation against reporters.

Journalists also observe that for many reporters, raised in the culture of the alternative press, signing reports was unusual and if signed, articles carried a nom de plume. Signatures not only endangered the personal safety of journalists but were also seen as unbefitting a journalism that had political, rather than professional, goals. In the world of alternative journalism, bylines were seen as a vice of bourgeois journalism, a way to prioritize individual over collective work and glorify personal fame and recognition. The situation has changed. The abolition of systematic official censorship, the ebbing of violence against reporters, and the consolidation of career prospects have made individual bylines more frequent and important. There are exceptions due to concerns about the potential legal repercussions of exposés. If they lack full support from their news organizations, especially in extremely sensitive stories where lawsuits from implicated parties are expected, reporters are reluctant to sign, making publications assume full legal responsibility.

The creation of the so-called *unidades de investigación*, teams specifically dedicated to investigative journalism, seems to have helped the culture of celebrity journalism. In Colombia and Peru, critics charge that the compartmentalization of investigative journalism in units has elevated a handful of reporters above the rest, thus creating an elite of celebrated journalists above the *cargaladrillos* (brick carriers), the average reporters. In carving out a space for a special team of reporters specifically dedicated to investigate, the *unidades* institutionalized the star system of journalism.

Awards also foster celebrity journalism and also indicate the adoption of professional values. The growing number of awards suggests the gradual consolidation of a careerist mentality and the recognition of reporters on the basis of professional merits. Old-guard journalists think that these developments undermine the essence of journalism and its social mission, transforming it into any other profession. Younger reporters, instead, tend to judge them differently, seeing them as positive moves toward improving the quality of reporting and opening debates about the strengths and weaknesses of journalism.

If we consider the number of awards, publications devoted to the analysis of journalism as profession, and polls among reporters to choose "the best journalists," then the affirmation of a professional self-consciousness is more visible in Brazil than in other countries. Brazilian journalism features more awards than any other in the region including: the traditional Esso de Jornalismo (with categories in photography, reporting, specialized reporting and regional awards), Fiat Allis de Jornalismo Econômico (for economic reporting), Vladimir Herzog (named after the journalist tortured and killed by the military and awarded by the São Paulo Union of Journalists to reports on social, human rights, and citizenship issues), Jabuti (sponsored by the Brazilian Book Chamber), Líbero Badaró (given by the magazine *Imprensa* and sponsored by the Press Brazilian Association), AMB de Jornalismo (for reports on scientific and medical subjects), Simon Bolivar (sponsored by the Union of Journalists), and Icatu (awarded by Bank Icatu for economic reporting). Many investigative reporters have received awards, including the Esso award, one of the most traditional and prestigious prizes in Brazilian journalism. It was given to, among others, *ISTOE* reporters for the story about the driver/ whistle blower in the Collor scandal in 1992 and to *Folha de São Paulo* editor Fernando Rodrigues for exposing a vote-for-money scheme in Congress in 1997.

In all countries studied, a wide range of domestic and international awards has been granted to reporters who produced denunciations. The Rey de España (King of Spain) award, one of the most coveted and prestigious journalism awards for Latin American reporters, has been given to muckrakers numerous times. Some recipients included Argentine journalists Sergio Ciancaglini and Martín Granovsky for their reporting on human rights abuses and riots, a *Clarín* team for an investigation about the 1976 military coup, *Folha de São Paulo* columnist Janio Freitas for his exposé on corruption in the bidding for the construction of a rail system in Rio de Janeiro, and *El Tiempo* María Teresa Ronderos and Ernesto Cortés Fierro for reporting the linkages between Colombian politics and drug traffickers. Other awards that South American journalists received for muckraking work include the Columbia University-based Maria Moors Cabot Prize for journalistic contributions to Inter-American understanding, the International Women's Media Foundation award for journalistic courage, the Hellman-Hamwett's freedom of expression award, the Committee to Protect Journalists's Press Freedom award, the International Planned Parenthood Federation's Rosa Cisneros award for reporting on population issues, and other regional and domestic prizes given by professional and human rights organizations.

FROM WALSH TO WOODSTEIN

Another aspect to consider in surveying the growing influence of the ideology of professional journalism and the rise of journalistic celebrities are the icons that seem to embody journalism's ideals. Journalism, like any other cultural community, upholds "constitutive myths," stories about what it is and what it wants to be. Individuals and events are catapulted to the highest level as embodiments of the loftiest ideals, the defining moments, the most glorious hours. They are the yardsticks that distinguish good from bad reporting. They condense aspirations and stand as beacons of professional merit. They are fun-house mirrors that distort yet somewhat reflect real actions and principles. As with legendary heroes, virtues are aggrandized and weaknesses are minimized or ignored.

No doubt, "the press in Watergate" and journalists Bob Woodward and Carl Bernstein are the "constitutive myths" of contemporary investigative journalism (Schudson 1995). Watergate, as the "key incident in the annals of journalism," defines the identity not just of investigative reporting but, more generally, the ideology of professional journalism (see Zelizer 1993). Woodstein, the nickname for the Woodward and Bernstein team, have been enshrined in the pantheon of U.S. journalism as the little reporters that could, the reporting duo that was able to root out evil by dethroning a powerful president, the journalistic Davids who, equipped with only a typewriter, defeated the government Goliath.

Woodward and Bernstein were not the only or most obvious candidates to be put in the highest pedestal. Revered and resented during their time, muckrakers Ida Tarbell or Lincoln Steffens could have fit the bill, too. But their denunciations of social conditions and wealth accumulation fit uneasily in the liberal ideology of the U.S. press, to whom the government, not industrial barons or corporations, is the seat of wrongdoing. Steffens's proximity to President Theodore Roosevelt and his own political career also made him unsuitable for the post-1920s journalistic model that prizes neutral reporting and distance from government. Roosevelt's "muckraker" moniker stuck longer than the names or the work of turn-of-the-century reporters as constitutive myths of watchdog journalism. Seymour Hersch's investigation of My Lai could have been other possibility but, as sociologist Michael Schudson (1995: 164) suggests, the massacre of Vietnamese civilians "was too bloody and devastating and divisive to hold up as the epitome of American enterprise journalism." Instead, at least in the versions presented in their work and interviews and immortalized by Hollywood, Watergate and Woodstein corresponded to the tradition of objective, professional, fourth-estate journalism. It did not hurt, either, that the official portrayals resonated with the quintessential American myth of principled individuals who struggle and succeed against the system.

The symbolic power of Woodstein and Watergate transcends the frontiers of U.S. journalism. South American watchdog journalism is filled with references to Watergate. Its presence is detected in multiple forms. As a cultural and political referent, Watergate is many things simultaneously: a source of inspiration, a language, a script, a master narrative of journalism, an image bank.

Watergate is a source of inspiration. If Camilo Taufic's *Periodismo y Lucha de Clases* (Journalism and Class Struggle) or Lenin's writings on journalism were typically found in the bookshelves of journalists in the 1960s and 1970s, today, instead, *All the President's Men, The Final Days,* and other best sellers by U.S. journalists are more likely to be cited and displayed. For journalist Gerardo Reyes, the foundation of the *unidad investigativa* at Colombia's *El Tiempo* in 1977 was a direct byproduct of Watergate. "Having caught the Watergate fever, journalist Daniel Samper returned from the United States with the idea that an independent, critical and investigative press, like the American, was needed in Colombia" (1996: 55). After completing a masters degree in journalism at the University of Kansas at a time when the experience of the press in Watergate was all the rage in schools of journalism, Samper assembled a team of young journalists to replicate the deeds of Woodstein.[1]

José Arrieta (1998), a prominent Peruvian journalist who went into exile in 1997 after receiving threats, defines *All the President's Men* as "the Bible of investigative journalism, a manual to understand how to deal with sources, how not to rely on one source, how to be patient and careful about details." Investigative reporters in South America are, to Reyes (1995), "the sons of Watergate." The former managing editor of the newsweekly *Semana* confesses, "Every investigative journalist has the dream of Watergate" (in Luna 1995). South American journalists fully subscribe to what Schudson calls "the myth of journalism in Watergate," the idea that *Washington Post* reporters were "responsible for Nixon's fall" as an Argentine journalist observes (Wiñazki 1996).

Watergate even provides a dictionary of words and phrases. Like elsewhere around the world, South American journalists attach the suffix "gate" to transform political events into political scandals. The list is as long as the list of recent scandals including Argentina's Swiftgate, Milkgate, and Narcogate; Brazil's Collorgate; and Colombia's Sampergate. Beyond gate, Watergatese surfaces in other instances. After Fernando Color de Mello's vice-president was sworn in, the Brazilian newsweekly *ISTOE* announced in its cover the "Fim do pesadelo," a paraphrase of Gerald Ford's, "Our national nightmare is over." Watergatese also cropped up *in All the Faces of the President* and *All the Partners of the President,* books about the Collor de Mello scandal.

Watergate offers the master script to follow and explain the evolution of scandals. It is a dramatic shortcut that, correctly or not, allows us to understand quickly the events in question by assuming a stock of common knowledge. An editor recalls that in explaining the *Proceso 8,000* to a U.S. reporter he said "Medina is Dean," comparing Medina, Samper's campaign manager, to John Dean as the whistle-blowers. But in contrast to Watergate, he added, the tapes were released at the beginning of the scandal in Colombia (Vargas 1996). An editorial in the conservative daily *El Nuevo Siglo* compared the narcotape scandal to Watergate and asked, "will it have the same consequences as that historical drama? It would be a logic conclusion." Like all scripts, Watergate features a cast of characters with different names, places and felonies. An article in the *Jornal do Brasil* (1992) established a one-on-one comparison between the main actors in Watergate and Collorgate. PC Farias was described as a kind of John Mitchell but, unlike the latter, he became enriched as a consequence of illegal activities during the election campaign. Claudio Vieira was a sort of H. R. Haldeman, controlling and distributing money and covering-up for his boss. Pedro Collor resembled John Dean for throwing mud everywhere but, in contrast to Dean, he did it during the early stages of the investigation; and secretaries Ana Acioli and Rosinette Melanias, like Rosemary Woods, stoically stood by their bosses.

In a country where Bob Woodward is the most admired journalist, play-by-play comparisons between Watergate and Collorgate were typical (Gutenberg 1998). "The futurist Watergate building on the margins of the Potomac in Washington was for Richard Nixon, twenty years ago, like the modern-like Casa da Dinda on the margins of Paranoá Lake in Brasilia for Fernando Collor de Mello. Nixon's Alagoas, differences aside, was the University of Southern California as it gave many names for the White House staff. Ron Ziegler, his Claudio Humberto, was a USC graduate. H.R. Haldeman, Nixon's Claudio Vieira, too. It was said that the group was the White House mafia, an adjective that is not even close to what is being said today about the gang of Alagoan thieves in power in Brazil" (Pontes 1992; also see Skidmore 1999).

Watergate is also the master narrative for deciphering journalism history.

Brazilian journalists compared Collorgate's effects on their press to Watergate's on the U.S. press. "The commonalities between Watergate, responsible for Nixon's resignation, and the PC Farias case are not limited to the crimes. Here and there, the press guaranteed a quality of the information despite threats and pressures," writes a Brazilian journalist (Ferreira 1992). For another journalist, "The congressional investigation of PC Farias is as important for the Brazilian press as Watergate was for the North American. Beginning with the investigations of the Washington Post, investigative journalism spread in the U.S. press (Pereira 1992). According to a retrospective article about press criticism in *Folha de São Paulo* (1997), after the impeachment of Collor de Mello, a journalism emerged that was "based on investigation, not always conscientious, that deals with wrongdoing in government. The impeachment had, among us, a position comparable to Watergate in the evolution of the U.S. press in two ways: the revitalization of the political-institutional function of journalism and the revelation of mistakes [of the press] that became apparent due to the growing influence of the media."

Watergate is also a repository of images. At the height of the *Proceso 8,000*, a Colombian cartoonist portrayed Richard Nixon gradually transmuting into Ernesto Samper. A sign that the confusion of fact and fiction was not unique to the American mind in the aftermath of Hollywood's *All the President's Men*, stills from the movie replaced images from actual events and participants. On the twenty-fifth anniversary of Watergate, Argentina's *Clarín* published an extensive article recapping the major events that featured a well-known picture of Dustin Hoffman and Robert Redford in front of a Washington Post sign. A review of Ben Bradlee's book, *A Good Life*, in a Brazilian newspaper was illustrated with a movie photo of Jason Robards in his Oscar-winning performance as Bradlee in *All the President's Men* (*Jornal do Brasil* 1995).

What's the appeal of Watergate? What purposes does Watergate serve as a constitutive myth in journalistic cultures where conditions for practicing watchdog journalism are diametrically different? Unlike the United States, most South American countries lack an equivalent of the Freedom of Information Act that can facilitate access to public information, and in the countries where similar legislation does exist, reporters consistently run against official rejection and hurdles. Congressional or judicial bodies are less likely to take journalistic denunciations and pursue investigations further. News organizations assign limited, if any, resources to devote extended time to investigate stories. And journalists have no reassurance that the publication of exposés would not put their lives on the line.

Despite these differences, making references to Watergate gets South American journalism closer to the dominant myth of contemporary watchdog journalism. Watergate confers credibility to hard-hitting, fact-grounded reporting. It legitimizes the actions of local journalists as true heirs of the best journalistic tradition. It allows reporters to bask in the glow of one of the most ubiquitous and powerful myths of contemporary journalism. It serves to put the tradition of journalism of opinion at a distance and to inch closer to the model of professional muckraking.

The ambition for credibility and legitimacy as Watergate-worth muckraking is illustrated by the decision of the newsweekly *Noticias* to pay a reportedly substantial sum of money to Carl Bernstein to write a report on the state of Argentine journalism after *Noticias* (and *Página/12*) broke major scandals that shook the Menem administration in the early 1990s. Bernstein, not a specialist in Latin American journalism, produced a long piece based on a number of interviews with local reporters. A picture of him in the historic Plaza de Mayo was featured in the cover. Why did *Noticias,* a newsweekly that mixed variety news with exposés on Menem's associates, need to hire a Watergate hall-of-famer if not to gain legitimacy, to dignify its reporting by getting the stamp of a blue-ribboned muckraker? In journalistic cultures where there are no journalists with similar cachet of professional muckraker, Woodstein is a towering presence.

Muckrakers identified with a different journalistic tradition such as Argentina's Rodolfo Walsh, Rogelio Garcia Lupo, Gregorio Selser or Raul Scalabrini Ortiz, who penned a number of exposés between the 1940s and 1970s, do not quite fit the new cultural imagination of journalism. They investigated and denounced foreign monopolies, U.S. intervention in Latin America, and military violence among other subjects. Consider Walsh, upheld as the epitome of investigative journalism by an older generation of Argentine journalists who were his friends and colleagues (Garcia Lupo in Walsh 1995; Verbitsky 1997). Walsh considered "exactitude and quickness" to be a journalist's essential qualities. His meticulousness for facts and details was evident in his investigations on corruption, human rights abuses, and corporate practices. Mixing investigative techniques with fictional narratives, his books became both literary and journalistic classics. Walsh did not conceive journalism without a political mission. His allegiance to facticity was put in the service of political militancy that took him to work for the Cuba-based Prensa Latina news service soon after the 1959 revolution and for the newspaper of the CGT Argentinos, the left-wing union organization that broke away from the one controlled by union leaders who cozied up with the military in the mid-1960s. In 1973, he joined the Montoneros, the main Peronist guerrilla group, and participated in the founding of their newspaper.[2] Whether Walsh took part in Montoneros' armed actions, or only collaborated in some of them as a member of its intelligence unit, is an open subject. After the March 1976 military coup, Walsh continued denouncing the juntas. As a member of a guerrilla group that became a clandestine organization, Walsh's reporting also went underground. The intended reader of his reporting was not a news consumer but someone who belonged to an underground network of news distribution. On the first anniversary of the 1976 coup, Walsh wrote an open letter to the military junta, an article that chronicled and denounced atrocities that became the final testimony of his watchdog reporting. The following day a death squad ambushed and killed him in a Buenos Aires street.

Published in small partisan publications as well as in mainstream newspapers and magazines, Walsh's writing combined literature and journalism, which were, in his words, "impossible to be done apart from politics in today's Argentina" (Walsh 1995: 352). He best embodied the tradition of the muckraker as political militant, a tradition that does not sit well with basic tenets of the ideology of professional journalism represented by Watergate and Woodstein. Although he continues to be an important referent for 50- and 60-something Argentine muckrakers, only few reporters in the region fashion themselves in the mirror of the journalist-as-political-crusader that Walsh represented. As a potential constitutive myth of journalism, Walsh is too politically committed for a contemporary tradition that prizes neutrality, too closely identified with the violence of the 1970s for today's antiviolence zeitgeist, and too leftist for a watchdog journalism that has gone mainstream.

PROFESSIONALISM AND THE MAINSTREAMING OF WATCHDOG JOURNALISM

The prominence of Watergate and Woodstein as cultural referents of professional muckraking is one of the most telling signs of the mainstreaming of watchdog journalism in South America. The growing concern with professional standards and practices are part of the shift of watchdog reporting from the margins to the center of press systems. Practiced by underground and under-funded publications two decades ago, muckraking has moved to mainstream news media. Having had a precarious life in leftist publications, it found room in economically solid and politically mainstream news organizations. Political persecution and the lack of interest in profit-making meant that the alternative press, and thus watchdog journalism, faced chronic economic difficulties. When practiced by alternative publications in the 1960s and the 1970s, watchdog journalism neither expected nor fit the bill of professionalism. Contributors typically included individuals with a vast range of backgrounds who rarely received a salary or monetary compensation. Political ideals more than economic or professional rewards motivated them: it was journalism as a form of political participation than as a job. Many journalists reminisce that, in the past, they held jobs in mainstream news media to earn an income while moonlighting for alternative publications to write about issues without the pressures and restrictions typical of the big press (Verbitsky 1995). Brazilian columnist Luis Nassif (1997a) recalls, "in the 1970s, we wrote for the big press and sent denunciations to the alternative press."

The result is that the big press gradually incorporated subjects and hired reporters who previously worked for alternative publications (Barcelo in Marques de Melo and Lins da Silva 1991; Nassif 1997a). The reflections of journalist Antonio Nunes about the Brazilian case apply elsewhere as well: "the big newspapers absorbed the voices, the journalists, the intellectuals, the techniques that renovated language, that is, absorbed the plurality that the alternative press had introduced" (in Medina 1987: 30). "The big press incorporated 'the journalism of denunciation' that was practiced by alternative publications in the past," according to a Colombian journalist (Santos 1996). In all countries, some of today's best-known watchdog journalists previously wrote for alternative publications that were, in the words of a veteran Argentine journalist (Garcia Lupo 1996), "schools for muckraking reporting."

As it gained room in mainstream publications, watchdog journalism experienced important changes. One transformation has been the subject of denunciations, as discussed in chapter 4. "The filth of the floor" that contemporary muckrakers rake, to use Theodore Roosevelt's expression, is mostly government malfeasance rather than corporate delinquency or social/working conditions. Related to the subject changes of reports is the fact that contemporary watchdog journalism is less impregnated by old-time ideological conflicts. "There are no ideological values today. Revolution has been replaced by accommodation. . . . It's individuals against individuals" bitterly observes a Brazilian journalist and college professor, veteran of many alternative publications (Kucinski 1997). In light of these changes, it is not surprising that Watergate, rather than turn-of-the-century U.S. muckrakers or South American journalists closer to the model that Walsh represented, fits better as the paragon of watchdog journalism. Such model represents a reporting that discloses official abuses without ties to partisan causes and only committed to professional values and standards.

Considering these transformations, watchdog journalism's growing concern about facts is not coincidence. When "news are no longer in the service of political proselytism," a Brazilian columnist writes, "journalistic rigor becomes more important" (Nassif 1997b). Journalistic rigor basically means the production of news based on facts following solid newsgathering methodologies and toning down personal politics. Although they continue to have ambiguous feelings about journalism's claiming professional mantra, journalists agree that reporters, above all, should mobilize facts to denounce wrongdoing. If nothing else, professionalism means a growing concern with facticity.

Various legal reasons account for why facts have become more important. Stories based on shreds of evidence put reporters, editors, and news organizations in legal danger. Facts are believed to be incontestable evidence of wrongdoing and legal shields protecting news organizations and journalists in libel lawsuits. As Carlyn Romano (1986: 52) writes, "With investigative stories, a gaining maxim holds that 10 percent of the story is for readers and 90 percent for lawyers. A reader may wonder why in the midst of a critical story the paper devotes so much space to a dubious person's background or to some attractive character trait. In fact, the story is being written with the jury in mind, so the paper will be able to demonstrate during a libel trial how it bent over backward to be fair." Aside from differences in the judicial systems in the United States and Latin America, Romano's observation is relevant to understand the appeal of facts. The impeding threat of expensive lawsuits has made news organizations more cautious and inclined to report wrongdoing only when facts are available.[3]

With this in mind, it comes as no surprise that journalistic evidence often needs to fit the requirements of legal evidence. Although what qualifies as legal evidence is ultimately determined by judges and congressional commissions, journalists need to be keenly aware of the potential legal implications of stories and be familiar with stipulations that decide whether the evidence of wrongdoing they had gathered can be admitted in court proceedings.

Here the connection between the requirements of legal evidence and the mainstreaming of watchdog journalism becomes apparent. Unlike alternative publications, mainstream news organizations are more concerned about legal protection. The former had an underground existence in situations of illegality created by the suppression of constitutional rights, and were intended to challenge the then-ruling news order, "to break the news blockade" as Walsh put it. The latter, instead, are well established and profit-making (rather than essentially partisan) organizations interested in the bottom line rather than championing any specific party line. With a host of legal advisors aboard, they approach any subject of investigation more cautiously than the alternative press, a press whose function was precisely the opposite, to take risks and push political boundaries. No wonder, then, that facts become mandatory for this new watchdog journalism. Journalistic facts that potentially double as legal facts are the best safeguard to fend off plaintiffs and threats of lawsuits.

Aside from providing a legal safety net, facts are the anchor of professional credibility. "You are more respected," says *Folha de São Paulo*'s managing editor, "the higher you are above political sympathies [and] political parties" (de Souza 1997). The yardstick for measuring good journalism is now etched with professional categories. And nothing is better than facts to show colleagues and readers a good professional job. Personal politics cannot be left out of reporting, journalists readily admit, but if politics overshadows the facts, the credibility of a reporter suffers. Professionalism, above all, means reporting "facts without adjectives."

Changes in the political culture are acknowledged as responsible for stressing the relevance of factual information. "Today there is more information, less ideological and more respectful of the reader," states an Argentine journalist (Tenembaum 1996). A Colombian journalist notes, "Public opinion demands the media to offer more proofs" (Padilla 1995: 26)."We used to confuse bohemia and journalism until not so long ago. The transformation came because people ask for veracity and credibility," says a Colombian editor (Torres 1996). An Argentine journalist who disclosed the Yomagate, the scandal involving relatives and associates of President Menem in drug-money laundering, states: "Opinion doesn't go in the report. The information weighs more. There are less adjectives. . . . You can't have a militant attitude. If you do, people don't believe you" (Lejtman 1996). This testimony is particularly telling considering that Lejtman investigated the story as a *Página/12* reporter, a daily that does not conceal its political sympathies in the language of objectivity and has overtly criticized the Menem administration and pounded on military officers accused of human rights abuses. Even in situations where the news media adopted clearly different political standings such as during the *Proceso 8,000,* the former managing editor for the newsweekly *Semana* observes that "credibility is compromised if you are too *antisamperista*" (Vargas 1996).[4]

As discussed in chapter 5, the foregrounding of facts does not mean that objectivity is necessarily deemed possible or desirable. What should Argentine reporters investigating human rights abuses during the last military government call Jorge Videla — assassin, dictator, former president, or general? Did Colombian journalists violate the principles of professionalism by offering facts about Pablo Escobar's illegal activities while calling him a criminal? No consensus exists in this regard. Different reporters and news organizations opt to use different adjectives some prefer an aseptic language. What seems certain is that reporting changes when citizens move away from old partisan causes and are less willing to believe the press on the basis of political sympathies. Fact-oriented reporting responds to the need of journalism to find new ways to become and be legitimate once the political world and readers' relations with news have changed.

NEW POLITICS, NEW JOURNALISM

The preceding pages indicate that the culture of professionalism has lately made significant strides in South American journalism. The requirement of licenses (in some countries) and the entrance of college graduates have changed the profile of the newsroom. The opening of more jobs fueled by the explosion of news media coupled with the existence of better remunerated positions have made possible the emergence of occupational mobility. Also, even in markets with low salaries, it is increasingly likely that journalists can earn at least a modest living. The consolidation of a system of professional inducements (awards, prestigious jobs) and the rise of celebrity journalism have fostered careerism.

How can we understand these changes? The adoption of standards identified with the tradition of professional journalism is fundamentally connected to the breakdown of traditional partisan and ideological rifts and the consolidation of news companies as market-driven organizations. Studies have argued that the emergence of a political consensus provided the backbone for the development of professional journalism in the United States (Hallin 1994). In South America, the situation has been historically different as journalism was embedded in larger political confrontations that made the achievement of political consensus impossible. As journalism was infused with the same ideological divides that tore societies apart, an agreement about professional norms was unthinkable. Political tensions and open confrontations reverberated in newsrooms. The press could not escape the political milieu that shaped its practices and identities. This situation has profoundly changed in recent years as the traditional faults of the region's politics have virtually been eliminated. The shelving of welfare-state populism and the disappearance of revolutionary politics and military intervention have been turning-point events in the history of South American politics. Most notably, the crumbling of the cold war order has resulted in the cooling off of international and domestic confrontations prevalent since the end of World War II. The attenuation of ideological conflicts has spawned a new political scenario upon which it is possible for journalism to reach a consensus around some professional principles.

There have been changes in the political cultures of both journalists and news organizations. Traditional leftist causes that gripped the identity of many journalists have become less influential. Having worked for alternative publications and participated in leftist politics during the agitated politics of the 1960s and 1970s, many of today's best-known muckrakers have shed past ideological leanings. This has not been isolated process but a reflection of the general disarray of the left in the region after the defeat of assorted domestic movements that waved the banners of socialism and communism coupled with the worldwide collapse of real socialisms. Calls for proletarian revolution and guerrilla insurrection, calls that sounded loudly two decades ago, have become relegated to marginal cultural-political pockets. This has been responsible for the virtual disappearance of alternative publications that in the past offered outlets for progressive journalism.

The culture of traditional news organizations has also changed. Newsrooms that historically featured conservative editorial lines are now populated by journalists identified with different political positions. The ebbing of leftist and populist movements and the end of cold-war confrontations have toned down red scare fears among the upper brass. A Brazilian scholar and journalist writes, "The biggest difference between the journalists of the 1980s and 1990s (especially in the last years) and those of the previous period (until the late 1970s) are the changes in the confrontations between journalists and owners" (Lisboa 1995). Today, instead, the race for prestige and market competition among news organizations has prodded traditional newspapers to weigh journalists' professional qualifications more heavily than political orientations.

Traditionally inclined to hire journalists from "inside the house" instead of weighing professional' merits, conservative news organizations were not very enthusiastic about recruiting reporters with leftist sympathies (Gilbert 1996). Nor were left-oriented journalists generally interested in working for status-quo news media. If they did, it was not unusual that they also worked for other publications more aligned with their own political convictions. For those who approached journalism as an occupation and a form of political militancy all wrapped in one, writing for conservative newspapers meant selling out, betraying their own beliefs. Not that established news organizations were too keen in hiring such reporters. In the context of cold-war witch-hunting and ideological rigidity, they were reluctant to recruit journalists who participated or sympathized with socialist and populist causes or were active in union movements. Not surprisingly, reporters generally preferred to (and sometimes could only) work for publications whose editorial policies were consistent with their political positions. This changed as newspapers are no longer identified with a press caudillo and editorial positions are not substantially different across news media. A veteran Peruvian journalist notes, "My generation was the last one of people identified with the publisher of a newspaper" (Thorndike 1995).

Nowadays it is not unusual to find journalists and columnists with past militancy in leftist causes in the newsrooms of big news media. Today's reporters are more willing to work for news organizations regardless of editorial positions. A Colombian journalist states, "I worked for *Semana, El Tiempo, El Espectador,* and *El Siglo.* This was impossible before."(The first three have been identified historically with the Liberal party and *El Siglo* has been a Conservative daily). This change means that editorial and personal politics are displaced in favor of professional concerns. While news organizations are more interested in hiring journalists and columnists on the basis of professional excellence or getting a reputation as open publications, reporters are more likely to make employment decisions on the basis of professional conditions and opportunities. As an example of these changes, Brazilian journalists point out that *O Estado de São Paulo* featured columns written by Frei Betto and *Jornal da Tarde* (owned by *O Estado* group) counted Luis Inacio da Silva ("Lula") among other columnists.[5] Another sign of the breakdown of past ideological rigidities, reporters suggest, are the many cases of journalists, formerly active in leftist politics, now holding top editorial positions in the country's most influential newspapers.

The connection between the disappearance of traditional partisan confrontations, the affirmation of a business logic among news companies, and the gradual influence of the ideal of professional journalism somewhat resembles the situation Colombia experienced in the late 1950s after the signing of the *Pacto Nacional.*[6] *El Tiempo* columnist Enrique Santos Calderón (1989) writes, "During the National Front, Colombian newspapers entered a period of professionalization. The calming down of party passions [and] the search for impartiality coincide with a period of great technological advances in which the newspapers competed like business and became consolidated as big companies. In the 1960s, reporters and columnists developed a higher professional consciousness." At that time, a similar process could not be found elsewhere in the region. The rising of the political temperature simultaneously with a wave of military coups, social unrest, and guerrilla insurrection undermined any chances of political détente that could have served as the basis for the emergence of professional journalism.

Brazil presents an interesting case, however. Personal memoirs and assorted testimonies describe the growing professionalism of Brazilian journalism, especially in the post-war years. If one of the dimensions of professional journalism is that a journalist's skills are more important than his politics and that subjectivity is downplayed, there were visible signs of professionalization. In the late 1950s, it was hard to find many countries where a journalist with known Trotskyist sympathies such as Claudio Abramo was the managing editor of a conservative and influential newspaper like *O Estado de São Paulo*. Nor was it common, especially at a time when publishers not only carefully avoided being tinted with red politics but also straightforwardly condemned radical politics, to find a media mogul like Roberto Marinho, who declared "Nobody messes with my communists." Owner of the conglomerate *Globo* and a staunch supporter of the military dictatorship, Marinho made this remark in relation to the fact that the *Globo* newspaper protected many journalists from official persecution (Dines 1993). These anecdotes reveal that the big Brazilian news organizations, although they overwhelmingly sided with the military dictatorship in the 1960s, were attuned to the culture of professional journalism earlier than their counterparts elsewhere in the region.

A strict division between professionalism and politics seem less likely in situations when news organizations decidedly take partisan standings, especially in conflictive political conditions such as the daily *La República* or the newsweekly *Caretas* in contemporary Peru. Without hiding their political inclinations, both publications have openly challenged the Fujimori administration on several fronts. A related example is Argentina's *Página/12*, described by some of its former journalists as being "militants with typewriters" (Lejtman 1996). Jettisoning any pretense of objectivity, that daily adopted an oppositional attitude vis-à-vis the Menem government and consistently disclosed cases of wrongdoing. Reporting for media explicitly committed to specific politics implies that the personal convictions of journalists are consistent with editorial standings. But even news organizations that often practice crusading reporting are concerned with facticity as a central dimension of professional journalism.

JOURNALISTIC IDENTITY IN FLUX

In summary, the ascendancy of the ideology of professional journalism is perceptible. This does not mean, however, that there is an inevitable move toward professionalism or a consensus among journalists about the legitimacy and desirability of journalism's aspiration to professional status. South American journalism cannot fully reach the ideal type of professions suggested earlier; the impulse toward an increasing, but *manqué* professionalism seems inevitable, however. Journalism continues to be plagued with contradictions that make the affirmation of professional journalism difficult, if not impossible. The historical ambiguities of journalism have not been resolved yet. If professionalism is understood in terms of training, monetary compensation, prestige system, and careerism, South American journalism does seem to have inched closer to meeting those standard definitions. But if other elements of the culture of professional journalism are considered, it becomes apparent that journalism is still being pulled in multiple directions, rather than evolving toward an ideal, U.S. model of professionalism. Contradictory tendencies shape journalistic identity in ways that escape clear-cut categories. Professional journalism means autonomy but autonomy is different across media organizations and typically restricted according to editorial interests. Professional journalism assumes that journalists can make a living as journalists but most salaries, with a few exceptions, are extremely low. Professional journalism implies the observance of a minimal set of ethical precepts, but according to newsroom grapevine, corruption has not disappeared.

No wonder many journalists experience a professional crisis caused by personal expectations clashing with newsroom limitations. The anxieties and doubts created by this situation are part of the larger shift by which journalistic identity, once defined in terms of social responsibility, has increasingly became understood along the lines of professional responsibility. Under the present circumstances, however, both understandings of journalism run against the conditions prevalent in newsrooms and the interests of news organizations. Reporters who identify with socially responsible journalism confront the reality of news organizations primarily concerned with economic gain and, only strategically with disclosing wrongdoing. Nor is the ideal of professional responsibility fully embraced. It is deemed unfeasible as long as working conditions in newsrooms are inhospitable to journalistic autonomy and while editorial interests inevitably constrain the subjects of watchdog reporting. Moreover, many journalists continue to harbor doubts about the adequacy of the professional model of journalism in countries that do not offer a suitable environment for a dispassionate reporting that is situated above the political fray. As contradictory personal desires and organizational demands shape journalistic identity, journalists hold mixed views about the purpose of journalism.

The transformations of the last two decades do not imply a total break with the past. Nor did they crystallize into a unified set of principles that defines and rules journalistic work. Torn between antagonistic expectations and shaped by the different interests of news organizations, journalism remains ambiguously defined. Although the concept of professional reporting is more visible, it has not become hegemonic. Journalism cannot be categorized either as a profession or a craft. Both the ideology of professional journalism and the tradition of crusading reporting conform differently to the diverse realities of existing *journalisms*.

PART III

WATCHDOG JOURNALISM AND
THE QUALITY OF DEMOCRACY

CHAPTER 7

Can Watchdog Journalism
Tell the Truth?

What do journalists and news organizations expect from exposés? How far or close are expectations from results? What are the intended and unintended consequences of reports? What is the impact of watchdog journalism, a kind of journalism that perhaps more than any other one explicitly sets out to have political goals? As discussed in previous chapters, a mix of professional and political motivations drive press denunciations. News organizations and journalists do harbor political goals but journalists rarely spend considerable time thinking about potential results. Journalists typically care about professional matters rather than the grand democratic goals that analysts usually assign to the press. In the mind of journalists, meeting standards of accuracy, beating deadlines, juggling sources, and scooping competitors rank more prominently than bringing political reform or democratic accountability. If concerned about consequences, the preoccupation of journalists and news organizations tend to be instrumental rather than idealistic.

Concerns about professional prestige or personal safety, for example, tend to overshadow the search for the elimination of power abuses. Hopes of achieving Woodstein fame do exist among journalists who expect to "eat president" (as they say in Colombia) or "hit a politician" (in the jargon of Argentine journalists). Some journalists may expect exposés to reach hell-of-a-story status that would get attention from colleagues, sources, and the public; others enjoy the thrill of the chase of reporting on sensitive issues. Only in the minds of paranoid officials are journalists obsessed about outcomes and decided to go out and get them. Generally, however, journalists are likely to be more concerned about the newsworthiness of a story, the opinion of editors and the upper brass, and the reaction of sources than about the outcome of a story. Even those who acknowledge political motivations are too busy to ponder what could happen, and only have a vague perception of possible effects. Critics who charge the press for irresponsibly publishing accusations are correct in observing that, for journalists, the impact on politics and personal reputation is an afterthought. Many journalists consider that devoting time to forecast outcome is a futile exercise when the future of stories is contingent on a series of unpredictable factors that are beyond their control or of any news organization. Stories may land nowhere, take unexpected turns, open a Pandora's box, or trigger further investigations. Thinking of results, however, is mostly a post-facto activity. Only in retrospective, after the dust of exposés settles, do journalists and analysts engage in discussions about the consequences of exposés. In the heat of the moment, however, when stories are in progress and the adrenaline rush is running high, reporters rarely draw arrows linking causes and effects or think about the potential impact of watchdog reporting.

The last section of this book analyzes the consequences of reporting wrongdoing. Having examined why and how watchdogs bark in the previous two sections, the analysis moves to understand the effects of watchdog journalism. This question is the common concern of the next two chapters. The intention is to discuss whether and how watchdog journalism contributes to democratic life, by exploring the outcomes of watchdog reports in regard to truth and political accountability. These are two of the ideals that, according to classic and contemporary theories, the press should cultivate and follow in a democratic order: bringing the truth and holding powers accountable. The common thread of the arguments presented in chapters 7 and 8 is that watchdog journalism positively contributes to opening discussions about truth and accountability. Limitations grounded in political-economic factors and the culture of professional journalism, however, narrow its potential to find the truth and to make the powerful responsible to citizens.

JOURNALISTIC TRUTH

Demands for truth-telling and truth-searching have characterized Latin American politics in recent decades. The agenda of human rights movements, in particular, has centered on finding out the truth about violations committed by police and military officers during the authoritarian regimes in the 1970s and 1980s. In the heyday of military dictatorships, the repression of dissident voices and widespread censorship excluded any possibility of knowing what happened to thousands who were kidnapped, tortured, and murdered. Where are the disappeared ones? Who killed them? How did security and intelligence forces operate? Such questions dealt with issues that were systematically distorted by military dictatorships. The "truth commissions" formed in many countries after democratic administrations took power expressed the increasing relevance of truth searching. The goal of those commissions was to produce accounts of past events based on testimonies from victims and relatives.

Beyond the agenda of human rights movements, the demand for truth expanded throughout Latin America. For the last two decades, truth has been the rallying cry for other social movements and political crusades, including citizens' groups that inquire about police abuses in Brazil, the roughing up and assassination of journalists in Colombia and Guatemala, the massacres of peasants in Peru, the murder of an Argentine schoolgirl in a northwestern province, and the murder of a presidential candidate in Mexico, to name a few examples. The widespread calls to know the truth, buried underneath official misinformation, attest to the legacy of human rights movements in the political culture and the centrality of demands for justice in post-authoritarian Latin America.

If truth is continually sought, perhaps it is because truth is believed to be absent. Skepticism is not new in societies where governments have chronically manipulated news. This is hardly a period of the end of innocence, when citizens realized that governments have lied to the public. Unlike in the United States in the early 1970s, this is not a post-Pentagon Papers, post-Watergate situation in which press revelations rip the veil of official deception and bring down confidence in public institutions. The magnitude of recent events has arguably intensified a preexisting belief that the truth is usually sacrificed. The tragic legacy of assassinations and disappearances disclosed in the aftermath of the military dictatorships offered a version of reality that contradicted the intense propaganda of the authoritarian regimes. Personal testimonies of victims and military officers, the discovery of mass graves, and the exhumation of corpses directly challenged official statements that rejected or minimized accusations of human rights abuses in the past.

The rise of watchdog journalism in South America is inseparable from this cultural climate. In turning truth into a widespread demand, human rights movements tilled the ground for a journalism interested in bringing out the truth hidden underneath official deception and silence. The emergence of watchdog journalism needs to be placed within this new cultural sensibility in which, for many, the search for the truth has become a priority. Like organizations pushing to know about human rights violations and police brutality, watchdog journalism is concerned with truth-telling. This is particularly remarkable considering the pervasive cynicism in the region's democracies. Enduring expectations and demands for truth telling are confronted with the persistence of wrongdoing, lies, and manipulation. "In the kingdom of lying," an Argentine editor observes (Zunino 1999), "truth-telling is revolutionary."

If lying is pervasive (as exposés demonstrate), can muckraking be the exception? Isn't journalism crossed by the same moral and political contradictions that affect the credibility of other institutions and sacrifice the truth? An observer of the Brazilian press writes, "What is happening in Brazil is a unique phenomenon in the history of the world press, a strange phenomenon responsible for the introduction of the word 'ethics' in Brazil's popular vocabulary that has become the unifying ideal of an entire nation. Never a word originated in intellectual circles became extended in a continent without anyone questioning the speed in which it has spread out. How is it possible that among all powers that rule national life, only the press has escaped the web of corruption and now it's free to denounce it?" (de Carvalho 1994).

De Carvalho's thoughts raise a number of questions about the holier than thou stand taken by many muckrakers. Can we expect watchdog reporting to deliver the truth when, as news stories reveal, no one does? Does journalism fall to attempts to falsify and hide information? Is truth-searching just a rhetorical strategy to legitimize journalism as a respectable profession and muckraking as the journalistic genre that embodies the sacrosanct values of the press? Or does truth telling genuinely reflect the intentions and the achievements of muckrakers? Does truth telling straitjacket the mission and potential contribution of journalism to a democratic society? If truth is always questioned and disputed, as philosophical relativism suggests, can it still be held as journalism's goal?

In this chapter I argue that watchdog journalism is an effort, modestly successful at best, to steer (rather than to confine) and to open (rather than to conclude) debates about truth. Watchdog journalism only constitutes an approximation to the truth, given the constrains on reporting practices and the conditions it confronts, namely the weighty role of powerful sources, the uncertainty surrounding the subjects of investigative reporting, and tacit and explicit commercial and political pressures on the newsroom. These practices, I argue, blunt muckraking's potentially sharp edge, making its relation to truth inexorably half-hearted, inconclusive, and mired in contradictions.

DEBATED TRUTHS

Truth-telling is one of the founding fictions of the democratic press. We are told that without it, the press would lose its raison d'être, becoming indistinguishable from fiction writing, preaching, or political crusading. In the canon of Western democracies, the association between press and truth harks back to classic texts that outlined the mission of the press in the modern world. Milton's (1967) *Areopagitica* still provides much of the justification to defend the indivisible relation between truth and journalism. His passionate defense of freedom of the press is informed by the conviction that, if censorship is abolished, truth will necessarily prevail over falsehood. Dismantle the system of regulations that suffocates the press and let the marketplace rule, Milton argued, and the victory of truth is guaranteed. Only through free debate a transcendental truth can be discovered. The other influential view is John Stuart Mill's argument that the pursuit of truth is inseparable from freedom of the press. The latter implies freedom of discussion, indispensable for the truth to emerge, although Mill did not believe in the discovery of transcendental truth. No opinion should be silenced because the truth results from free exchanges of ideas. Likewise, no opinion can claim to be the whole truth because "it is only by the collision of adverse opinions that the remainder of the truth has any chance of being supplied" (Mill 1975: 50). No skepticism is found in either Milton or Mill. The founding fathers of the libertarian tradition of modern journalism had no question about the existence of truth. If unattainable under existing conditions, it is because of tyrannical governments and burdensome weights on the press.

Contemporary news organizations are similarly convinced that the search for the truth presides over the newsroom. If the media are one of the most glaring examples of the elusiveness and the impossibility of truth, as postmodern authors insist, no one has told the press. Journalists and the reading public castigate or applaud the performance of the news media on the basis of whether they accurately serve truth-telling. Walter Lippman's (1922: 203) observation that "we expect the newspaper to serve us with truth however unprofitable the truth may be" still applies. Recent mainstream criticisms of U.S. journalism (Fuller 1996; Weaver 1994) continue to hold truth telling as the benchmark to evaluate the performance of the press. Professional practices, a cynical culture, and bottom-line pressures, they argue, currently undermine journalism's duty. Leftist critics also frequently blast the news media for failing to report the truth, for deceiving the public into believing that the truth is presented while serving capitalist, rather than democratic, interests. Regardless of ideological sympathies, the pursuit of truth continues to be upheld as the defining obligation of journalism.

Flushed with enthusiasm, the South American news media also typically proclaim that the search for the truth defines its mission. Lying is what wrongdoers do, not what good journalism does. One of the functions of the press is to drag out the truth tucked inside the pleats of official power. The headline celebrating the twentieth-fifth anniversary of *Veja,* the Brazilian newsmagazine that had a decisive role in the scandal that brought down former president Fernando Collor de Mello, read "25 years in search of the truth." "Truth is our permanent goal, week after week, when reporters go hunting for news to present them quickly and as clear as possible. When the news is urgent, we don't wait for the end of the week — we publish extra editions. The search of truth is never over" (*Veja* 1993). "The Business of Truth" was the title of an article in the Argentine newsweekly *Noticias* that reviewed the growing interests of the press in revealing corruption (Majul 1992). Peru's *El Comercio* (1993) applauded a congressional proposal to investigate the murder at the University of La Cantuta "to get closer to the truth." Colombian journalist and scholar Dario Javier Restrepo clearly articulated this view in calling the news media to tell the truth after revelations were made about the linkages of Liberal politicians and the Cali cartel. Restrepo (1995: 92–95) writes, "There can't be calculated silences, half-truths, or public relations spin. Truth is a right and a need in this moment. . . . The right to the truth is demanding because the [political] institutions lack credibility. . . . In a situation of crisis, surrounded by confusion and chaos, anything that it's not only the truth adds more confusion, distrust and demoralization. . . . Only the truth: that's the contribution of the media to society. . . . Doctors produce health, judges produce justice, teachers produce education, the media produce the truth."

Such statements resonate with popular and romantic versions, according to which muckraking best represents the fourth estate tradition carried forward by intrepid reporters who cut through government lies and manipulation and emerge triumphant with the truth. This is articulated in common expressions such as "the unmasking of power," "tearing the veil of secrecy," or "revealing hidden truths" that are used to describe muckraking's mission or reporters' own definition of their work. Even though the process of finding out the truth is full of lies, of individuals muddling the waters by tossing false information, obstructing investigations, and lying to the press and the public, it is believed that the truth can finally emerge, thanks to the press.

The insistence that truth is the professional rallying cry of journalism, the calling of good reporting, runs against the grain of postmodern scholarship that questions the idea that the truth can be grasped. Media scholar John Hartley (1996) has argued that tabloid and trash news best illustrates the "post-truth tendency" in journalism. They collapse the neat boundaries between true and false propositions traditionally maintained by the canon of Western journalism. Although valuable to understand the place of truth in tabloid journalism, Hartley's argument does not translate to watchdog journalism. Muckraking deliberately sets out to reveal the truth and assumes that it can be effectively brought out. Perhaps more than any other journalistic genre, it remains a solid defender of modernity unmoved by relativist views that insist on the constructed character and the absence of truth. In embracing the ideal of journalistic veracity, it takes for granted clear-cut distinctions between fabrications and accuracy, reality and unreality. This confidence in truth telling contrasts with public skepticism and the outright opposition of pessimist philosophers to the idea that the truth can ever be known. How to reconcile such skepticism with journalism's belief that the truth can effectively be attained?

THE TRUTH AND THE FACTS

Journalism assumes that truth equals the definition of facts. Even those critical voices inside the journalistic community that blame colleagues for falling short of truth telling assume that facts are the basis of truth. Relativist concepts of the truth are unlikely to shed doubts on a newsroom's faith in truth-telling as long as reporters remain convinced that news facts can be immediately identified and presented to the public. Such theories have no impact on journalism. Impenetrable bunkers against postmodernist attacks, newsrooms are seemingly impervious to the notion that facts do not exist. Anthony Smith (1980) has correctly observed that the training of journalists is shielded against relativist positions. Journalism adopts a realist position, one that holds that truth means the correspondence between information and reality: The truth can be grappled when facts are apprehended. Even in South American journalism, where the distinction between facts and opinion has always been murkier than in the United States, there is the belief that reporting consists of presenting facts and that "the truth lies at the level of facts" (Gavin 1991). The veracity of facts supports the claims to truth.

South American journalists generally reject the argument that the press simply reports reality. Most readily admit that journalism manufactures different versions of reality. They are convinced, however, that facts exist, that they can be known, that they are synonymous with true information, and that the truth is possible when all facts and information are available. This is why print reporters spend countless hours chasing sources for testimonies and paper trails that put in evidence that wrongdoing was committed. That assumption also underlies the unshakable belief that pictures forge a transparent relation between evidence and truth. For journalists, it is difficult to dispute images that show, for example, that, a presidential decree authorized the illegal sale of weapons or that the campaign treasurer wrote down the amounts of drug-money doled out to regional candidates. Photographic discourse, as William Mitchell (1992: 28) writes, "seems to provide a guaranteed way of overcoming subjectivity and getting at the real truth." Such conviction is particularly stronger among broadcast muckrakers who, because of television's requirements, are forced to assemble visual evidence that reveals the truth. A Peruvian journalist remarks, "On television you can't rely on hearsay. The people want to see, want corruption caught in the act. . . . This is why many investigations [that we did] were never broadcast. Information about torture, for example, was impossible to put it on the screen. Sixty percent of the investigations, I would say, were shelved because of that" (Arrieta 1998). "It is more difficult to prove cases on television" (Elguezabal 1999), observes an Argentine journalist, anchor and producer of many investigations for an evening newscast.

Consensus over what constitute journalistic facts makes possible to render reality visible. Even if journalists accept the idea that facts are constructed following certain rules, relativism has no room in journalism. It undermines the very basis upon which professional news reporting is organized. Like any other system devoted to the production of knowledge, journalism firmly subscribes to a specific set of rules to separate facts from nonfacts. Information that acquires fact-status such as statements from high-powered sources and audiovisual testimonies are above suspicion. Empirically observed and manipulated, they are reality itself. This is why journalism's epistemological edifice collapses if we remove the pillar of "realism as facticity." To accept the full implications of relativism, journalism would have to radically reconsider its founding principles.

To analyze muckraking's relation to truth, then, it is necessary to examine more closely how it constructs the facts of investigative stories to buttress claims of truth. This requires us to address information management practices (Schlesinger 1990), the routines and strategies that dominate news making. As sociologist Andrew Barry (1993: 492) writes, "truth is constructed through discursive practices of media institutions and the interaction between media and sources." My intention is to show that even if we follow journalism's concept that truth emerges when all facts are available for public inspection, truth would still remain elusive, out of newsroom's reach.

Truth implies perfect conditions of knowledge, absolute transparency and complete access to information. This may be inevitably utopian because knowing all the facts eludes journalism, or for that matter, any other knowledge community.

OFFICIAL SOURCES

Watchdog journalism faces more difficulties than regular reporting in defining the facts. The latter deals with routinely packaged facts, regularly covered by reporters in their beats, and industrially processed by newsrooms. It is rarely questioned that "the president addressed Congress," "two trains collided," or "the police captured a suspect in a bank robbery." The facts of these three examples are obvious, at least from a journalistic point of view. Watchdog reporters face a different animal. Facts are not immediately evident precisely because they are unknown to reporters and the public at large. The facts of wrongdoing are not daily manufactured by official sources and relayed to newsrooms. Nor do reporters come in contact with them on a daily basis. Defining the facts is the first task of investigative reporters. What happened? Who was involved? Where was wrongdoing committed? When did it happen? Why? How did it evolve?

To analyze reporters' answers to these questions it is necessary to investigate the constitutive rules of investigative reporting. Following Mitchell (1992), if we consider reporting as a speech act, it entails an understanding of the principles reporters follow to "provide evidence or arguments for the truth." The intention is to offer facts that per se, without any intervention, would reveal wrongdoing. The truth is not constructed on the basis of reporters' opinions but on what they deem to be absolute evidence that wrongdoing was committed. The truth appears authorless, sustained on proof that unanimously indicates falsity and reality. But reporters do not rely on their own opinions to proclaim that something has effectively happened (and thus is real) but on someone else's personal statements. Truth is what others declare to be true. The requirements of professional journalism dictate that they are restrained from becoming an authoritative source to declare the authenticity of claims. Only the testimonies of official sources can make the transition from personal and subjective to true and objective statements.

As discussed in chapter 4, on- and off-the-record testimonies from high-level sources are fundamental to construct the facts of watchdog reporting. Presidents, ministers, leading senators and representatives, prominent business executives, police and military chiefs, and influential presidential aides have a tremendous advantage in triggering stories of wrongdoing. Their confessions and documents not only prod newsrooms to pursue stories but are also the bread-and-butter of exposés. They have the capacity to turn hidden secrets into public truths. Had they not came forward with sensitive and compromising information, most reporters agree, it is doubtful that most exposés would have ever surfaced. Information handled down to newsrooms by high-powered sources has generally triggered exposés. Even though they are perceived to have vested interests in the reported events, powerful sources become de facto authoritative voices in defining truth. Truth equals the testimonies of powerful sources. The truth in press denunciations depends on the willingness of insiders to leak and stand behind certain information. If they are uninterested in volunteering facts, the truth does not come out. In relation to the difficulties for the press to know all details about the connections between campaign financing and the Cali cartel, Colombian columnist Maria Isabel Rueda (1996) remarks, "Perhaps we will never know the truth because the only two people who can tell the whole story are President Samper and former minister Botero." Truth in watchdog journalism is inseparable from the relation between power and knowledge. Only those in power are able to declare the truth. In turn, the capacity to establish the truth constructs and reinforces power hierarchies. Journalism defers to establish the truth or to dispute previously held truths to those in power. Asymmetric power relations inform the conditions for the production of truth.

Journalists value information that can be demonstrated according to journalism's rules of facticity, to the principles that determine what pieces of information acquire the status of facts. There is no impartial information, they say. Personal interests always drive sources to contact newsrooms so what is needed is to filter the information through strictly journalistic criteria. "Only a few denounce for patriotic reasons," observes a Colombian muckraker (Donadío 1998). Journalists are less interested in weighing the morals or the politics of sources and more inclined to evaluate the quality of information on the basis on empirical principles, and to consider whether the information conforms to editorial criteria and interests. The function of journalists, a Brazilian editor observes, is "to publish what can be proven" (de Carvalho 1997). Can a source back up his or her denunciations with evidence that is journalistically acceptable? Reflections on the morality of sources are largely absent, mainly because quid pro quo relations are assumed to be intrinsic to source-reporter contacts. Assuming the inevitability of such relations, sources and reporters push to exploit them to their advantage. For journalists, what matters is that the information is reliable and sufficiently solid to jump over editorial and legal hurdles. They balk at the idea that they need to be concerned about the motivations of sources. So what if sources generally care about themselves rather than benefiting the public, journalists observe, I have my own goals, too. Considerations about the ethics of sources are dismissed as "academic speculations" disconnected from the routines and the chaotic process of decision-making in the newsroom.

Consequently, as Edward Epstein (1975) rightly observes, self-serving sources, not reporters, establish what passes as truth. The alleged truth results not from the altruistic pursuit of the truth but from personal calculations. To Epstein, this practice deeply questions journalism's claim to truth telling. Reporters cannot challenge sources unless they want to risk relations with those who regularly act as expert testimonies and information leakers. Even though responsible reporters double-check and compare information, journalism is not designed to test the veracity of sources. Its function is to gather and circulate information. Consequently, Epstein advises, journalism should renounce truth telling. The practices of news making, he suggests, make journalism and truth two separate enterprises.

Epstein's argument suggests that morality and truth in journalism are divorced: Journalists consider information to be valuable as long as it meets professional expectations no matter what motivations prompt sources to leak information. The resulting system of truth is analogous to a Smithian social order in which the public good is achieved only when individuals pursue their own interests. The truth comes out not because sources, the ultimate definers of what passes as true, tenaciously seek the truth but because they purposefully follow self-interested goals. The world that watchdog journalism dwells on is not populated by officials or journalists inspired by ethical principles that establish that truth-telling is always necessary and desirable regardless of circumstances, but by self-interested individuals who, while searching for private advantages, may unintentionally contribute to the public good. In the name of informing the public about secret matters, journalists adopt a utilitarian attitude that justifies the methods used to obtain information regardless of why informers leak information. Journalists matter-of-factly accept that virtue in politics or in journalism is rare. Both are morally ambiguous worlds and, consequently, those individuals who pass solid information contribute to truth telling. Not surprisingly, then, the interests of strange bedfellows commonly converge in press denunciations. Reporters disgusted at human rights violations rely on information passed by military officers who, motivated by personal rivalries or philosophical differences with hard-liners, contact newsrooms. Anti-Mafia press crusaders team up with turncoats to reveal corruption schemes. Journalists opposed to drug traffickers turn to members of intelligence and drug enforcement services to get facts to catch drug barons.

But questions of truth and morality in newsgathering practices, particularly in watchdog reporting, require rethinking the utilitarian logic that elevates truth telling to the highest pedestal without any further consideration. In watchdog journalism, the process of finding the truth is plagued with moral questions that are at the core of the functioning of the press. What specifically sets watchdog journalism apart from other forms of journalism is its interest in denouncing actions that are believed to challenge certain moral principles. Wrongdoing is intelligible only against an established set of ethics. Public corruption is news because public officials are not expected to be corrupt even though citizens widely assume that official corruption is widespread. The murder of poor teenagers and street children at the hands of trigger-happy police is news because the police are supposed to protect, not to victimize, citizens. Human rights abuses contradict expectations that the military should not behave like gangs of criminals without regard for international and domestic legislation, not to mention the sanctity of human life. Wrongdoers are the subjects of news because they are perceived to affront society's rules and to betray the public trust. Watchdog journalism essentially deals with "moral disorder news" (Gans 1979), that is, news about behavior that contradicts moral expectations. It attests to the role of the media as an agent for the communication of moral values, a channel through which citizens learn about moral problems and form ideas about acceptable and nonacceptable behavior (Tester 1997). Muckrakers are crafters of society's moral order, to paraphrase media scholars James Ettema and Theodore Glasser (1998), having largely become "the collective conscience of their nations," as journalist Peter Eisner (1990) observes about Colombian muckrakers.

Although it disregards nihilist calls that we live in a postmoral world and believes, instead, in a perfectible moral world, watchdog journalism implicitly assumes that certain actions are morally reprehensible without asking why. Exposés are based on a seeming moral consensus that is rarely questioned. Considering that it is primarily concerned with public morality and truth, muckraking is not interested in delving into the ethical principles that presumably define wrongdoing. While busy trying to understand immoral activities, journalists are largely disengaged from the moral complexities and ambiguities involved in the process of newsgathering. They are not expected to weigh ethical concerns but, instead, to report information that can be presented as incontestable evidence of truth. Muckrakers assume that society can be morally better but pondering the ethics of sources and muckraking has virtually no room in journalism. Such questions sit uncomfortably in newsrooms rushed to churn out stories that are expected to meet standard norms of facticity rather than to question accepted practices.

LONG AND WINDING STORIES

Notwithstanding the efforts to render the truth transparent, the nature of the subjects of investigative stories makes it difficult for reporters to grasp all facts. Even those who can devote an exceptional amount of time to research and remain relatively isolated from pressures to produce materials regularly hardly come to know all details. The typical subjects of exposés are complex and information is tightly guarded. An Argentine journalist who uncovered the Carrasco murder says that the subject was extremely complex to investigate, for "it involved almost two hundred characters including the military, the police, the judiciary, two army garrisons, and eighty members of [Omar] Carrasco's squad" (Urien Berri 1998). Colombian journalists offer similar opinions on investigating topics like the connections between drug cartels and politics. An *El Tiempo* editor observes, "*narcoterrorism* is very difficult [to work]. After eight years we still didn't know anything. Information considered to be valid during that time was not the deepest" (Torres 1996). Covering drug issues in Colombia has always been extremely difficult given the illegal nature of operations and the almost impenetrable cloud of secrecy hovering over drug activities. The *Proceso 8,000* was complex as it essentially involved the inscrutable connections between the main political parties and the drug cartels.

The reconstruction of influence-peddling schemes offers similar problems. It involves finding out tightly kept information. Tracing money trails, for example, requires reporters to find information about foreign and local bank accounts. This information is vital to demonstrate, for example, that deposits largely exceed declared income or that balance figures contradict suspects' claims. Financial institutions are usually reluctant to report names, balance, and general movements on their accounts. According to the Peruvian newsmagazine *Caretas* (1995a), this has been a main difficulty in the investigation of corruption during the García administration: "Access to bank accounts in the 'fiscal paradises' of Gran Cayman, Panama, or Luxembourg, is extremely difficult and almost impossible for Third World countries like Peru. For U.S. officials is different given the fact that the United States has agreements with those countries." A journalist observes that official rejection of cooperation has been one of the main obstacles in the progress of investigations (Valenzuela 1997). In Argentina, many investigative reports and judicial cases have also run against similar obstacles. U.S. banks have denied requests to have access to accounts where funds were presumably deposited in relation to the bribes that executives of the Banco Nación received from IBM in exchange for a multimillion dollar contract, the illegal sale of Argentine weapons to Ecuador in 1995, and drug-money laundering operations. An editorial in the daily *Clarín* (1997) denounced the double standards of U.S. authorities who prioritize the battle against corruption and drug trafficking in bilateral relations yet are reluctant to cooperate in lifting restrictions on the secrecy of bank accounts. Without the latter, the editorial suggests, "it would be like expecting water to come out of the faucet without opening the master pipe."

The meager support of news organizations to watchdog journalism also makes difficult for journalists to gain a fuller understanding of the stories they investigate. With few human and materials resources available, they can hardly keep up with all intricacies of one story or follow-up leaks about countless cases of corruption. "There are many cases and few journalists," observes *Folha de São Paulo* managing editor (de Souza 1997). Assigning journalists to follow stories for a long time is costly, and news organizations, even those that have set up investigative teams, are generally disinclined to spend considerable resources on reporting that would not necessarily bring new, high-impact findings. Journalists observe that owners prefer quick reports that are cheap not only in terms of original investments but also that would not result in lawsuit threats and financial headaches. The decisions of some newspapers to dismantle investigative teams are revealing of the ambivalent commitment to detailed, in-depth muckraking. Editorial expectations about reporters cranking out denunciations with meager means go against what for many journalists are the essential elements of investigative reporting: time and patience to excavate the ins and outs of a maze of facts, names, and actions.

Reporters work in conditions of incomplete information at the same time that they try to outline the shape of acts of wrongdoing. Reporters are like the blind men in the Sufi tale: They might know it's a trunk, a leg, or an ear but ignore the fact that it's an elephant and do not know what the elephant looks like. They weave together events, compare inconsistencies, and consider potential ramifications of different stories. What the story really is about, where it starts, where it ends, or whether it is one or multiple stories remains unknown for quite some time. Only gradually do the contours of the story become more distinct as more information is brought to the surface.

Such situations of incomplete information persist even when reporters become more familiar with new facts. They do not wait until all pieces are put together to file a story. The urgency of journalism, its obsession with breaking news and beating the competition, demands quick results. The principle of getting the news fast and first does not escape watchdog reporting. South American muckrakers rarely have the luxury of working on particular stories full time and for extended periods. Often, they are expected to turn out stories daily. They cannot wait until the story has been fully researched. To avoid sacrificing expediency for accuracy, editors expect reporters to provide legitimate and tangible information and to take necessary precautions to avoid blunders and lawsuits. Delivered in episodes, stories remain unfinished and can take different twists, remain dormant for a while and be resuscitated later, or simply die out. New and unknown sources can potentially spring up and be willing to feed information, shedding light on other facts or challenging what was hitherto known. The evolution of the stories might prod people who were reluctant to give information to come forward. Further revelations might jump-start investigations that were abandoned for lack of attention-grabbing, eye-catching information. The lack of all details and the chance of unexpected revelations make it impossible to anticipate the future evolution and conclusion of any story. If we consider that full disclosure is a necessary condition for truth, the fact that exposés hardly meet the requirement of substantial completeness (Klaidman and Beauchamp 1987: 35) undermines muckraking's goal of reaching the truth.

Although often associated with solving a puzzle, watchdog reporting is a more unpredictable and sloppy process than putting a jigsaw puzzle together with the help of a photographic reproduction of the finished model. Reporters might have double-checked known informers and occasionally combed other sources, but suspicions linger on. The impossibility of ever fully knowing all aspects makes truth provisional and temporary. Walter Lippman singled out this problem as the Achilles' heel of journalism. For him, news is different from truth and should be kept separate from it. To record all facts is virtually impossible. If information is incomplete, then the truth is out of reach. To judge the press on the basis of its observance of truth, Lippman (1922: 228) warned, is to "misunderstand the limited nature of news, the illimitable complexity of society."

Lippman perceptively tells us that society is too difficult to pretend that the press can render comprehensive explorations of all lies and truths. But we also need to stress that journalism's proclivity to fly over extremely complex stories, to take aerial shots rather than close-ups of intricate events, does not contribute to a better grasp of the partial truths it aims to reveal out of a vast number of cases of wrongdoing. A journalistic culture engrossed with quickly produced stories that are rapidly replaced by others with equally short life spans does not help us know the truths of the "illimitable complexity of society" that journalism sets to investigate. Unless stories keep political or judicial interest or bring out new, arresting details, editors often grow impatient and are reluctant to maintain stories. The actions of prosecutors and representatives are often the respirators that provide oxygen for press denunciations after stories lose public interest and editors conclude that there are no new details forthcoming. A newsroom culture that punishes reporters who work on stories for long periods of time does not help to extend the life of stories either. Mastering the details of a prominent story, no doubt, is prized as a sign of professional distinction and excellence. But persevering on an investigation for too long, to the point that a reporter becomes identified with only one denunciation, does not help to solidify professional credentials. Reporters do not want to come across as, in the words of an Argentine journalist, "the widow of a story" (Lejtman 1996). They may be seen as single-minded, solely interested in waging personal crusades against one institution or individual, and this is unbefitting a "professional" journalist. Furthermore, it also speaks of narrow journalistic talents. When news organizations are constantly hungry for new and spellbinding stories, there are no incentives to lavish too much attention on one story. Rather, the incentives are to move quickly from story to story.

UNDER PRESSURE

The existence of *journalisms,* rather than a unified consensus around what journalism should be, makes it problematic to speak of truth in singular terms. As discussed in previous chapters, economic and political interests set the boundaries of the selection of news stories, sources, and angles. They have exposed different cases, paid different attention to the same denunciations of wrongdoing, and played different roles in bringing up and following charges.

Antithetical commercial and political interests of news organizations obscure watchdog journalism's relation to truth. Can we think of a transparent, immediate relation between reported reality and reality when the production of news cannot be separated from commerce and politics? When sales are the goal of news organizations, isn't the truth compromised, sidetracked, ignored, often sacrificed? When news organizations carefully turn some stones and leave others unturned, isn't the articulation of claims to truth entangled in politics? When the possibility of journalistic objectivity is widely questioned in the South American press, as argued in chapter 5, what are bases upon which truth can stand? When muckraking often becomes crusading journalism, can we still understand truth along the lines of a journalistic culture that rejects politics? Truth is not produced in pristine laboratories but in newsrooms subjected to internal and external down-and-dirty politics, the commercial interests of upper management, and the expectations of advertisers. The truth that watchdog journalism professes to serve is contaminated by political and business factors which slant newsgathering in different ways. Journalism, as a knowledge community, does not operate in a vacuum, but within certain constraints that determine its relation to the truth.

The relation between truth and journalism is not as seamless as journalists publicly acknowledge it to be. Journalists often know more than what they publish. Self-censorship, "the scissors in journalists' heads" as some call it, is the first filter, informed by reporters' expectations about what might hit editorial snags or require waging an uphill battle to get published. Some are sporadically willing to take that fight. The belief that potential problems inside news organizations would inevitably arise, however, discourages journalists from putting their investigative teeth into specific stories. Self-censorship is not limited to reporters. News organizations also opt to avoid rocking the boat with stories that are likely to enrage political and economic powers. Peruvian journalists, for example, talk about the negligence of media owners to criticize the Fujimori administration in the aftermath of the *Frecuencia Latina* experience in 1997 that ended with the decision of the government to revoke the citizenship from then-owner Baruch Ivcher. Aside from the painful consequences for all journalists and media owners involved, that experience sent shock waves through the news media. It was a powerful warning that patently showed the likely consequences that any news organization may suffer if it decided to peruse into official secrets in the future.

The idea of a consensus inside the press undergirds the concept of journalistic truth, but when such consensus is missing, when the truth of some news organizations and journalists is not fully embraced by others, it becomes necessary to rethink the place of truth-searching in journalism. Consider the position of the Colombian news media during the *Proceso 8,000*. For news organizations, there was not a single truth that was unanimously accepted even though the facts that were publicly available were the same. Not all news organizations reacted similarly when facts of the linkages between the 1994 Liberal election campaign and the Cali cartel were publicized. Conservative news media such as *La Prensa* and *El Siglo* seemed eager to conclude that evidence was sufficient to charge then-President Samper; their liberal counterparts, instead, warned that it would be wrong to rush to infer that the facts unequivocally stood for the truth (Ronderos and Cortés Fierro 1996).

In Peru, news media sympathetic to the Fujimori administration virulently criticized news organizations and journalists that denounced official wrongdoing. For example, the truth that some media found in excavating documents that allegedly raised doubts about the Peruvian nationality of President Fujimori (which legally made him unable to be president), was not shared by other news organizations. After *Caretas* journalist Cecilia Valenzuela reported that Fujimori was born in Japan and César Hildebrandt, the host of a television show and outspoken critic of the government, echoed her report, news organizations such as the daily *Expreso* and the newsweekly *Si* relentlessly attacked them. Articles published in *Si* accused Hildebrandt of lying and tolerating unethical reporting practices after he approved Valenzuela's decision to steal documents from the National Archives for her investigation (Ricketts 1997). Valenzuela was dubbed a "frustrated investigator" and "a novel journalist"; the episode was called "a dark page for our journalism" (Vitali 1997). A cover story read, "The investigators lied and acted maliciously" (*Si* 1997).

Dissent inside the press about the truth of denunciations was also visible in Brazil during Collorgate. The facts that, to some news organizations, exposés revealed the truth behind the corruption scheme that implicated then-president Fernando Collor de Mello did not seem so convincing to the *Globo* media group. *Globo* timidly covered the denunciations and only changed its position, throwing its support for the impeachment movement at the same time that influential political and economic actors began to criticize and take distance from Collor.

Reporters recognize that autonomy in reporting the alleged truth is strongly conditioned by the agenda of news organizations. They pragmatically assume that constraints on journalistic work are different in different media. Boundaries are in flux, not settled indefinitely, and vary across the media landscape. James Curran's (1990:133) observation is relevant here: "the extent of influence generated directly and indirectly by owners varies greatly from one news organization to another, and perhaps from one period to another." Sudden changes in the relation between the upper brass and political and economic interests, for example, might open or close opportunities to touch on different subjects. Reporters recognize that editorial policies are not necessarily written in stone and sometimes it is possible to carve out space by confronting and arm-twisting editors. Reporters are usually caught on a crossfire between the expectations of sources and the demands of editors. The emergent stories, then, are often the product of intense negotiations and diverse agendas rather than of a quixotic search for the truth.

IS THERE TRUTH?

The limitations analyzed heretofore make it necessary to rethink watchdog journalism's relation to truth telling. Watchdog reports do not stop when somehow it is decided that the truth has been finally exposed. The life span of investigative stories hinges on a number of circumstances, not on the conviction that the truth has finally emerged. What passes for truth often becomes what a handful of legitimate sources publicly agree on a given subject. Political pressures and commercial interests often influence the decisions of news organizations to abandon, resuscitate, or stretch stories indefinitely. In summary, the overwhelming weight of official sources and political and economic compromises make muckraking's allegiance to truth telling problematic. As a system that produces truth, journalism cannot escape different constraints.

One way out of this problem is to conclude that watchdog journalism should set out moderate goals rather than to uncritically proclaim to serve the truth. The whole truth, conceived as a "full depiction of reality" (Fuller 1996: 91), may never be reached but it can be approximated. It is worth preserving the notion of truth because it is desirable no matter how difficult, or impossible, it is for journalism to really attain it. Press scholar Everett Dennis (1990: 7) writes, "no matter which interpretation of the news best fits our needs and biases, most of us agree that what we really want is 'the truth,' however illusory that notion might be." If we take this position, then, journalism has to accept its limitations but should not renounce truth telling. As an institution devoted to knowledge, journalism cannot model itself after the scientific paradigm, but should strive to do its best in coming close to the truth. One of the grand goals of democratic journalism, the search for the truth needs to be maintained. The key problem here is how to approximate the truth if conditions of perfect knowledge are absent. Who determines that the truth has been finally reached? What standards should be used to measure how far or close journalism is from the truth? The exposés examined in this book suggest that the manufacture of truth is inseparable from the exercise of power. Power articulates relations of access to the process of news making (and setting the record on what the truth is) as well as the position of news organizations vis-à-vis competing economic and political forces.

An alternative solution modeled along the lines of philosophical pessimism is to eliminate truth telling from journalism's to-do list. Like any other system of knowledge, journalism can never approximate the truth basically because the production of truth is inextricably related to the production of power as Michel Foucault forcefully argued. Power always produces one-dimensional 'truths' that reify certain forms of knowledge as if they were universal. Power is inescapable from the production of knowledge information is necessarily partial, an expression of those with the capacity to determine "what passes for true" (Allen 1993). Thus journalism's relation to truth is suspicious.

But to write off truth altogether is problematic. Without any notion of truth, on what basis can we value the work of reporters who, uninterested in flattering power, put their lives on the line and strive, however imperfectly, to bring out information that challenge official versions? If we abolish truth, how can we distinguish between news organizations and journalists who diligently go along with autocrats obsessed about suppressing public discussion and those that seek to tease out official deception? The elimination of truth would lead to equate official deception with attempts from civil society, however fraught with problems, to challenge them. It would empty out the significance of struggles against official lies and repression that imagine "a good society" in which transparency, if slippery and unattainable, is still worth pursuing. Such conviction informs the admirable work of some muckrakers who earnestly believe that their work contributes to finding out what is not publicly said about official actions that are relevant to the lives of citizens. They are convinced that, as Peruvian editor Gustavo Gorriti (1998b) says, "the truth, that is, the correct representation of the facts, harms powerful individuals prone to [respond] by threats and deaths." One of the most important lessons of recent South American politics is that fights for the truth have empowered citizens from all walks of life even when knowing the full truth is seemingly out of reach and constantly vitiated by official lies. Demands to search for the truth repeatedly surface even in the face of public skepticism and disillusionment that result from previous experiences. Truth-telling needs to be preserved as a desirable ideal for the best possible democracy even though the Truth preached by the canon of U.S. journalism is inevitably contested and never fully achieved.

What is necessary is to rethink journalism's relation to truth without throwing it out. Truth telling constantly eludes journalism the same way the possibility of complete knowledge and full transparency escapes any cultural and political discourse. The whole truth can never be told, as philosopher Sissela Bok (1978) suggests. The news media, however, can have a more modest, but by no means less important role in stimulating debates about truth rather than claiming truth-telling as its province. Journalism could be on more solid ground if conceived of as a catalyst for public debate and the provider of multiple and dissident voices rather than as the flag-carrier of truth. As press scholar James Carey (1993) advocates, journalism's best hope is to preside over and within the public conversation. The truth does not belong to reporters but to public discussion. In a way, this would mean a return to liberalism's classic understanding of the relationship between the press and truth. Truth not as what should be expected in terms of journalistic accuracy, the yardstick to separate good from bad reporting, but rather the result of what Milton defined as "the conditions for a free and open encounter" among citizens.

But public debates cannot reach the truth either. Aren't cases legally closed and journalistically dead yet permanently open to debate in the public sphere? Almost three decades later and after a barrage of books, columns, a Hollywood movie and documentaries, the truth is still debated over what motivated the break-in at the Watergate offices of the Democratic National Committee and the events that brought down Richard Nixon's presidency. Likewise, can Peruvians know all details of corruption inside the Alan García administration or all abuses committed by the armed forces and intelligence agencies during the Fujimori administration? Can Argentines know all nuances of the country's corruption-ridden political system or of the instrumentation of the disappearance of thousands in the 1970s by the military juntas? Can Colombians fully know the extent of the linkages between the drug economy and political and economic powers?

Absolute truth might never be reached not only because full disclosure is unattainable, but because it would require a consensus about values and interpretations among citizens. Such consensus requires certain conditions —

absolute transparency and complete knowledge — that would make reaching the truth possible. Such conditions neither exist nor seem possible in contemporary societies. If we believe that the permanent openness of debate in the public sphere should be a fundamental aspiration of democratic societies characterized by competing and antagonistic values, we cannot expect one universal truth to emerge. Opaqueness rather than transparency, incomplete rather than full information, moral difference rather than convergence, characterize South American societies. The idea of truth that underlies arguments that assign the press the duty of truth telling requires closure, that is, premises and conclusions accepted as valid by all citizens. But, as philosopher Richard Rorty (1991) suggests, given that the definition of ground norms to establish the truth is a futile project, we should abdicate the possibility of a normative regulation upon which the truth can exist. The rational foundation of consensus leaves the possibility that criticism will always be present, making the truth, as political philosopher Jean-Marc Ferry states (1994: 207), "perpetually on trial." Truth remains forever in the eye of the beholder. Neither can moral and political differences be bridged nor can journalism bring out all the facts it pursues.

Truth is not only conditioned by the constraints of watchdog journalism but also by the impossibility of overcoming differences and reaching a permanent consensus in the public sphere. In a pragmatist mode, citizens conceive the truth of journalism as the truth that they think is good for them to believe in. Truth is understood to be what agrees with personal ideas that are not necessarily shared by others. Watchdog journalism has the capacity to open and to stimulate debates about wrongdoing but it can hardly appropriate the truth as its trophy. Its responsibility needs to be to sustain the openness of public discourse by mobilizing information that can be a springboard for debates about wrongdoing in different social realms.

CHAPTER 8

WATCHDOG JOURNALISM AND
DEMOCRATIC ACCOUNTABILITY

The idea that the press should promote accountability is enshrined in the normative ideals of the Anglo-American tradition of journalism. It is central to the liberal model that casts the press in the role of the fourth estate and assigns check-and-balance functions to news organizations. The lore of journalism as well as academic studies frequently remind us that holding government accountable is one of the most fundamental tasks of the press in a democratic order (Dennis, Gillmor, and Glasser 1989; Schudson 1995).

Accountability asks who is responsible for transgressions that are deemed to affect the public good. It assumes the need for a minimal degree of openness of the political process to the public and also that powerful interests should be subjected to the rule of law. The press is assumed to have a central role in making government open and accountable (Bernstein 1992: 38). Classical theorists such as James Bentham and James Mill conceived liberal democracy as equipped with mechanisms to ensure accountability of the governors to the governed. The responsiveness of government to citizens, a characteristic of democratic systems, requires institutions for policing state activities. As a system of rights and obligations, democracy assumes that, as political theorist Norberto Bobbio (1988: 12) writes, "Public power is regulated by general norms (fundamental or constitutional laws) and must be exercised within the framework of the laws which regulate it, while citizens have secure rights of recourse to an independent judiciary in order to establish and prevent any abuse or excessive exercise of power."

The question of political accountability is particularly relevant in the context of contemporary South American democracies. The new democracies of the region fit accepted definitions of liberal democracy: Free and competitive elections are regularly held, different parties peacefully rotate in government, and rights of freedom of association and expression are minimally observed. Notwithstanding its many limitations and imperfections, the affirmation of a liberal democratic order is not a small feat considering the proclivity of former periods of constitutional rule to be interrupted by military coups. To acknowledge these transformations is the first step to analyze the contributions of the news media to the quality of present-day democracies.

Any optimistic outlook of the contemporary situation rapidly turns sour when considering the persistent difficulties or, more pessimistically, the absence or weakness of accountability mechanisms, that is, as political scientist Guillermo O'Donnell (1997) writes, of "institutions that monitor, control, correct and/or sanction illegal acts of state institutions." This deficit is by no means new in countries where, historically, a vast array of power abuses existed unchecked and perpetrators rarely had suffered prosecution or punishment. The weakness of accountability networks has been a constant rather than a distinctive shortcoming of today's democracies in the region (see Stokes 1997).

Lately, this issue has received increasing attention. Corruption, public morality, and judicial reform have vaulted into the center of political debates. Scholars have also turned to the issue of accountability by examining, among other subjects, political graft, judiciary systems, and the effectiveness of the rule of law. Diagnoses emphasize the persistent obstacles for establishing a sturdy and effective system of control of government actions, and also indicate the urgency of this problem. Positions range from half-full glass to half-empty glass arguments. While some call attention to recent gains such as congressional and judicial investigations and the centrality of justice as a public demand, others find troubling the fragility of institutional mechanisms in monitoring abuses, prosecuting suspected criminals, punishing convicts, and, generally, limiting state powers (Ratliff and Buscaglia 1997).

In the context of this emerging debate, my interest is to analyze the relation between watchdog journalism and political accountability. How does watchdog journalism contribute to accountability? How good of a job is the news media doing in raising accountability? What difference does watchdog journalism make to dealing with a major problem of contemporary South American democracies?

POLITICAL ACCOUNTABILITY AND SKEPTICISM

Any discussion of watchdog journalism's impact on accountability needs take into consideration the sense of frustration among journalists about the state of accountability mechanisms. In my interviews, journalists offered downcast portrayals of the present situation. They were highly skeptical about the ability of press disclosures to crystallize in effective change when institutions are largely inattentive to press denunciations and are ineffective or uninterested in conducting further investigations. They offered soul-searching thoughts and wondered whether their reporting makes a difference when the performance of democratic institutions abysmally falls short of public expectations and constitutional rules. Individuals reportedly involved in wrongdoing are rarely investigated or prosecuted; if found guilty, they are not punished or receive minor sentences; and if jailed, they often get reduced sentences. Such impressions resonate with the conclusions of the first investigative team of Colombia's *El Tiempo,* which found out that its denunciations only had limited political consequences (Reyes 1998).

Even considering that the culture of South American journalism is typically described as politically skeptical, disillusion runs high. There are exceptions, however. One Brazilian journalist recognizes that although Congress and the Executive successfully blocked the creation of investigative commission to look into his denunciation of representatives involved in the votes-for-money scheme (the Senhor X story), the fact that most of them were voted out of office in the October 1998 elections suggested that watchdog reporting does make a difference (Rodrigues 1998). Some Colombian reporters find comfort in the fact that as a result of the *Proceso 8,000,* in which the press had an important role in uncovering information about linkages between drug lords and politicians, over one hundred officials have been tried and two dozens convicted (Ronderos 1998).

But the sense of failure prevails. A sample of quotes culled from my interviews with journalists attest to that. "What do we get with so many journalists killed? I am not a martyr, I have a family." "Is it worthwhile to put my head in the mouth of the wolf?" "When reporters are unprotected and other institutions neither respond nor fulfill their responsibilities, is not watchdog reporting like going to the moon without a spacesuit?" "No one was caught. I risked so much, family, friends, for what? So they can remain entrenched in power?" The thoughts of an Argentine journalist who investigated the murder and cover-up of an army private fairly represent widespread frustration and doubts: "Without the division of powers, journalism is reduced to fattening the archives that historians might use. Is it worth risking your life for a story that, at best, will be a footnote in a volume in a remote future?" (Urien Berri 1994).

It would be hard to dispute that there are sufficient reasons for such feelings. In Argentina, none of the seventy-one officials of the Menem administration legally accused of corruption between 1990 and mid-1995 have been convicted. By 1996, only three individuals received sentences out of 108 legal cases that implicated so-called "friends of power" in wrongdoing (Zunino and Amato 1996). All individuals charged in the Yomagate (the investigations about the involvement of aides to President Menem in drug-money laundering) were cleared and the cause was annulled. Judge Maria Servini de Cubria was accused of mishandling the process and received a sixty-dollar penalty from the Supreme Court. Two associates of President Menem charged with selling rotten milk to a government children's program were absolved. In Brazil, none of the eighteen members of Congress investigated in relation to corruption in the Budget Commission were indicted. Four resigned, eight were absolved, and six were banned from holding public office. The title of an account of the case expressed the sense of frustration among the journalists who authored the investigation: "The Owners of Congress: The Farce of the Congressional Investigation of the Budget [Commission]" (Krieger, Rodrigues, and Bonassa 1994).

Certainly, journalists are not alone in feeling disappointed and skeptical about the solidity of accountability mechanisms and about the failure of the justice system in meeting expectations of fairness and impartiality. The sentiment of impunity is widespread in South American democracies. Typically, whenever a case of corruption surfaces, the public is doubtful that institutions will act effectively. Brazilians who petitioned the impeachment of President Fernando Collor were concerned that the investigations would not result in legal sanctions and feared that "everything [would] be amicably resolved" (Giannotti 1992). Argentines who mobilized to pressure authorities to investigate the murder of an army private were also preoccupied about that, like in previous cases of official wrongdoing, nobody would be punished (Urien Berri 1994: 6). A poll taken in Lima and Great Lima in July 1995 showed that only 17 percent of the public had a good image of the judiciary, 50 percent thought they did an adequate job, and 30 percent had a bad image (Datum 1995). In Argentina, the credibility of the judiciary fell to 7 percent in 1996 (Zunino and Amato 1996). A survey shows that only 25 percent of the population trusts the justice system in the region (*Wall Street Journal* 1998).

Are expectations about the ability of press denunciations to raise accountability too ambitious in societies that have deep-seated problems in monitoring official actions and establishing independent judicial systems? Can journalism foster accountability regardless of the actions (or inaction) of other institutions? What should we credit journalism for?

OUTRAGE AND REFORM

To delve into these questions, we need to approach investigative journalism in terms of its political consequences. This is one of the merits of the study by David Protess (1992) and co-authors: In moving the analysis of investigative journalism from methodological and procedural matters to consequences, they open a rich area to reflect upon the actual and potential contributions of the press to political change. This is expressed in the authors' understanding of investigative journalism as "the journalism of outrage." They argue that the primary goal of muckraking is building policy agendas and generating policy reforms. Success in achieving such goals depends, they contend, on the participation of journalists in coalitions that can introduce and shepherd reforms. Only when journalists form coalitions with policy makers, investigative reporting has better chances of having wider repercussions. This argument is offered as an alternative to the "mobilization model" that posits that reform follows an outraged public that demands change and puts pressure on policy makers. Policy reform, instead, results from the combined actions of journalists and government officials rather than from direct or indirect public outcry activated by press denunciations.

This study offers valuable insights to frame the analysis about the linkages between watchdog journalism and political accountability in South America. Two sets of questions can be raised.

First, what happens when press revelations of wrongdoing do not generate outrage? What qualifies as an outraged public? Should non-stop media attention be accepted as a telling sign of outrage? What about attitudes measured in opinion polls? Is public mobilization against individuals and/or institutions suspected of having committed abuses necessary to conclude that revelations have triggered outrage? Furthermore, whose outrage determines that a given exposé is, indeed, outrageous? It does not require particular brilliance to assert that regardless of the substance of the denunciations, different publics react differently to revelations. What some publics may find shocking, others may tolerate or simply ignore. Although some transgressions are more likely to meet public response, reactions are unpredictable, no matter how offensive the content may seem to some observers and audiences. Here the issue is not that outrageousness varies across political cultures but, rather, that the same subject does not provoke similar reactions even in the same country within a short period of time. Because reactions cannot be assumed or predicted from press disclosures, it is problematic to view outrage as the defining characteristic of watchdog journalism. What needs to be explained is, under what conditions press disclosures are more likely to outrage publics and have a large political impact?

Second, what happens when watchdog journalism does not result in policy reforms? Arguably, none of the major denunciations in contemporary Latin America has crystallized in substantial reforms. Of all stories analyzed in this book, only the investigation of the murder and cover-up of Army private Omar Carrasco in Argentina contributed to a major reform, the end of the 1901 law that established the mandatory military service for 18-year-old males. Journalists did not imagine or expect that their coverage would add efforts to substantial change. Nor was reform the consequence of press denunciations, according to a journalist who extensively investigated the events (Urien Berri 1998). The denunciations and intense media attention, however, gave impetus to existing proposals to modify the military service and to a groundswell movement that finally inclined the Menem administration to push for the abolition of the service two months after the scandal broke. The administration, however, rejected the argument that the Carrasco murder was an important factor in its decision. Observers concluded that the move responded to an electoral strategy to appeal to young voters and families in the 1995 presidential election (Barcelona 1994).

Aside from this case, policy reforms have not been implemented despite continuous exposés and grandiose official promises. There are no convincing signs that police violence has receded in Brazil, that drug trafficking cartels have less influence in Colombian politics, that the power and autonomy of Peruvian intelligence services has been curbed, or that official corruption has been eradicated in Argentina. No question, it would be foolish to assume that press exposés could single-handedly ameliorate (let alone eliminate) ingrained problems in South American societies. Even if we take a minimally optimistic standpoint, the resolution of these problems requires formidable political will and appropriate conditions. As a leading columnist for Colombia's *El Tiempo* notes, "To extirpate official and private corruption is a monumental challenge, a serious, methodical and long-term task that demands a clear and persistent strategy and an intelligent and skillful tactic. Neither occasional actions nor press headlines can remove such a deep-rooted phenomenon" (Santos Calderón 1998).

The lack of reform in the aftermath of press revelations can hardly be attributed to journalism's disinterest in collaborating with officials, or the lack of public pressure to put an end to specific violations. Survey research shows wide public discontent about official corruption (*Wall Street Journal* 1998). Reasons for the absence of substantial changes in assorted political and social areas are too complex to be fully discussed within the limits of this study and certainly await extensive attention. In light of this persistent difficulty, then, it is worth asking whether muckraking is a toothless tiger. Given the tangible limitations of journalism, the ingrained nature of different forms of wrongdoing, and the sluggish attempts for passing reforms, how does watchdog journalism contribute to political accountability?

Casting a wide analytical net is necessary to deal with this question. Possible contributions of press exposés can be many. It is exceedingly complicated to attribute to watchdog journalism direct responsibility in specific political developments. Denunciations can embolden reporters and news organizations to disclose wrongdoing (and thus add efforts in the scrutiny of powerful interests), especially when persistent antipress violence drives journalists to self-censorship. They can sharpen public awareness about the ineffectiveness of institutions that monitor abuses and sanction transgressors. Watchdog journalism can deter potential acts of wrongdoing by showing that some news organizations have a relentless appetite for juicy leaks on certain issues. Denunciations can strengthen the role of the news media as an institution with check-and-balance functions. And they can sustain momentum and give visibility to social movements, electoral alliances, and wide political coalitions that push anti-corruption and human rights issues in contemporary South American democracies.

The difficulty of offering conclusive evidence to support these speculations is related to the larger problem of grasping the long-term effects of watchdog journalism. What are the results of press denunciations over an extended period of time? In democracies where wrongdoing and legal impunity have been pervasive, does watchdog journalism nurture a sense that accountability is absent? If reforms are notoriously absent, does it fuel sentiments of political inefficacy and deepen the crisis of credibility of political institutions? Because watchdog journalism actually contributes to a variety of political outcomes, it is necessary to analyze its relation to political accountability beyond whether it does (or not) generate political reforms.

WATCHDOG JOURNALISM AND PUBLIC OUTRAGE

Let me first explore the issue of public outrage in press disclosures. Outrage needs to be kept separate from watchdog journalism for it belongs to the dynamics of political scandals and cannot be predicated as a necessary outcome of press denunciations. Scandals and muckraking have a close affinity but are not identical. Denunciations of extensive corruption or atrocious crimes that barely leave a ripple in public opinion attest to the fact that watchdog reporting does not necessarily lead to scandals. Likewise, scandals are not always born out of press denunciations. The actions of prosecutors, for example, also initiate and maintain scandals. A brief incursion into the definition of scandals may help to clarify this point.

Although scandals have been defined as "corruption revealed" (Lowi 1988), more than publicized corruption is required for scandals to materialize. Just because the press catches a government official embezzling funds or involved in human rights violations, scandals do not consistently follow. Sociologist John B. Thompson's concept of scandals offers valuable ideas to examine this issue. He suggests that scandals have four characteristics. First, they involve "transgressions of certain values, norms, or moral codes." Second, such transgressions "are known or strongly believed to occur or exist by individuals [non-participants] other than those directly involved." Third, "some non-participants disapprove of the actions or events and may be offended by the transgression." Fourth, "some non-participants express their disapproval by publicly denouncing the actions or events" (Thompson 1997: 39).[1]

Watchdog reporting plays a fundamental role in regard to the second requirement. It turns private affairs into public issues by revealing transgressions that were known only to participants and insiders. Simply put, no public knowledge, no scandal. This is why the news media have an essential role in the dynamics of contemporary scandals. All scandals are media scandals. In times when the media have unmatched capacity to be linchpins between disparate social worlds, at both national and global levels, news organizations are the catalyst in the process by which secret illegalities become public affairs. Whether revealed transgressions meet public condemnation and are followed by expressions of disapproval is only tangentially related to press denunciations. Disclosures of "scandalous" behavior do not always scandalize publics. What publicized transgressions scandalize publics and are the catalysts for scandals? What makes an outrageous story outrageous?

A combination of endogenous and exogenous factors may determine whether a story jolts public opinion, is followed by public indignation, or is lost on the public's radar. It seems virtually impossible to produce a parsimonious explanation that could account for all possible variations in reactions to press denunciations. The complexity of the formation and changes in public opinion present formidable obstacles to suggesting a set of infallible principles that would explain (much less anticipate) reaction to press exposés (Lemert 1981). What we can aim, however, is to map out different aspects that need to be considered to understand the potential impact of watchdog stories.

Are there certain topics that are more likely to generate public outrage and prompt political action? Consider the 1994 press denunciations of linkages between Liberal politicians and drug barons in Colombia. If we follow several indicators of the public mood, from opinion polls to public mobilization, it would be hard to argue that the story captured the attention of large segments of the population even though journalists call it "the biggest scandal of political corruption in Colombia's history" (Vargas, Lesmes, and Tellez 1996: 13), and, for a member of the opposition, it was "the biggest electoral scandal that the nation had ever experienced" (Victoria 1997: 13). After taped conversations between drug lords and Liberal politicians were made public, the story hit a lull and public opinion seemed unaffected by the brewing scandal. At the height of the *Proceso 8,000*, as the scandal became known, an analyst observed, "[There is] a notorious deficit of citizenship, of civil society, an alarming apathy of the community" (Cepeda Ulloa 1996). A journalist concluded: "The Colombian people are sitting this crisis out. In any other country in the hemisphere, a government scandal of these dimensions would have the population in the streets, yelling for the heads of the crooks. But that requires hope that things can change and that an alternative exists. There is alienation, silence, indifference" (Carrigan 1996: 10). Moreover, there were signs that citizens grew tired of the scandal. The remarkable amount of attention that the media devoted to the issue could not get the interest of jaded and confused readers, noted *El Tiempo* ombudsman (Villar Borda 1996).[2]

In contrast, Argentine journalist Horacio Verbitsky's story about death flights during the last military dictatorship jolted public opinion. Adolfo Scilingo, a former Navy captain, offered Verbitsky a chilling account of regular flights in which scores of individuals kidnapped by military squads were dumped live into the Rio de la Plata. Thanks to the labors of the 1984 truth commission appointed by then-President Raul Alfonsín, the gavel-to-gavel broadcast of the 1985 trial of the military juntas, and press reports, plenty of information about the planning and execution of the dirty war had come out since the end of the authoritarian regime. Scilingo's testimony, however, got much attention and renewed debate about one of the most dramatic chapters of Argentine history. One of the most important consequences was that armed forces commander General Martin Balza declared in front of large television audience that "mistakes" were made in the "conflict among

Argentines." It was the very first time that a military officer, let alone the country's top military official, publicly dissented, even in a carefully parsed language, with the line that the armed forces had pushed for over two decades about the repression of political dissidents in the 1970s.

Of course, we cannot infer from these examples that revelations about human rights abuses are more likely to trigger public indignation than about graft or linkages between elected officials and criminals. Some exposés of graft and influence-peddling have recently resulted in public indignation; other stories about human rights violations had limited repercussion. Public indifference to revelations implicating Liberal politicians in receiving funds from the Cali cartel could be accounted on the fact that it was essentially a political insider's story removed from most people's lives. In a country where a minority of citizens regularly votes, it is not surprising that revelations about linkages between drug traffickers and the political class did not receive much attention beyond elite circles. Likewise, in Brazil, the fact that that the scandal surrounding the Budget Commission in 1993 caused few ripples was particularly remarkable in contrast to the public uproar and mobilization during Collorgate the previous year. The same Congress that swiftly undid the Collor administration was engulfed in a wide-ranging scandal that did not generate public commotion.

Does political impact depend on whether the subject of denunciations affects large numbers of citizens? In their study of Watergate and public opinion, Kurt and Gladys Lang (1983) argue that public interest and involvement are higher when the issue at stake is a "low threshold" problem. Such problems affect almost everyone and are of personal concern to sizable segments of the population. This could be the reason why most Colombians were unruffled about the disclosures that funds from the Cali cartel were funneled into the 1994 Liberal election campaign. The revelations were of interest and directly affected political elites. The newsweekly *Semana* concluded: "It seems that the *Proceso 8,000* is a scandal for the ruling class. Members of the social class of [president] Ernesto Samper and [defense minister] Fernando Botero more than the people find drug trafficking and 'hot monies' outrageous. High society is polarized like never before around the five billion pesos of [drug barons] Rodriguez Orejuela. In those circles, there is a Puritanism vis-à-vis the influence of drug trafficking that has broken the monolithic unity that has always ruled. . . . In those high circles, drug politics was though to be real among regional bosses, not inside the world of the Samper Pizano o Botero Zea. Outside that social group, the majority of Colombians are not outraged" (*Semana* 1995b: 51). According to news reports, primarily middle-class students and upper-class women participated in the demonstrations that petitioned the resignation of President Samper (also see Leal Buitrago 1996).

Conversely, the visibility and impact of the investigation of the murder and cover-up of private Omar Carrasco in Argentina can be attributed to the fact that it was a low-threshold issue. Even though it originally began as a police story involving the confusing death of an army private in the southwestern province of Neuquen, the revelations quickly gained national attention and gave way to a full-fledged scandal involving high-ranking military authorities. The abuses of army draftees are legendary in Argentine culture, especially after the rampant mistreatment of recruits during the 1982 Malvinas/Falklands war was widely publicized. *Colimba,* the popular name for the now-defunct service, expressed the widespread belief that privates were subjected to abuses. It stands for running (*COrrer*), cleaning (*LIMpiar*) and sweeping (*BArrer*). The Carrasco story resonated with a public opinion familiar with the infamous plights of privates through first-hand knowledge or accounts of friends and relatives. Soon after the story broke, broadcasting and print media featured testimonies of parents and privates about abuses. The daily *La Nación* (1994) stated, "The diffusion of the Carrasco case triggered reactions about the treatments of citizens in the military service."

The low threshold variable as litmus test of political impact, however, does not apply consistently to all press denunciations. Exposés on subjects that affect larger numbers made no political splash. *Folha de São Paulo*'s investigation on racism in Brazil, for example, virtually left no political traces and faded out shortly after publication (Rodrigues 1998). Some revelations that presumably only affected or were of immediate interests to a minority instead generated wide reactions. In Argentina, the scandals that followed revelations about the unlawful sale of weapons to Ecuador in 1995 and about the illicit dealings between executives of IBM Argentina and the *Banco de la Nación Argentina* in the negotiation of a multi-million dollar sale of computer equipment to the country's largest financial institution has been in the front pages for years, even though large segments of the population have not shown tremendous interest in the story. Neither story has it ranked high in opinion polls nor have mobilizations been staged to repudiate illegalities. Although the news media have devoted nonstop attention to these issues, the public did not seem terribly interested in whether officials pocketed large sums of money by negotiating arms deals or computer equipment.

The low threshold argument assumes that all citizens are somewhat equal in the court of public opinion. This goes against the conclusion that citizens with unequal economic means, cultural capital, media access, and consumption power have dissimilar political influence and weight in public opinion. This raises the question of who needs to be outraged for a denunciation to have sustained media and political life. Does the political bite of exposés depend on whether the subject of wrongdoing is of immediate interest to influential political and economic elites? Or is it contingent on whether it affects the so-called attentive public, middle- and upper-middle class citizens who form the bulk of the readership of newspapers and newsweeklies? Are denunciations of the plights that affect large numbers of citizens removed from mainstream public opinion condemned to have little, if any, repercussion?

The production values of a story may also determine the political impact of press denunciations. The presence or absence of specific news "hooks" — such as titillating details, media celebrities, or human drama — are important in shaping the kind of public reaction and political impact. It is hard to predict the right mix of ingredients that would inevitably guarantee wide repercussions. Yet journalists generally believed that stories that combine elements of celebrity and sensationalism are likely to garner more attention than those full of legalese and paper trails. On-the-record testimonies by prominent officials or prominent individuals are more likely to create a commotion than accusations that do not identify the source or feature accusers who are unknown to most readers and audiences. *Folha de São Paulo*'s disclosures about illegalities involving Fernando Collor's campaign treasurer Paulo Cesar Farias that were published during the 1989 election campaign barely registered in the radar of public opinion. Yet *Veja*'s interview with Pedro Collor in May 1992 caused a commotion and triggered the political and judicial process that ended with his brother's presidency. Denunciations that appeal to voyeuristic appetites and allow the public to peek at wrongdoers caught in the act leave a mark too. This is what many denunciations of Argentina's newscast *Telenoche Investiga* have featured. Images of bribe-taking police officers and mayors or a judge participating in smuggling operations, unaware of the presence of hidden cameras, have generated much commentary and, arguably, have become ingrained in the public perception as emblematic examples of official corruption.

Timing also determines the impact of stories. Brazilian observers state that the wide repercussions of the exposés on Fernando Collor hit a nerve in 1992, and not earlier because of the economic situation at that time. The public seems more willing to tolerate behavior in exchange for lower inflation or lower unemployment. In contrast, when inflation runs high and other economic indicators are out of control, elites and citizens rapidly lose patience and are less willing to look the other way when public officials are embroiled in acts of wrongdoing. In addition, the timing of a particular story in relation to other press exposés on the same subject is important. When public opinion has already been exposed to denunciations on similar subjects, it is less likely that public reaction would be comparable to the first denunciations. Desensitized to public corruption and human rights violations after exposure to atrocities and all imaginable possible forms of graft, the public becomes inoculated to press denunciations, unfazed by new exposés that reiterate that another official has acted illegally. Particularly when legal punishments are rare and the sense of impunity is pervasive, the paradox is that a succession of denunciations engenders a public anaesthetized, instead of increasingly alert, to wrongdoing. Press denunciations become a sort of the white noise of contemporary democracies in South America, regularly present but ignored by the vast majority.

The identity of the journalist and the news organization may also determine the political ramifications of a story. A story published in a local newspaper is unlikely to receive wide attention or have great repercussions. Denunciations made by Colombian regional dailies, for example, only got national attention when Bogotá-based papers (Ronderos and Cortés 1996) picked them up. Likewise, the fact that some journalists are household names and enjoy considerable influence in elite circles may determine the political reach of a given exposé. A little-known reporter, especially if she works for a small publication or media company, lacks sufficient cachet to turn her denunciations into high-profile stories. Unfortunately, some stories often get attention only when reporters become victims of violence. Argentine reporter Hernán López Echagüe asserts that his investigation about the ties between political bigwigs and gangs in the Buenos Aires central food market only received attention after he was roughed up and the media extensively covered the event (in Vázquez 1998). The long investigation of the newsweekly *Noticias* on businessman Alfredo Yabrán, suspected of having ties to Mafia-like groups and to the Menem administration, rapidly gained widespread attention and entered in a different phase after news photographer José Luis Cabezas, who was covering the story, was murdered in January 1997. Media attention on Cabezas' gruesome murder and subsequent public mobilization to demand justice heightened the political impact of the investigation. The post-mortem prominence of the slain photojournalist, fueled by intense public mobilization and the actions of news organizations, catapulted the exposé to the center of Argentine politics and accelerated judicial and political actions on the Yabrán case.

In summary, journalists may determine that a given exposé is a political bombshell but the public would not necessarily react as expected. The subject of the denunciation and its resonance with the public mood, the production values of stories, the timing of disclosures, and the visibility of the muckraker and news organization shape the potential political outcome of a given exposé.

WATCHDOG JOURNALISM AND SCANDALS

But even in cases when press denunciations trigger public outrage, should we conclude that journalism effectively increases political accountability? What if sizable portions of the public become outraged, but there are no further investigations, or individuals found guilty of criminal activities are not legally punished? What yardstick should we use to measure the contributions of the press to accountability?

The political evolution of press denunciations does not strictly march to the beat of public opinion. What happens after an exposé is published is contingent on unforeseen reasons and processes that are only tangentially related to the performance of the news media. Factors intrinsic and extrinsic to the stories may determine whether press denunciations stir the public blood or disappear without a trace. The analysis of press and accountability, however, needs to look beyond the presence or absence of outrage. Exposés may touch off congressional and judicial investigations and spark public mobilization demanding partial or substantial changes and political crises which, subsequently, may result in judicial and political resolutions. Watchdog journalism is likely to have a stronger political bite when institutions coalesce together and collectively contribute to making perpetrators publicly responsible for their crimes.

Against popular and scholarly media-centric approaches that conclude that the news media have exceptional powers in bringing down ministers or presidents, it is necessary to analyze the balance of congressional forces, the configuration of the judiciary system, and the response of organized interests to gauge the consequences of media exposés. Especially in countries where the news media have not historically kept distance vis-à-vis powerful interests but offer channels for doing politics by other means, it is a mistake to examine the relations between press and accountability independently from larger political dynamics. The response of Congress and prosecution offices and the position of major pressure groups (business organizations, armed forces) are crucial in determining the political impact of press exposés.

Congressional Actions

Congressional response is fundamental in shaping the political impact of exposés. There have been countless cases in which press denunciations met congressional inaction. For example, congressional stonewalling of initiatives to pursue denunciations that involved members of the Menem and Fujimori administrations explains why many exposés in the last decade did not have longer political lives. Both administrations counted on congressional majorities that opposed investigations into denunciations of corruption and human rights abuses. The Brazilian congress rejected the petition for the formation of a committee to investigate charges of influence peddling denounced by *Folha de São Paulo* in 1997. In June 1996 in Colombia, when the presidentially appointed Commission of Accusations concluded that there was no evidence to indict President Ernesto Samper the course of the political and judicial processes changed. In a decision that was highly criticized by some (including business groups and the U.S. government) and supported by others (unions and grassroots organizations), a Liberal-dominated congress voted 111 against 43 to conclude the *Proceso 8,000* investigations (see Cepeda Ulloa 1996).[3]

Conversely, the role of Congress was partially responsible for the greater response to press denunciations about the illegal dealings of then-President Fernando Collor de Mello. *Veja*'s explosive interview with Pedro Collor de Mello in May 1992 is usually credited with having sparked the scandal that eventually brought down the government. The accusations circled around Fernando's right hand Paulo Cesar (PC) Farias of influence-peddling, extortion, and electoral fraud. Before Pedro went public, there were lingering suspicions that Fernando Collor not only took political advantage in extorting funds from contributors in return for future favors but that he also personally enriched from the operations. The interview generated momentum for congressional investigation. A few weeks later, *Veja* pulled a one-two punch with a story about the tax files of PC Farias based on information reportedly passed by a prominent representative of the *Partido dos Trabalhadores* (PT), Collor's main opposition in Congress. Immediately after, the opposition requested an investigation into press revelations about Farias' activities and

Collor's involvement. Some of its members went as far as calling the president to resign: Luis Inacio "Lula" da Silva, former PT presidential candidate, was quoted as saying that "the exit of Collor is the only exit out of the crisis" (*Jornal do Brasil* 1992b). The PMDB, the party with the largest representation in Congress, endorsed the request. It was here, early in the process, that the lack of a solid congressional majority became one of Collor's most serious political liabilities. The fragile electoral coalition that carried him to the presidency was insufficient to reject or postpone further investigations. In a highly fragmented party system, the firm determination of the PMDB and the PT to investigate and criminally charge Collor was decisive.

The *Commissão Parlamentar de Inquerito* (CPI, the Congressional Commission of Inquiry) held its first meeting on June 1, 1992. The Collor administration intended to prevent the investigation from reaching the president by framing the process as a question of tax evasion involving Farias rather than a matter of influence peddling or extortion. The first witness called by the CPI, Pedro Collor, confirmed his early accusations of Farias but toned down the charges on his brother. Later, prominent businessmen also testified and fired heavy ammunition at Farias and other members of the Collor government. They confirmed that Farias headed an influence peddling scheme and described in detail its organization and dealings. Toward the end of June, calls for impeachment from congressmen and a few governors began to sound louder. Luiz Fleury, then-governor of São Paulo, was quoted as affirming that "there is already proof against Collor" (*Folha de São Paulo* 1992b). Collor's strategy did not seem to work and the tables seem to be turning against him as most CPI members declared that they were willing to extend the investigations to Fernando Collor even though the original mandate was to investigate Farias. By the beginning of July, Collor became the target of investigations. This shift was clear in the press: the *Jornal do Brasil* coverage of the crisis featured a bull's eye with "Collor" at the center, *Folha*'s reporting was entitled Collorgate, the paper displayed an image that combined Collor's and Farias's faces. The secretaries of the two men and driver Eriberto França were crucial witnesses in the CPI investigations. Their testimonies provided the smoking gun, showing that monies from Farias's illegal operations were funneled into Collor's accounts. After several testimonies and mounting criticisms of Collor de Mello from different groups, the CPI finished its investigations at the end of August. It concluded that Fernando Collor knew about PC Farias's illegal activities, benefited from the influence peddling scheme, lied when he asserted that he paid all his personal accounts, and used funds from Farias's scheme to pay for renovations in his mansion. The testimony of driver Eriberto França, who has been previously interviewed by newsweekly *ISTOE*, was decisive and particularly damaging to Collor's political and legal situation. As he did in the interview, França reiterated that he transported and personally deposited funds from Farias's operations into ghost accounts owned by Collor's secretary. He also contradicted Collor's assertion that he had not met or talked with PC Farias in several years.

The president of the Brazilian Press Association, together with the president of the main lawyers organization, presented the formal request for impeachment on August 28, 1992. The request was not exceptional in Brazilian history: It was the sixth time in the hundred year-old Republic that Congress had asked for impeachment. The petition stated, "if Collor wants to serve Brazil, he must resign," and stressed the danger of the absence of governability and civil disobedience. It also expressed that Collor lost moral authority to govern the country. Two-thirds of the votes in Congress were needed for impeachment proceedings to move forward. It became clear that there was a move in favor of impeachment. On September 30, 441 congressional representatives voted for trial and destitution, 38 against, 1 abstention, and 23 absent. In early December, the Senate overwhelmingly passed a resolution to pursue political charges. On December 27, the Supreme Court denied Collor's request to postpone the Senate's proposal. Soon after impeachment proceedings began, Collor resigned and the Senate decided to ban him from holding public office for five years.[4] Compared to several requests for investigations that were stonewalled by congressional majorities in Argentina, Colombia, and Peru, Collor's unfavorable balance of forces in Congress, tilted further by public mobilization and criticisms from influential actors, resulted in a different political outcome.

Judicial Actions

The response of judicial offices is also decisive in shaping the outcomes of press denunciations. Argentine muckraker Horacio Verbitsky (1993) has argued that the manipulation of the judiciary has considerably limited the effects of press denunciations. The decision of the Menem administration to stack the Supreme Court by increasing the number of justices from five to nine and appointing most members, was aimed to protect the government from the legal consequences of press exposés. In many cases, Verbitsky shows, the connivance of judges with government officials was responsible for the mishandling of legal processes and the exoneration of individuals accused of wrongdoing, or the application of mild sentences.

In Colombia, many observers concluded that the creation of the office of the chief prosecutor, the retirement of prosecutor Gustavo de Greiff, and the appointment of Alfonso Valdivieso were crucial for moving forward the investigations about the linkages between the Cali cartel and Liberal politicians. Political scientist Francisco Leal Buitrago (1996: 34) writes, "Most public opinion expectations are on the Chief Prosecutor's office" despite the fragility and institutional weakness of the office. In contrast to De Greiff's opposition to the prosecution of druglords and the possibility of extradition and trial in the United States, Valdivieso aggressively confronted drug trafficking. In August 16, 1994, two days before he stepped down, De Greiff shelved the cause of the *narcotapes* that was opened in June after Conservative politician Andrés Pastrana gave the tapes to then-President César Gaviria. One of the first decisions of the newly appointed chief prosecutor was to bring the *Proceso 8,000* from Cali to Bogotá in September. Valdivieso reopened the investigation on the *narcotapes* in April 1995. At a press conference, he announced the beginning of the investigation of nine Liberal representatives and two other officials to establish whether they had received monies from the Cali cartel. Five more congressmen were added to the list in June. Valdivieso's decision to call Santiago Medina (treasurer of the 1994 Liberal campaign) and then-defense minister Fernando Botero (Samper's former campaign manager) to testify was both a political and judicial watershed. Both Medina and Botero were later arrested. Botero's testimony was particularly important because it became the main legal evidence that incriminated President Samper. In February 1996, after months of investigations and citations ordered by his office and the Supreme Court, Valdivieso filed charges against President Samper for illicit enrichment, cover-up, and fraud. Leal Buitrago (1996: 35) argues that the prosecution tried to strengthen its position by "politicizing the investigation and encouraging public condemnation of the politicians involved [in the cause], even of president Samper. . . . Against the opposition of individuals and groups that used the protection of different institutions (e.g. the Executive, the Council of State, the National Electoral Council), the [prosecutor] was pushed to politicize the process as a defense mechanism."

Pressure Groups

In countries where, historically, diverse political and economic interests have exerted clear influence, it is not surprising that their attitude has also been decisive in shaping the outcomes of press denunciations. The positions of business groups, the military, foreign interests, trade unions, and organized publics are key to understand what happened after press exposés. My intention is not to discuss whether the response of one group has more weight than others but, instead, to pinpoint at pressure groups whose reaction can be decisive in shaping the political outcomes of watchdog journalism.

Business associations have a crucial role in pushing and sustaining investigations. Their response to press exposés and judicial and congressional investigations is often considered one of the most reliable signs to gauge the possible political impact of news stories. During Collorgate, the decision of influential business groups to distance themselves from the embattled administration was seen as an indication that Collor was in political trouble. The fact that influential interests openly expressed opposition to the president was a telling sign that Collor was rapidly losing support. The willingness of prominent businessmen to testify against Farias indicated that dominant economic groups were withdrawing support. The comments of Roberto Civita, CEO of publishing powerhouse Editora Abril, also reflected changes in attitude. Interviewed on television on June 22, he defended the investigative process and declared: "The country has reached a limit in terms of government corruption. We have to avoid that the investigation ends nowhere. There are too many people ashamed about what is going on. Brazil will continue with or without that mister" (*Folha de São Paulo* 1992a). In early August, José Roberto Marinho, head of *Globo* radio, was quoted saying that "Collor's impeachment was likely" (*Folha de São Paulo* 1992c).

In Colombia, different business adopted contrasting positions vis-à-vis the *Proceso 8,000*. The Santo Domingo group, one of the country's largest corporations, did not raise its voice against the government. The fact that the newsweekly *Cromos,* owned by the group, repeatedly defended president Samper was generally interpreted as a sign of Santo Domingo's solid support. In contrast, the association, which represents fifteen leading businesses, issued a communiqué that stressed the importance of "reaching the truth" when Liberal politicians were called to testify and the press extensively covered the actions of prosecutor Valdivieso in August 1995. Fearful of U.S. sanctions that would have damaging consequences, business groups openly distanced themselves from the Samper administration by October 1995. The withdrawal of support from business took place at a much slower pace than in Brazil's Collorgate, however. By early 1996, newsweekly *Semana* (1996a) observed, "Samper's problem is not massive popular opposition. His real problem is that he practically lost his credibility with the establishment and without the establishment he cannot govern." The decision of *El Tiempo*, the country's most influential daily, to ask for Samper's resignation on July 1996 was interpreted as a sign that political and economic elites had completely withdrawn support from the embattled president.

U.S. embassies and agencies also played an important role. In Colombia, observers pointed out that prosecutor Alfonso Valdivieso had strong support from the U.S. government and that U.S. agencies provided his office with access to important information (Carrigan 1996). A U.S. Senate Foreign Relations Committee (1996) report in February 1996 described Valdivieso and deputy chief prosecutor Adolfo Salamanca as "honest Colombians" who "have brought some of this corruption to light and are attempting to purge the Colombian political system of narcocorruption. Their brave efforts are to be commended and supported." The evolution of neither press denunciations nor the *Proceso 8,000* can be understood without considering the active role of the United States. The transition from De Greiff to Valdivieso as the head of the prosecutor's office occurred amid debates in the U.S. Senate over the certification of Colombia in the fight against drug trafficking and the dissatisfaction among U.S. policymakers with De Greiff's performance. On September 30, 1995, the declarations made by Joe Toft, former director of the Drug Enforcement Agency in Colombia, in a television interview attested to the uneasiness in Washington about Bogota's position. Toft declared, "In my opinion, there are no doubts that the campaign of Ernesto Samper received money from drug traffickers. My opinion is based on what I know, in intelligence information. I do not know for sure if he was aware. But I would be surprised if he were not. [People] talked about millions of dollars, many millions of dollars. . . . There is a lot of information about it. The narcocassettes are only a part but an influential one. They are conclusive evidence. What worries me is that they are not for the Colombian justice" (in Vargas et al. 1996, 78).

It openly revealed the opposition of an influential U.S. agency to the decision of prosecutor de Greiff to shelve the investigations about the *narcotapes*. Subsequently, other high U.S. officials similarly questioned the commitment of Colombia to fighting drug trafficking. During the early months of 1995, ambassador Myles Frechette was skeptical about the likelihood that Washington would approve the certification; attorney general Janet Reno criticized Colombia's judiciary; Secretary of State Warren Christopher stated that Colombia's efforts against drug trafficking were not satisfactory; and senator Jesse Helms, head of the Foreign Relations Committee, virulently attacked Colombia's antidrug policies.

This overview suggests that to measure the impact of watchdog journalism by considering success or failures in shaping policy agenda is important but too confining. Consequences cannot be gauged only on the basis of whether exposés are the catalyst for reform movements. The potential effects of press denunciations are subordinated to larger political processes including, the ripeness of a given political situation, the position of powerful interests, and public support for transformations.

To recognize that journalism has limited impact in inciting public outrage and triggering further investigations and judicial actions suggests that the political accomplishments of watchdog journalism need to be analyzed independently from larger reactions. From this perspective, it would be wrong to conclude that muckraking has not furthered political accountability even when, in many cases, exposés failed to generate wide public reaction, to prod congressional and judicial inquiries, or to lead to legal sanctions of individuals suspected or found guilty of wrongdoing. Its achievements cannot be minimized because the public seems largely unperturbed about revelations of influence peddling dealings or heinous crimes, political institutions ignore press denunciations, and there is a widespread sense of impunity. Accountability hinges on the combined actions of a network of institutions rather than on the solitary actions of one organization. Each institution may have different or even overlapping roles but it is necessary for them, if not to act collectively, certainly to follow each other's actions. If journalism has limited power, then, how does it effectively increase accountability?

PUBLICIZING STATE SECRETS

One way in which the press contributes to accountability is through publicizing official wrongdoing. In so doing, it contributes to accountability in the context of democracies where state secrecy continues to be a serious problem. Watchdog journalism offers public knowledge of illegal actions, a fundamental resource for accountability. Without it, it is hard to envision that demands on individuals and organizations to take responsibility for certain acts would exist. This refers to the "answerability" dimension of accountability. Political scientist Andreas Schedler makes a distinction between answerability and enforcement as two dimensions of accountability. The former refers to asking questions to give information and explain decisions, and the latter alludes to the punishment of illegal behavior. Accountability, then, requires both answers to questions and sanctions. In Schedler's (1999:17) words, "A is accountable to B when A is obliged to inform B about A's (past or future) actions and decisions, to justify them, and to suffer punishment in the case of eventual misconduct."

To contribute successfully to democratic accountability as answerability, then, the task of the press is seemingly straightforward: The dissemination of information about wrongdoing that is not available in the public domain. In bringing out information that someone wants to keep hidden, the press also contributes to the people's right to know and the creation of a better informed citizenry. The denunciations analyzed in this book show that the news media revealed information that specific government offices and individuals tried to keep out of public view. Watchdog journalism breaks official silence about sensitive issues, forces involved parties to speak, and undercuts potential attempts to manage public opinion. To borrow Erving Goffman's (1959) concepts, watchdog journalism brings out the back region that stands in opposition to the front region of public officials. The latter is the place were "a performance is given" and the former is "the place where the impression fostered by the performance is knowingly contradicted . . . and the performer can reliably expect that no member of the audience will intrude" (Goffman 1959: 110, 112–13). In politics, as in the social realms analyzed by Goffman, the back region is kept outside of public view and access is closed. Watchdog journalism shows inconsistencies between the back region and the front region by reporting, for example, that a president who promised to eliminate government corruption is himself involved in a influence peddling ring, that a president who made calls to fight drug trafficking received drug monies to finance election campaign, or that an army general who proclaims to defend human rights knew about the cover-up of the murder of a private. If the media function as a propaganda machine in contemporary democracies, as many critics have argued, these cases suggest that, occasionally and with limits, some news media publicize information about the hidden side of power, the side where citizens have restricted, if any, access.

It goes without saying that officials involved in wrongdoing were not exactly interested in volunteering information about corruption and human rights abuses. Not only they were not willing to allow disclosures to be published, but reportedly tried to suppress stories. Journalists tell plenty of anecdotes about telephone calls from government officials who tried to persuade or forcibly demanded newsrooms to kill stories. Reactions range from sweet-talking editors and reporters into being patriots and warning them that revelations would damage the international image of the country to death threats from identified and unidentified sources.

News organizations do more than bring out information hidden from public view. In several opportunities, they actually pushed congressional and judiciary offices to investigate and prosecute. Against staunch opposition from other actors to look into charges, they kept pressure on the authorities that eventually ordered investigations. In Colombia, journalist Maria Cristina Caballero's reporting for newsweekly *Cambio 16* was credited with having revived the judicial investigation about drug monies in early 1995, months after former chief prosecutor De Greiff had dismissed the cause (Ronderos 1998; Vargas et al. 1996). She reported that a team of military and police forces raided the office of the accountant of the Cali cartel and found lists with names of two dozen politicians and Samper's campaign treasurer Santiago Medina, numbers in front of each name, and addresses (*Cambio 16* 1995). Asked about the meaning of the numbers, Medina replied that they corresponded to the number of T-shirts distributed during the campaign and former representative Rodolfo Garavito gave confusing versions. A copy of the list was made to drug baron Miguel Rodriguez Orejuela. Felipe Lopez, the Cali prosecutor who was investigating the cause the previous years when the narcotape story broke, initially denied that he had the lists. After *Cambio 16*'s story, however, López backtracked and announced that he found them. The document published by *Cambio 16* became the basis for the *Proceso 8,000,* after top prosecutor Valdivieso petitioned the Supreme Court to transfer the cause from Cali to Bogotá.

In Peru, it is hard to imagine that without the press, either the congressional inquiry or the judicial process about the disappearances of nine students and a professor at La Cantuta University would have ever moved forward. Incomplete and fraught with suspicions as they were, the investigations would have not materialized had the press not brought information to the fore. The congressional investigation was stalled in mid-1993. In early April, opposition representative Henry Pease presented an explosive document. It identified the Grupo Colina and high-ranking army officers as responsible for the disappearances and murders. Pease had received the information from the organization León Dormido (Sleeping Lion), which claimed to represent officers critical of human rights violations. General Rodolfo Robles later publicly confirmed the denunciations and fingered presidential advisor Vladimiro Montesinos, Army Commander General Nicolás Hermoza and others. In August, Ricardo Uceda, then-managing editor of the newsweekly *Si,* received a map where the remains of the students and professor of La Cantuta were supposedly buried. After verifying the information, Uceda and two journalists contacted human rights organizations and other media, reported the findings, and led them to the burial site. After it was proven that the remains were of La Cantuta victims, *Si* published a follow-up report about the place where the murders were committed and the corpses were originally buried.

These revelations, corroborated by judge Victor Cubas Villanueva, forced Congress to reopen the investigation against the ardent opposition from Fujimori's bloc. *Sí* journalists not only investigated the events but also played the role of the forensic team that excavated the site. Newsweekly *Caretas* also helped to keep the story alive. Interviews with La Cantuta students and with General Robles, who went into exile in Buenos Aires, contradicted the official line that the army did not participate in the actions. Eventually, the army chief admitted the responsibility of his institution. In May 1994, a military court found three officers guilty of the murders; they were absolved by the 1995 Amnesty law passed by the Fujimori administration. Peruvian editor Gustavo Gorriti (1998b) notes that even though the government granted amnesty, the press "established the truth about [the events at] La Cantuta."

The news media not only performs publicity functions by conducting and publishing investigations that contradict official statements but also by making visible the actions of several actors whose combined actions contribute to accountability. As Brazilian scholar Antonio Fausto Neto (1994b: 173) remarks about the impeachment process of ex-President Collor de Mello, "The media did not act just as mediator among powers . . . but also as a mechanism for the functioning of the political sphere." In times of mediated politics, the news media gives existence to ideas and demands of pressure groups and social movements. This does not mean that media representations are necessarily faithful and balanced but rather that without media attention they would be invisible.

Media coverage of judicial investigations is crucial. This typically happens in situations when the news media rely on leaks from prosecutors' offices for its own denunciations. Such kind of coverage is not often recognized as "media coverage" because it violates rules about the secrecy of judicial inquiries but, de facto, it works in such a way. Media dependency on confidential legal information strengthens the already powerful position of prosecutors as newsmakers. When news organizations are too passive and overwhelmingly rely on the actions and leaks of prosecutors, as happened during Colombia's *Proceso 8,000*, judicial testimonies are often taken at face value and the news media rarely takes time to verify the facts and conduct independent investigations. This is another sign that the news media too often kowtow to the maneuvers of interested parties (in this case, prosecutors and judges) and are prone to news management. Such dynamics reflect the location of news organizations vis-à-vis powerful interests: They are solidly entrenched in the spheres of power and closely linked to the production of official information. The news media also put the spotlight on the judiciary by publishing witnesses' testimonies and findings. *El Tiempo*'s publication of the extensive testimony of Santiago Medina, Samper's campaign treasurer, is perceived as a landmark in the unfolding of the *Proceso 8,000* not only given the tenor of Medina's accusations but as a telling indication that Colombia's most influential daily legitimized and brought to the forefront the actions of prosecutor Valdivieso, who was harshly criticized by the Executive and other government offices.

The news media also contribute to accountability through covering public mobilizations. If public opinion needs visibility to be influential, as Kurt and Gladys Lang (1983) suggest, press coverage gives existence to the sentiments of the majority of the population that lacks access to newsrooms. In some cases, media coverage of demonstrations had a decisive impact. The Argentine media only sporadically conducted original investigations on the murder of a schoolgirl that implicated government higher-ups in the northwestern province of Catamarca. Wide-scale coverage of regular demonstrations and vigils, however, contributed to keeping the story alive and, in the minds of some analysts, to the downfall of the Saadi administration, a political dynasty that had ruled the province for decades (Rey and Pazos 1991).

Brazilian observers concluded that extended media attention to anti-Collor rallies across the country were decisive in putting pressure on Congress and pushing swing votes to support investigations and impeachment (Keck 1992; Mendes 1993). Moreover, media coverage of the rallies indicated that powerful groups, including the dominating *Globo* network, were shifting gears and "abandoning Collor's ship." If the slowness of the *Globo* network in covering prodemocracy rallies in the early 1980s was interpreted as a sign that elites continued to support the authoritarian regime, the coverage and positive spin of anti-Collor demonstrations suggested that political and economic elites were withdrawing support.

In none of these cases does the performance of news organizations fit the orthodoxy of investigative journalism that says that investigative reporting "is work done by reporters." If we take this perspective, journalists are frequently passive rather than active in bringing out information unavailable in the public realm, as reports are based on information not only gathered from reporters' sources but also sponged from the inquiries of prosecutors and congressional committees. South American journalists, however, find the concept of active journalism in the standard definition of investigative journalism in the United States too narrow and inapplicable to their context. Instead, they believe that muckraking always requires active reporting no matter what sources and methods are used to gather information. The conditions for doing investigative reporting (as understood in U.S. manuals) in the region are abysmally different, so that definition is not useful either analytically or normatively. In their mind, muckrakers who rely on different sources of information and newsgathering methods (including leaks) practice investigative reporting. Investigative journalism is less about methods and more about consequences.

An important shortcoming of the performance of the news media is the narrow lens used in uncovering wrongdoing. They generally put the spotlight on official illegalities but overlook business crimes and matters of social justice. Rarely do they publicize corporate graft and social inequalities, which, for the most part, are undetected. Nor do they make efforts to illuminate how the illicit acts of government officials affect the life of ordinary citizens. Only sporadically news reports analyze how wrongdoing affects the lives of ordinary citizens (Bless 1997). Sure, attention to government delinquency is not misplaced. It continues to be badly needed when the lack of accountability of state powers still dogs present-day democracies. Watchdog journalism, no doubt, has made important efforts in this regard by revealing the sorry state of accountability mechanisms and reporting that law enforcers and lawmakers are lawbreakers. Its inattention to wrongdoing in other spheres, however, does not contribute to identify and understand other important issues.

Editorial considerations are arguably responsible for why muckraking generally turns away from issues such as corporate practices, labor conditions, the exploitation of children, environmental issues, or the social conditions of immigrants and indigenous populations. News organizations are not interested in offending large advertisers or business linked to their own corporate structure involved in fraudulent commercial practices and social abuses. The boundaries between reporting and editorial interests are porous. The conviction of a good part of U. S. journalism about the past existence of a solid division between church and the state in newsrooms, now under threat due to increasing bottom-line pressures created by conglomerization, has been hardly present in the South America press. Journalists observe that, in some cases, confrontations between certain individuals and media companies motivated the few denunciations that highlighted business wrongdoing. Aside from economics, the restricted coverage of wrongdoing expresses an organizational culture that puts its magnifying glass on official news and primarily taps into elites conflicts to produce exposés. What underlies the thematic agenda of watchdog journalism is the intimacy between the news media and power. If the state eclipses the realms of commerce and social life as the target of press denunciations, this is the consequence of newsrooms that are dependent on distillations of intra-elite rivalries and the existence of reporting templates that are restricted by a professional culture enamored with official dealings. Both the political economy of the news media and a journalistic culture oriented toward official news are the bookends of watchdog journalism.

Some journalists justify media's infrequent attention to social inequalities by stating that it is too obvious for anyone living in South American societies to be presented as news. In societies with high levels of inequality, anyone easily comes across poverty, undernourishment, and other social ills. Because such problems are so visible, they are not news. Journalistically, there is less interest in such stories than in catching an official with his hand in the cookie jar. Moreover, reporters comment, middle-class readers are not terribly interested in gaining knowledge about the situation of downtrodden and marginal citizens. Corporate graft as a subject of exposés is different, journalists explain. Its absence responds to news organizations uninterested in ruffling feathers of prominent elites that even if they may not control large advertising budgets, are part of the same political and social circles of publishers and editorial board members.

The lukewarm and ambiguous interest of news organizations in watchdog journalism conditions the possibilities of reporting on issues other than official crimes. When they assign limited resources to watchdog journalism, picking up the phone and checking facts with a handful of sources are certainly easier than shoe-leather reporting to produce denunciations. Because the routines of news making and newsroom culture privilege news about government officials, reporters are more likely to have contacts in government rather than in corporate boards, unions, or neighborhood associations. And, in turn, officials are more likely than executives or workers to maintain steady contacts with journalists and pursue media outlets to fight out internal rivalries.

If corporate delinquency and social injustice are largely invisible in the eyes of the news media, the potential of watchdog journalism to be a catalyst for understanding different peoples and problems and for generating debates about a vast range of issues is limited. This does not mean that those issues are completely absent from public discussion if journalism neglects them. Their presence is less significant, however, when muckraking's radar does not register them. The news media do not tell us what to think but what to think about, as agenda-setting studies insist. They have the power to initiate discussions in the public sphere about an unlimited number of issues

by foregrounding specific problems. That potential is unrealized when journalistic practices and media interests narrow down the agenda of watchdog
journalism. For the news media to contribute effectively to the formation of
a critical public, as press scholar James Carey (1993) has observed, it is necessary that nothing should be taken for granted and that everything should
be subject to argument and evidence.

THE POLITICS OF SHAMING

Aside from publicizing state secrets, journalism also contributes to accountability by setting in motion political developments that result in punishments, Schedler's second dimension of accountability. These refer to "sanctions against particular persons or entities, including prosecutions, firings
and demotions" (Protess et al. 1991). In putting stories about wrongdoing in
front of a wide audience, watchdog reporting is able to unleash processes
that have culminated in resignations and legal actions. At times, press denunciations are enough to build pressure that results in public officials quit-
ting their jobs even before congressional investigative committees are
formed and prosecutors initiate actions.

Examples are not short in supply. The long and unfinished list of legal actions and resignations in the last decade makes it almost impossible to com-
pile an exhaustive record. Cabinet members, representatives, police chiefs,
and others resigned soon after exposés hit the newsstands. In Argentina,
scores of first- and second-level officials of the Menem administration and
local governments resigned after exposés were published. Defense minister
Oscar Camillion and Air Force commander Juan Paulik resigned in the aftermath of press revelations and congressional investigations about the illegal
sale of weapons to Ecuador in 1995. Three middle-ranking Army officers were
demoted and sentenced in relation to the Carrasco murder. Minister of Justice Rodolfo Barra resigned on July 1996 after newsweekly *Noticias* revealed
that he had been a member of Nazi organization in his youth. In Brazil, president Collor resigned after a six-month scandal. In Colombia, then-Defense
Minister Fernando Botero resigned and was sentenced to 63 months in prison
and to pay 2.2 billion pesos. Former campaign treasurer Santiago Medina was
sentenced to 64 months in prison on charges of illicit enrichment on behalf
of a third party and received a fine of 3 billion pesos. Several cabinet members were charged with complicity in the cover-up of drug money contributions. One hundred seventy representatives were investigated, dozens were

called to testify, and ten went to prison for illicit enrichment. As of the time of this writing, the judicial process has not concluded. In August 1998, the Supreme Court decided to investigate 111 representatives that exonerated former President Samper.

In regard to resignations and judicial processes, the value of watchdog journalism in terms of political accountability can be analyzed in two dimensions. It contributes to changing the political standing of individuals who relinquished public positions of power after press denunciations came out. These are not groundbreaking reforms that drastically overturn existing conditions, yet they help to raise awareness about whether officials are responsible and other institutions effectively hold them accountable.

Another way muckraking adds efforts to accountability is through the symbolic punishment of individuals and organizations. Accountability should be understood not only in political or legal terms, but also as moral liability "for the results, mostly harmful, of a given form of behavior or event" (Bovens 1998). Even when, as in most cases here analyzed, there have mostly individual changes and individuals guilty of wrongdoing are rarely prosecuted or legally punished, the significance of moral sanctions should not be minimized. Watchdog journalism deals a powerful blow to the reputation of individuals who may have successfully avoided legal processes or even were exonerated but, in the public mind, continue to be associated with immoral and illegal behavior. Sociologist John B. Thompson has rightly called attention to this issue in reference to scandals. He writes that scandals are phenomena "where individual reputations are at stake. Of course, the threat to reputation is not the only issue at stake in many scandals. If the covert activities involve the contravention of legally binding norms or formally established procedures, the individuals may also face criminal prosecution and/or dismissal from their posts. Revelations often result in an array of criminal prosecutions, sackings and broken careers; for the individuals involved, the marring of reputation is by no means their only concern. Nevertheless they know very well that, just beyond the legal wranglings, just above the fray and fury of courtroom proceedings and special congressional inquiries, lurks the question of reputation, of one's 'name'" (Thompson 1997: 46).

One can scarcely doubt that Fernando Collor and members of the 1993 Budget Congressional Commission, former Peruvian president Alan García and his former right-hand man Alfredo Zanatti, scores of former members of the Menem administration in Argentina, and a long list of Colombian politicians involved in the drug monies scandal are widely held as the epitome of government corruption in each country. Likewise, the military juntas in the 1970s and early 1980s together with retired and active officers in Argentina and members of death squads in Peru became symbols of human atrocities although they benefited from presidential pardons and lenient legal sanctions. Identified as symbols of official wrongdoing, these and many other individuals are part of the "hall of shame" of contemporary South American politics. It seems quite obvious how much the symbolic sanction of those individuals owes to press denunciations and sustained media attention on their alleged and confirmed criminal activities.

In this sense, watchdog journalism does something similar to the "outings" organized by *Hijos,* the organization founded by the children of individuals who were disappeared during the military dictatorship in Argentina. Critical of the presidential pardon that exonerated officers and the decree that put an end to judiciary processes dealing with human rights violations, *Hijos* frequently stages demonstrations in front of the private homes of military and police officers accused of human rights abuses. These public spectacles garner media attention and generate much commotion in the neighborhood. Demonstrators sing chants against officers and graffiti the walls with phrases such as "an assassin lives here." As actions to humiliate officers in public, these outings work similarly to scarlet letter punishments, reminding the public of the true identity of individuals. Such actions are not conceived as cheap and efficient alternatives to other forms of punishment, as argued in U.S. legal debates (Litowitz 1997), but as one of the available means through which citizens, convinced that justice has not been served, can raise public awareness about the existence of criminals. Likewise, press denunciations reveal the hidden side of public officials involved in wrongdoing. In dredging up information, journalism shames the shameless and tarnishes the reputation of public figures. Getting one's name back does not seem easy to accomplish. Judicial processes may be dismissed or overturned, sentences may be revoked, and authorities may pardon convicts. Symbolic punishments, however, are difficult to be erased. After news reports hammered that someone has been responsible for criminal acts, regaining prestige and public esteem seems difficult. It may be argued that officials who broke laws without any remorse are not ashamed of being stigmatized as wrongdoers, that just a minority of officials actually seeks rehabilitation, that many continue to exercise power behind the scenes, or that most vanish from the public eye and keep a low profile after judicial decisions and press denunciations lose steam. None of these possible responses minimize the relevance of press denunciations as symbolic sanctions particularly in political systems characterized by weak political accountability.

Columnists often remind us that regardless of political and judicial reso-lutions, individuals and administrations embroiled in denunciations of wrongdoing confront the problem of tarnished reputations. Congress and the judiciary system may clear a politician of any responsibility but, as a *New York Times* correspondent observed after Colombian president Ernesto Samper was exonerated, his name "is not in the clear" (Schemo 1996b). "Shame" was one of the rallying cries during the anti-Collor demonstra-tions. Companies seem particularly vulnerable to such labelings. It was ob-served that regardless of actual consequences, the scandal involving IBM in bribing executives of Banco de la Nación Argentina stained the company's image (*Wall Street Journal* 1995). Press denunciations may have only limited effect in ushering in political reforms or furthering judicial sanctions but they cast a huge shadow that forever clouds the political stature and prestige of individuals and organizations. The importance of public reputation is glaringly obvious in cases of individuals who, absolved from all criminal charges, relentlessly strive to get their name back.

Exonerated by Congress, Colombian President Ernesto Samper managed to complete his four-year mandate, but remained politically wounded. Under the cloud of the scandal, the political credibility of his administration was badly damaged. Survey research showed that the public did not support impeachment, but was rapidly losing confidence in Samper. His positive image went from 76 percent to 51 percent and his negative image climbed from 12 percent to 30 percent. More damaging than public reaction was the decision of the Department of State to revoke his U.S. visa and to decertify Colombia in the war against drugs. In a country extremely sensitive to U.S. reactions, these were two loud slaps in the face of the embattled Samper gov-ernment, especially given the delicate state of bilateral relations in relation to drug-trafficking and the extradition of drug barons (*Semana* 1996b). Al-though Samper avoided criminal charges and potential impeachment pro-ceedings, both decisions were signs that the scandal had inflicted irreparable political harm. Borrowing a page from Richard Nixon's post-Watergate po-litical life, Samper has devoted efforts to clear up his name and to regain re-spectability but apparently without much success. Public opinion surveys re-flected that even though Colombians were divided about whether he should resign, most believed that he was guilty even after Congress exonerated him. While 29 percent believed that he had to resign in August 1995, 54 percent were inclined to that decision in January 1996.

The problem of press denunciations as symbolic punishments is that, as a consequence of the drive toward the personalization of news, wrongdoing is treated as personal failing rather than as an institutional pattern. Watchdog journalism tends to frame wrongdoing as an individual failure but rarely addresses structural factors that facilitate and protect officials engaged in delinquent activities. What is scrutinized and debated is the morality of individuals rather than the morality of the political and economic system. The tendency to personalize wrongdoing can be interpreted positively as a way to understand deep trends. Colombian columnist Enrique Santos Calderón (1998) observed, "maybe we should thank [president] Samper for having brought us the *Proceso 8,000* so we can understand better, through his personal and political torment, how entrenched and resistant is that illness that eats us." An opposite interpretation is to conclude that personalization leads to an impoverished understanding of wrongdoing. In regard to Collorgate, Brazilian journalist Alberto Dines (1992) was one of the many voices that criticized the press for narrowly covering official wrongdoing as a problem that involved a few individuals. Dines noted, "The campaign against corruption shrunk into a campaign against Collor's corruption, which resulted in a surgical removal, a symbolic cure rather than a complete cleansing." How we evaluate the real impact of watchdog journalism ultimately hinges on different concepts of accountability.

WHAT QUALIFIES AS ACCOUNTABILITY?

Should we conclude that journalism effectively contributes to accountability when its major achievements are to publicize official secrets, to put in motion individual changes, and to symbolically punish wrongdoers? Whether resignations, demotions, or other similar actions are considered evidence of accountability depends on the definition of democratic accountability. If we understand, along the lines of liberal arguments, that accountability involves a series of procedures to instrument the rule of law, the press has unquestionably helped to raise accountability by publicizing information and actions that resulted in "throwing the rascals out," whether through the resignation or the voting out of individuals suspected or charged of corruption.

Publicity is central to the notion and the process of accountability. Combining utilitarian and Kantian arguments about the desirability of publicity for democratic accountability, political scientists Amy Guttman and Dennis Thompson (1996) suggest that publicity deters public officials from engaging in unlawful behavior and invites citizens to deliberate about public issues. It also forces officials to answer for their actions, to disclose to citizens the reasons for their behavior. This has potentially positive consequences for democratic deliberation, they argue, because "making reasons public contributes to the broadening of moral and political perspectives that deliberation is supposed to encourage" (1996: 100). Deliberation is central to a concept of democracy in which citizens and officials can clarify moral disagreements and governments can adopt policies that are publicly justified, and even negotiate the rules and the conditions for secrecy. From a perspective that endows the news media with a pivotal role in stimulating public conversation, the significance of watchdog journalism in terms of its contribution to the publicization of wrongdoing is enormous. It has the ability to bring public attention to unlawful actions and to set in motion debates about the nature and the responsibility for such acts; to prod government institutions to investigate and instrument legal sanctions; to energize citizens to search for information and official responsibility, and to unleash political processes that result in the removal from office of individuals suspected or convicted of crimes.

In an optimistic tone, some observers have concluded that, in fact, the news media has effectively contributed to fostering accountability through the publicization of abuses in several cases in recent years. In regard to the role of the press during Collorgate, for example, analysts opined that the process did work: The media denounced, Congress investigated and sentenced, and Collor (and other officials) resigned (see Rosenn and Downes 1999). The system of checks and balances worked. Such dynamics are new in countries accustomed to military coups as mechanisms to force officials out of office. No need for a whole administration to go down in flames to conclude that the press plays its part in making politics more accountable. Accountability deals with roles and procedures. The function of the press is to be a mechanism of publicity and it should be evaluated in those terms. It should not be made responsible for the shortcomings of Congress or the judiciary system. If an administration enjoys a clear congressional majority that vehemently opposes any investigation or the Supreme Court systematically throws out any petition to investigate presidents and close collaborators, the political ceiling of press denunciations is clearly low. The press neither prosecutes nor judges but, at best, submits fair and accurate information for public consideration that may (or not) trigger further investigation and legal actions. It is constrained to the provision of news and, consequently, should be judged in terms of its unique and constitutionally protected functions. Journalists insist that in societies with weak political accountability the press is often miscast in the role of prosecutor or full-fledged investigator (Gallo 1997). Its very nature makes it inadequate to take on other functions. Furthermore, if the press takes on other attributes, this inevitably has damaging consequences for democratic life, namely, the blurring of constitutional boundaries. Considering the checkered record of constitutional rule and persistent institutional weakness, this danger is particularly heightened in the Latin American context. Thus watchdog journalism does make a difference to democratic life.

Such conclusions are not satisfying to those who are less inclined to see accountability procedurally and are more concerned about its contribution to solving structural problems. These positions, more aligned with leftist critiques of liberal democracy, suggest that press denunciations result in, at best, the punishment of a few individuals. Such sanctions work as moments for the purification of the system but leave basic political and social inequalities untouched. They symbolically exorcise immorality and illegality and remove the rotten apples from the fruit basket but the rules and workings of the system still work. Examples of this position are also found in critical evaluations of Collorgate. The resignation of Fernando Collor was interpreted as a process in which the elites opted to change individuals but maintain the fundamentals of the system (de Oliveira 1992; Mendes 1993). Vito Giannotti writes: "What was behind the proposal or resignation was a big deal for the elites to save themselves and save the president they elected, save their own skin because a big part of that elite is as guilty as Collor. What was important was to guarantee that continuity of the neoliberal project without shocks, without risks. Neoliberal policies of adjustment, unemployment and hunger will continue. Debates would finish and the bourgeoisie would return to normalize production, just the way it wanted" (1992: 165, 168).

The first position rightly directs attention to the question of accountability as requiring a set of institutional procedures that publicize the opaque affairs of the state and submits power-holders to public scrutiny. It also correctly distinguishes the responsibilities and limitations of the news media from the functions of other institutions. It would be unfair to judge the performance of the press solely based on its contribution to substantial reforms for, as mentioned earlier, the implementation of substantial changes depends on larger political developments and institutions. To conclude that the lack of reforms is a sign that watchdog journalism has been politically fruitless would be shortsighted.

CONCLUSION

High hopes are placed on the democratic press. The press is expected to monitor power, to express a diversity of opinions, to make citizens informed, and to foster public debate, in other words, to be a conduit for the dissemination of information, the lifeblood of democratic life. Such expectations have inherited from the Enlightenment the idea that information is good. "No information, no democracy" is the underlying premise. Authoritarianism looms in the horizon as the bogeyman, the big beast synonymous with secrecy and the suppression of information. Democracy, instead, assumes the availability of information that allows citizens to participate in the public sphere as members of a political community. More (and more diverse) information is assumed to increase democratic prospects.

From this view, investigative reporting is the depositary of the highest expectations of all things that news organizations do (or should do). In the imaginary of the democratic press, investigative journalism is the good journalism, the poster child of the normative ideal that outlines its political mission. The disclosure of information about illegal activities is investigative journalism's unique contribution to democracy. It incarnates some of the key functions assigned to the press: holding back the runaway power of the state and informing citizens about acts of public relevance. Out of the barrage of news and entertainment that the press churns out daily, investigative journalism shows the press dressed in its democratic best. The press features classified ads, advertising-made sections, sensational news, and marketing tricks for its own economic health. Investigative reporting, instead, is what the press does for the health of the republic. Marketing executives and publishers solely concerned about bottom-line results take pride in the former, but true-blooded journalists find personal redemption and professional legitimacy in the latter. Investigative journalism, the incarnation of the fourth estate ideal, wears the robes that clothe the romantic ideal of the free press.

It is the medal of chest-thumping publishers interested in exhibiting democratic credentials. It is the virtuous professional ideal held aloft by editors
and reporters.

CHANGE OF THE GUARDIANS

This book has shown that the fourth estate notion of the press has gained
currency in South American journalism. Whereas investigative journalism
qua "the journalism of exposé" had a sporadic, marginal existence in the past
and was limited to the ups-and-downs of alternative publications, it found
room in the mainstream press in the 1980s and 1990s. This process has been
the result of the combination of several developments. Despite the persistence of antipress attacks, the consolidation of liberal democracy ushered in
a political context that encouraged news organizations and journalists to report on touchy subjects. Violence against the press has not disappeared but
the situation is better than when military censorship and repression ruled.
But even the imperfect reestablishment of constitutional rights (most evident in Fujimori's Peru) has brought about substantial changes that positively affect muckrakers' work.

Other factors have contributed to muckraking journalism, too. Leading
news organizations, particularly the largest Brazilian newspapers, cautiously
approached muckraking as a marketing strategy as they faced a shrinking
market of readers. Political convictions also motivated denunciations but,
unlike during the heyday of the alternative press, such convictions do not express partisan leanings. Instead, they typically represent political conflicts
among governing elites, divergences between news organizations and individuals at the center of exposés, and journalists' personal convictions and
professional ambitions. One does not need to take a lyrical vision of journalism to acknowledge that it is not just self-serving goals that animate
muckrakers. Moral principles also drive many journalists to lift the rug to
uncover official deceit, notwithstanding difficulties inside and outside newsrooms. Internally, resources assigned to investigative reporting are scarce,
editorial boards and publishers are timid, and pressures are not uncommon;
outside newsrooms, verbal and physical threats and the absence of legal
mechanisms to have access to official records add other obstacles.

Muckraking also represents the search among news organizations and
journalists to redefine professional identity. It helps to cement claims to
cherished fourth estate credentials, the mirror that South American journal-

ism holds high. As watchdog journalism went mainstream in the 1980s and 1990s, a new set of ideals emerged to buttress the professional legitimacy of news organizations and reporters. The crusading tradition represented by the alternative press during dictatorial periods was unsuitable for a different journalism. Watchdog journalism is no longer housed in publications founded with the mission of propagating partisan ideals, resisting military juntas, and opposing oligarchies, capitalism, and imperialism. Instead, it found room in market-oriented news businesses with center-right, moderate, and left-center editorial sympathies. The ideology of U.S. journalism, particularly as crystallized in the Watergate trope, fits readily the presentation of muckraking as politically disinterested, nonideological, fact-based reporting.

The adoption of such ideals is notable among a new generation of journalists. These are journalists who hold college degrees (many in journalism), did not participate in the politically effervescent 1960s and 1970s (or only caught the tail end), and, like the citizenry at large, are skeptical of partisan politics. Many hold attitudes that attest to a different view of journalism. An editor for the leading Argentine newsweekly chooses not to vote because, as he says, "journalists should not take sides." A Brazilian muckraker confessed that he felt uncomfortable when President Fernando Henrique Cardoso, who was dear to his political sympathies, was first elected in 1994. Cardoso's victory made it difficult to fulfill the journalistic obligations of neutrality and criticism, he says. Muckrakers of the past would not likely have made similar confessions about keeping partisan inclinations at bay, honoring fourth estate principles, and serving the public interest.

But as politics changed and the economics of media organizations started to change, newsrooms have experienced important transformations. Nonpartisan, professional editors-in-chief have taken the helm of leading newspapers, and publishers-cum-press-caudillos (who used to run tight partisan ships) gradually followed the path of the dinosaurs. These changes need to be understood in the context of the gradual shift in the economics of leading news organizations, and the growing distance between news organizations and partisan politics. Such changes are far from complete and have barely began. Contemporary watchdog reporting still straddles different journalistic traditions. The transformations are more perceptible in metropolitan media in Argentina, Brazil, and Colombia. In Peru, a smaller advertising market, a sizable amount of official advertising (compared to private investments), a repressive political atmosphere in the post-1992 coup years, and the open confrontation between the Fujimori administration and some news organizations have produced a different situation. The conditions for muckraking in most cities and towns in the interior have not experienced major changes as old-time clientelistic politics and state coffers still exercise substantial influence on the press.

In this book I have also explored the actual and potential consequences of watchdog journalism for democratic life. Unlike in the United States, where the press has been the punching bag of media critics for decades and journalists have repeatedly made calls for soul-searching (particularly after *l'affaire* Lewinsky), the chorus of public opinion unanimously congratulates the press in South America. In the latter, neither public condemnation nor self-flagellation among journalists is found. Quite the contrary: Judging by its standings in polls in country after country, it seems that the press has been doing an outstanding job in the 1980s and 1990s. Political observers and journalism analysts also compliment the press. Despite problems, it is noted that the "glass should be viewed as half full rather than half empty" (Buckman 1996:34). Journalists also applaud the performance of the press. Some harbor mixed feelings and point at strengths and shortcomings, successes and mistakes, but most (including reporters' and publishers' organizations) overwhelmingly recognize that the press must be doing something right to enjoy such wide public esteem.

Watchdog reporting is widely credited for much of the prestige that the press enjoys. Its merits are particularly remarkable considering the poor performance of other institutions that have the constitutional mission of monitoring power. In contrast to slow-moving and manipulated judiciary systems and subservient and lapdog parliaments, the press has broken major cases of corruption and contributed to the removal of corrupt officials. Although the press meets its fourth estate obligations, despite limitations and obstacles, other estates conspicuously stop short from fulfilling their mandates.

It is not necessary to find the ideology of the fourth estate completely persuasive to recognize that watchdog journalism, no matter its many imperfections, has contributed to the quality of South American democracies. This is particularly so amid the deterioration of civic liberties and the deepening of absurd social inequalities in the region in the late twentieth century. The contributions of watchdog journalism are of no small importance. It has raised questions about the transparency of governments, shined its flashlight in dark political corners, and brought attention to acts of wrong-doing, while other institutions showed a dubious commitment to monitoring abuses or were napping while abuses happened and were reported. These actions should be commendable in any political context, but they are especially important in democracies with bulging files on abuses but spotty accountability records.

The contributions of watchdog journalism have been limited, however. Watchdog journalism, like the press in general, is wrapped in contradictions. It offers a Rorschach blot representing the tensions that characterize the press. It is endowed with the mission to serve the public interest, but its feet are firmly placed in the market. Democratic expectations are deposited in news organizations that, if interested in exposing wrongdoing, pursue it as long as it does not come in conflict with powers that directly affect their own commercial interests. One of the paradoxes of liberal democracy is that it is premised on the public availability of information and the free flow of information, but private parties manufacture the bulk of the information required for democratic citizenship. This contradiction becomes visible in the methods and the repertoire of muckraking.

Methods

South American watchdog journalism looks northward for inspiration but finds the orthodoxy of U.S. investigative journalism (as defined in manuals and books) impossible. Journalists are not persuaded by the concept of investigative journalism that emphasizes specific methods and, instead, prefer to understand investigative reporting in terms of its consequences. The reality of South American journalism, they justify, is worlds apart from the milieu that informs canonical definitions. In any case, investigation is not (or should not be) unique to some forms of reporting. For them, muckraking's unmatched value is the disclosure of illegalities: it divulges secrets that citizens do not know and powerful parties want to keep hidden.

Although journalists' doubts about the prescriptive dimensions of U.S.-based definitions are warranted, the question of how journalists gather information about wrongdoing should not be minimized. Are all newsgathering methods valid to disclose abuses? Should wrongdoing be revealed regardless of how information was obtained? What if information (as countless exposés insinuate and journalists admit) not always comes from morally upright individuals but from connivers, accomplices, and turncoats who give information on the condition they remain anonymous?

Borrowing a page from John Stuart Mill's ethics, journalists tend to adopt a utilitarian perspective to deal with these questions. They suggest that in societies plagued by corruption and deceit what matters, above all, is truth telling. When the press lacks legal and economic resources that underlie the catechism of investigative journalism, and journalists are repeatedly targets of pressures and attacks, the priorities are different. Publicizing information, no matter its origin or how it was secured, is preferable to silence. "Sources-have-their-interests-I-have-mine" and "You-cannot-identify-sources" are baseline rules that journalists follow rather than running the double risk of losing sources and their own lives. Keeping the identity of informants secret is accepted as part of the quid pro quo of source — reporter transactions. Conventional newsroom wisdom says that individuals who participated in illegal dealings are likely to have the best information. Journalism should care about the credibility of the information rather than about the motives of sources.

Should it? When I asked journalists whether such practices presented any political or ethical problems, they threw the pie of newsroom reality at my academic face, and proceeded to explain matter-of-factly: Drug dealers have the best information about the operations of drug barons, military officers and intelligence agents know about human rights abuses and other illegal operations, and corrupt politicians and businessmen know inside-out influence-peddling schemes mounted by government officials. Information always comes with one string attached: anonymity. And, just as there is no free lunch, there is no free information. Self-interested individuals leak information to grind their personal axes, to ruin political careers, and to pursue other nonheavenly goals. All other considerations belong in academic territory and ethics classes, not in the realms of *realpolitik* and down-and-dirty journalism.

My interest is not to take supposedly higher academic ground but, instead, to call attention to the contradictions embedded in evaluating investigative journalism *solely* in terms of its consequences. The disregard for newsgathering practices implicitly legitimizes certain kinds of politics, which flies in the face of the very goals that many muckrakers so eloquently articulate and pursue. The pervasive use of anonymous sources allows invisible hands to throw political stones without going public. Citizens may benefit by getting information that perhaps would not be available otherwise, but such practices favor those in power with fluid access to newsrooms. It perpetuates official news management and political dynamics that reinforce the power of governing elites. Muckraking gives us a peek into the secret workings of power but tells us little about itself. It discloses other people's practices, not its own. It shows us how political sausage is made but reveals little (if anything) about how news sausage is made. And the making of news sausages is closely linked to the "politics by other means" that are increasingly dominant in South American democracies. Citizens are often left in the dark about such dynamics, which become the subjects of permanent speculation and suspicion, precisely because little is revealed about them. The challenge for watchdog journalism is if it can resolve the contradiction of searching for transparency in public affairs while keeping its own affairs opaque.

Repertoire

Contradictions are also embedded in the repertoire of watchdog journalism. This book has shown that muckrakers generally scrutinized official malfeasance but only exceptionally looked into corporate wrongdoing or social inequalities. It would be utterly wrong to minimize the importance of denouncing government misdeeds. Reports on official crimes are of tremendous significance, especially considering the extent of official wrongdoing, the weakness of accountability mechanisms, and institutional malaise. The infrequent attention paid to abuses in other areas is problematic, and raises questions about the commitment of news organizations to muckraking.

Exposés of shady business practices, for example, might offend powerful editorial board members, interests intertwined with media conglomerates, and large advertisers. News organizations, regardless of their economic prowess, are rarely inclined to lock horns with powerful businesses unless, as some journalists observe, they unleash the news hounds to attack competitors. But even as part of a commercial strategy the exposure of business crimes is rare. The rarity of business exposés or, for that matter, investigations of social conditions, is not just the result of the unwillingness to put commercial and political interests at risk. News organizations are not terribly interested in producing denunciations that require the investment of substantial resources. Access to information that documents business venality is extremely difficult. It would require prolonged efforts that might not bring any scoop or newsworthy material. Access to government records is not easy either, but ax-grinding officials offer a cheap solution by volunteering information. News about official crimes can be produced without extra resources. For a journalism that gravitates towards officials news and puts them on the highest professional pedestal, ready-made, leaked dossiers and telephone calls provide an inexpensive and quick way to produce exposés.

No wonder, then, that with little time and resources invested, exposés generally offer fleeting treatments of wrongdoing. They concentrate on individual crimes rather than on the long-term concentration of power, and present superficial rather than in-depth reports about abuses in a variety of spheres. Professional templates and newsgathering routines that privilege official wrongdoing leave out the investigation of social conditions and the examination of how political abuses and business greed affect the lives of ordinary citizens. The challenge for watchdog journalism is to expand its thematic agenda, to investigate wrongdoing beyond official intrigue and back stabbing among political elites.

In closing, I have argued that muckraking does not eliminate corruption but raises awareness about its existence. It does not create accountability but adds efforts to a more vigilant society. It does not make power-holders responsible for their misdeeds but forces them to give answers for their acts. It does not bring reform but can call attention to areas that badly need reform. It does not legally sanction criminals but symbolically punishes them. It does not cure society's ills but may contribute to debates and the search for solutions. It does not have all the answers to the many deficits of contemporary South American democracies but can point them out.

The upshot is that potential contributions are severely limited by economic and political interests and a journalistic culture obsessed about squabbles among officials. Watchdog journalism exists within the confines of news organizations and journalistic cultures. Media organizations expect to achieve business success rather than to enrich public debates. The culture of newsrooms tends to follow formulaic narratives and issues rather than to expand attention to different matters of public interest. Journalism largely focuses on powerful newsmakers and official dealings rather than on issues that might open readers to worlds that are largely unfamiliar.

Like the press at large, muckraking is charged with contradictions. Its merits show the potential to contribute to democracies in which public deliberations cover a wide variety of subjects, political and economic power-holders are monitored and accountable, and policymakers and citizens do not lose sight of the urgency of pursuing legal and social equality. The question remains if watchdog journalism can overcome the contradictions that blunt its potentially sharper edge or if those contradictions are irresoluble.

NOTES

1. WATCHDOG JOURNALISM IN A HISTORICAL PERSPECTIVE

1. For Curran, the civic media has three components: media linked to collective organizations for a general audience, subcultural media belonging to a constituency, and organizational media that serves as a channel for communication in a group. Professional media refers to journalists who work for adversarial media linked to organized interests, public service institutions, and profit-driven organizations.

2. This conclusion is based on the fact that the leading newspapers were part of family-owned industrial conglomerates, with the exception of *El Comercio,* which was owned and operated by a journalistic dynasty.

3. La Violencia refers to the period from 1946 and 1958 that pitted the two traditional parties in an all-out confrontation, especially in the countryside and left 200,000 dead.

4. In July 1980, two months after the military government stepped down and Fernando Belaúnde Terry came back to the presidency, *Expreso* (as well as other expropriated papers) was returned to its previous owner. In a reprise of the situation pre-1968 coup, Ulloa was appointed finance minister. He aspired to lead *Acción Popular*'s ticket for the presidential elections but he did not win the nomination. Instead, he successfully ran as senator for the same party.

5. The military have long criticized the press, seeing it as inherently divisive and antinational, an evil that needs to be controlled or extirpated. "The media are a balcony of subversion," a statement made by Colombian Minister of Defense General Luis Camacho in the early 1980s, illustrates the deep-rooted feelings of distrust among the military.

6. These newspapers had originally supported the 1964 coup.

7. The original owners of *Marka*, leftist parties, unions, and partners originally formed the company that controlled the newspaper. Continuous shifts in stock holding distribution, which to some extent reflected the internecine struggles within the Peruvian left, were responsible for changes in the editorial line. Two projects uneasily

coexisted at El *Diario de Marka*: one approached the daily basically as a commercial enterprise with political goals while the other prioritized political ideas and relegated business considerations. Despite its changes, it remained essentially a political newspaper that cultivated an aggressive, in-your-face style that clashed with the establishment newspapers that were returned to their previous owners in 1980. In reaction to the paper's denunciations, the Belaunde government stopped official advertising (Gargurevich 1991).

8. Together with Nobel laureate Gabriel García Márquez and others, Walsh participated in the founding of *Prensa Latina*, a news agency that intended to break the news blockade established by Western agencies during the Cuban revolution. Later, he founded many alternative publications such as the newspaper of a dissident union organization, *Noticias* (the newspaper of the Peronist guerrilla organization Montoneros), *Semanario Villero* (a newspaper for slum-dwellers and conceived as a school of journalism to train "popular journalists") and *ANCLA* (an underground news service during the military dictatorship in the 1970s).

2. DENOUNCING WRONGDOING

1. Yabrán boasted that although he was highly influential and had close connections with prominent officials, he maintained a low profile. In November 1994, when his confrontation with minister Cavallo was surfacing, *Noticias* interviewed him but he didn't want to be photographed. With a smirk in his face, Yabrán asserted "Taking a picture of me is like shooting me in the forehead" (Gallo 1998).

2. The story about how *Veja* obtained the interview with Pedro Collor has been told numerous times in the Brazilian press. According to managing editor Mario Sergio Conti (1992),

"We had a reporter, Luis Costa Pinto (Lula), editor of the Recife branch, a 23-year-old guy (that is, within the press the boy was almost nothing) who cultivated Pedro Collor, called him every week. Because he's a good professional, Lula was transferred to Brasilia and maintained contacts with Pedro Collor. He knew there was some confusion in Alagoas with the Collors' newspaper. *Veja* initially published Pedro Collor's dossier in February 1992 in which he said that he was gathering documents about PC [Farias]. The article came out but nobody paid much attention, except for [Fernando] Collor and PC who tried to reach an agreement with Pedro. They had several meetings. PC even sent us a letter questioning the information but we didn't publish it because the information was right. The reporter kept in contact with Pedro who was becoming more upset with PC. When he decided it was time to tell all, Pedro Collor told it to somebody he trusted, to a publication he trusted, who always treated him right and never feared his brother's attacks. Let's remember, that week everyone wanted an interview with [Pedro] Collor. But he didn't; he only talked to us. If he wanted repercussion he would have talked to *Rede Globo* [Brazil's largest TV network]. It was our reporter's merit; he established a relationship based on trust with the source . . . . Lula interviewed Pedro Collor in Maceio [Alagoas capital and the Collor's home town]. Then he called me and gave me a summary. I said: 'This is very serious. I want to meet Pedro. Can you bring him to Sao Paulo?' And Lula did. There were more than one hundred reporters waiting Pedro Collor at the airport and we could bring him, with his wife and his sister to the newsroom. Lula, editor Tales Alvarenga, executive director Paulo Moreira Leite and myself talked to him for two and half hours. Then I was sure that Pedro was speaking the truth, that he wasn't crazy or irresponsible. It wasn't *Veja*'s merit but the reporter's. It wasn't a big name of the press who discovered it [but] a reporter in Recife.'

3. In a return to his reporting roots, Colombian Nobel laureate Gabriel García Márquez (1997) has masterfully narrated these events in his *News of a Kidnapping*.

4. In mid-September, Medina reiterated and expanded his testimony on the role that Ms. Sarria had in the Samper campaign.

5. Sarria, considered a key witness in the case, was found dead in February 1996.

6. The relations between Montesinos and *Caretas* became conflictive. Montesinos initially brought a lawsuit against *Caretas* in 1989, which was dismissed by the Supreme Court. As the magazine began to put more attention into his activities, he offered publisher Enrique Zileri to provide first-hand intelligence information in exchange for not delving into his business. Zileri requested an on-the-record interview but Montesinos ignored it and sued the news weekly for defamation (the publication dubbed him "the new Rasputin").

7. In Brazil, the average of 3.2 persons per month killed by police before mid-1995 rose to 20.5 in the first months of 1996 (Human Rights Watch 1997).

3. WHY WATCHDOGS BARK

1. In Peru, then-Defense minister General Victor Malca sued Ricardo Uceda for his report on the Barrios Altos massacre and General Clemente Noel brought a lawsuit against Cecilia Valenzuela who accused him of having witnessed tortures.

2. Similar situations happened in other countries in the region. According to Eleazar Diaz Rangel, former president of the *Colegio Nacional de Periodistas* (National Association of Journalists), in Venezuela the state has threatened to withhold advertising and offered subsidized exchange rates to put pressure on editors (Fernandez 1993. In Chile, the economic recession of the 1980s almost brought down two media conglomerates. The Pinochet government initially approved the loans

that saved them from bankruptcy, but later, close to the democratic transition, canceled the debts and transferred them to the state bank (Gonzalez 1992).

3. This refers to the mobilization for direct elections in the early 1980s that culminated in the 1985 electoral contest.

4. The decision of the Collor administration to raid *Folha*'s offices and investigate the newspaper's tax returns was interpreted as retaliation for *Folha*'s disclosures.

5. After years of persistent economic difficulties, the Cano family has accepted the offer of the Santo Domingo group to take over *El Espectador*. The irony is self-evident: the same newspaper that vigorously resisted the attacks of drug-traffickers and denounced corporate venality in the past became part of one of the country's largest business. At the time when the deal was closed *Semana* (1997) observed, "For some [observers], it was a paradox that a newspaper that took the role of the crusader against the power of economic groups in the 1970s, ended in the hands of the most powerful groups that ever existed in Colombian history."

6. Menem's tirades against the press have been frequent in the 1990s (Verbitsky 1997; Zunino 1995). He has called journalists who disclosed wrongdoing "stupid, liar and miserable paid by some opposition group." His criticisms have not been limited to the local press. After the *New York Times* published information about official corruption, Menem energetically declared that the newspaper "publishes lies, attributes to authorities things they never said, and it is motivated by the interests of the opposition. It is unjust, shoots with heavy ammunition, and makes terrible mistakes."

7. At the peak of the *Proceso 8,000* scandal, Santos Castillo, know to have been close to President Samper, was reported to have sarcastically remarked to the editor-in-chief (who was also his son) and a top editor, "the campaign against the president is going very well. You guys have published three front-page articles against him. Tell me how many more pages you need and I will make sure that they have few ads" (*El Tiempo* 1999).

8. After stepping down from the presidency in 1990, Alan García left Peru.

9. Francisco Igartua founded *Oiga* in the 1940s and the magazine had an on-and-off existence shaped by the country's politics. Persecuted by the military, Igartua was forced to go into exile. Together with Doris Gibson, Igartua created *Caretas* in 1950 and later left it to revamp *Oiga* in 1962. Enrique Zileri, Gibson's son, became editor of the then bimonthly. The military governments of Velasco Alvarado and Morales Bermudez shut down the magazine twice and Zileri was deported.

10. I thank John Nerone for having suggested the expression.

4. THE POLITICS OF SOURCES

1. A survey among Brazilian journalists shows that only 26 percent of reporters consider it indispensable to write stories that present facts supporting statements and

83 percent admit the use of confidential documents without authorization (Cardoso 1995).

2. The four tapes made public in July 1994 were part of over 800 hours of phone conversations recorded by U.S. and Colombian intelligence services who tapped the telephone lines of people linked to the Rodriguez Orejuela drug lords.

3. *Petista* refers to *Partido dos Trabalhadores* (PT), the coalition of leftist and center-left parties that ran against Fernando Collor in the 1989 presidential election.

5. PARALLEL IDEALS: FACTICITY AND OBJECTIVITY IN EXPOSÉS

1. The pictures were obtained from a photographer originally hired by Fernando Collor who, according to journalists, decided to turn the film to *Veja* after Collor did not pay him.

6. PROFESSIONAL CRUSADERS: THE POLITICS OF PROFESSIONAL JOURNALISM

1. A minor stockholder at *El Tiempo*, Samper had sufficient clout to convince the upper brass that the project was worth trying and to push specific investigations.

2. The newspaper was shut down by the Peronist government after Juan Perón died in office in July 1974. The decision was another manifestation of the consolidation of right-wing forces within Peronism that launched an open confrontation against guerrilla organizations, including Montoneros.

3. This carefulness, no doubt, has been fueled by continuous legal actions against reporters and press companies. Implicated individuals, especially government officials, have typically and quickly resorted to legal threats to respond to press accusations of wrongdoing. It doesn't help either, reporters observe, that judges have favored plaintiffs. Such a legally belligerent climate has turned watchdog reporting into an extremely problematic proposition, with potentially damaging and expensive results for journalists as well as publishers.

4. *Semana* was widely identified as supporting a Liberal faction opposed to then-president Ernesto Samper.

5. *O Estado de São Paulo*, the flagship of one of the leading publishing groups in the country, has historically defended conservative interests that viewed Frei Betto and Lula as the personification of the red menace in Brazil. Frei Betto has been one of the best-known advocates of theology of liberation and Lula is the former union leader who led the presidential ticket of the leftist coalition in 1989, 1994, and 1998.

6. The *Pacto Nacional* was a power-sharing agreement between Liberals and Conservatives.

8. WATCHDOG JOURNALISM AND DEMOCRATIC ACCOUNTABILITY

1. Thompson also mentions a fifth characteristic of scandals, the damaging of the reputation of individuals responsible for the transgressions. Because, as he argues, it is not always present I do not include in the definition. I will return to this point later.

2. Between July 1994 and March 1996, *El Tiempo* featured 721 stories on the subject, 133 in front page (Villar Borda 1996).

3. The editors of newsweekly *Semana* observed, "the government has intervened in the process with classic instruments of Colombian politics: the distribution of public funds and political favors to the representatives who voted in favor of Samper" (Vargas et al. 1996: 451).

4. Needless to say, the resolution of Collorgate was not the result solely of Collor's unfavorable balance of forces in Congress. A convergence of factors was ultimately responsible for his resignation, as many authors have argued (Keck 1992; Neumanne 1992; Neves and Fagunes 1992; Weyland 1993). It is clear, however, that Congress had a decisive role in the fact that Collor de Mello was forced out of office in a relatively short period of time. Only six months passed since Congress decided to pursue press disclosures further and his resignation. Even after Collor resigned, the impeachment process continued. The Supreme Court eventually acquitted him.

REFERENCES

BOOKS, JOURNAL ARTICLES, AND
NEWSPAPER ARTICLES IN ENGLISH

Abbott, Andrew. *The System of Professions: An Essay on the Division of Expert Labor.* Chicago: University of Chicago Press, 1988.

Ades, Dawn. *Photomontage.* London: Thames and Hudson, 1986.

Allan, Stuart. "News and the Public Sphere: Towards a History of Objectivity and Impartiality." In Michael Bromley and Tom O'Malley, eds., *A Journalism Reader,* pp. 296–329. London: Routledge, 1997.

Allen, Barry. *Truth in Philosophy.* Cambridge, Mass.: Harvard University Press, 1993.

Alves, Rosental Calmon. "Democracy's Vanguard Newspapers in Latin America." Paper presented at the International Communication Association Conference, Montreal, May 1997.

Anderson, David. *Investigative Reporting.* Bloomington: Indiana University Press, 1976.

Aucoin, James L. "The Reemergence of American Investigative Journalism." *Journalism History* 21, no. 1 (Spring 1995): 3–15.

Barry, Andrew. "Television, Truth and Democracy." *Media, Culture and Society* 15, no. 3 (July 1993): 487–96.

Benjaminson, Peter. *Investigative Reporting* Ames: Iowa State University Press, 1990.

Bennett, W. Lance. *News: The Politics of Illusion,* 3rd ed. New York: Longman, 1996.

Bernstein, Richard J. *The New Constellation: The Ethical-Political Horizons of Modernity/Postmodernity.* Cambridge, Mass.: MIT Press, 1992.

Bledstein, Burton J. *The Culture of Professionalism: The Middle Class and the Development of Higher Education in America.* New York: Norton, 1976.

Bobbio, Norberto. *Liberalism & Democracy.* London: Verso, 1988.

Bovens, Mark. *The Quest for Responsibility: Accountability and Citizenship in Complex Organizations.* Cambridge, Mass.: Cambridge University Press, 1998.

Bok, Sissela. *Lying.* New York: Random House, 1978.

Boyce, George. "The Fourth Estate: The Reappraisal of a Concept." In G. Boyce,

J. Curran, and P. Wingate, eds., *Newspaper History: from the Seventeenth Century to the Present Day*, pp. 19–40. London: Constable, 1978.

Broddason, Thornbjörn. "The Sacred Side of Professional Journalism." *European Journal of Communication* 9, no. 3 (September 1994): 227–48.

Buckman, Robert T. "Current Status of the Mass Media in Latin America." In R. R. Cole ed., *Communication in Latin America*, pp. 3–36. Wilmington, Del.: SR Books, 1996.

Campbell, Richard. *60 Minutes and the News: A Mythology for Middle America*. Urbana: University of Illinois Press, 1991.

Cane, James. "Shattering the Ink Mirror: The Expropriation of La Prensa and the Question of 'Freedom of the Press' in Peronist Argentina, 1943–51." Paper presented at the 91st annual meeting of the American Historical Association, Pacific Coast Branch, San Diego, August 1998.

Carey, James. "The Communications Revolution and the Professional Communicator." *Sociological Review Monograph* 13 (1969): 23–38.

——. "The Mass Media and Democracy: Between the Modern and the Postmodern." *Journal of International Affairs* 47, no. 1 (Summer 1993): 1–21.

Carrigan, Ana. "An Unlikely Hero: Valdivieso's Crusade Against Drug Corruption." *NACLA Report on the Americas* 30, no. 1 (July/August 1996): 6–10.

Chalaby, Jean K. "No Ordinary Press Owners: Press Barons as a Weberian Ideal Type." *Media, Culture & Society* 19(October 1997): 621–41.

Cohen, Stanley. *Folk Devils and Moral Panics: The Creation of the Mods and Rockers*. New York: St. Martin's Press, 1980.

Conaghan, Catherine. "Fear, Loathing and Collusion: Press and State in Fujimori's Peru." Paper presented at the 21st Congress of the Latin American Studies Association, Chicago, September 1998.

Corradi, Juan, Patricia Wiss Fagen, and Manuel A. Garretón, eds. *Fear at the Edge: State Terror and Resistance in Latin America*. Berkeley: University of California Press, 1992.

Curran, James. "Cultural Perspectives of News Organizations: A Reappraisal and a Case Study." In M. Ferguson, ed., *Public Communication: The New Imperatives*, pp. 114–34. London: Sage, 1990.

——. "Mass Media and Democracy Revisited." In James Curran, ed., *Mass Media and Society*, 81–119. London: Arnold, 1996.

Dahlgren, Peter, and Colin Sparks. *Journalism and Popular Culture*. Thousand Oaks, Calif. : Sage, 1992.

Daston, Lorraine. "Marvelous Facts and Miraculous Evidence in Early Modern Europe." In J. Chandler, A. I. Davidson, and H. Harootunian, eds., *Questions of Evidence: Proof, Practice, and Persuasion Across the Disciplines*, pp. 243–74. Chicago: University of Chicago Press, 1994.

de Certeau, Michel. "History: Science and Fiction." In R. Bellah et al., eds., *Social Science as Moral Inquiry*, pp. 125–52. New York: Columbia University Press, 1983.

de Leon, Peter. *Thinking about Political Corruption*. Armonk, NY: M.E. Sharpe, 1993.

de Lima, Venicio. "The State, Television and Political Power in Brazil." *Critical Studies in Mass Communication* 5 (1988): 108–28.

Dennis, Everett. "In Allegiance to the Truth: News Ethics and Split-personality Journalism," *Nieman Reports* (Summer 1990): 4–8 and 36.

Dennis, Everett, Donald Gillmor, and Theodore L. Glasser, eds., *Media Freedom and Accountability*. New York: Greenwood Press, 1989.

Dimenstein, Gilberto. *Brazil: War on Children*. London: Latin America Bureau, 1991.

Duzán, María Jimena. *Death Beat: A Colombian Journalist's Life Inside the Cocaine Wars*. New York: Harper Collins, 1994.

Eisner, Peter. "Colombia's Killing Fields." *The Quill*, September 1990.

Elliott, Philip. "Professional Ideology and Organizational Change: The Journalist Since 1800," in G. Boyce, J. Curran and P. Wingate, eds., *Newspaper History from the Seventeenth Century to the Present Day*, pp. 172–91. London: Constable, 1978.

Entman, Robert M. *Democracy Without Citizens: Media and the Decay of American Politics*. New York: Oxford University Press, 1989.

Epstein, Edward. *Between Fact and Fiction*. New York: Vintage, 1975.

Ettema, James S., and Theodore L. Glasser. *Custodians of Conscience: Investigative Journalism and Public Virtue*. New York: Columbia University Press, 1998.

Ferry, Jean M. "Modernization and Consensus." In M. Lilla, ed., *New French Thought*, pp. 201–11. Princeton, NJ: Princeton University Press, 1994.

Fishman, Mark. *Manufacturing the News*. Austin: University of Texas Press, 1980.

Fleischer, David. "Political Corruption in Brazil: The Delicate Connection with Campaign Finance." *Crime, Law and Social Change* 25, no. 4 (1996/1997): 297–321.

Freidson, Elliot. *Professional Powers: A Study of the Institutionalization of Formal Knowledge*. Chicago: University of Chicago Press, 1986.

Frus, Phyllis. *The Politics and Poetics of Journalistic Narrative: The Timely and the Timeless*. New York: Cambridge University Press, 1994.

Fuller, Jack. *News Values: Ideas for an Information Age*. Chicago: University of Chicago Press, 1996.

Gaines, William. *Investigative Reporting for Print and Broadcast*. Chicago: Nelson-Hall, 1994.

Gans, Herbert. *Deciding What's News: A Study of CBS Evening News, NBC Nightly News, Newsweek, and Time*. New York: Pantheon, 1980.

García Márquez, Gabriel. *News of a Kidnapping*. New York: Knopf, 1997.

Gauthier, Gilles. "In Defense of a Supposedly Outdated Notion: The Range of Application of Journalistic Objectivity." *Canadian Journal of Communication* 18 (1993): 497–505.

Gavin, Thomas. "The Truth Beyond Facts: Journalism and Literature." *The Georgia Review* 45, no. 1 (Spring 1991): 39–51.

Geddes, Barbara, and Artur Ribeiro Neto. "Institutional Sources of Corruption in Brazil," *Third World Quarterly* 13, no. 4 (1992): 641–61.

Ginsberg, Benjamin, and Martin Shefter. *Politics by Other Means: The Declining Importance of Elections in America.* New York: Basic Books, 1990.

Ginzburg, Carlo. "Checking the Evidence: The Judge and the Historian." In James Chandler, Arnold I. Davidson, and Harry Harootunian, eds., *Questions of Evidence: Proof, Practice, and Persuasion Across the Disciplines,* pp. 290–303. Chicago: University of Chicago Press, 1994.

Glasgow University Media Group. *Bad News.* London: Routledge, 1982.

Glasser, Theodore and James S. Ettema. "When the Facts Don't Speak for Themselves: A Study of the Use of Irony in Daily Journalism," *Critical Studies in Mass Communication* 10, no. 4 (December 1993): 322–28.

Gleason, Timothy W. *The Watchdog Concept: The Press and the Courts in Nineteenth-century America.* Ames: Iowa State University Press, 1990.

Goffman, Erving. *The Presentation of Self in Everyday Life.* Woodstock, N.Y.: Overlook Press, 1959.

Golding, Peter, and Philip Elliott. *Making the News.* London and New York: Longman, 1979.

Gorriti, Gustavo. "Where Journalists Still Get Respect," *New York Times*, July 21, 1998 p. A15.

Gusfield, Joseph. *The Culture of Public Problems.* Chicago: University of Chicago Press, 1981.

Guttman, Amy, and Dennis Thompson. *Democracy and Disagreement.* Cambridge, Mass.: Harvard University Press, 1996.

Hackett, Robert A. "Decline of a Paradigm? Bias and Objectivity in News Media Studies," *Critical Studies in Mass Communication* 1, 3 (1984): 229–59.

Hackett, Robert A., and Yuezhi Zhao. *Sustaining Democracy? Journalism and the Politics of Objectivity.* Toronto: Garamond Press, 1998.

Hall, Stuart. "The Determinations of News Photographs." In Stanley Cohen and Jock Young, eds., *The Manufacture of News: Deviance, Social Problems & the Mass Media,* pp. 85–94. London: Constable, 1978.

Hall, Stuart, et al. *Policing the Crisis: Mugging, the State, and Law and Order.* New York: Holmes & Meier, 1978.

Hallin, Daniel C. *The "Uncensored War": The Media and Vietnam.* New York: Oxford University Press, 1986.

——. *We Are on Top of the World: Television Journalism and the Public Sphere.* New York: Routledge, 1994.

Hartley, John. *The Politics of Pictures: The Creation of the Public in the Age of Popular Media.* London: Routledge, 1992.

——. *Popular Reality: Journalism, Modernity, Popular Culture.* London: Arnold, 1996.

Hess, Stephen. *The Government/Press Connection.* Washington, D.C: Brookings Institution, 1984.

——. *News and Newsmaking.* Washington, D.C.: Brookings Institution, 1996.

Heuvel, Jon Vanden, and Everette E. Dennis. *Changing Patterns: Latin America's Vital Media.* New York: Freedom Forum Media Studies Center, 1995.

Human Rights Watch. *Police Brutality in Urban Brazil.* New York: Human Rights Watch, 1997.

Jackson, John D. "Analyzing the New Evidence Scholarship: Towards a New Conception of the Law of Evidence." *Oxford Journal of Legal Studies* 16, no. 2 (1996): 309–28.

Janowitz, Morris. "Professional Models in Journalism: The Gatekeeper and the Advocate." *Journalism Quarterly* (Winter 1975): 618–26.

Jobim, Danton. "French and U.S. Influences upon the Latin American Press." *Journalism Quarterly* 1, no. 1(1954): 61–66.

Johnson, Terence J. *Professions and Power.* London. Macmillan, 1972.

Katz, Ian. "From Inky Presses to Outer Space." *Business Week* (May 20, 1996): 18.

Keck, Margaret. "Brazil: Impeachment!" *NACLA Report on the Americas* 26 (1992): 4–7.

Klaidman, Stephen, and Tom Beauchamp. *The Virtuous Journalist.* New York: Oxford University Press, 1987.

Klitgaard, Robert. *Controlling Corruption.* Berkeley: University of California Press, 1988.

Knudson, Jerry W. "Licensing Journalists in Latin America: An Appraisal." *Journalism & Mass Communication Quarterly* 73, no. 4 (Winter 1996): 878–89.

Kuhn, Thomas. *The Structure of Scientific Revolutions,* 2nd ed. Chicago: University of Chicago Press, 1970.

Lang, Gladys Engel, and Kurt Lang. *The Battle for Public Opinion: The President, the Press, and the Polls during Watergate.* New York: Columbia University Press, 1983.

Larson, Magali Sarfatti. *The Rise of Professionalism: A Sociological Analysis.* Berkeley: University of California Press, 1977.

Latin American Weekly Report. "U.S. Takes Action on Corruption," January 24, 1991, p. 2.

Lemert, James B. *Does Mass Communication Change Public Opinion After All?: A New Approach to Effects Analysis.* Chicago: Nelson-Hall, 1981.

Limor, Yehiel, and Dan Caspi. "It Takes Two to . . . Leak." Paper presented at the conference of the International Communication Association, Montreal, Canada, May 1997.

Lippman, Walter. *Public Opinion.* New York: Free Press, 1922.

Litowitz, Douglas. "The Trouble with 'Scarlet Letter' Punishments," *Judicature* 81, no. 2 (1997): 52–57.

Little, Walter. "Political Corruption in Latin America," *Corruption and Reform* 7, no. 1(1992): 41–66.

Lowi, Theodore. "Foreword." In Andrei S. Markovits and Mark Silverstein, eds., *The Politics of Scandal: Power and Process in Liberal Democracies,* pp. vii–xii. New York: Holmes & Meier, 1988.

Maingot, Anthony. "Confronting Corruption in the Hemisphere: A Sociological Perspective," *Journal of Interamerican Studies and World Affairs* 36, no. 3 (1994):49.

Mancini, Paolo. "Old and New Contradictions in Italian Journalism," *Journal of Communication* 42, no. 3 (1992): 42–47.

McClintock, Cynthia. "The Media and Re-democratization in Peru," *Studies in Latin American Popular Culture* 6 (1987): 115–34.

Megill, Allan. "Introduction: Four Senses of Objectivity," in Allan Megill, ed., *Rethinking Objectivity*, pp. 1–20. Durham: Duke University Press, 1994.

Mill, John Stuart. *On Liberty*. London: Oxford, 1975 [1859].

Milton, John. *Areopagitica*. New York: St. Martin's Press, 1967.

Miraldi, Robert. *Muckraking and Objectivity: Journalism's Colliding Traditions*. New York: Greenwood Press, 1990.

Mitchell, William. J. *The Reconfigured Eye: Visual Truth in the Post-photographic Era*. Cambridge, Mass.: MIT Press, 1992.

Negrine, Ralph. *The Communication of Politics*. London: Sage, 1996.

Nerone, John. "The Mythology of the Penny Press." *Critical Studies in Mass Communication* 4 (1987): 376–404.

———. *Violence Against the Press: Policing the Public Sphere in U.S. History*. New York: Oxford University Press, 1994.

O'Connor, Robert. "The Media and the Campaign," in Howard R. Penniman, ed., *Venezuela at the Polls*, pp. 171–90. Washington, D.C.: American Enterprise Institute.

Orme, William A. *A Culture of Collision: An Inside Look at the Mexican Press*. Miami: North-South Center Press, 1996.

Paletz, David L., and Robert M. Entman. *Media, Power, Politics*. New York: Free Press, 1981.

Panizza, Francisco. "Human Rights in the Processes of Transition and Consolidation of Democracy in Latin America." *Political Studies* 43 (1995): 168–88.

Phelan, Peter, and Peter Reynolds, *Argument and Evidence: Critical Analysis for the Social Sciences*. London: Routledge, 1996.

Protess, David, Fay Lomax Cook, Jack C. Doppelt, James S. Ettema, Margaret T. Gordon, Donna R. Leff, and Peter Miller. *The Journalism of Outrage: Investigative Reporting and Agenda Building in America*. New York: Guilford, 1992.

Ratliff, William and Edgardo Buscaglia. "Judicial Reform: The Neglected Priority in Latin America." *Annals of the American Academy of Political and Social Science* 550 (March 1997): 59–71.

Robins, Kevin. *Into the Image: Culture and Politics in the Field of Vision*. London: Routledge, 1996.

Romano, Carlin. "The Grisly Truth about Bare Facts," in Robert Karl Manoff and Michael Schudson, eds., *Reading the News*, pp. 38–78. New York: Pantheon, 1986.

Rorty, Richard. *Objectivity, Relativism and Truth: Philosophical Papers*, Vol. I, Cambridge: Cambridge University Press, 1991.

Rosenn, Keith, and Richard Downes, eds. *Corruption and Political Reform in Brazil: The Aftermath of Fernando Collor de Mello.* Miami: North-South Center, 1999.

Rothblatt, Sheldon. "How 'Professional' are the Professions?" *Studies in Comparative Society and History* 37, no. 1 (1995): 194–204.

Saba, Roberto Pablo, and Luigi Manzetti. "Privatization in Argentina: The Implications for Corruption." *Crime, Law and Social Change* 25, no. 4 (1996/1997): 353–69.

Sage, Colin. "Drugs and Eonomic Development in Latin America: A Study in the Political Economy of Cocaine in Bolivia." In Peter Ward, ed., *Corruption, Development and Inequality: Soft Touch or Hard Graft?* London: Routledge, 1989.

Salwen, Michael B., and Bruce Garrison. *Latin American Journalism.* Hillsdale, N.J: Lawrence Erlbaum Associates, 1991.

Shapiro, Barbara J. *"Beyond Reasonable Doubt" and "Probable Cause": Historical Perspectives on the Anglo-American Law of Evidence.* Berkeley: University of California Press, 1991.

Schedler, Andreas. "Conceptualizing Accountability." In Larry Diamond, Marc F. Plattner, and Andreas Schedler, eds., *The Self-Restraining State: Power and Accountability in New Democracies,* pp. 13–28. Boulder: Lynne Rienner, 1999.

Schemo, Diana Jean. "Colombia's Leader, Cleared by Congress, Still Isn't In the Clear." *New York Times,* June 14, 1996a, p. A5.

———. "To Punish Colombia, U.S. May Revoke Air Route." *New York Times,* August 4, 1996b, p. A10.

Schiller, Dan. *Objectivity and the News: The Public and the Rise of Commercial Journalism.* Philadelphia: University of Pennsylvania Press, 1979.

Schlesinger, Philip. "Rethinking the Sociology of Journalism." In Marjorie Ferguson, ed., *Public Communication,* pp. 61–83. London: Sage, 1990.

Schlesinger, Philip and Howard Tumber. *Reporting Crime: The Media Politics of Criminal Justice.* Oxford: Clarendon Press, 1994.

Schudson, Michael. *Discovering the News.* New York: Basic Books, 1978.

———. *The Power of News.* Cambridge, Mass.: Harvard University Press, 1995.

Schultz, Julianne. *Reviving the Fourth Estate: Democracy, Accountability, and the Media.* Cambridge: Cambridge University Press, 1998.

Schwartz, Dona. "To Tell the Truth: Codes of Objectivity in Photojournalism." *Communication* 13 (1992), 95–109.

Sigal, Leon. *Reporters and Officials.* Lexington, Mass.: Heath, 1973.

Sives, Amanda. "Elite Behavior and Corruption in the Consolidation of Democracy in Brazil," *Parliamentary Affairs* 46, no. 4 (1993): 549–62.

Skidmore, Thomas. "Collor's Downfall in Historical Perspective." In K. Rosenn and R. Downes, eds. *Corruption and Political Reform in Brazil,* pp. 1–20.

Smith, Anne-Marie. *A Forced Agreement: Press Acquiescence to Censorship in Brazil.* Pittsburgh: University of Pittsburgh Press, 1997.

Smith, Anthony. "Is Objectivity Obsolete?"' *Columbia Journalism Review* (May/June 1980): 61–65.

Soloski, John. "News Reporting and Professionalism: Some Constraints on the Reporting of the News," *Media, Culture & Society* 11, no. 2 (April 1989): 207–28.

Sparks, Colin, and Slavko Splichal. *Journalists for the 21st century: Tendencies of Professionalization among First-year Students in 22 countries.* Norwood, N..J.: Ablex, 1994.

Stokes, Susan C. "Democratic Accountability and Policy Change: Economic Policy in Fujimori's Peru," *Comparative Politics* 29, no. 2 (1997): 209–26.

Streckfuss, Richard. "Objectivity in Journalism: A Search and a Reassessment," *Journalism Quarterly* 67, no. 4 (1990): 973–83.

Tester, Keith. *Moral Culture.* London: Sage, 1997.

Thompson, John B. "Scandal and Social Theory." In J. Lull and S. Hinerman, eds., *Media Scandals,* pp. 34–64. New York: Columbia University Press, 1997.

Thompson, Kenneth. *Moral Panics.* London and New York: Routledge, 1998.

Tuchman, Gaye. *Making News.* New York: Free Press, 1978.

Tunstall, Jeremy. *Journalists at Work.* Beverly Hills: Sage, 1971.

Ullmann, John, and Jan Colbert. *The Reporter's Handbook: An Investigator's Guide to Documents and Techniques.* New York: St. Martin's Press, 1991.

United States Senate Foreign Relations Committee. *Corruption and Drugs in Colombia: Democracy at Risk.* 96-S382-2, S. Prt 104–47.

Verbitsky, Horacio. *The Flight: Confessions of an Argentine Dirty Warrior.* New York: The New Press, 1996.

Wall Street Journal. "Scandal Tarnishes IBM's Image." December 11. 1995.

——. "Mirror on the Americas," special edition, 1998.

Waisbord, Silvio. "Investigative Journalism and Political Accountability in South American Democracies." *Critical Studies in Mass Communication* 13, 4 (1996): 343–63.

——. "Argentina." In Alan Albarran and Sylvia Chan-Olmsted, eds., *Global Media Economics,* 81–96. Ames: Iowa State University Press, 1998A.

——. "Bad News: Violence against the Press." Paper presented at the conference of the Association for Education in Journalism and Mass Communication, Baltimore, 1998b.

Weaver, Paul. *News and the Culture of Lying.* New York: Free Press, 1994.

Weyland, Kurt. "The Rise and Fall of President Collor and Its Impact on Brazilian Democracy," *Journal of Interamerican Studies and World Affairs* 35, no. 19 (1993): 1–37.

Zelizer. Barbie. *Covering the Body: the Kennedy Assassination, the Media, and the Shaping of Collective Memory.* Chicago: University of Chicago Press, 1992.

——. "Journalists as Interpretative Communities." *Critical Studies in Mass Communication* 10 (1993): 219–37.

——. "Words Against Images: Positioning Newswork in the Age of Photography." In Hanno Hardt and Bonnie Brennen, eds., *Newsworkers: Toward a History of the Rank and File ,* pp. 135–59. Minneapolis: University of Minnessota Press, 1995.

BOOKS AND JOURNAL ARTICLES IN PORTUGUESE AND SPANISH

Abramo, Claudio. *A regra do jogo: O jornalismo e a etica do marceneiro* São Paulo: Companhia das Letras, 1989.

Alves de Abreu, Alcira, and Fernando Lattman-Weltman. *A imprensa em transição: O jornalismo Brasileiro nos anos 50.* Rio de Janeiro: Fundação Getulio Vargas, 1996.

Arocha, Jaime, et al. *Colombia: Violencia y democracia.* Bogotá: Colciencias, 1989.

Barcellos, Caco. *Rota 66: A historia da policia que mata.* São Paulo: Editora Globo, 1992.

Bastos de Quadros, Itanel. "El Desarrollo Publicitario de Brasil." *Revista Latina de Comunicación Social* 2 (February 1998).

Blaustein, Eduardo, and Martín Zubieta. *Decíamos ayer: La Prensa Argentina bajo el Proceso.* Buenos Aires: Colihue, 1998.

Buarque de Gusmão, Sérgio. *Jornalismo de in(ve)stigação: O caso Quércia.* Rio de Janeiro: Civilização Brasileira, 1993.

Burgos, Hernando. "La libertad condicionada." *Quehacer* (September/October 1997): 14–26.

Burgos, Manuel. "Una constante en nuestra historia." *Quehacer* (May/June 1995): 54–57.

Camaño, Juan C., and Osvaldo Bayer. *Los periodistas desaparecidos.* Buenos Aires: Norma, 1998.

Capelato, Maria Helena. *Os arautos do liberalismo: Imprensa paulista 1920–1945.* São Paulo: Brasiliense, 1989.

Castillo, Fabio. *Los jinetes de la cocaína.* Bogotá: Editorial Documentos Periodísticos, 1987.

———. *La coca nostra.* Bogotá: Editorial Documentos Periodísticos, 1991.

Castro Caycedo, Germán. *Colombia amarga.* Bogotá: Carlos Valencia Editores, 1976.

Cepeda Ulloa, Fernando. *La corrupción administrativa en Colombia: Diagnóstico y recomendaciones para combatirla.* Bogotá: TM Editores, 1994.

———. "El congreso colombiano ante la crisis." In Francisco Leal Buitrago, ed., *Tras las huellas de la crisis politica,* pp. 75–95. Bogotá: FESCOL/IEPRI, 1996.

Chagas, Carmo, Jose M. Mayrink, and Luiz A. Pinheiro. *Tréz vezes trinta: Os bastidores da imprensa Brasileira.* São Paulo: Nova Cultural, 1992.

Collor de Mello, Pedro. *Passando a limpo: A trajetória de um farsante.* Rio de Janeiro: Editora Record, 1993.

Cotta, Pery. *Calandra: O sufoco da imprensa nos anos de Chumbo.* Rio de Janeiro: Bertrand Brasil, 1997.

Datum . "Estudio de Opinión Pública," July 1995. Lima: Datum.

de Marco, Miguel et al. *Orígenes de la prensa en Rosario.* Santa Fe, Argentina: Colmegna, 1969.

De Oliverira, Francisco. *Collor: A falsificação da ira.* Rio de Janeiro: Imago, 1992.

Dimenstein, Gilberto. *A guerra dos meninos: Assassinatos de menores no Brasil.* São Paulo: Editora Brasiliense, 1990.

———. *Meninas da noite: A prostituição de meninas-escravas no Brasil.* São Paulo: Editora Atica, 1992.

Dines, Alberto. *O papel do jornal.* São Paulo: Summus, 1986.

Donadío, Alberto. *Banqueros en el banquillo.* Bogotá: El Ancora Editores, 1983.

———. *Por qué cayá Jaime Michelsen?* Bogotá: El Ancora Editores, 1984.

Duarte, Paulo. *Julio Mesquita.* São Paulo: HUCITEC, 1977.

Donnegra, Gabriel. *La prensa en Colombia.* Bogotá: El Ancora, 1984.

Filgueira, Carlos H. "Prensa y cultura política en Uruguay." In Carlos H. Filgueira and Dieter Nohlen, eds., *Prensa y transición democrática: Experiencias recientes en Europa y América Latina,* 80–105. Frankfurt: Iberoamericana, 1994.

Folha de São Paulo. *Racismo cordial.* São Paulo: Editora Atica, 1995.

Fonnegra, Gabriel. *La prensa en Colombia: Cómo informa? De quenes? A quien le sirve?* Bogotá: El Ancora Editores, 1984.

García Márquez, Gabriel. *Periodismo militante.* Bogotá: Son de Máquina, 1978.

Gargurevich, Juan. *Historia de la prensa Peruana, 1594–1990.* Lima: La Voz Ediciones, 1991.

Giannotti, Vito. *Collor, a CUT e a pizza.* São Paulo: Página Aberta, 1992.

González, José. *La prensa como reflejo de desarticulación social.* Lima: CICOSUL, 1992.

Herrán, María Teresa. *La industria de los medios masivos de comunicación en Colombia.* Bogotá: FESCOL, 1991.

Instituto Prensa y Sociedad. *Prensa y justicia en una sociedad en conflicto.* Lima: Instituto Prensa y Sociedad, 1994.

Jose, Emiliano. *Imprensa e poder: Ligações perigosas.* Salvador: EDUFBA, 1996.

Krieger, Gustavo, Fernando Rodrigues, and Elvis C. Bonassa. *Os donos do Congresso: A farsa na CPI do orçamento* . São Paulo: Atica, 1994.

Kucinski, Bernardo. *Jornalistas e revolucionarios: Nos tempos da imprensa alternativa.* São Paulo: Scritta Editorial, 1991.

Lanata, Jorge. "Introducción." In *Página/12 , el nuevo periodismo.* Buenos Aires: Editorá, 1987.

Leal Buitrago, Francisco. "Alcances y dilemas de la crisis politica." In Francisco Leal Buitrago, ed., *Tras las huellas de la crisis politica,* pp. 21–45. Bogotá: FESCOL/IEPRI, 1996.

Lejtman, Roman. *Narcogate.* Buenos Aires: Editorial Sudamericana, 1993.

Lins da Silva, Carlos Eduardo. "As brechas da industria cultural Brasileira." In Regina Festa and Carlos E. Lins da Silva, eds., *Comunicação popular e alternativa no Brasil,* 33–52. São Paulo: Paulinas, 1986.

———. *O adiantado da hora: A influência Americana sobre o jornalismo Brasileiro.* São Paulo: Summus, 1991.

López Chang, Miguel. *Periodismo de investigación: Entre la credibilidad y la duda.* Lima: Coordinadora Nacional de Radio, 1995.

López Martinez. *150 años de El Comercio, 1839–1989.* Lima: El Comercio, 1989.

Marques de Melo, José, and Carlos E. Lins da Silva. *Jornalismo Brasileiro: Perfis de jornalistas.* São Paulo: ECA, USP, 1988.

Marticorena, Katia. La prensa como poder fiscalizador: El caso de La Cantuta. Manuscript, Universidad de Lima, 1996.

Mattos, Sérgio. *Um perfil da TV Brasileira-40 anos de história: 1950–1990.* Salvador: ABAPA Tarde, 1990.

Medina, Cremilda, ed. *O jornalismo da Nova Republica.* São Paulo: Summus, 1987.

Mello Mourao, Gerardo et al., eds. "Imprensa alternativa: Historico e desdobramento." In *Imprensa alternativa & literatura: Os anos de resistencia,* 9–44. Rio de Janeiro: Rioarte, 1987.

Mendes, Candido. *Collor: Anos luz, ano zero.* Rio de Janeiro: Nova Fronteira, 1993.

Napp, Guillermo. *Para la historia del periodismo.* Buenos Aires: El Cronista Comercial, 1987.

Neto, Antonio Fausto. "A sentença dos media: O discurso antecipatorio do impeachment de Collor." In Jose L. Braga and Sergio Porto, eds., *Nação, cultura & politica.* Rio de Janeiro: Diadorim, 1994a.

———. "Vozes do impeachment." In Heloiza Matos, ed., *Midia, eleiçoes e democracia,* pp. 159–189. São Paulo: Scritta, 1994b.

Neumanne, Jose. *A república na lama: Uma tragedia Brasileira.* São Paulo: Geração Editorial, 1992.

Neves, Newton Jose de Oliveira, and Milton Fagundes. *Collor: O artifice do caos.* São Paulo: Icone, 1993.

O'Donnell, Guillermo. "Rendición de cuentas horizontal y nuevas poliarquías." *Nueva Sociedad* 152 (November/December 1997): 143–67.

Orrillo, Winston. *Periodismo, política, literatura: La palabra en el tiempo.* Lima: Causachun, 1986.

Pacheco, José Emilio. "Nota preliminar."' In Rodolfo Walsh, *Obra Literaria Completa,* pp. 3–7. Mexico City: Siglo XXI, 1985.

Pease García, Henry. *Los años de la langosta: La escena política del Fujimorismo.* Lima: La Voz Ediciones, 1994.

Peirano, Luis, Eduardo Ballón, Leyla Bartet, and Gilberto Valdez. *Prensa: Apertura y limites.* Lima: DESCO, 1978.

Pinheiro Manchado, A. *Opinião x censura: Momentos da luta de um jornal pela libertade.* Porto Alegre: L&PM, 1978.

Pinto Gamboa, Willy. *Sobre fascismo y literatura.* Lima: Cibeles, 1983.

Restrepo, Javier Darío. "Los medios ante la crisis." *Signo y Pensamiento* 27 (1995): 91–96.

———. "Medios de comunicación en la crisis politica." In Francisco Leal Buitrago, ed., *Tras las huellas de la crisis política,* pp. 235–61. Bogotá: FESCOL/IEPRI, 1996.

Rey, Alejandra, and Luis Pazos. *No llores por mi, Catamarca: La intriga política de un Crimen.* Buenos Aires: Sudamericana, 1991.

Reyes, Gerardo. *Periodismo de investigación.* Mexico City: Trillas, 1996.

Reyes Matta, Fernando. *Comunicación alternativa y búsquedas.* Santiago: ILET, 1983.

Ribeiro, Alex. *Caso Escola Base: Os abusos da imprensa.* São Paulo: Editora Atica, 1995.

Rodrigues Pereira, Raimundo. "Viva a imprensa alternativa. Viva a imprensa alternativa!" In Regina Festa and Eduardo Lins da Silva, eds., *Comunicação popular e alternativa no Brasil.* pp. 53–75. São Paulo: Edições Paulinas, 1986.

Ruiz, Emilio Juan. *Cuarto poder: Cómo el poder económico se inserta en los medios de Comunicación Colombianos.* Bogotá: Colección Rotativa, 1996.

Samper, Daniel, Fernando Umaña, Gerardo Reyes, María Cecilia Silva, and Olga Pinilla. *Por quien votar?* Bogotá: Editorial Oveja Negra, 1982.

———. *Por quien votar?,* second edition. Bogotá: Editorial Oveja Negra, 1986.

Santa Cruz, Eduardo. *Análisis histórico del periodismo Chileno.* Santiago: Nuestra América Ediciones, 1988.

Santoro, Daniel. *Venta de armas, Hombres del gobierno.* Buenos Aires: Sudamericana, 1998.

Santos, Eduardo. *La crisis de la democracia en Colombia y "El Tiempo."* Mexico City: Gráfica Panamericana, 1955.

Santos Calderón, Enrique. "El periodismo en Colombia, 1886–1986." *In Nueva historia de Colombia,* vol. 6, pp. 109–36. Bogotá: Planeta, 1989.

Saáita, Sylvia. *Regueros de tinta: El diario Crítica en la década de 1920.* Buenos Aires: Sudamericana, 1998.

Sodré, Nelson Werneck. *História da imprensa no Brasil.* Rio de Janeiro: Civilização Brasileira, 1966.

Taschner, Gisela. *Folhas ão Vento.* Rio de Janeiro: Paz e Terra, 1992.

Trindade, Húgio. *Revolução de 30: Partidos e imprensa partidária no RS (1928–1937).* Porto Alegre: Núcleo de Pesquisa e Documentação da Política Rio-Grandense, 1980.

Urien Berri, Jorge and Dante Martin. *El ultimo colimba: El caso Carrasco y la justicia arrodillada.* Buenos Aires: Sudamericana, 1995.

Vargas, Mauricio, Jorge Lesmes, and Edgar Tellez. *El presidente que se iba a caer.* Bogotá: Planeta, 1996.

Verbitsky, Horacio. *Robo para la corona: Los frutos prohibidos del arbol de la corrupción.* Buenos Aires: Planeta, 1991.

———. *Hacer la corte: La construcción de un poder absoluto sin justicia ni control.* Buenos Aires: Planeta, 1993.

———. *Un mundo sin periodistas.* Buenos Aires: Planeta, 1997.

Victoria, Pablo. *Yo acuso: Un documento pliego de cargos contra el Presidente Samper.* Bogotá: Ediciones Temas de Hoy, 1997.

Villalba, Alejandro. Entrevista a Horacio Verbitsky: Rodolfo J. Walsh y el periodismo politico. Manuscript, Universidad de Córdoba, 1991.

Virtue, John et al. *Los periodistas en los paises Andinos.* Miami: Florida International University, 1995.

Walsh, Rodolfo. *El violento oficio de escribir: Obra periodística 1953–1977.* Buenos Aires: Planeta, 1995.

NEWSPAPER AND MAGAZINE ARTICLES
IN PORTUGUESE AND SPANISH

ABC Color. "Corrupción & Impunidad: Desde el . . . Stronismo Hasta Nuestros Dias." December 31, 1997.
Alzugaray, Domingo. "Interview." *Imprensa* (June 1993): 31–36.
Barcelona, Eduardo. "Menem quiso ganar de mano con lo de la conscripción." *La Nación,* June 11, 1994, p. 8.
Biasatti, Santo. "La libertad de prensa en terapia intensiva." *Clarín,* May 7, 1997.
Bless, Karina. "Impuesto a los honestos." *Noticias,* January 4, 1997, p. 24–27.
Brickman, Carlos. "Corrupção velha de guerra." *Imprensa* (July 1992): 36.
Bruschtein, Luis. "Los alcances del 'fenómeno real.'" *Página/12,* 1997.
Caballero, Maria Cristina. "Un bloque tras 15 capos." *Cambio 16,* July 18, 1994, p. 20–22.
Caballero, Antonio. "La tarjeta profesional de la discordia." *El Espectador,* February 19, 1998.
Cambio 16 . "En la cúpula del cartel." August 8, 1994, p. 20–22.
——. "Tretas del cartel." January 30, 1995, p. 14–17.
Cardoso, Adalberto. "Jornalistas: Ética e democracia no exercício da profissão. *Novos Estudos* 42 (July 1995):130–40.
Caretas. "Prensa acosada." September 30, 1993, p. 28–30.
——. "Las nuevas cuentas." August 10, 1995a.
——. "Que tal raza!" September 14, 1995b.
——. "Duro de callar." December 26, 1997, online edition.
Carta, Mino. "Sejamos honestos." *Correio Braziliense,* October 6, 1996a.
——. "Jornalismo, ontem e hoje." *Correio Braziliense,* November 10, 1996b.
Cepeda Ulloa, Fernando. "Las otras formas de corrupción." *El Tiempo,* April 15, 1996.
Clarín . "Los días de una semana diferente." January 13, 1991, p. 3.
——. "Pons va a reabrir la investigación." May 11, 1991, p. 9.
——. "El gobierno nunca investigó a los intermediarios de la venta de armas," March 19, 1995, p. 2–3.
——. "Operación Claridad," March 24, 1996.
——. "Cuando los Estados Unidos retacean información," January 10, 1997.
Conti, Mario Sergio. "Interview." *Imprensa,* October 1992, p. 25–30.
Cony, Carlos Heitor. "Politicamente incorreto." *Isto E ,* November 24, 1993.
Crucianelli, Sandra. "Unidades de periodismo de investigación: Condenadas al fracaso? *Pulso del Periodismo* (1998), *www.fiu.edu/~imc/investigativo.html*
Cunha Pinto, Guilherme. "Por dentro da Folha." *Playboy* (November 1993).

de Carvalho, Olavo. *Imprensa,* (May 1994).

Diament, Mario. "La otra libertad de prensa." *Pulso del Periodismo* (April/June 1994), p. 31–33.

Dimenstein, Gilberto. "A revolução que estamos vivendo." *Imprensa* (December 1993): 34–36.

Dines, Alberto. "O circo da noticia" *Imprensa* (1992), p. 51.

———. "Interview." *Imprensa* (November 1993), pp. 35–42.

———. "A imprensa no banco dos reus." *Correio Braziliense,* December 18, 1994.

Donadío, Alberto. "El derecho a la información." *Pulso del Periodismo* , October/December 1995, p. 21–22.

El Comercio . "La verdad en el caso de 'La Cantuta.'" April 16, 1993, p. A2.

Fernández, Carmen Alicia. "Corrupción y denuncia periodística,' *Chasqui,* no. 45 (April 1993): 74–78.

Ferreira, Argemiro. "As regras de um jogo pesado." *Imprensa,* August 1992, p. 18–20.

Folha de São Paulo. "Roberto Civita defende processo contra Collor." July 23, 1992a, p. 10.

———. "Ja ha provas contra Collor, diz Fleury." June 30, 1992b, p. 9.

———. "Para diretor da *Globo,* impeachment é provável." August 5, 1992c. p. 8.

———. "Como PC financiou Canhedo." May 8, 1995, p. 4.

———. "Um jornalismo cada vez mais critico e mais criticado." August 8, 1997a.

———. "Projeto editorial 1997." 1997b, www.uol.com.br/fsp/brasil/fc170808.htm.

Franciscato, Carlos, and Gil Campos. "Mata-se jornalista: Tratar aqui." *Imprensa* (February 1995), p. 22–27.

Frias Filho, Otavio. "Interview." *Imprensa* (August 1993): 31–40.

Gallo, Dario. "Fiscales de papel." *Noticias* , July 5, 1997, p. 24–31.

———. "Había una vez un cartero sin rostro." *Noticias* , May 21, 1998.

Gandour, Ricardo. "Para onde estamos indo?" *Imprensa* (November 1993), p. 78–79.

García Márquez, Gabriel. "El mejor oficio del mundo." *Pulso del Periodismo* (January/March 1996), p. 14–17.

O Globo. "No Congresso, Ibsen já admite CPI." May 19, 1992, p. 3.

González, Fernando, and Gabriel Michi. "Fuego contra fuego." *Noticias,* March 3, 1996, p. 22–28.

González, Gustavo. "La pendiente democratización de la prensa." *Chasqui* 43 (October 1992): 62–64.

Gorriti, Gustavo. "El hombre de hierro," *Pulso del Periodismo* (January/March 1994): 16–19.

———. Presentation at the conference of the Centro Latinoamericano de Periodismo, Coronado, Panamá, August 1998.

———. "El periodista frente al miedo." *Pulso del Periodismo,* 1998b, www.fiu.edu/~imc/miedo.htm.

Imprensa . "A cabeça do jornalista do Brasil." March, 1993, p. 18–27.

———. "Acima da lei e dos simples mortais," January, 1995, p. 20–23.

Instituto Gutenberg. "A imprensa-fiscal pode receber dinheiro dos governos que ela fiscaliza?" March 1, 1995. www.igutenberg.com.br/emquest1.htm.

———. "Com as melhores normas técnicas do jornalismo." May/June, 1997, 15.

———. "Quem escreve as notícias." 1998, www.igutenberg.com.br/notas3.htm.

Jornal do Brasil . "Ha algo em comum entre os frequentadores dos porões de poder, de lá e de ca." 1992.

———. "PT promove seis comicios." May 26, 1992, p. 2.

———. "A biografia de um mito da imprensa." October 21, 1995.

Kirschbaum, Ricardo. "Papeles para la historia." *Clarín,* November 1, 1998.

Koop, David. "Un día en la vida de un periodista peruano." *Crónica.* (Mexico). September 29, 1997.

Krieger, Gustavo, Elvira Lobato, and Ari Cipola. "PC enriquece junto com ascenso de Collor." *Folha de São Paulo,* 1992, p. 1:8–9.

La Nación. "Provoca repercusiones en todo el país el caso del soldado Carrasco." April 15, 1994, p. 7.

———. "La autocensura en los medios, un debate que nadie escapa." February 28, 1998.

La República. "Cual es el problema, las denuncias o la corrupción?." August 5, 1996a.

———. "SIN ejecuta plan para amedentrar a periodistas," December 8, 1996b.

Lauer, Mirko. "Resistencia Militar." *La República,* July 10, 1993.

Lefcovich, Sandra. "Vale-tudo na Colombia." *Correio Braziliense,* November 10, 1996.

Leite, Roberto. "*Folha,* 75 anos: A ordem e pensar big." *Imprensa* (April 1996), www.vol.com.br/imprensa/texto/103t07.htm.

Leuco, Alfredo. "Periodismo por periodistas." *Página/12,* May 26, 1997, p. 7.

Lisboa, Marcia. "Qualidade une jornalistas e empresários." *Imprensa* (January 1995): 18–19.

Lofredo, Gino. "Periodismo Investigativo." *Chasqui* 45 (April 1993): 1.

Luna, María del Pilar. "Jorge Lesmes: La piedra en el zapato de Samper." *Pulso del Periodismo* 24, 1995, p. 34–35.

Majul, Luis. "El negocio de la verdad." *Noticias,* 1992, p. 19.

Meio & Mensagem. "Os 20 maiores anunciantes em revistas em 1993." May 9, 1994.

Moisés, Jose Alvaro. "A que serve o 'denuncismo' da *Folha?" Folha de São Paulo,* June 12, 1996.

Moreno, Graciela. "Un regalo todos los dias." *Noticias,* September 19, 1996, p. 46–47.

Motta, Cunha. "São Paulo, década de 30: Pequena história de jornais e jornalistas." *Jornal da Tarde,* May 5, 1975.

Nader, Alceu. "A etica entre o amor e o odio." *Imprensa* (May 1994), p. 7–9.

Nassif, Luis. "A patota do 'Pasquim.'" *Folha de São Paulo,* January 24, 1997a.

———. "Estilos de jornalismo." *Folha de São Paulo,* March 30, 1997b.

———. "Retranca." *Correio Brasiliense,* 1997c.

———. "Os Rambos do jornalismo." *Folha de São Paulo,* 1997d.

Noblet, Ricardo. "Pool informal de jornalistas domina Brasilia." *Imprensa* (May 1995).

Nogueira de Sa, Junia. "A quem interessa o 'denuncismo,'" *Folha de São Paulo* November 14, 1993.

Noticias. "Las pruebas de la corrupción." November 13, 1994.

Oiga . "Las mil y una de Alan y El Assir." September 30, 1991.

Padilla, Nelson Freddy. "Periodismo patas arriba!" *Cambio 16,* December 25, 1995, p. 26–27.

Páez, Angel. "Revelar documentos secretos que prueban corrupción no es traición ala patria."' *La República,* October 21, 1996.

Página/12. "Una misión de la SIP constató en 1978 que para los editores de diarios la seguridad nacional tenía prioridad sobre la libertad de expresión." www.página12. com/1998/98-06/98-06-07/pag10.htm.

Pedreira, Fernando. "Interview." *Imprensa,* August 1992, p. 27–34.

Pereira, Merval. "A pedagogia do escandalo." *Imprensa.* August 1992, p. 14–17.

Pombo, Roberto. "La onda James Bond." *Semana,* September 5, 1995, p. 17.

Pontes, Marcelo. "Da Casa Branca a Casa de Dinda." *Jornal do Brasil,* August 8, 1992, p. 8–9.

Radar. "Informação chapa branca." 8, 1995, p. 6–12.

Reyes, Gerardo. "Los hijos de Watergate." *Pulso del Periodismo,* October/December 1995, pp. 7–12.

Ricketts Rey de Castro, Patricio. "Tiro de gracia." *Si,* August 11, 1997, p. 7–11.

Ronderos, María Teresa, and Ernesto Cortés Fierro. "El proceso a los medios: Destape, confusión y poder," *El Tiempo,* May 10, 1996, p. 1B.

Rossi, Clovis. "Imprensa tem pouco a comemorar no seu dia." *Folha de São Paulo,* September 10, 1990, p. 5.

Rueda, María Isabel. "La verdad." *Semana,* February 13, 1996, p. 40 and 42.

Santos, Rafael. "A la hora de cierre." *El Tiempo,* February 4, 1996, p. 5A.

Santos Calderón, Enrique. *El Tiempo,* June 23, 1994, 4A.

———. "Que persigue Andrés Pastrana?" *El Tiempo,* June 17, 1994, 4A.

———. "Realidad y ficción del 8000." *El Tiempo,* February 19, 1998, 4A.

Seaton, Edward. "Es saludable la colegiatura obligatoria de periodistas? No!"' *Pulso del Periodismo* (April/June 1990), p. 27–28.

Semana. "Primera conversación: Ernesto Samper-Elizabeth de Sarria." August 8, 1995a, p. 48.

———. December 12, 1995b, p. 51.

———. January 30, 1996a, p. 35.

———. "El costo de la bofetada." March 5, 1996b, p. 32–34.

———. "El tiempo del grupo." November 17, 1997.

Si!. "Los investigadores mintieron y actuaron de mala fe," August 11, 1997, p. 1.

Somos. "Angeloz/*Página/12* socios?" December 23, 1991, p. 5.

Tamayo de Echeverry, Gloria. "La tarjeta profesional de la discordia." *El Espectador,* February 19, 1998.

El Tiempo. "Itinerario de un narco-vuelo," January 30, 1996a, p.A1-3.

——. "Congresistas recibieron la plata," January 31, 1996b, p. A1-3.

——. "Su vida transcurrió siempre en *El Tiempo,*" April 21, 1999.

Tijman, Gabriela. "La situación del periodismo en América Latina." *La Maga,* November 15, 1995, p. 42.

Urien Berri, Jorge. "Las Amenazas del Poder." *La Nación,* December 10, 1994.

——. "Piden el proceso para Anzorena por presunto coautor del crimen." *La Nación,* December 13, 1995.

Valenzuela, Cecilia. "El disparadero de La Cantuta: Buscando detrás de Martín Rivas." *Caretas,* December 2, 1993, p. 10–14.

——. "Barrios altos: Nueva pesadilla." *Caretas,* July 13, 1995, p. 30–34.

Valverde, José Luis. "Es saludable la colegiatura obligatoria de periodistas? Si!" *Pulso del Periodismo* (April/June 1990), p. 26, 28.

Veja. "Raio X na Renda," May 20, 1992, p. 16–24.

——. "A hora de PC." July 7, 1993.

——. "Em nome da imagem." October 29, 1997, p. 28.

Vázquez, Luciana. "Una investigación adquiere repercusión en los medios cuando el periodista es agredido." *Perfil,* June 2, 1998.

Villar Borda, Leopoldo. "Estamos Jartos con el Proceso 8,000." *El Tiempo,* March 17, 1996, p. 2B.

Vinhas, Alessandra. "O golpe que a imprensa apoiou." *Imprensa,* March 1994, p. 17–20.

Vitali, Roberto. "Apología del delito." *Si,* August 11, 1997, p.12–13.

Vivas, Fernando. "Periodismo de investigación," *Caretas* 1439, 1995.

——. "Quién anuncia quién? *Caretas* 1574, 1999, *www.caretas.com.pe/1999/1574/cine/cine.htm.*

Vomero, Maria Fernanda. "Vida de foca." *Imprensa,* 1999, www.vol.com.br/imprensa/bancas/nesmat.htm.

Wiñazki, Miguel. "Prensa y Poder." *Noticias,* April 6, 1996, p. 58–61.

Zunino, Edi. "Su enemigo favorito." *Pulso del Periodismo* (May 1995), p. 36–41.

——. "Un Hombre sin límites." *Noticias,* March 1, 1997, p. 26–33.

Zunino, Edi, and Francisco Amato. "Las manos de la justicia." *Noticias,* March 10, 1996, p. 22-31.

Zunino, Edi, and Joe Goldman. "Mano de Obra Ocupada." *Noticias,* December 21, 1996, p. 34–37.

INTERVIEWEES

Adrianzen, Alberto. August 1, 1995. Lima.

Alcantara, Euripides. February 28, 1996. New York.

Aquino, Wilson. 1997. Rio de Janeiro.

Arrieta, José. September 1, 1998. Telephone conversation.

Barcellos, Caco. July 2, 1997. São Paulo.

Barraza, Gerardo. August 4, 1995. Lima.

Bustamante, Carlos. July 29, 1995. Lima.

Caballero, Maria Cristina. March 16, 1996. Bogotá.

Ciancaglini, Sergio. July 17, 1996. Buenos Aires.

Cortés, Ernesto. September 28, 1998. Telephone conversation.

Costa, Caio Tulio. July 2, 1997. São Paulo.

de Althaus, Jaime. August 3, 1995. Lima.

de Freitas, Janio. June 26, 1997. Rio de Janeiro.

de Carvalho, Joaquim. July 1, 1997. São Paulo.

de Souza, Josias. July 4, 1997. São Paulo.

Diament, Mario. December 19, 1995. Telephone conversation.

Dimenstein, Gilberto. February 21, 1996. New York.

Donadío, Alberto. 1998. Electronic mail communication.

Duzán, Maria Jimena. March 12, 1996. Bogotá.

Elguezabal, Sergio. January 8, 1999. Buenos Aires.

Garcia Lupo, Rogelio. July 22, 1996. Buenos Aires.

Gilbert, Isidoro. July 15, 1996. Buenos Aires.

Gómez, Ignacio. March 14, 1996. Bogotá.

Gorriti, Gustavo. September 25, 1995. Telephone conversation.

Gullo, Marcelo. August 1, 1995. Lima.

Igartua, Francisco. August 4, 1995. Lima.

Kirschbaum, Ricardo. July 24, 1996. Buenos Aires.

Kucinski, Bernardo. July 3, 1997. São Paulo.

Lejtman, Roman. July 25, 1996. Buenos Aires.

Lesmes, Jorge. March 11, 1996. Bogotá.

Leuco, Alfredo. July 16, 1996. Buenos Aires.

Lins da Silva, Carlos Eduardo. March 1, 1996. Telephone conversation.

Lobato, Elvira. June 26, 1997. Rio de Janeiro.

Majul, Luis. July 15, 1996. Buenos Aires.

Nassif, Luis. July 14, 1997. Electronic mail communication.

Pacheco Jordão, Rogerio. July 17, 1997. Electronic mail communication.

Paredes Castro, Juan. August 3, 1995. Lima.

Pasquini Durán, José María. July 24, 1996. Buenos Aires.

Rey, Alejandra. July 25, 1996. Buenos Aires.

Reyes, Gerardo. February 10, 1996. Telephone conversation.

Rodrigues, Fernando. June 10, 1997. Electronic mail communication.

Rodriguez, Andrea. November 16, 1995. Telephone conversation.

Rodriguez, Mario. March 11, 1996. Bogotá.

Ronderos, María Teresa. 1998. Telephone conversation.

Rosales, Blanca. August 1, 1995. Lima.

Rospigliosi, Fernando. November 1, 1997. Lima.

Rossi, Clovis. July 2, 1997. São Paulo.

Santoro, Daniel. July 25, 1996. Buenos Aires.

Santos, Alejandro. March 12, 1996. Bogotá.

Santos Calderón, Enrique. 1998. Electronic mail communication.

Tenembaum, Ernesto. February 13, 1996. Telephone conversation.

Thorndike, Guillermo. August 4, 1995. Lima.

Torres, Edgar. March 13, 1996. Bogotá.

Uceda, Ricardo. July 27, 1995. Lima.

Urien Berri, Jorge. 1998. Telephone conversation.

Valenzuela, Cecilia. October 30, 1997. Lima.

Vargas, Mauricio. March 14, 1996. Bogotá.

Verbitsky, Horacio. September 30, 1995. Washington, D.C.

Viau, Susana. July 24, 1996. Buenos Aires.

Zileri, Enrique. August 1, 1995. Lima.

Zunino, Edi. January 8, 1999. Buenos Aires.

INDEX